Curtain Time

THE STORY OF THE AMERICAN THEATER

by Lloyd Morris

SOCIAL HISTORY

Postscript to Yesterday: America: the Last Fifty Years
No So Long Ago
Incredible New York: High Life and Low Life of the Last Hundred Years
Ceiling Unlimited (with Kendall Smith)

BIOGRAPHY

The Rebellious Puritan: Portrait of Mr. Hawthorne
A Threshold in the Sun

DRAMA

The Damask Cheek (with John van Druten)

FICTION

Procession of Lovers
This Circle of Flesh

CRITICISM

The Celtic Dawn
The Young Idea
The Poetry of Edwin Arlington Robinson
William James: The Message of a Modern Mind

TRANSLATION

The New Carthage (from the French of Georges Eekhoud)

"Good my lord, will you see the players well bestowed? Do you hear, let them be well used, for they are the abstract and brief chronicles of the time . . ."

HAMLET, Act II, Scene 2

CURTAIN TIME

THE STORY OF THE
AMERICAN THEATER

by Lloyd Morris

Random House *New York*

TO **ROBERT N. LINSCOTT**
IN GRATEFUL FRIENDSHIP

ACKNOWLEDGMENT

In the New York of my childhood there still lived elderly people who remembered the American theater of the early nineteenth century. My great-grandfather was one. As an indigent youth he haunted the pit and gallery of the Park and the Bowery Theaters. He saw Junius Brutus Booth and the elder Wallack in the fullness of their fame. He followed, almost from the beginning, the careers of James H. Hackett and Edwin Forrest, the first native-born stars to grace our stage. As a man in the prime of life he attended the performances of Miss Charlotte Cushman and Mrs. Mowatt, the first American actresses to achieve international celebrity. He was a witness of the sanguinary Astor Place riot, climax of the bitter feud between Forrest and the British star, Macready. My great-grandfather remembered Rachel, and the startling realism of Miss Matilda Heron's *Camille,* which shocked playgoers nearly a century ago.

Bundles of playbills and programs were in the storeroom of the gaunt brownstone house where I lived in boyhood—souvenirs of a passion for the theater shared by my grandparents, parents, aunts and uncles. They were my delight on stormy afternoons, vivified by the reminiscences of my elders and their table talk, which often ran to dispute about the relative merits of the stage favorites of two generations. All the splendors of the past, now so distant, were lively then, providing a background for my personal adventures in the theater which began at the turn of the century. I can scarcely recall a time when the theater was not a romantic experience, familiar but forever new; when the darkening of an auditorium, and the first glow of footlights on a curtain, did not set my heart to racing. They still do, and that is my reason for writing *Curtain Time.* A love of the stage and an admiration for its people, a sense of enchantment by our theater today, a desire to revive the glories of its yesterdays—these have shaped the book.

My warm appreciation is offered to many people who generously helped me. I am especially indebted to Miss May Davenport Seymour, Curator of the Theater and Music Collections of the Museum of the City of New York. Miss Seymour made available to me the invaluable resources of those collections. Her interest in my work never flagged, and her patience with my inquiries was boundless. To her solicitude *Curtain Time* owes many fine illustrations. And I am greatly in her debt for information about the Davenports and the Seymours, two families whose members have added luster to the American stage. Mr. John Walden Myer, Director of the Museum of the City of New York, kindly facilitated my work there. My friend George Freedley, Curator of the Theater Collection of the New York Public Library, permitted me to use its massive archives, library, and collection of pictures and memorabilia. He gave me also the benefit of his scholarship whenever I requested it. To him, to Mrs. Elizabeth P. Barrett, and to Paul Myers, my thanks.

When announcement was made that I was working on this book, I had the good fortune to receive, from people interested in its subject, offers of material and information which they possessed. To Mr. George Middleton, distinguished playwright and a founder of the Dramatists' Guild, I am indebted for data which amplified information contained in his illuminating autobiography, *These Things Are Mine*. To Miss Meta von Bernuth I am most grateful for a collection of programs, originally made by her friend Mrs. Eugenie Woodward, which she sent to me. It was a very useful source of reference. Professor Arthur Hobson Quinn of the University of Pennsylvania, historian of the American drama, courteously provided the solution of a problem that arose in my research. Miss Suzette G. Stuart graciously found for me, in the archives of Trinity Church, New York, data leading to the solution of another problem. Mr. Crawford A. Peffer, long associated with the Redpath Bureau, sent me some information which, but for his kindly thought, I might not have obtained. The extensive resources of the New York Society Library were of great value in my research, and my thanks are due to Miss Edith Crowell, Miss Helen Ruskell and Mrs. Frederick G. King for their friendly co-operation.

For other assistance, I am grateful to Miss Grace Mayer, Curator of the Print Collection of the Museum of the City of New York; Miss Nannine Joseph, my friend and agent; Mr. Rodman Gilder; Mr. Arthur Todd; Miss Mary Barber, Mrs. Bruce Bliven, Jr., and Miss Jean Ennis of Random House; and friends professionally connected with the theater.

I acknowledge, gratefully, my indebtedness to these works by contemporary scholars: George C. D. Odell's monumental *Annals of the New York Stage;* Arthur Hobson Quinn's *A History of the American Drama;* William G. B. Carson's *The Theater on the Frontier* and *Managers in Distress;* George R. MacMinn's *The Theater of the Golden Era in California;* and Edmond M. Gagey's *The San Francisco Stage*.

LLOYD MORRIS

July, 1953

CONTENTS

LIST OF ILLUSTRATIONS

Curtain Time

THE STORY OF THE AMERICAN THEATER

Alas, Poor Yorick

TOWARD evening on June 4, 1821, while New Yorkers strolled on Broadway from the Battery to City Hall Park, two men were inspecting a new, imposing monument in the churchyard of St. Paul's Chapel, adjacent to the fashionable promenade. One of the men was slender and markedly undersized. The other, more robust, appeared tall by comparison, though only of medium height. Many strollers on the avenue would have recognized them instantly.

The taller man, Dr. John Wakefield Francis, was a distinguished physician. A lover of the arts and an inveterate patron of the theater, he considered it a privilege to give his services, without fee, to authors, painters and actors. Moreover, he enjoyed their society and cultivated their friendship. This unconventional taste was condoned by many of his patients because of his professional skill. Dr. Francis' companion had recently given cause for scandal. This had launched a stormy controversy in the New York and Boston newspapers, and public resentment was rising against him. Edmund Kean, the most famous of English actors, had made a brilliantly successful American tour that ended, abruptly, in disaster. Denied a last engagement in New York, Kean was about to take ship for England, yielding, as he said, to "a torrent of hostility."

As the summer evening closed in, the two men lingered at the new monument. Elevated from the ground by two steps, it was a four-sided pedestal surmounted by a flaming urn carved from marble; the sculptured flame pointed

George Frederick Cooke as King Lear

toward the Park Theater, on nearby Park Row, north of Ann Street. The
pedestal displayed an inscription:

ERECTED TO THE MEMORY OF

GEORGE FREDERICK COOKE

BY EDMUND KEAN

OF THE THEATRE ROYAL, DRURY LANE

1821

"THREE KINGDOMS CLAIM HIS BIRTH,
BOTH HEMISPHERES PRONOUNCE HIS WORTH."

Before leaving the churchyard, Edmund Kean sang softly, "Those Evening
Bells" and "Come o'er the Sea."

The monument was the first in the United States to commemorate an actor.
Permission to erect it had not been gained easily.

In the northern states, many influential people retained a strong prejudice
against the theater. The first Boston theater, opened in 1794, was equipped with
a separate entrance to the gallery, and opponents of the playhouse contended
that, by affording a special door to this portion of the house, "usually the resort
of the vile of both sexes, a premium on vice was offered." The custom of allow-
ing prostitutes to frequent the upper boxes and ply their trade there still flourished at the Park Theater in New York and the Chestnut Street Theater in
Philadelphia. Francis Wemyss, an English comedian who joined the Philadelphia stock company in 1822, deplored the theater's fine new chandelier because
it exposed to view "the third tier of boxes, where licentiousness prevails in its
worst form." In New York, conservative citizens approved of the stand taken
by the Reverend Gardiner Spring, pastor of the Brick Presbyterian Church.
One of his young daughters had attended the Park Theater without his knowledge. At services on the following Sunday, when it came time for the usual
announcements from the pulpit, she heard her father proclaim that, "Eliza
Spring, having recently visited one of those profane and sinful places of carnal
recreation, commonly called theaters, is hereby cut off from the communion
of the Church of Christ."

In general, clergymen of all denominations condemned the theater. Typical
of their attitude was a merciless attack on the alleged immorality of a tragedy
entitled *Bertram* produced in Philadelphia in 1816. The author of this play
was an English clergyman, and the work had been licensed for performance

A View of George Frederick Cooke's Tomb, 1821, by I. R. Smith

in London by the Lord Chamberlain. But in one Philadelphia church, on a Sunday morning, the congregation listened in acute embarrassment while the rector denounced the shameful production. What, he inquired, could be thought of the morals of the actress who was willing to impersonate the heroine? The unfortunate actress in question was a member of the congregation. She was present at the service, seated in her accustomed place, in full view of everyone. She was Mrs. William B. Wood, wife of the manager of the theater, whose exemplary domestic life and high moral principles were widely known.

An equally disagreeable experience was suffered by Mr. and Mrs. Bartley, players brought from England in 1818 to appear in the theaters of New York, Philadelphia and Boston. In the course of their journey by stagecoach from New York to Boston, they stopped at Hartford, Connecticut, where a group of prominent citizens had invited them to provide an evening's entertainment of recitations and readings. Hartford possessed no theater, so the program was to be given in the ballroom of the city's principal hotel. But the more puritanical elements of the community set up an outcry against this innovation, and demanded that the Attorney General of Connecticut enforce the "blue law" prohibiting theatrical performances and circuses. On the evening of the entertainment, the landlord of the hotel was notified by the Attorney General that he intended to prosecute the actors if they carried out their illegal project. This information was withheld from the Bartleys who, unaware that they were defying the law, fulfilled their contract. At midnight, after they had retired, an emissary of the Attorney General arrived at the hotel with a warrant for their arrest. Members of the committee responsible for their performance were still present and, by depositing $500 as bond for the appearance of the Bartleys in court, postponed their arrest. Although their legal defense was provided for by their indignant sponsors, the actors were detained in Hartford, to their financial loss, until a decision in their favor was eventually rendered by the court.

In spite of the hostility of extreme conservatives, the theaters of New York, Philadelphia and Boston flourished, for in these cities members of the wealthy class, eager for entertainment and not averse to social display, erected luxurious playhouses and rented them to intrepid managers whose efforts they supported by occupying the lower tiers of boxes. Nevertheless, the operation of a theater was, at best, a precarious enterprise and managers had already learned that, in order to earn profits, it was necessary to extend their activities. They therefore devised the "circuit" system. In summer, when the Boston Theater closed, its managers took the company on a tour of New England cities that usually included Providence, Newport, Portsmouth, New Hampshire, and Portland, Maine. The managers of the Chestnut Street Theater, in Philadelphia, conducted spring, summer and autumn seasons in Baltimore and Washington. There were also theaters in Albany, New York; in Richmond and Petersburg, Virginia; in Charleston, South Carolina, where optimistic managers periodically assembled companies, and to which they often lured leading players from the theaters of New York, Boston and Philadelphia for brief engagements.

The wealthy class which supported the theaters retained a traditional social prejudice against the players who performed in them. The belief prevailed that actors and actresses led dissolute lives, and although their talent might be applauded their profession was considered disreputable. With very few exceptions, they were excluded from good society. In 1821, recording the death of Snelling Powell, the first successful theater manager in Boston, a newspaper called attention to "the private worth and respectability" of Powell and his wife, and declared that "they have at least proved that actors do not *necessarily* belong to the inferior ranks of society; for they have been examples of industry and prudence, rising from a depressed condition to affluence and respectability." Most players on the American stage had been brought from England, where social barriers against the profession were gradually being leveled, and they bitterly resented the humiliations to which they were exposed in the young republic. "The physician, the barrister, the clergyman, the soldier, are all received with the honor due to their occupation," Francis Wemyss noted aggrievedly. "The player, whose toil is equal, and whose task to gain eminence is more severe, is only received as a clever buffoon, tolerated, but not accepted in the bosom of society." But to be tolerated was itself a privilege for, as Wemyss recorded, in the United States members of the theatrical profession were usually "condemned and despised." This was why the veteran comedian Joseph Jefferson, long a favorite with Philadelphia audiences, invariably rejected invitations from gentlemen of the city to join them at taverns after the play. Since they were unwilling to receive him in their homes, he refused to let himself be made a source of amusement at their convivial parties.

Thomas Abthorpe Cooper was one of the few actors who had been admitted to good society. The most highly paid player on the American stage, his immense popularity with audiences began to wane only after they had seen Edmund Kean. A native of England, Cooper had been adopted and educated by his distant relative, the political radical William Godwin. Finding this association detrimental to his career, Cooper accepted an American engagement in 1796, at the age of twenty. He quickly achieved celebrity as a tragedian and his services were in such constant demand that, unlike other actors, he did not have to identify himself with any single theater. Instead, he traveled from one theater to another, as the first touring star. For these engagements Cooper exacted larger sums than managers had ever before paid. He made his home in New York, and indulged in the luxuries that wealth made possible. Even the city's wealthiest men were impressed by the fact that Cooper, when he went to play engagements in Boston and Philadelphia, always made the journey in his own costly carriage and with his own horses. For a considerable period, he was also manager of the Park Theater; this venture, supposed to be very profitable, gave him the status of a reputable man of affairs. It was at this time that he married Miss Mary Fairlie, a young woman of excellent family. The alliance established Cooper in fashionable circles to which neither his talent, his celebrity, or his exceptional physical beauty would have made him acceptable.

It was Cooper who brought to the United States the famous English tragedian George Frederick Cooke, the first foreign star to venture on an American tour. Cooke died in New York City on September 26, 1812, and on the following day his remains were committed to the "stranger's vault" of St. Paul's Chapel. There, forgotten, they reposed for nine years until Edmund Kean and Dr. Francis conceived the project of honoring Cooke with a monument. Kean had never known Cooke personally, or seen him play, but Dr. Francis had been his friend as well as his physician. To execute their plan, they found that they would have to obtain the consent of the Bishop of New York. When Bishop John Henry Hobart received them, his embarrassment was obvious. "You do not, gentlemen, wish the tablet inside St. Paul's?" he inquired. "No, sir," Dr. Francis replied, "we desire to remove the remains of Mr. Cooke from the stranger's vault and erect a monument over them on some suitable spot in the burying ground of the church." While Bishop Hobart pondered this, Dr. Francis offered a persuasive assurance: "It will be a work of taste and durability." After further reflection, Bishop Hobart gave his decision. "You have my concurrence, then," he said, "but I hardly knew how we could find a place inside the church for Mr. Cooke."

Neither Kean nor Dr. Francis would have had the temerity to propose burying an actor's remains inside a church. They were aware that the privilege of burial in consecrated ground was an exceptional concession. They may have realized that the monument which Kean erected would have, for people of the theater, a peculiar significance. To future generations of players, it recorded an early victory in the long struggle to win prestige for their profession. There was, however, a touch of irony in its symbolic importance. Few actors had given greater cause for prejudice than George Frederick Cooke, and almost none had been as contemptuous of social approval.

Cooke's fame had preceded him across the Atlantic. At the Theater Royal, Covent Garden, he played leading roles with Mrs. Siddons, the "Tragic Muse," and her equally eminent brother, John Philip Kemble. The London critics had acclaimed him as Kemble's sole rival. But Cooke's dissolute habits soon became notorious. His affairs with women repeatedly involved him in scandals, and an irresistible addiction to drink alienated the public. Cooke often attempted to play when drunk, incapable of remembering his lines or moving about the stage. If his efforts were roundly hissed by the audience, he berated them. Then the curtain would be rung down, the audience dismissed with an apology and their money refunded. Sometimes Cooke failed to arrive at the theater, and the scheduled performance could not be given. The press began to attack him savagely, and Cooke, finding himself unwelcome in London, made tours of the provincial theaters. On one of these, in 1810, he met Thomas Abthorpe Cooper, who had come to England to recruit players for the Park Theater in New York. Cooper proposed that Cooke make an American tour under the management of Cooper and his astute partner in the business of the Park Theater, Stephen Price. Cooper undertook to pay Cooke a weekly salary of 25 guineas for a period of ten months; to pay his Atlantic passage; to allow him traveling expenses of 25 cents a mile in the United States. Cooke would be required to play engagements in New York, Philadelphia, Baltimore and Boston, having a "benefit" performance in each city from which he would receive the profits. Cooper's personal experience as a touring star indicated that these terms would bring enormous profits to himself and Price. As Cooper surmised, Cooke was badly in need of money and easily persuaded that American triumphs would revive his popularity in England. Nevertheless, he was surprised by Cooke's eagerness to undertake the tour. Cooke's departure from England was kept secret until he was on the Atlantic, and when the news leaked out Cooper found himself compelled to publish a denial of "the absurd and calumnious report" that he had kidnapped Cooke after making him drunk and irresponsible.

In New York, the announcement of Cooke's impending arrival caused extreme excitement. It was widely disbelieved, and many people predicted that the visitor would turn out to be an impostor. That the great English tragedian should come to America appeared as impossible as that "St. Paul's Cathedral could be brought across the ocean." On the night of his first performance at the Park Theater, a huge crowd waited in the streets for many hours before the doors were opened, and Cooke faced the largest audience yet collected in New York. He was in his fifty-fifth year, and his talent had greatly deteriorated. But American playgoers had never seen an actor of comparable power and brilliance, or one capable of such terrifying impersonations of human malignity. Cooke's opening performance in *Richard III* received a spectacular ovation, and he aroused wild enthusiasm when he played Shylock in *The Merchant of Venice,* and the villainous Sir Giles Overreach in Philip Massinger's *A New Way to Pay Old Debts.*

Cooke had been lodged at the Tontine Coffee House on Wall Street, and he soon reverted to his intemperate habits. Once, when Cooke was announced to play *Richard III,* Dr. Francis was summoned shortly before curtain time. He found Stephen Price with the actor, and in a fever of anxiety. Cooke had been drinking steadily for thirty hours, and lay crumpled over a table filled with empty decanters. "Let him only get before the lights, and the receipts are secure," Price wailed. Dr. Francis administered restoratives. Then the two men bundled Cooke into a coach and drove him to the theater. Practically voiceless and helplessly unsteady, Cooke whispered his way through the play. The audience showed no resentment. "Have I not pleased the Yankee Doodles?" the tragedian asked after the final curtain, and left the theater to return to his drinking. In

George Frederick Cooke as Richard III

his eagerness to protect the box office, Stephen Price installed Cooke in his own home, where the manager and his wife made every effort to keep the star in a state of partial sobriety. But frequent ructions occurred when Cooke became drunk and abusive, and these scenes sometimes terminated in physical violence. Once, Cooke ran away and failed to return for twenty-four hours; he was found, disgracefully drunk, only in time to be taken to the theater for his benefit performance in Addison's *Cato*. An immense audience awaited him, but Cooke "could not remember one line after having delivered the other," and his performance was "the most shameful exhibition ever witnessed in New York." His explanation was candid, if not reassuring. "Heaven help me, if you ever heard anything of me, you have heard that I always have a frolic on my benefit day. If a man can't take a liberty with his friends, who the devil can he take a liberty with?" But apparently Cooke had exhausted the patience of the New York public. During the remainder of his engagement receipts at the box office fell off alarmingly.

When Cooke departed on tour, he was accompanied by William Dunlap, whom the harassed Price had persuaded to assume the unenviable office of watchdog and guardian. Painter, playwright and novelist, Dunlap was a close friend of Washington Irving and James Fenimore Cooper. He had been one of the projectors of the Park Theater and, for a long period, its sole manager. Except for Dr. Francis, Dunlap was the only American for whom Cooke ever demonstrated any fondness. The roistering old actor requested Dunlap to write his biography, and Dunlap performed the task after Cooke's death. Dunlap had an acute sympathy for the eccentricities of genius, particularly for those of geniuses whom he had never met. But daily association with Cooke soon became exasperating, even to Dunlap. He confided an increasing disenchantment to his diary. "Alas, Cooke is again a wretched drunkard!" he lamented. On the following day, "The old drunkard sallied forth again." Ten days later he noted bitterly, "The old wretch went forth to his whores again as soon as I was gone"; his annoyance was the greater because, on the previous night, Cooke had "played *Lear* very wildly." Soon afterwards, Dunlap set down his appraisal of Cooke's character. "A coward, a braggart, a hypocrite, a man of repentance without amendment, forming resolutions only to break them, fearing death with womanish pusillanimity, yet rushing to meet him with the frenzy of desperation, formed by nature for the attainment of every virtue without possessing one—I fear not one!"

In Philadelphia, Baltimore and, later, in Boston, Cooke's early performances were unprecedently successful; the huge revenues of the box office astounded the managers. But, invariably, the fatalities of New York recurred. While Cooke was playing in Philadelphia, Thomas Abthorpe Cooper returned from England and was immediately sent to Philadelphia to bolster a failing attraction. The two tragedians alternated in the roles of Othello and Iago. They appeared together in *The Gamester* and *Venice Preserved*. In *Henry IV*, Cooper played Hotspur to Cooke's Falstaff; in *The Merchant of Venice*, Antonio to Cooke's Shylock. The opportunity to see two great stars for the price of one proved irresistible; receipts mounted again. But Cooke could not refrain from "scandalous excesses" for which "he never betrayed the least shame or remorse." When his offenses were mentioned, "he was silent and affected perfect unconsciousness." William B. Wood, the sorely tried manager in Philadelphia and Baltimore, was astonished by the actor's "perfect indifference to public opinion." Whenever Cooke was in his cups, he delighted in abusing all things American. "I'm preparing a pamphlet," he would shout. "When I get to London, I'll blow up your managers and your actors and your blasted country. I can hold a pen. I scourge your damned Yankee manners."

In Baltimore, at a convivial party, one of the guests told Cooke that President James Madison intended to come from Washington to see him act. "If he does," retorted Cooke, "I'll be damned if I play before him! What? I, George Frederick Cooke, who has acted before the Majesty of Britain, play before your Yankee President? No!" Relations between the United States and Great Britain were rapidly worsening, and in a few months war was to be declared. But Cooke was already at war with the "rebellious Yankee Doodles" before whom he found it "degrading enough to play." In Baltimore, he defaulted at a performance; thereafter his audiences dwindled. In Boston he brawled in low taverns and, when trying to play while in a drunken stupor, was hissed off the stage. In New York, there was an uproar when Cooke "married," without her father's knowledge, Mrs. Behn, daughter of James Bryden, proprietor of the Tontine Coffee House. The marriage was almost certainly bigamous, and the poor lady, after Cooke's death, was reduced to keeping a theatrical boarding house. Meanwhile, Cooke's health was rapidly failing. In the summer of 1812, just after the declaration of war on Great Britain, Cooke played an engagement in Providence with the Boston company. His audiences were humiliatingly small, though Cooke remained sober throughout the engagement and his performances were magnificent. Already fatally ill when he returned to New York, the old tragedian lingered for two months under the care of Dr. Francis and two older, eminent physicians. One of them later reported the young doctor's exemplary devotion to his patient. Dr. Francis remained at Cooke's bedside, quite alone, throughout the last night of Cooke's life. His older associate joined him early in the morning. He recorded that Cooke's mind was perfectly clear; he knew that he was dying.

When, nine years later, permission was obtained for the erection of a monument to Cooke, Dr. Francis supervised the transfer of the actor's remains to their new resting place. This gave him an opportunity to exercise his surgical skill for a somewhat unusual purpose. He took advantage of it. Thereby, inadvertently, he caused Cooke's ghost to haunt the American theater for more than a century. An inkling of the odd affair reached the public in 1832, when William Dunlap published his *History of the American Theater*. In this work, Dunlap made a guarded allusion to the monument which Kean had erected. "Although it may hereafter be found that his surgeon possesses his skull, and his successor, Kean, the bones of the forefinger of his right hand—that dictatorial finger— still the monument covers the *remains* of George Frederick Cooke." A kindly soul, Dunlap had no desire to injure the reputation of Dr. Francis, who was his physician, friend and tactful benefactor.

By the time that Dunlap published his *History,* literary and artistic circles in New York were fully aware that Dr. Francis kept Cooke's skull hidden away in his office. Some years after the monument had been erected, a benefit performance of *Hamlet* was announced at the Park Theater. At a late hour, it was discovered that the stage manager had neglected to provide a skull for the scene of the grave diggers. A messenger was hastily sent to Dr. Francis, who loaned Cooke's skull for the performance. On the following morning, the skull was returned and again locked away. That evening Dr. Francis attended a meeting of the Bread and Cheese, a dining club founded by James Fenimore Cooper in 1824 to bring together the city's leading writers, painters and men of intellectual attainment. Dunlap was a member, and was probably present, for the club's guest on this occasion was Daniel Webster. Perhaps the great statesman's presence stimulated Dr. Francis to tell how Cooke's skull had returned to the stage as Yorick's, in the very theater where the great star had won his first American triumph. In any case, the incident became known to certain members of the Bread and Cheese. Phrenology, at the time, was arousing popular interest, and these gentlemen expressed a desire to examine Cooke's skull. Dr. Francis was willing to gratify them. The tragedian's head made its second public appearance at a banquet table.

In 1858, toward the end of his long, very distinguished career, Dr. Francis published a volume of reminiscences, *Old New York,* in which he acknowledged his possession of the skull. Rather perversely, he neglected to explain by what right he had severed the skull from the actor's skeleton. It was not until 1930—one hundred and eighteen years after Cooke's death—that Dr. Francis' acquisitive surgery was vindicated by his granddaughter, Mrs. Louise Francis Lyon, a retired actress. Shortly before Cooke's death, Mrs. Lyon related, the actor told his physician, "Dr. Francis, I have nothing to leave you but my love and gratitude for all you have done for me, but if you would care to have my skull for science's sake, I'll gladly leave it to you."

At his death in 1861, Dr. John Wakefield Francis left the tragedian's skull to his elder son, Dr. Valentine Mott Francis, who kept it in his office, locked in a glass case. During the summer of 1885, while residing at Jamestown, Rhode Island, Dr. Francis fell down a flight of stairs in his home, sustaining a severe injury to his head. Dr. George McClellan, a neighbor, was called to attend him. Dr. McClellan was a nephew of Lincoln's general, and the Dean of Jefferson Medical College in Philadelphia. Under his skillful care, Dr. Francis soon recovered from his injury. When Dr. McClellan refused to accept any fee for his services, Dr. Francis made a humorous allusion to Cooke's bequest to his father. Since Dr. McClellan's skill had deprived him of any immediate prospect of securing Dr. Francis' head, the patient would present him with another, of possibly greater interest.

While Dr. Valentine Mott Francis was packing Cooke's skull for shipment to Philadelphia, one of the teeth became detached. Like his father, Dr. Francis was a lover of the theater. He especially admired Edwin Booth, then the most famous of American actors. In token of his admiration, he sent Cooke's tooth to Booth as a gift. Booth had the tooth mounted as a scarf pin and, with his usual care for realistic effect, caused the root of the tooth to be stained blood red. Some time after Cooke's skull came into Dr. McClellan's possession, Booth played *Hamlet* in Philadelphia. Legend asserts that, shortly before the curtain rose, he was handed a skull with the request that it be used in the scene of the grave diggers, to gratify a member of the audience. Booth, so the story goes, complied with this request but did not learn, until after the performance, that Yorick's skull was the skull of George Frederick Cooke.

In 1929, after the death of Dr. McClellan's widow, and according to the terms of his will, Dr. Ross V. Patterson, his successor as Dean of Jefferson Medical College, inherited the skull of George Frederick Cooke. By that time, the story of the skull's wanderings had long been forgotten. News of the bequest aroused a brief flurry of interest in the American press. Then the affair of the skull was again forgotten until 1936, when Daniel Frohman, veteran theatrical manager and president of the Actors' Fund of America, proposed that Dr. Patterson consent to "the replacement of the skull with Cooke's body, as a tribute to the first great actor in the American theater." Nothing came of this reverential project. Dr. Patterson, who died two years later, bequeathed the skull to Jefferson Medical College in Philadelphia. It has reposed, ever since, in an exhibition case in the library of the college, not too remote from the streets in which the old bacchanalian "went forth to his whores." The other grim relic of George Frederick Cooke has also been preserved, but over this the theatrical profession exercises an indirect guardianship. Edwin Booth bequeathed the scarf pin which he had fashioned from Cooke's tooth to The Players, the club for actors which Booth founded in 1888. Booth's scarf pin has been placed, by The Players, in the Theater Collection of the Museum of the City of New York. The bones of Cooke's dictatorial forefinger, which Dr. John Wakefield Francis gave to Edmund Kean, met a less ceremonious fate. It is said that during a quarrel with Kean, his unfortunate wife revenged herself by adding the cherished relic to her household trash pile.

Time and weather often defaced the monument erected by Edmund Kean. In 1846 his son, the actor Charles Kean, had it restored. In 1874 another English star, Edward A. Sothern, defrayed the costs of a second restoration. By 1890, the monument had again become dilapidated, and Edwin Booth undertook its repair. Two other restorations were made before 1948, when the Edmund Kean Club of New York City affixed a bronze plaque to the monument on which the earlier obliterated inscriptions are reproduced. There, a generation of American playgoers to whom the name of George Frederick Cooke is largely unknown can read a record of the theater's piety to its high traditions, and of the acting profession's faith in the dignity and social value of their art.

CHAPTER 1

The Makers of Tradition

SHORTLY after 1815, Stephen Price conceived a daring project which revolutionized the American theater. His former partner, Thomas Abthorpe Cooper, had retired from management to devote himself to the more profitable career of a touring star and Price had taken into partnership Edmund Simpson, a member of the Park Theater's acting company. Unlike his new associate and his fellow-managers in other cities, Price was not by profession an actor. New Yorkers knew him chiefly as a man about town, a connoisseur of food and wines, a generous host and jovial companion; he was frequently in the company of editors and writers for the press. His somewhat frivolous reputation was deceptive, for Price was primarily a businessman, the first strictly "commercial" producer to appear in the United States. To Snelling Powell and James H. Dickson in Boston, to William Warren and William B. Wood in Philadelphia, their managerial activities offered the hope of increased incomes and the assurance of permanent employment as actors. But Price was exorbitantly ambitious. He had notions of making a fortune. He saw in the theater a field of enterprise which, from the commercial standpoint, had not been adequately exploited. What the theater required was the services of a master showman, a merchant of talent capable of keeping public curiosity about his wares at fever heat. Price felt confident that he could do this. He considered himself singularly free of illusions about the theater. On the whole, he was right, for this belief was the only illusion that he cherished.

Thomas A. Cooper as Pierre in
"Venice Preserved."
By C. R. Leslie

Price surmised that a strong appetite for novelty could be developed in the playgoing public. As things stood, the theaters were not equipped to satisfy it. Yet George Frederick Cooke had brought huge audiences into the theaters, and whenever Cooper played a starring engagement managers could count on large profits. To Price, these facts suggested a magnificent opportunity. Why not import, one after another, the reigning favorites of the London stage, about whom the American public was being informed by the press? These great stars must be brought over under exclusive contract to Price. They would perform first at the Park Theater, thereby establishing it as the leading playhouse in the country. Through his contacts with editors and journalists, Price could whip up excitement in New York about the visiting stars. This would compel the managers in other cities to engage them, because of the pressure of public demand. The prospect was dazzling. In addition to his profits in New York, Price would receive an income from audiences in Boston, Philadelphia, Baltimore, Washington and elsewhere.

Undaunted by the financial hazards of his project, Price carried it out with extraordinary success. In England the theatrical profession soon described him as "Star Giver General to the United States." The title was an apt one, for Price was the only man in American theatrical history ever able to create a virtual monopoly. But this exploit did not satisfy his ambition. Visiting London frequently on his star-gathering raids, he acquired an intimate knowledge of English theatrical affairs. Presently, he began to consider a more beguiling possibility. Why not invade the London theater, become the first producer to operate establishments on both sides of the Atlantic? Price eventually leased the Drury Lane Theater. Indignant at his effrontery, London managers determined to put him out of business and to this end stimulated resentment of the "American invasion" by the press and public. For one season, Price fought gallantly. The adventure proved ruinous. Although a British court granted him a legal discharge, he insisted on paying all his creditors. Since in England, as in the United States, bankruptcy was the usual recourse of managers in distress, Price's action greatly enhanced his prestige in theatrical circles.

Eliminated as a producer in London, Price remained the leading supplier of talent to the American theater. Only the assurance of enormous earnings, not to be equaled in Great Britain, could reconcile London favorites to the reported discomforts and infelicities of an American tour. British travelers had enumerated them. Filthy inns, unpalatable food, rickety stagecoaches, river boats deficient in privacy; rude manners that made social intercourse difficult; an exasperating republican condescension toward foreigners; a savage climate. In addition to these, actors could expect poorly equipped theaters, inferior supporting companies and ignorant audiences. But the terms which Price offered washed with gold all envisaged horrors. This might not have been the case, for Americans were assumed to exaggerate whenever they talked about money, and were notorious for sharp practices in business. Yet, oddly enough, Price had paid his debts, though legally released from doing so. Few English managers had ever behaved so honorably. Clearly, Price was a man to be trusted. If he hadn't been an American, you might have mistaken him for a gentleman.

In 1818, Price made a cautious, preliminary test of his project by bringing to the United States a young actor who, for six years, had been a favorite with audiences at Drury Lane. Particularly, he enjoyed high favor with the ladies, by whom he was considered as romantically handsome as Lord Byron. At twenty-four, James William Wallack justified this comparison with the celebrated poet. He was dark-haired and dark-eyed; his features were delicately molded; he was of medium height, had a fine figure, and his bearing was remarkably graceful. He had, on the stage, a trick of rapid, agile movement that was distinctively his own, and it produced the effect of vivacity and exuberance which came to characterize his acting. Price quickly aroused curiosity by feeding information about Wallack to the press. Wallack's father was an actor, his mother an actress who had played with David Garrick. The boy was sent to a theatrical school founded by Queen Charlotte and there attracted the attention of Richard Brinsley Sheridan, the playwright, who obtained an engagement for him at Drury Lane. Lord Byron, who served on the board of management for one year, considerably advanced young Wallack's career. Wallack's mother had taught him the acting methods of Garrick. He had personally studied the performances of Mrs. Siddons and John Philip Kemble before their retirement. At Drury Lane he played secondary roles to Robert William Elliston and Edmund Kean. The very names of these great players quickened the imaginations of Americans. Wallack needed no other recommendation than that he had learned his art from them; and who would not wish to see a man who had won the favor of Sheridan and the friendship of diabolical, fascinating Byron?

Nobody asked why, since he enjoyed such exceptional advantages in London, young Wallack chose to try his fortunes in the United States. Money was not his object. He had recently married and his wife had brought him a dowry of £20,000. Mrs. Wallack was the daughter of John Johnstone, a popular Irish singer and comedian, a member of the raffish set with which the Prince Regent surrounded himself at Carlton House. She had accompanied Wallack to the United States and, as the year turned, was to present him with a son whom they named John Lester. Probably neither parent surmised that the Wallacks, father and son, were to occupy a commanding position in the American theater until nearly the end of the century. For James William Wallack had come to the United States solely to improve his fortunes in London. So long as Kean and Elliston dominated the stage of Drury Lane, he could look forward to playing only secondary roles. But, if Americans acclaimed him, could he not return to London as a star?

This fixed purpose soon resulted in difficulties at the Park Theater. It came time to announce the role in which Wallack would make his first appearance. He knew that Cooper was considered pre-eminent in Shakespearian roles. "What was Cooper seen in last?" he inquired. He was told that Cooper had played Macbeth, his best role. "Then I'll play Macbeth!" Wallack declared, to the consternation of Price and Edmund Simpson.

They explained the obvious dangers of inviting comparison with the mighty Cooper. In vain; Wallack was intractable. On September 7, 1818, he opened his American tour in *Macbeth,* pleasing a large audience. During the ensu-

ing fortnight he appeared in *Coriolanus,* as Rolla in Sheridan's *Pizarro,* in *Romeo and Juliet, Hamlet* and *Richard III,* not only challenging Cooper but seeking to prove his own aptitude for variety. Opinion in the press was divided. One critic complained that Wallack was too melodramatic; another found him wanting in dignity. But he drew crowded houses and, in spite of the critics, his success with the public was impressive. Price took advantage of this situation by exploiting Wallack's unspoken challenge to Cooper. The veteran tragedian was engaged to follow his new rival at the Park Theater, and to enact three of the Shakespearian roles just performed by Wallack. Immediately afterwards, Wallack began a second engagement. This time he was seen in four new roles, none Shakespearian or identified with Cooper. He scored an even greater success than before. As Price had foreseen, the approval of New York stimulated curiosity in other cities. Boston, Baltimore, Philadelphia, Washington and Charleston gave the new star a hearty welcome and crowded houses. Wallack remained in the United States to play a second season, during which he obtained three engagements in New York. On one of his visits to the Park Theater, his high claims as a star were eloquently confirmed by a series of joint appearances with Cooper—a man so little given to generosity that, as Francis Wemyss said, his "haughty demeanor and rudeness, amounting almost to insult to his brother actors, rendered him an object of fear instead of admiration." For his benefit performance in New York before taking ship for England, Wallack provided the kind of program that most delighted American audiences. He performed single acts of three of Shakespeare's plays and two acts of *Pizarro.* He then offered imitations of George Frederick Cooke, John Philip Kemble, Charles Mathews and other celebrated English actors. He concluded the evening with a farewell address to an audience still unwearied and clamoring for more.

The success of his American tour brought Wallack leading roles on his return to Drury Lane. London received him as an established star. But a career in his native land no longer satisfied him, although he remained an Englishman to the end of his long life. Within a year of his return home he again embarked for the United States. In the next thirty years he was to cross the Atlantic more than thirty times, often making long sojourns in the United States but always renewing his professional career in England until, white-haired, portly and famous as "the elder Wallack," he determined to settle permanently in New York. On his second American tour, Wallack revealed his talent as a comedian. In time, high comedy became the field in which he excelled, and in which his polished, urbane, lightly romantic characterizations established the tradition followed by American actors.

Two years after bringing Wallack to the United States, Price announced the forthcoming American tour of Edmund Kean, England's foremost tragedian

James William Wallack as Gloucester in "Richard III"

and idol of the London public ever since his sensational first appearance, in 1814, at Drury Lane. Americans traveling in Europe sent home glowing accounts of Kean's performances, often quoting the saying of the poet Coleridge that seeing him act was like reading Shakespeare by flashes of lightning. There had also crossed the Atlantic the strange tale that Lord Byron, one night in his box at Drury Lane, was "seized with a sort of convulsive fit" induced by the terrifying realism of Kean's climactic scene in *A New Way to Pay Old Debts*. Kean sometimes boasted that he was the natural son of the Duke of Norfolk and that he had been educated at Eton. But many American theatergoers already knew that both these claims were falsehoods. He was, in sober fact, the bastard child of Nancy Carey, a strolling actress who had abandoned him in infancy. Adopted by Miss Tidswell, a veteran member of the Drury Lane company, Kean when still a child escaped into the underworld of vagrant players. His youth was spent working as an acrobat, harlequin and actor of small parts. At the age of seventeen, in Belfast, he was given the role of Young Norval in John Home's *Douglas* when Mrs. Siddons appeared as Lady Randolph. In the full tide of his fame, Kean frequently told how, after the performance, the great actress had graciously patted his head, saying, "You have played very well, sir, *very* well. It's a pity, but *there's too little of you to do anything.*" His insignificant stature, like his illegitimacy, was a bitter humiliation, and Kean, still nettled by Mrs. Siddons' prophecy, felt impelled to remind people that he had triumphantly refuted it. His triumph had come when the management of Drury Lane, on the verge of bankruptcy, offered to try him out in the role of Shylock and, almost overnight, he restored the fortunes of the failing theater. Nevertheless, so London gossip had it, Kean continued to suffer from long years of failure, neglect and desperate poverty, during which he had made a wretchedly unhappy marriage and had lost a beloved child. These years of misery poisoned fame and success. Perhaps this explained the rumor—it had already reached America—that Kean, although courted by the English aristocracy, delighted in snubbing them; that he chose his associates from the lowest dregs of society; that he was given to erratic bouts of drunkenness and dissipation when, for days or weeks, he would vanish into the stews of London.

The legend of his wayward genius enchanted the younger generation. They had succumbed to the new romantic mood that was sweeping over Europe. Particularly, they were ardent champions of Byron's poetry, condemned by their elders because of its licentiousness and its startling doctrine that the individual should give free rein to his natural impulses, should defy any convention or authority that curbed his freedom. Wasn't Kean the Byronic hero incarnate, a creature of stormy passions, a victim of profound melancholy, possibly tainted with madness, that goaded him into depravity? And wasn't he, appropriately, the exponent of a new kind of acting that repudiated the classical purity, the formal elegance and "poetical" refinement cultivated by his illustrious predecessors on the English stage? Kean's art promised to speak for the living present, not the dead past, and the younger generation, even before they saw him play, were prepared to acclaim him.

Kean began his American tour in New York, on November 29, 1820, with a performance of *Richard III*. The theater had been sold out long in advance, and many in the audience were skeptical, for it seemed improbable that any actor, however great, could justify the fanatical enthusiasm which Kean evoked in England. But, as on his first night at Drury Lane, he roused his audience to the highest pitch of excitement, receiving ovation after ovation during the progress of the play. Kean's engagement, extended by popular demand to an unprecedented four weeks, gave the New York public an opportunity to see him in many of his most celebrated roles. He appeared as Othello, Shylock, Hamlet, Lear and Richard II; as Sir Giles Overreach; as Brutus in the tragedy of that name written for him by John Howard Payne and first produced in London two years earlier; as Sir Edward Mortimer in George Colman's melodrama, *The Iron Chest*. "The people don't know exactly what to make of him," Edmund Simpson, Price's partner, recorded; "his strange manner surprises them, but his style gains converts every night." Critics and public alike acknowledged Kean's extraordinary power. His torrential outbursts of passion held them spellbound. They were electrified by the rapidity of his transitions from one emotion to another, by his ability to convey, through a single word or look or gesture, the most subtle shades of thought or feeling. Sometimes even the actors who were playing with him were themselves overcome by the intensity of the dramatic illusion that he projected. Yet Kean never varied his playing of any role. He patiently rehearsed each bit of business, tried the tones of every speech over and over again; carefully practiced every gesture, movement and facial expression; then, having regulated all these details, he read his lines as if from a musical score, and the effects so precisely composed in advance thrilled the audience by their seemingly marvelous spontaneity.

At first, as Simpson noted, audiences were perplexed by Kean's "style." Clearly this was a radical innovation, as yet unique, and they could hardly foresee that it was establishing a tradition that would dominate acting for the remainder of the century. Kean rejected the classical style which, attempting to stress the universal elements of human nature, assimilated any role to a general type and subordinated the personality of the actor to it. The universal, the typical, the fundamental resemblances of men, had little interest for Kean. He was concerned with the qualities that differentiate one man from another, with the specific individuality of characters, and his effort to particularize each of them led him, inevitably, to subordinate his roles to his own personality. "He never seems to me to intend to be any one of his parts, but I think he intends that all of his parts should be *him*," young Fanny Kemble was soon to record, after an intensive study of Kean's performances. "So it is not Othello who is driven frantic by doubt and jealousy, nor Sir Giles Overreach who is selling his child to hell for a few years of wealth and power; it is Kean, and in every one of his characters there is an intense personality of his *own* that, while one is under its influence, defies all criticism." Kean founded the tradition of self-expression which, in time, brought audiences into the theater rather to see a favorite star than to see the play in which that star was performing.

Kean's occasional eccentric behavior bewildered the gentlemen who met him socially. While in New York he expressed a desire to be taken to the asylum for

the insane far out north on Manhattan Island at Bloomingdale. Dr. John Wakefield Francis and another physician arranged to show him the institution. Driving out there, they stopped at Vauxhall Gardens, a summer amusement park
then closed for the winter. The caretaker was summoned and Kean asked permission to enter the park. In buoyant spirits, he passed through the gates—a
small, black-haired man whose dark eyes seemed to blaze out from the extreme
pallor of his thin, haggard face. Quick as a flash, he performed a double somersault, delightedly showing off his agility in a harlequin feat that he had learned
as a boy. When the party arrived at the asylum, Kean was presented to the
officials, who guided him among the deranged patients, explaining the various
forms of insanity from which they suffered. At the end of this tour, Kean was
invited to ascend to the roof of the building, which commanded a beautiful
view. On the roof, he stood for a few moments in silent contemplation. Then,
suddenly, he said, "I'll walk the ridge of the roof and take a leap. It's the best
end I can make of my life." He started quickly toward the gable end of the
building, and was about to climb up to the ridge when Dr. Francis and his associate rushed after him, seized him by the arms, and forcibly persuaded him to
return to safety. What accounted for Kean's sudden impulse to commit suicide,
Dr. Francis wondered; but he was never able to decide. Other prominent New
Yorkers were impressed by Kean's modest deportment and lack of affectation;
these were the reverse of what they had been led to expect. He won the warm
friendship of Manuel Mordecai Noah, editor of the important *National Advocate,* and a playwright whose recent drama *She Would be a Soldier* had been
successfully produced in New York and Philadelphia, and was destined to hold
the stage for many years. Noah became Kean's principal eulogist, and before his
departure from New York arranged a dinner in his honor attended by distinguished residents of the city, probably the first public banquet ever tendered an
actor in the United States.

In Philadelphia, where Kean played next, his success was as great as in New
York. The enthusiasm of his audiences introduced a new custom; that of calling
the star before the curtain at the end of a performance to receive a tribute of
extra applause. This innovation was bitterly disapproved by the manager of the
theater, William B. Wood. "Can anything be more ridiculous," he objected,
"than that an actor, after laboring through an arduous character—a protracted
combat, and the whole series of simulated expiring agonies, should instantly
revive, and appear panting before the curtain to look and feel like a fool, and
to destroy the little illusion which he has been endeavoring to create?" But the
custom quickly spread from Philadelphia to other cities and in time led to even
more dubious practices. Wood especially deplored "the liberal bestowal of
wreaths, bouquets (with or without rings enclosed) upon insignificant as well
as upon distinguished stage artists," since "these in most cases are openly prepared and paid for by the 'grateful recipients' of their own purchases," and
"formed an unconcealed part of the dressing apparatus for the evening." Even
though it might delude the public, this form of professional quackery was des-
picable.

In his intimate contact with Kean, Wood noticed a major weakness of char-

Edmund Kean as Richard III,
from a painting by S. Drummond

acter which ultimately contributed to the great tragedian's swift decline. Kean permitted himself to be beset by a crowd of idlers eager to attach themselves to any new theatrical celebrity. In Philadelphia, these persons were in the habit of calling at the stage door to waylay Kean and carry him off to a late supper or party at the moment when he was most exhausted. The following morning found Kean weak and weary; he would rally for the night's exertion in the theater, then repeat the same indiscretion. "Unlike Cooke, who could bear two or three bottles of port wine, Kean would be overset by as many glasses," Wood noted. "He was aware of his folly in submitting to these midnight wastes of time and health, but wanted firmness to resist them. I frequently remained with him in his dressing room after performance for several hours, in order to tire out these persevering tempters, who would remain in their carriages at the stage door with the most indelicate pertinacity. On one occasion we stayed inside the building until nearly three o'clock, before the rumbling of the carriages announced the departure of his persecutors. It was impossible not to feel a deep interest for a man who, too weak to resist temptation, possessed sensibilities of conscience and character which brought the deepest contrition and shame on every occasion of offense."

The star's tour took him from Philadelphia to Boston, where the "Kean fever" had already broken out and was raging furiously. Tickets for the opening night had been sold out far in advance; those for subsequent performances were sold at auction, and the premiums above box office prices were donated to local charities by J. A. Dickson and John Duff, the managers of the theater. Kean's acting became "the all-engrossing topic of fashionable discussion" in Boston, and such was the rush to see him that his engagement for nine performances was extended by an additional six. On his closing night, he was called before the curtain and the audience clamored for him to prolong his stay. In acknowledging this ovation, Kean promised to revisit "the literary emporium of the New World" as soon as possible—a promise which he was soon to repent.

Meanwhile, he rejoiced in his conquest of America. "Everything both on and off the stage in this country has exceeded my most sanguine expectations," he wrote home. "I am living in the best style, traveling magnificently, and transmitting to England £1,000 each month." After playing a second triumphant engagement in New York, Kean rejoined the Philadelphia company to close its season there, then went with the company to play in Baltimore. From that city, early in May, 1821, he notified the Boston managers of his intention to return there immediately for a second engagement. Dickson promptly replied, urging Kean to postpone his visit until autumn since the theatrical season was drawing to a close and many people of fashion had already left the city. But Kean was not to be dissuaded; he was convinced that he could draw capacity audiences at any time.

Accordingly, he went to Boston. His first two performances drew small audiences. On his third night, looking through a peephole in the curtain shortly before the performance was to begin, Kean saw that there were only about twenty people in the auditorium. Although Dickson urged him to keep faith with the public, he declined to play and left the theater for his hotel. Soon after his departure the boxes filled and other portions of the house were well occupied. Word was sent to Kean, with a request that he return to the theater; this he refused to do. Duff went before the curtain, explained the situation to the audience, offered either to refund their money or, if they chose, perform the play with a substitute in Kean's role. There was some disorder, but eventually the play was performed. Early next morning Kean took the stagecoach for New York.

In Boston, there was general indignation at his refusal to play, which was considered a deliberate insult to the community, and the newspapers published attacks on Kean as well as several savage lampoons. By the time he reached New York, the feeling against him had spread to that city. The New York newspapers took up the quarrel, making an international issue of the affair as a British affront to the American nation. In the *National Advocate* Kean published a long letter defending himself and, "as the servant of the public," offering a disingenuous apology. He lived by his professional exertions, he asserted; he could not afford to give his talents away. Nobody had warned him "that the arts in this country were only encouraged periodically, or that there could be any season in which Shakespeare was diminished in value." The Boston managers countered with an impressive rebuttal. Resentment against Kean rose swiftly in New York, and a riot was feared if he played again. The *National Advocate* soon published his "Farewell to America;" and, on the day following his departure for England, another letter in which he declared, "I shall return again."

To the surprise of many Americans, Kean returned to New York in the autumn of 1825, under conditions that offered slight promise of a successful tour. His troubles in the United States had produced an unfavorable reaction in England, and audiences at Drury Lane received him coldly when he first performed there. Perhaps he believed himself to be a victim of persecution, and succumbed to the abiding melancholy that had flared up in his attempted suicide at Bloomingdale. He began drinking more immoderately than ever before, and ugly rumors about other forms of debauchery were soon circulating, made credible by his notorious ill-treatment of his wife. To make matters worse, Kean became so flagrantly careless on the stage that, during several performances, the audience repeatedly hissed him. Finally, an unsavory scandal completed his disgrace. For many years, Kean had been involved in an affair with the wife of Alderman Robert Cox, a retired London banker. Charlotte Cox had initiated the affair and kept it going, and circumstances suggested that her husband knew all about it and was complaisant. Then, unexpectedly, he brought suit against Kean and, after a sensational trial, was awarded a verdict with damages. The scandal had rocked London, but Kean, with foolish audacity, insisted on performing at Drury Lane immediately after the conclusion of the trial. A riot of such violence broke out in the theater that Kean's temporary exile from the British stage seemed imperative. It was under these conditions that, in urgent need of money, he decided to undertake a second American tour, apparently hoping that the old hostility to him had subsided.

The hope was ill-founded. Accounts of the Cox trial had appeared in the American press, and editors who had previously used the Boston incident to stir up popular fury thoroughly exploited the scandal. When announcement was made of Kean's forthcoming tour, these editors launched a campaign to wreck it. Reviving the Boston issue, they urged their readers, as patriotic Americans, to avenge a gross British insult. This appeal was designed to inflame the working classes and the more turbulent elements of the urban population, patrons of the gallery and pit. The editors also insisted that Kean, having been guilty of the vilest moral turpitude, must be banned from the stage. This argument was directed to the clergy, the conservatives hostile to the theater, the wealthy, fashionable people and respectable middle classes who supported it. When Kean arrived in New York, the campaign against him was in full blast.

On the night of Kean's first performance, the Park Theater was crowded. Obviously, trouble was anticipated for, as a newspaper later reported, "not a single respectable female appeared in the house." The play was *Richard III*. Kean's first entrance unleashed a storm of catcalls and hisses. After a long wait for silence, he left the stage. When he reappeared, the din broke out again and he was pelted with decaying fruit. Several gentlemen in the boxes rose to demand that Kean be given a hearing. They were shouted down. Manager Edmund Simpson came on the stage to plead with the rioters; in vain. While the uproar continued, a conference was held in the greenroom. Simpson gave orders for the performance to proceed. Though no word uttered on the stage could be heard by the audience, the actors valiantly carried on. Kean was repeatedly struck by missiles hurled by the rioters, and his death scene was performed under a volley of rotten apples. When the curtain fell the rioters, having accomplished their purpose, left the theater without further disorder.

Two days later, on the morning before his second performance, Kean published in the *New York Gazette* an apology for his former misconduct in Boston, sadly appealing to the public for clemency. "I visit this country now under different feelings and auspices than on a former occasion," he explained. "Then I was the ambitious man, and the proud representative of Shakespeare's heroes; the spark of ambition is extinct, and I merely ask a shelter in which to close my professional and mortal career." But even before *The Gazette* reached its readers powerful forces were already at work in Kean's behalf. Men of influence in the community had been appalled by the disgraceful riot. Clearly, it was intended to be an ominous show of power; the power of a lawless rabble to impose its will on the city. This was a contest between slums and mansions, between the Five Points and the Battery. However little they sympathized with Kean, New York's merchants and bankers felt compelled to rally to his support. Law and order must prevail over anarchy. Ironically, embarrassingly, the cause of an actor notorious for his total lack of moral principles had become the cause of moral principle itself. At his second performance, Kean played to an audience that had come to the theater for the purpose of crushing any further attempt to drive him from the stage. There were some half-hearted efforts to interrupt the performance, but these were drowned out by applause. Nobody had to be ejected from the theater. At the end of the play, Kean addressed the audience. His speech of abject contrition was warmly applauded. The rest of his engagement, well attended by the city's prosperous classes, passed without incident.

In Boston, the managers of the theater, encouraged by this favorable turn of events in New York, announced Kean for an engagement of four performances. For the first of these, the house was entirely sold out in advance. That morning, the city's newspapers published Kean's appeal to the public for "liberality and forbearance," and the editors advised those who were opposed to Kean to demonstrate their resentment by remaining away from the theater. However, a rumor soon circulated that Kean would not be allowed to play. As soon as the doors of the theater were opened, the house filled quickly; but not even one woman appeared in the audience. Henry James Finn, one of the actor-managers, came before the curtain and announced that Kean intended to make a speech of apology to the citizens of Boston. An uproar immediately broke out in the gallery. Kean came before the curtain, dressed in his everyday clothes. A shower of missiles descended on him; someone hurled a bottle of evil-smelling fluid; the clamor increased, and Kean left the stage without uttering a word. Stockholders of the theater, from their boxes, tried to quell the disturbance, without effect. Meanwhile, a mob that had gathered outside the theater began smashing the lamps and windows of the building. In this turmoil, a placard was brought on the stage announcing that Kean had left the theater; he had, in fact, made his escape through an adjoining house. Armed with brickbats and clubs, the mob outside soon stormed its way into the theater. Occupants of the boxes and pit, stricken with panic, rushed for the stage, seeking to leave the building by the stage door. Some people jumped out of windows. The mob began to destroy the furnishings of the theater. A justice of the peace who was present climbed up on the stage, read the riot act twice and attempted to address the rioters. Hours later, having wrecked much of the theater, the mob melted away.

While the riot was in progress Thomas Kilner, one of the managers, drove

Kean into the suburbs of Boston, whence the actor made his way by stagecoach
to Worcester and to Albany. Here Kean was announced to play *Othello,* and
the role of Iago was assigned to the company's juvenile lead, Edwin Forrest, a
nineteen-year-old native of Philadelphia who had been serving his apprenticeship in the rude theaters of the frontier. Forrest called on the great tragedian at
his hotel to receive his instructions concerning stage "business." They proved
to be brief. "My boy, all I ask of you is to keep in front of me and never let your
attention wander," Kean said, and dismissed him. But at rehearsal, Forrest gave
one of his speeches a novel emphasis. "My God, who told you to do that?" Kean
demanded. The startled young actor confessed that it was his own idea, and
awaited a sharp rebuke. "Well, my boy," Kean said, "everyone who plays Iago
after you will have to do it, too." On the strength of this commendation, young
Forrest was cast to support Kean in two other plays, and his acting apparently
impressed the star deeply. In Philadelphia, where Kean went from Albany,
certain gentlemen arranged a dinner in his honor. During the course of a speech
which he made at this banquet, Kean remarked, "I have met one actor in this
country, a young man named Edwin Forrest, who gave proofs of a decided
genius for his profession and will, I believe, rise to great eminence." This high
tribute soon brought Forrest his first decisive opportunity.

Kean's tour, meanwhile, continued to bring him misery. In Philadelphia,
warnings of a demonstration against him caused his engagement to be postponed for one week while Warren and Wood, the managers, negotiated for
police protection. There was a noisy outbreak on his opening night; a few
rotten eggs and other missiles were thrown at Kean. But he finally succeeded in
dominating the audience, and when he left the theater at the end of the performance the rioters who had tried to drive him from the stage cheered him
lustily as he drove away in his carriage. In Baltimore, however, a frenzied clash
between Kean's supporters and opponents finally resulted in a riot as violent as
that which had occurred in Boston. Early the following morning, a respected

Edmund Kean as Hamlet,
by Cruikshank

Baltimorean, Colonel Benjamin Edes, advised Francis Wemyss to get Kean out of the city immediately, for "if he attempts to play tonight, we shall tar and feather him, and he may think himself lucky if he escapes with no further injury." Kean was hurriedly put on a boat for Philadelphia, and after consultation with lawyers and the municipal authorities, Warren and Wood closed the theater. Although he was cordially received in Montreal and Quebec, the only American cities where Kean enjoyed any measure of success were Philadelphia and New York. And even in these cities he resorted to desperate expedients to attract the public. Having given a magnificent performance of *Henry VIII,* he also appeared in the afterpiece, choosing to put on Colman's familiar farce, *New Hay at the Old Market.* In this, playing the role of Sylvester Daggerwood, he offered impersonations of celebrated English actors, and made his final exit with a somersault. Similarly, he astounded his admirers by following another of his great tragic roles with *The Waterman,* a musical farce in which he sang the role of Tom Tug. It sometimes amused Kean, in private, to show off his acrobatic skill. But these public exhibitions were different, and many playgoers found them even more pathetic than tasteless. For, whatever your opinion of his character as a man, Kean remained incontestably the greatest of living actors. It was sad to realize that, long before leaving America forever, Kean had been reduced to displaying himself, on the same evening, as a supreme tragedian and a proficient clown.

One night, at the conclusion of a performance of *Richard III,* and before the curtain rose on the afterpiece, you might have observed a slight stirring in the audience. Everybody had noticed that one of the boxes was occupied by Junius Brutus Booth and his wife. Booth suddenly left the box. Was he going to Kean's dressing room? If so, drama of a high order was about to begin backstage. All playgoers knew that the two men had been professional foes for the past eight years, and the rumor went that they bitterly detested one another. Booth was absent from his box for a long time. He returned while the farce was in progress and immediately left the theater with his wife. She saw that his eyes glistened with tears, but he refused to answer any questions. Days passed before Mrs. Booth persuaded her husband to talk about his interview with Kean. He told her, at last, that when he announced himself at Kean's dressing room Kean immediately dismissed his valet, then embraced his old enemy. Hot toddies were sent for; the two men talked amicably for a while; then, seeing that Kean was greatly fatigued, Booth helped him to disrobe and left him. Many years later Mrs. Booth told this incident to her son, Edwin, and he always remembered her comment on it. "I am positive from your father's eyes and long silence on the subject," she said, "that there was more of pain than of pleasure in their parting."

The feud between Kean and Booth—which brought Junius Brutus Booth to the United States in 1821—had been the talk of London in 1817, and its noisy echoes crossed the Atlantic. Its real ground, as perhaps neither of the actors understood, was their uncanny physical resemblance. Both were undersized and slight of figure; they were of about equal height; on the stage, disguised by costume and the black wig traditionally worn when playing tragedies, they were

almost exact counterparts. Their voices were unlike. Kean's, in the upper register, was apt to be harsh or shrill; Booth's was exceptionally musical and resonant. Kean's hair was black, his eyes were very dark; Booth's hair was brown,
and his eyes were blue-gray. Though Booth was Kean's junior by almost ten
years, their likeness, in manner as well as appearance, was startling.

In 1817, when Kean reigned unchallenged at Drury Lane, Booth was given
a trial night at Covent Garden. He elected to perform *Richard III,* one of Kean's
most celebrated roles. Little was known about Booth except that he had
achieved some success in provincial theaters. The son of an attorney, Richard
Booth, he had received a good classical education, had developed an aptitude
for languages, and at the age of seventeen had shown his wayward temperament by joining a company of strolling players, though none of his forebears
had ever been connected with the theater. He played a long tour on the
Continent. He married, fathered a son. After his return to England, two years
passed before he was given his chance to invite the verdict of a London audience. William Hazlitt, the most influential of London critics, pronounced judgment on Booth's Richard. "Almost the whole of his performance was an exact
copy or parody of Mr. Kean's manner of doing the same part. It was a complete,
but at the same time, a successful piece of plagiarism. . . . We do not blame
Mr. Booth for borrowing Mr. Kean's coat and feathers to appear in upon a
first and trying occasion, but if he wishes to gain a permanent reputation, he
must come forward in his own person." All London was soon talking about the
new, "ingenious facsimile" of Kean. The management of Covent Garden, eager
to put Booth under contract, haggled over the terms which he felt his sudden
notoriety justified him in demanding. While discussions were in progress, Kean
became alarmed; what could be worse than the prospect of ceaseless competition with one's very counterfeit? Taking matters in his own hands, the great
tragedian personally invited Booth to leave Covent Garden and join him at
Drury Lane. A contract was quickly drawn up; Booth signed it—as he later
claimed, without having read it.

Presently, Kean and Booth were announced for *Othello;* Kean in the title
role, Booth as Iago. In one of his letters John Howard Payne, actor and playwright, reported the event. "The house was packed from pit to gallery; it was
a great performance, and a grand sight. The new little man behaved himself
like a great hero. Kean seemed to feel the force of the newcomer, and performed
up to the full height of his wonderful powers. In the jealous scene their acting
appeared like a set trial of skill, and the applause that followed the end of each
of their speeches swept the house like a tornado. The effect was almost bewildering. At the end of the play, both of the actors appeared to be exhausted
from the extraordinary effort they had made. Kean appeared to take much
delight in bringing Booth before the curtain. He seemed to enjoy Booth's
success just as much as the audience did." But did he? Booth concluded that
he did not. The Drury Lane contract, Booth realized, might be used to eliminate him as Kean's rival by deliberately restricting him to minor roles. As im-
pulsively as he had left it, Booth returned to Covent Garden. The competing
theaters at once went to law and carried their warfare into a battle of pam-

phlets. Public excitement became intense when Covent Garden announced Booth's reappearance in *Richard III*. The patrons of pit and gallery, however, had determined to punish Booth for his defection. They kept the theater in a continuous uproar; the play proceeded as if in pantomime. Similar riots broke out at three subsequent performances. Finally, Booth was permitted to address the audience; he made an abject apology; thereafter, no disorder occurred when he played. The memory of his humiliating plea never ceased to haunt him. Later, in the United States, he refused to take curtain calls, no matter how insistently the audience shouted, even though, whenever an audience displeased him, he would interrupt the play to scold them angrily.

Before Booth left England other humiliations aggravated his latent morbidity, his already strong tendency to erratic behavior. He was sensitive about his short stature; even more so about the fact that he was slightly bandy-legged. There was a night when, while the audience hung breathlessly on one of Booth's most impassioned scenes, an oaf in the gallery cried out, "Ha, Ha! You're a pretty fellow to stop a pig!" Never thereafter would Booth undertake a role that he believed to be beyond his physique. He could not look "heroic," he protested. In time, this became an obsession which prejudiced him against playing Macbeth and Othello; although his success in these roles was great, he performed them as seldom as possible. During the years that followed his imprudent contest with Kean, the charge of deliberate plagiarism was constantly revived. Whenever Booth played roles in which he had been preceded by Kean, critics raised the cry of servile imitation. When he undertook roles that Kean had never attempted, critics made the same point in another way, declaring that Booth was deficient in the ability to create characters, as Kean did, by conceiving them in original terms. Vain, high-tempered, abnormally proud, Booth suffered the more because he was able neither to ignore the critics nor refute them. People thought that Booth was firmly—perhaps excessively— convinced of his own genius. Yet his conviction was fitful and never quite absolute; he was driven to magnify it by the obstinate persistence of his doubts. It became clear that, in England, he could not hope to displace Kean, or even be accepted as Kean's equal, and nothing less would satisfy his inordinate ambition. Early in 1821, having become involved in a love affair with Mary Anne Holmes, Booth took her on a vcyage to Madeira. After a sojourn there, he decided not to return to England. Instead, he suddenly embarked with her for the United States. They landed in Norfolk, Virginia, on the last day of June, 1821, three weeks after Kean, driven from the American stage by the hullabaloo over his conduct in Boston, took ship for England.

So unpremeditated was his decision to begin a new career in America that Booth failed to procure the letters of introduction to Price or the Boston and Philadelphia managers which would have assured him a suitable debut and the aid of the press in preparing audiences for him in the eastern cities. He applied for employment at the theater in Richmond, where a summer season was in progress, and made his first American appearance in *Richard III,* billed as "the great tragedian from the London theaters—Covent Garden and Drury Lane." In nearby Petersburg, also, James H. Caldwell was giving a season, with a company brought from the theater that he had opened in New Orleans the previous winter. Caldwell sent a representative to Richmond to attend Booth's first performance; this man, impressed by Booth's acting, engaged him for Petersburg.

On the day that he was supposed to arrive in Petersburg for the sole rehearsal to be held before his scheduled evening performance, Booth failed to appear at the theater. The company proceeded to run through three acts of *Richard III,* and were about to begin the fourth, when—as Noah M. Ludlow, one of the actors, noted—"a small man that I took to be a well-grown boy of about sixteen years of age came running up the stairs, wearing a roundabout jacket and a cheap straw hat, both covered with dust, and inquired for the stage manager." It developed that Booth had missed the stagecoach from Richmond and had walked the twenty-five miles to Petersburg. "He ran through the rehearsal very carelessly," Ludlow recorded, "gave very few special or peculiar directions, tried the combat of the last act over twice and said 'That will do,' and the rehearsal was over." This astonished the actors, but Booth's performance that evening shocked and disgusted them. During the first three acts, he delivered his lines "with seeming indifference, after the manner of a schoolboy repeating a lesson of which he had learned the words, but was heedless of their meaning." It was not until the fourth act, and the scene in which Richard hints at the murder of the young princes, that Booth began revealing his power. Thereafter, Ludlow found his acting "unique and wonderful," and superior even to that of Cooke in the same role. At the final curtain, there was prolonged applause from the audience, in which the actors also joined. Actors in all the principal cities were soon to find that Booth loathed the drudgery of rehearsals, usually turned up late for them, was flagrantly careless. For, as audiences presently learned, Booth was not only a star, but a soloist; he lacked the sense of ensemble. He performed the level scenes of any play mechanically, as if bored by them, saving his energy for the climaxes. Then, suddenly, he was all ablaze; a monster, a madman, who held you breathless in terror. Playgoers called him "the little giant."

Always on the lookout for novelty, Stephen Price gave Booth a brief New York engagement at the Park Theater. To prepare the way for him, Price revived the old story of the feud with Kean. This was a disservice. It concentrated the attention of playgoers and critics on a comparison with Kean, whom they had seen frequently during the previous season. Misguidedly, Booth made this comparison easier by playing the roles in which Kean had enjoyed his greatest triumphs: Richard, Hamlet, Lear and several more. The New York newspapers quickly took up the London charge of servile imitation; newspapers in other cities followed their lead; the accusation cropped up for years. Patrons of the Park Theater were so little impressed by Booth's acting that Price, significantly, did not offer him the customary return engagement. In Baltimore and Philadelphia, however, Booth caused a mild sensation, adding to his repertory the role of Sir Edward Mortimer in *The Iron Chest,* which remained a favorite with his admirers for thirty years. Hostility to Kean predisposed Boston audiences to receive Booth enthusiastically, and his failure to win acclaim in New York also counted in his favor. In deciding questions of taste, cultivated Bostonians acknowledged no superiors; they considered the judgment of New York peculiarly dubious. They promptly proclaimed that Booth's acting "always evinced genius," and forever after abided by this verdict. (Years later, when told of Booth's death, the eminent lawyer Rufus Choate spoke for Boston with characteristically Bostonian finality. "There are no more actors!" he declared.) Charleston and New Orleans, which had not seen Kean, were lavish in their praise of Booth. The pattern of his subsequent career was being set by his first American tour. Booth would always make his greatest success, and attain his highest prestige, out of New York: in the cities of New England and the South, and the frontier towns of the West. New York's fashionable audiences and leading critics never accepted him as an artist of the first rank. But he came to be idolized by the patrons of the Bowery Theater, where the vogue for "heavy tragedy" afforded him unlimited opportunity to exploit his particular style of acting. It was the opinion of William B. Wood, the Philadelphia manager, who knew all the greatest stars of the era, that Booth "suffered the misfortune to be overvalued by some persons, and undervalued by others. He was seldom justly appreciated."

Certainly the feeling of misfortune oppressed him almost continuously. In part—but only in part—this prompted the innumerable eccentricities which quickly brought him notoriety in and out of the theater, making him, in the end, a national legend familiar to Americans who had never seen a play. Soon after concluding his first tour, Booth bought a farm in Maryland, near Baltimore. There with the woman he now called his wife, he eventually fathered ten children, four of whom died very young. He professed great reverence for all forms of life; cherished the notion that mortals, after death, would be held accountable to animals for their treatment of them; therefore permitted no animal, domestic or wild, to be killed. The family would probably have starved had not expediency suggested that his reverence make a unique exception of vegetable life. Booth became an inflexible, though reluctant, vegetarian. He abhorred contact with strangers and the isolation of his farm seemed not to assure sufficient privacy. So, deciding to retire from the stage and the world, he applied for a post as keeper of a lighthouse, but failed to obtain it. This reflected his curiously ambivalent attitude to his profession. He did not think it an unworthy one, but he wished none of his children to follow it, preferring, so his son Edwin recorded, that they engage in "anything that was *true*, rather than that they should be of that unreal world where nothing is but what is not."

Perhaps it was his own approach to his art that persuaded him that the world of art, a world of illusion, is a realm of essential falsity. The everlastingly reiterated comparison with Kean galled him. Americans demanded that an artist be "original," did they? Booth determined to show them that he could be more original, more individual, more peculiar than any other actor. Nothing could be easier; he was a man of many idiosyncrasies; he had only to give all of them free play. He felt that he did full justice to his work only if "inspired." If the mood failed, why not merely refuse to act or, without a word of warning, suddenly leave the crowded theater and disappear, perhaps for days? Booth left behind him a trail of capricious refusals to perform, and desertions of the theater while a play was in progress. Once, when playing Iago at the Bowery Theater, when the Othello of the evening was awaiting Booth's entrance, he stalked across the stage without uttering a word, made an irregular exit through a back door, quit the theater and forced the management to ring down the curtain until a substitute Iago could be costumed. After several days, Booth returned and persuaded the manager to let him continue his engagement. A notice was posted in which Booth explained that his "sad unconscious act" was due to "a serious visitation, affecting and enfeebling my nerves, and a long deprivation of sleep, acting on a body debilitated by previous illness and a mind disordered by domestic affliction; occasioning a partial derangement." Noting the incident in his diary, Philip Hone surmised that "there is no doubt that public sympathy will be excited to fill the house and give the poor fellow not only the forgiveness of the audience, but a kind and generous reception." There was, as Booth well knew, no doubt whatever. He could take these risks with impunity. His partisans idolized him and, for them, his bewildering extravagances merely thickened the romantic aura of "originality" that surrounded him. Wherever he was admired, he could count on crowded houses and, if he wished, hold audiences spellbound.

Not, however, without painful effort. He had to identify himself with his roles, actually live into them before performing. His method, a century later, would be taught in American schools of acting as that of Stanislavsky and the Moscow Art Theater. If Booth was scheduled to play Othello, Edwin Booth recalled, "he would, perhaps, wear a crescent pin on his breast that day; or, disregarding the fact that Shakespeare's Moor was a Christian, he would mumble maxims of the Koran. . . . If Shylock was to be his part at night, he was a Jew all day, and if in Baltimore at the time, he would pass hours with a learned Israelite, who lived nearby, discussing Hebrew history in the vernacular." He had a flair for playing villains; he was at his best, he knew, in such roles as Richard III, Sir Edward Mortimer, Sir Giles Overreach. In these, his deliberately cultivated originality was most obvious. He carried intensity of emotion to a pitch never before known on the American stage; the extreme realism of his scenes of terror, remorse, hatred, or vengefulness had never been approached. Early in his career, the American star James E. Murdoch played Wilford to Booth's Sir Edward Mortimer in *The Iron Chest,* and long afterwards reported the effect that Booth's acting produced on him in a climactic scene. "The heavy hand fell on my shoulder. I turned, and there, with the pistol held to my head, stood Booth, glaring like an infuriated demon. Then for the first time I comprehended the reality of acting. The fury of that passion-flamed face, and the magnetism of the rigid clutch on my arm, paralyzed my muscles, while the scintillating gleam of the terrible eyes, like the green and red flashes of an enraged serpent, fascinated and fixed me spellbound to the spot. A sudden revulsion of feeling caused me to spring to my feet, but, bewildered by fright and a choking sensation of undefined dread, I fell heavily to the stage, tripping Mr. Booth, who still clutched my shoulder."

The effort required to reach this exaggerated degree of realism was exhausting. Booth had to nerve himself to it, night after night. To stimulate his energy, he often took to drinking; a very little alcohol inebriated him, but gradually he had to increase the dosage. Eventually, singular things began to happen on stage. One night, when playing Richard at the Park Theater in New York, he chased the Richmond of the evening out of the stage door into the street. Playing the same role at the Bowery, he tried to murder the unfortunate Richmond in the duel scene, attacking him furiously in a frenzy of rage, foaming at the mouth, cursing wildly, refusing to die on cue, so that the actor playing Richmond had finally to throttle him and signal the prompter to drop the curtain. On another occasion, when playing the role of Othello, he prolonged the scene of Desdemona's death, so effectively stifling the actress that actors in the wings, finally realizing her peril, rushed onto the stage, overpowered Booth and tore him away from her. These strange fits came on him even when he had not been drinking. Audiences were electrified, but the actors knew that Booth had lost control of himself and his part. What he might do on the stage was unpredictable, for Booth, aware that Kean never varied the playing of any role, had adopted a contrary principle. Walt Whitman, who as a youth saw many of Booth's performances at the Bowery Theater, recalled in old age that he "was singularly spontaneous and fluctuating; in the same part, each rendering differed from any of his others. He had no stereotyped positions and made no arbitrary requirements on his fellow performers." But his extraordinary spontaneity only worked hardship on the actors of stock companies that he visited as a touring star. Most of them disliked the ordeal of having to play with him. Many of them feared the violence of his vagaries, and their apprehensiveness would not have been lessened had they understood that Booth's "oddities" had become, to him, only a source of suffering.

For these oddities, which he had deliberately assumed, eventually dominated him. He was swept by an irresistible impulse; he obeyed it; afterwards, there dawned on him the horrible certainty that other people had taken eccentricity to be aberration. So it was, too, with his efforts to create a supreme, overwhelming dramatic illusion. Was he losing the ability to distinguish simulation from reality? While he was expressing it, the simulated emotion became abso-

Junius Brutus Booth as Sir Giles Overreach in "A New Way to Pay Old Debts."
By W. Heath

lutely real, the false was suddenly made true. In earlier days, he had been able
to whip up a counterfeit of extravagant passion. But now, on the stage, he found
himself possessed by the villainies of the character he was playing. That way
lay madness, and he knew it. He no longer drank to nerve himself, but to
escape the demon he had conjured up. His drunken brawls were a terror to his
friends and, when he remembered them, a shame to him. And strangers, too,
were frightened by him even in his gentlest moods. One night, in a western
town, a young clergyman was summoned to Booth's hotel; the actor wished
him to conduct the funeral of a friend. For a long time, in Booth's private
parlor, the two men talked about theology, always a favorite subject with the
actor. Booth spoke of his belief in the transmigration of souls, of his belief in
human accountability to animals after death. Finally, the clergyman asked
about the proposed funeral. The corpse of his friend, Booth said, was in the
adjoining bedroom. They went into the bedroom. The bed and the floor were
covered with the carcasses of passenger pigeons. Booth explained. A migratory
flight of these birds had passed near the town; boys had wantonly slaughtered
them; Booth had bought them in the markets where they were exposed for sale.
They were his friends indeed, the friends of all mankind, and he insisted that
the young clergyman give them Christian burial. The clergyman never forgot
Booth's expression—was it melancholy, or some deep misgiving?—when, terrified by the discovery that his host was deranged, he refused and fled.

A few years later, Booth was traveling by ship to play an engagement in
Charleston. Suddenly, one day, he leaped overboard. He battled with the sailors
who rescued him; they had prevented him from carrying an important message
to a friend. Once back on the ship, he was overcome by dread that the vessel
was going to overturn; this shattering fear of disaster did not leave him until he
disembarked on the wharf. During the engagement in Charleston, Booth played
Othello to the Iago of his manager and beloved friend, Thomas Flynn. The
two men were sharing a room at the hotel, and after the performance Flynn
arrived there before Booth. Presently Booth entered, his face contorted with
rage. Still possessed by the character of Othello, he began the great scene with
Iago, "Villain, be sure thou prove . . ." Flynn tried to recall Booth from his
hallucination, but this only increased Booth's violence and he attacked his
friend wildly. In self-defense, Flynn seized the fire poker from the hearth, struck
at Booth's face. Though it broke the spell, the blow also broke Booth's nose.
The beauty of his face was permanently blemished, and his voice never recovered its magnificent resonance. Gradually it became clear to his associates that
Booth's mental instability was increasing, that he was passing beyond the
borderline of sanity. There came a time when Booth himself realized that
madness, final and incurable, might overtake him without warning; his only
certainty was that he never could be sure. He made his young son, Edwin,
accompany him on tour, nominally as his dresser, actually as his guardian.
Americans who flocked to see him as he wearily played across the country in
his later years may have agreed with Walt Whitman. Booth, Whitman declared,
"illustrated Plato's rule that to the forming an artist of the very highest rank
a dash of insanity (or what the world calls insanity) is indispensable."

CHAPTER 2

"Ours Is a Strange Trade"

DURING the decade that followed the first American appearances of Kean and Booth, Stephen Price brought to the United States all the most eminent stars of the British stage. In the autumn of 1822, the veteran comedian Charles Mathews arrived for a tour which astonished him by its unexpected success. A skillful player of high comedy, Mathews had won fame as an entertainer rather than an actor, offering an evening of short plays and sketches in which he assumed all the roles. In each city that he visited, he began his engagement by playing some of his most celebrated dramatic parts: Goldfinch, in *The Road to Ruin;* Sir Fretful Plagiary in *The Critic;* Morbleau in *Monsieur Tonson.* These delighted audiences everywhere but, to his amazement, they demanded that he also give them his "evenings" of monodrama. He had not supposed that his talents as a mimic, his skill in protean impersonation, or his strong bent for social satire would arouse any enthusiasm in America, but audiences never had enough of the "evenings." "I had only to hold up my crooked finger when I wanted them to laugh, and they obeyed my call," he wrote to his wife. "I was most agreeably surprised, indeed, at finding them an audience of infinitely

George Hanbel ("Yankee") Hill

more intelligence and quickness than I had expected." In Boston, Mathews played during a spell of intense cold; in his hotel room, the water in the pitcher froze to ice so solid that he was unable to break it with the leg of a chair; nevertheless, people came from as far as Salem in open sleighs to attend the "evenings." More remarkably still, when he concluded his engagement at the theater, he had to hire Boylston Hall and there repeat one of his "evenings," for the benefit of "those holy puritans who would not visit the theater to see an entertainment which they patronized in a hall." In the playing of comedy, Mathews established a tradition that was soon to be followed by the American comedian, James H. Hackett. And the pattern of his monodramas continued to be exploited, after more than a century, by such talented performers as Ruth Draper and Cornelia Otis Skinner.

Four years after Mathews, and one year after Kean's disastrous second tour, the tragedian William Charles Macready achieved such success that, during a tour prolonged to eight months, he had to return to every city that he visited and, in New York, played five engagements at the Park Theater. A star at both Covent Garden and Drury Lane, he was pronounced by William Hazlitt Kean's only rival in tragedy. This was sufficient to arouse curiosity, but interest in Macready was further excited by an element of novelty. In addition to the Shakespearian repertory common to all tragedians, Macready was to offer certain plays that had been written especially for him. Americans would thus see the original creator of the roles perform such celebrated dramas as John Banim's *Damon and Pythias,* and James Sheridan Knowles' *Virginius, Caius Gracchus* and *William Tell.* But while Macready was playing at the Park, the newly opened Bowery Theater pitted young Edwin Forrest against him. Forrest not only appeared in many of Macready's Shakespearian roles but, with defiant audacity, assumed those of Damon, Virginius and William Tell. The ill feeling born of this contest afterwards flared up in a feud which, more than twenty years later, culminated in an episode of violence and bloodshed that shocked the entire nation.

A tall, gaunt man, angular and awkward on the stage, Macready was in one respect an innovator. He had developed what he called "natural speaking"; when he declaimed blank verse, he uttered it as if it were colloquial prose. He professed to be an "intellectual" actor, unlike Kean and Booth, and contrived that every role should display his scholarship, and his talent for the subtle elaboration of character. All this brought him, in the United States as in England, the acclaim of sophisticated playgoers and people of fashion. To the patrons of pit and gallery, who rejoiced in "heavy tragedy," his studied, stiff way of acting appealed not at all. But weren't the high-pitched effects of heavy tragedians a little absurd, perhaps even a little vulgar? Playgoers who wished to believe that their taste was aristocratically fastidious rallied to the support of Macready. He became a cult with the social and intellectual élite of the cities where he played.

This taint of snobbery in his vogue would have caused Macready no displeasure had he been aware of it. He was rather proud of being, himself, a snob of the first water. His boyhood ambition had been to achieve a position of

Interior of the Park Theater, 1822, showing Charles Mathews and Miss Johnson in *Monsieur Tonson*

Charles Mathews as Monsieur Morbleu

social dictinction, but his father's financial misfortunes forced him onto the stage. He despised his profession as socially inferior to all others. He might be England's wealthiest, and even most famous, actor—but could he ever hope to be recognized as a "gentleman"? He thought not. His angry frustration vented itself in contempt for his professional colleagues. To actors who played with him he was insufferably arrogant, often insulting, sometimes downright brutal. In the United States, gossip about the "Macready tantrums" spread from greenrooms to the public. When he arrived in Philadelphia for his first engagement, William B. Wood gave a dinner in his honor, inviting as one of the guests old Joseph Jefferson, who had been cast to play the First Witch in Macready's opening performance of *Macbeth*. At rehearsal the following morning Jefferson, being lamed by gout, hobbled in leaning on a cane. Noticing this infraction of stage etiquette, Macready addressed the prompter. "Tell that person to put down his cane," he snapped. The prompter delivered the star's command. "Tell Mr. Macready," Jefferson retorted, "that I shall not act with him during his engagement," and he left the stage. Macready, he later explained, had ignored the fact that they were social equals and had previously met as such. "His purpose was to overbear and humiliate me, so as to subjugate the rest of the company." The incident was typical of Macready's behavior which, before the end of his tour, brought him permanent unpopularity with the American theatrical profession.

Even more extraordinary than the success of Macready was that of Charles Kean, who came over in 1830, at the age of nineteen, on a tour that kept him playing in the United States more than two years. Young Kean had not attained stellar rank in England and, in sending him over as a star, Stephen Price banked more heavily on his knowledge of his countrymen than on the fledgling's talents. Americans had come to feel shame and regret for their treatment of Edmund Kean, and their enthusiastic reception of his son, as Price foresaw, was partly dictated by conscience. Furthermore, they had peculiar reasons for being predisposed in Charles Kean's favor, irrespective of his capabilities as an actor. All playgoers knew that, three years earlier, in defiance of his father's prohibition, he had suddenly left school to support his mother and himself by the only livelihood open to him. The critics had been cruel to him, but young Kean persevered in spite of them and became reconciled to his father only after establishing his independence. This was the kind of grit that Americans admired; and Charles Kean's exemplary devotion to his mother, his personal probity, his scrupulously conventional conduct entitled him to approval. Undersized, like his father, young Kean was excessively plain. His voice was mediocre, his acting more strenuous than passionate. But his youth, his pluck and his obvious earnestness were ingratiating. Americans liked him the more for his temerity in playing Edmund Kean's most celebrated roles: Richard III, Hamlet, Sir Giles Overreach, Sir Edward Mortimer. Though comparisons were clearly unfair—and seldom made—the youth showed his spirit by not trying to evade them. The American moral sense, perhaps astounded by finding its ideals realized in so unlikely a subject, silenced all captious doubts about Charles Kean's talents. He was the first actor to win acclaim, not by his professional merits, but by his private virtues. This was a genuinely native criterion that many foreign stars were to find incomprehensible, but as the nineteenth century wore on, Americans resorted to it with growing confidence. And, having themselves promoted Charles Kean to international stardom, audiences in the United States, ignoring the reservations expressed by American and British critics, remained steadfastly loyal to him for more than thirty years.

In the spring of 1832, Charles Kean and James Henry Hackett were playing on alternate nights at the Arch Street Theater in Philadelphia. They met frequently, liked one another, and pooled their talents in a venture which provided Hackett with his most famous role. Kean suggested that they play Shakespeare's *Henry IV* together, Kean taking the part of Hotspur and Hackett that of Falstaff. Hackett had already attempted Falstaff at the Park Theater in New York four years earlier, but the results were so little gratifying that, in his later years, he always recorded the performance in Philadelphia as his first. Perhaps the memory of prior failure made Kean's suggestion the more provocative. In any case, the role appealed to Hackett—he could never resist an opportunity to play Shakespeare—and the production was made ready within a week. The first night gave scant promise that Hackett was subsequently to be accounted the greatest Falstaff of his era. His performance was so coolly received that the managers of the theater pleaded with Kean and Hackett to withdraw the play, but Hackett insisted on continuing and was rewarded, on the third night, by a warmly enthusiastic audience.

Hackett had been on the stage for only six years, but he was already able to

William Charles Macready as Iago,   from a painting by H. Pracey

impose his will on reluctant managers. As William Dunlap reported amazedly, "Without regular training, or the toil of *working up* in a company of comedians, he has seized the crown at a leap, and may say with Richard—'I am myself alone!' " For indeed, Hackett was in several respects unique. He was the first native American star, though Edwin Forrest followed him to stardom within the year. He was also the first American to appear, as a star, in London. At Covent Garden, in 1827, he had met with moderate success, much to the surprise of the English theatrical world, which was not only supplying the

American stage with stars, but nearly all other players also. Hackett's London engagement was brief and his welcome unspectacular, but the imputed approval of "Europe" greatly increased his prestige in the United States. He was the forerunner of all the American actors and actresses, musicians and opera singers who, in later years, were to find that the stamp of European approval enhanced their cash value at home.

At the age of thirty-two Hackett had already acquired a stately manner appropriate to the first—as yet, the only—American "gentleman" to adopt the profession of acting. People praised him, much to his discomfiture, as a "born comedian." His droll antics, his dry humor on the stage provoked explosions of laughter. Off the stage, he seemed like another man. He was handsome. His good looks would have had a fashionably "romantic" cast, had this not been erased by his monumental dignity. He set you to thinking, not of Byronic lovers, but of Websterian statesmen—there was, about him, an aura of beaver hat and flowered satin waistcoat, of scholarly erudition and senatorial eloquence; you expected him to communicate in a Ciceronian style studded with Shakespearian quotations; he did not disappoint you. Unlike Macready, Hackett never surmised that his profession could detract from his social standing. He was serenely aware of a gentility which, if not august, was more than adequately pedigreed. Was not his paternal grandmother the daughter of a Dutch baron? Was not his maternal grandfather Reverend Abraham Keteltas, whose exploits during the Revolution had made him honorably known as "the fighting parson"? The Keteltas connection allied Hackett with several distinguished families in New York's mercantile aristocracy: the Duanes, De Peysters, Roosevelts and Beekmans. The Beekman relationship was especially valuable, for Hackett's cousin, John Beekman, was John Jacob Astor's partner in ownership of the Park Theater. Its managers, Price and Simpson, were in no position to refuse any request made by Beekman, however little they liked it. This fortunate circumstance enabled Hackett to go on the stage.

He had hankered for a stage career during his student days at Columbia College, during a brief, unhappy clerkship in an attorney's office. Then, at nineteen, Hackett had married Miss Catherine Leesugg, a popular singing actress at the Park Theater—a misalliance that shocked his distinguished relatives. Clearly, something had to be done about this young maverick, whose only known talent was for mimicry; his imitations of celebrated actors were delightful. Cousin John Beekman set him up as a storekeeper in the upstate town of Utica, hoping that young Hackett would remain there until the scandal of his marriage had died down. Hackett prospered; he had an aptitude for business that eventually was to make him a wealthy man. Five years after his exile, he was back in New York, where an unlucky speculation reduced him to bankruptcy. In this emergency, Hackett's wealthy relatives came to his rescue, and Mrs. Hackett determined to return to the stage of the Park Theater, under her maiden name. Very likely John Beekman considered this decision financially prudent, though socially deplorable. It may have reconciled him to procuring, for Hackett, the long desired opportunity to make a professional trial of his amateur talent. Beekman forced Hackett on the mistrustful managers of the

William Charles Macready as Hotspur, by L. Haghe

Park. Then he rewarded them by using his influence to secure the presence of New York's aristocracy at the amateur's debut. This announced, to the public and press, that Hackett was no mere actor, but a gentleman whose odd ambition was endorsed by his eminent kinsmen and friends. On March 1, 1826, according to *The American*, Hackett's first appearance on the stage provided "the great attraction" at the Park Theater. The comedy *Love in a Village* was played, with Hackett in the role of Justice Woodcock and his wife in that of the heroine. In *The American* it was reported that Hackett "bore himself in the character more than respectably and gave a faint idea of what might be expected from a future display of talent which he is known to possess." This was scarcely an encouraging verdict, but he deserved no better. Overcome by stage fright, he performed so badly that certain august friends urged him never to risk another appearance. However, nine days later, he tried the role of Sylvester Daggerwood, which Kean had also used to display his talent for mimicry. Hackett offered impersonations of well-known actors, among them Kean and Mathews, and he also told a story in Yankee dialect. The audience received these efforts so enthusiastically that Hackett was immediately made a star.

His first stage laurels were won as a mimic, not as an actor. He undertook Charles Mathews' famous role of Morbleau, impersonating Mathews rather than playing the role. Morbleau was to become one of his most popular parts and he played it for many years, but it was only after he had gained assurance that he ceased to imitate Mathews and, instead, adapted Mathews' style of playing comedy to his own conception of the role. In a revival of *The Comedy of Errors* Hackett and the popular comedian John Barnes played the two Dromios. Hackett's mimicry of Barnes was so remarkably accurate in every detail of costume, make-up, gesture and intonation that bewildered but exhilarated audiences found it hard to tell the two actors apart. But in 1828, soon after his return from England, Hackett made the transition from impersonation to acting. The consequences extended far beyond his own career. He stimulated the development of a type of American comedy which was to hold the stage for more than a century.

Hackett had won great popular success with his stories told in Yankee dialect. Why not, therefore, try a play in which he could appear in the role of a Yankee character? Three years earlier there had been produced at the Park Theater *The Forest Rose,* a comedy by the New York playwright Samuel Woodworth. which continued to draw large audiences whenever it was performed. Woodworth had placed the action of his comedy in rural New Jersey, near New York, and had introduced in it a rustic character, Jonathan Ploughboy, that delighted the public. It was a play of this kind that Hackett wanted, with a fat part that would permit him to exploit his Yankee dialect. None being available, he decided to adapt *Who Wants a Guinea?,* a comedy by the British playwright George Colman, in which there figured a character, Solomon Gundy, described as a "French Cockney." By the simple expedient of transforming this character into a Yankee, Solomon Swop, and naming his version of the play *Jonathan in England,* Hackett created his required vehicle. (The author was gravely displeased when, some years later, as Examiner of Plays, he was called upon to license, for Hackett's performance in London, this perversion of his work, for which he had not given permission or received either credit or payment.) Hackett's success in this role was so prodigious that, during the next few years, he quickly added to his repertory other plays with Yankee characters. Some of these he wrote himself, or helped to write; others, he either commissioned from playwrights, or adapted from their works. Two of these plays—*The Times, or Life in New York,* and *The Moderns, or a Trip to the Springs,* laid in Saratoga— achieved an effect of social satire by introducing Hackett's salty, shrewd, self-respecting Yankee into the fashionable world. In *The Indian Wife,* which he adapted from *Montgomery,* a melodrama of the Revolution by the Boston actor-manager Henry J. Finn, he gave the comic Yankee a slightly heroic cast. But, with the exception of Solomon Swop, Hackett's two most successful Yankee roles displayed the New Englander against his native background. These were Major Joe Bunker in *Down East, or the Militia Training,* of which he was supposed to be the author, and Lot Sap Sago in *Yankee Land,* written for him by Cornelius A. Logan, an actor chiefly identified with the theaters in the West.

While gaining fame through his characterizations of New Englanders, Hackett diligently searched for other regional American types that would provide him with equally congenial and successful roles. In the spring of 1829 he appeared as Rip Van Winkle in a dramatization of Washington Irving's story, a part which won him high praise and which he continued to play for many years. A dramatic rendering of the story, by an anonymous playwright, had been produced in Albany one year earlier, but the version used by Hackett was the work of a British actor, John Kerr, and it had been played in London before Kerr, in 1827, came to the United States to join the company at the Chestnut Street Theater in Philadelphia. Five years after Hackett first assumed the role of Rip—he had meanwhile played a triumphant engagement in England—he discarded Kerr's version of the play and substituted another, written by the British playwright W. Bayle Bernard. Bernard also had a hand in the development of a role which, in point of popular success, far surpassed any of

James Henry Hackett,
by H. Inman

Hackett's Yankee characters. In 1830, Hackett offered a prize for a play on an American subject, by an American playwright. It was won by the New York novelist and essayist James Kirke Paulding, who submitted a drama entitled *The Lion of the West*. The central character was adroitly tailored for the comedian. Colonel Nimrod Wildfire, a Kentucky frontiersman, was an uncouth but authentic native type: reckless, humorous, prodigal, a notable fighter and teller of tall tales. Probably founded on Davy Crockett, who had already become a living legend to Easterners, Wildfire was the most vivid and vital contemporary character that had yet appeared in an American play. However, Paulding had not mastered the craft of writing for the stage and, shortly after the first performance of his play at the Park Theater, in the spring of 1831, Hackett proposed that it be revised by John Augustus Stone, an actor-dramatist who had recently won a prize offered by Edwin Forrest. Paulding consented, but the episode apparently left a sting, for he told William Dunlap that "Hackett overcharges the part for which the play is written and fills it with every cant phrase he can pick up," and suggested that he and Dunlap collaborate in writing comedies for the purpose of "upholding the American stage." But American playgoers didn't agree with Paulding's appraisal of Hackett's acting in the role of Nimrod Wildfire. Everywhere on tour *The Lion of the West* repeated its phenomenal success in New York, and when Hackett went to London in 1832 the play made a hit there also. As a result, Hackett commissioned Bayle Bernard to write *The Kentuckian,* another play about Nimrod Wildfire, as quickly as possible, for production in London. The play had a long run there and, after his return to the United States, Hackett played it for many years in every city that he visited.

The financial rewards won by Hackett with his Yankee roles made competition by other actors inevitable, and the demands of his rivals for new plays bore fruit in a school of rural drama that eventually exploited the regional peculiarities of other areas than New England. Three of Hackett's rivals in the field became celebrated touring stars in the United States and, like Hackett, also captivated British audiences. George Handel Hill, who soon came to be known as "Yankee" Hill, was a native Bostonian, an unsuccessful actor and barn-storming monologist who traveled the eastern circuit from Albany to Charleston. During Hackett's absence in England, Hill obtained an engagement at the Park Theater and, performing Hackett's role of Solomon Swop, scored an even greater success than its creator. Although Hackett had followed prevailing custom in appropriating the work of a British dramatist, he was furious at Hill's piracy of the play which he himself had pirated. Indignantly, he wrote to all American managers protesting against this "infringement of the most unalienable of literary rights, the spinning of one's own brains." Not content with this protest, he obtained an injunction prohibiting the performance of *Jonathan in England* by any other actor. But Hill had already become an outstanding, highly paid star, and he quickly developed a repertory of his own in which—always wearing a tow-colored wig, long-tailed coat, short vest and bell-crowned hat—he earned a substantial fortune. Hill was followed by Danforth Marble, a native of Connecticut who specialized in the Yankee type of that state. Marble was a favorite attraction on the western circuit and played in the eastern cities only infrequently. But during the first ten years of his career as a touring star he appeared in twenty-two comedies, most of them written to his order. Joshua Silsbee, like Hill and Marble, made his initial reputation in the western towns. He was more talented and more intelligent than either of his predecessors. They aimed at little more than a broad caricature of the Yankee, and their characterizations, in different plays, were repetitions of the same stereotypes. Unlike them, but like Hackett, Silsbee had acquired some technical proficiency before taking up Yankee comedy as a specialty. He was not content merely to delineate the Yankee as a type, to burlesque or caricature him. He aimed at individual portraiture in his characterizations, and developed a quiet, realistic style of acting that gave them the effect of life rather than farce. Silsbee attained great popularity in Boston and other New England cities, where playgoers considered his interpretations authentic. His most effective role was Solon Shingle in *The People's Lawyer,* a drama by Dr. Joseph Stephen Jones. Dr. Jones was a Boston physician and a prolific playwright; he was also an actor and manager. He was one of the best known American dramatists of the era, and some of his plays were produced, not only in theaters throughout the United States, but in Great Britain as well. All of these productions were pirated, and Dr. Jones was embittered by the fact that for them he "never received one dollar of remuneration." While this condition obtained, he declared, the United States would never have a native drama "creditable to our literature, and profitable to authors, managers and actors." It might have consoled him to know that *The People's Lawyer* would hold the stage for nearly fifty years, and that another of his New England dramas, *The Silver Spoon,* after a life almost as long, would again be made available for production, in revised form, during the second decade of the twentieth century.

The vogue of Yankee comedy was still new in the autumn of 1832, when

Fanny Kemble, the first great actress to appear on the American stage, arrived in New York with her father, Charles Kemble, the younger brother of Mrs. Siddons and John Philip Kemble. Was it conceivable, even in New York, that a manager should combine the distinguished art of the Kembles with the catch-penny vulgarities of "Yankee" Hill? Audiences at the Park Theater were not offended by incongruity. On two evenings, having been exalted by the Kembles, they waited to be diverted by Hill. He rewarded them, the first time, with a monologue, "The Yankee in Trouble, or Sephaniah in the Pantry"; the second time, he played the role of Solomon Swop.

An epidemic of cholera, during the summer, had ravaged New York, Boston, Philadelphia and Baltimore. The approaching presidential election was being hotly contested by President Andrew Jackson and Henry Clay; the whole country was in a turmoil. But in spite of these circumstances, the forthcoming tour of the Kembles provoked tremendous excitement. It could scarcely have been otherwise, since two generations of Americans had heard, not only about the genius, but the majesty of the Kembles. In England, the family commanded greater reverence than royalty. They were unique in theatrical annals; a dynasty, a national institution, a massive cultural treasure like the plays of Shakespeare or Westminster Abbey. The grandeur of Mrs. Siddons, in her prime, intimidated men who fancied themselves in love with her—one might as credibly make love to the ocean as to this auburn-haired goddess who froze the blood of her servants when she ordered a mutton chop. Of "Glorious John" Kemble, it was said that only after his retirement in Switzerland had he found a rival worthy of his notice; he was jealous of Mont Blanc. Lord Byron called the Kembles "supernatural," and the word was accurate; their scale appeared to be larger than life size. Their classic features, tall stature and regal carriage; their magnificent, ringing voices; even the family mannerism of measured diction which, when they spoke, made them seem to be declaiming blank verse—these attributes dwarfed any domestic frame, however spacious. The Kembles required a setting no less vast than Covent Garden, which they had built, managed, acted in, thereby establishing it as the first theater of Europe.

Disaster had finally come on Covent Garden, and this was why Charles Kemble and his daughter were undertaking an American tour. At fifty-seven, Kemble was still slender and vigorous; still known as the handsomest man in London; still regarded as the finest exponent of the classical style in tragedy, and as a master of high comedy also. But it was Fanny Kemble, not her father, about whom Americans were most curious. Three years earlier, when only nineteen, she had rescued her father from insolvency, averted the forced sale of Covent Garden, assured the livelihood of its seven hundred employees and, in one season, had become the acknowledged queen of the British stage. She had not been professionally trained for a theatrical career; her bent, and her ambitions, were literary. When her father turned to her for aid in his effort to stave off ruin, she agreed to go on the stage; with only three weeks to prepare for her debut, to appear in the role of Juliet. On the night of her first performance Covent Garden was filled by a brilliant, exacting audience. She held them spellbound, her triumph was absolute, and wild enthusiasm broke out as the final curtain fell. Old Mrs. Siddons, in her box, realized that no comparable demonstration had occurred since the night, forty-seven years earlier, when she had conquered London. Fanny Kemble played Juliet for an uninterrupted run of more than one hundred and twenty performances before London was willing to see her in another part. Then there followed a series of roles chosen for her by the management because they were identified with her illustrious aunt.

Only once, when a mere child, had Fanny Kemble seen Mrs. Siddons act, and her memory of the performance was vague. Terrified by the challenge, she accepted the roles without question. Conceiving them independently, she was acclaimed in all of them, even by people who remembered the splendor of her aunt's performances. One old family friend remarked that seeing her was "exactly like looking at Mrs. Siddons through the diminishing end of an opera glass." For Fanny, unlike her statuesque aunt, was slender and petite, and her hair and eyes were dark. Nevertheless, her resemblance to Mrs. Siddons was striking. She had the same beautiful brow, finely modeled features, noble throat and shoulders. But her voice was more musical than any other Kemble voice, and her temperament was her own. Every seat in Covent Garden was taken whenever she played. London shop windows displayed reproductions of Lawrence's portrait drawing. Plates and saucers, decorated with figures of Fanny Kemble as Juliet, appeared on the market. Gentlemen wore neckcloths imprinted with her portrait. She was amused to find herself "the small lioness" of the fashionable world. People were puzzled by her. Fancy an actress who was forbidden to enter the greenroom, and to whom nobody could be presented backstage! In society, she was always chaperoned by her father, mother, or spinster aunt. She delighted in dancing all night; she was a fearless horsewoman. Adulation enchanted her, but she refused to take it seriously, and nobody was prepared for a Kemble with a sense of humor. Moreover, what was to be thought of a reigning beauty who had written a poetic tragedy that was produced and published; who read "deep" books; who preferred the conversation of Sir Thomas Lawrence, the poet Campbell, or Washington Irving, to that of any beau? Fanny Kemble didn't seem to rate dramatic genius very high. "Certainly Mrs. Siddons was what we call a great dramatic genius," she recorded in her diary, "and off the stage gave not the slightest indication of unusual intellectual capacity of any sort." This was one thing that was never said about Fanny Kemble. Altogether, London didn't quite know what to make of her.

Nor, at first, did New York. The Kembles had brought letters of introduction to several prominent New Yorkers, among them Philip Hone, former mayor of the city and acknowledged leader of its fashionable society. Though neither was aware of it, Fanny and Mr. Hone had an interest in common; both kept very detailed, very candid diaries. Mr. Hone called promptly, and presently there arrived an invitation for Fanny, her father and her Aunt Dall, Miss De Camp, to dine at the Hone mansion on City Hall Park. Accustomed to "the innumerable invitations" of London society, Fanny did not realize that by giving a dinner in honor of an actress Mr. Hone was breaking, for the first time, an unwritten law of social exclusion. Her fellow guests, she surmised, represented "the best society in New York," but she did not know that, in

Fanny Kemble,
from a painting by Thomas Sully

securing their presence, her host had, in her behalf, put his social power to an extreme test. Her diary, that night, recorded—in an entry which later she was to regret deeply—some caustic observations on the company and the hospitality. The women had "an air of freshness and brilliancy," but she thought their costume, "a sort of French demi-toilette, with bare necks and long sleeves," peculiar. "The dinner was plenteous, and tolerably well dressed, but ill served; there were not half servants enough, and we had neither water glasses nor finger glasses. Now, though I don't eat with my fingers (except peaches, whereat I think the aborigines, who were paring theirs like so many potatos, seemed rather amazed) yet do I hold a finger glass at the conclusion of my dinner a requisite to comfort. After dinner we had coffee, but no tea, whereat my English taste was in high dudgeon." When the gentlemen joined the ladies in the drawing room after dinner, Fanny was led to "a tiny, old-fashioned, be-curtained cabinet piano stuck right against the wall," which was pitched too high for her voice; she disliked singing for strangers and was exasperated by singing badly. "I was very glad to come home," she noted, though she was appalled by the slovenliness of the American House and found its lack of privacy intolerable. Only a few days later, at another dinner party, she received an insight into the prejudice against the theatrical profession that prevailed in American society. One of the guests was Reverend Jonathan Mayhew Wainwright, "a very agreeable, good and clever man," and the rector of Grace Church, the most fashionable parish in the city. Dr. Wainwright "expressed great delight at having an opportunity of meeting us in private, as his congregation are so straitlaced that he can neither call upon us nor invite us to his house, much less set his foot in the theater. The probable consequence of any of these enormities, it seems, would be deserted pews next Sunday, and perhaps eventually the forced resignation of his cure of souls." To Fanny, this seemed incomprehensible; a number of eminent clergymen frequented the home of her parents in London.

Like Fanny, Philip Hone had also written up his diary. "Miss Kemble, like all young persons who have become celebrated, has many and strong admirers," he noted. "But many dislike her on first acquaintance. Her manners are somewhat singular. Allowance should be made for the peculiarity of her situation, just arrived among strangers, with a consciousness that she is viewed as one of the lions of the day, and as such the object more of curiosity than of affection. . . . She talks well, but will talk only when, and to whom, she chooses . . . She has certainly an air of indifference and nonchalance not at all calculated to make her a favorite with the beaux. I am confirmed in my opinion that she has astonishing requisites for the stage. Her features separately are not good, but combined they make a face of great and powerful expression. She is said to resemble her aunt, Mrs. Siddons. I am of the opinion that she does not like her profession. It is not her favorite theme of conversation; necessity, rather than choice, has led her to adopt it. Her father is a gentleman of fine manners and dignified deportment, somewhat stiff—for he is a Kemble—but evidently well bred and accustomed to good society." And Hone predicted that Fanny, at her American debut, "would make the most decided hit we have ever witnessed, or would fail entirely."

He was not only a good prophet, but an excellent reader of minds. Fanny was that most improbable of creatures, a great actress who disliked her vocation. "Ours is a very strange trade, and I am sorry to say that every day increases my distaste for it," she wrote while on her American tour. She had gone on the stage purely from a sense of duty to her parents. The theatrical profession was utterly distasteful to her, though acting, in the form of dramatic personation, was not; but she found every detail of her profession—from the preparations behind the scenes to the actual performances—more or less repugnant. Neither time nor custom diminished this aversion, and sometimes she marveled that, liking her work so little, being so devoid of enthusiasm, respect or love for it, she achieved any success whatever. "A *business* which is incessant excitement and factitious emotion seems to me unworthy of a man," she wrote; "a business which is public exhibition, unworthy of a woman." Then, too, she had a "constant consciousness of the immeasurable distance between a fine conception and the best execution of it," and, in any art, she could be satisfied with nothing less than "a noble ideal beauty." Far from stimulating her imagination, the conditions of her profession confined it. "Acting seems to me rather like dancing hornpipes in fetters," she summed it up. "Were it possible to act with one's *mind* alone, the case might be different." But in this, Fanny's achievement transcended her own estimate. "The great peculiarity of her acting is *mind,*" a New York critic wrote; "it is full of intellectual excellence. . . . This is, indeed, *acting.*"

The management of the Park Theater suggested that the Kembles make separate debuts, then form "a constellation." Charles appeared first, in *Hamlet.*

The audience was enthusiastic; the critics praised him highly; and Philip Hone, who thought him thirty years too old for the role, acknowledged that his acting "ought to improve the American stage." But it was Fanny that the public awaited, and she wondered about the quality of its taste. Did it only approve "the stamp-and-stare-and-start-and-scream school" of acting? "I am not sure that, upon the whole, our acting is not rather too quiet—tame, I suppose they would call it—for our present public," she wrote a friend in England. "Ranting and raving in tragedy, and shrieks of unmeaning laughter in comedy, are not, you know, precisely our style, and I am afraid our audiences here may think us flat." She was to make her debut as Bianca, in Reverend H. H. Milman's tragedy, *Fazio,* a powerful role and one of her best; Milman himself had told her that no other actress could approach her in the part. Unfortunately, the young leading man at the Park Theater, Mr. Keppel, hadn't been able to learn his role, and on the momentous night was too frightened to take advantage of Fanny's assiduous prompting. Had not the play been written practically as a monologue for the heroine, the performance would have gone to pieces. But Fanny touched supreme heights in her rendering of Bianca's love, hate and jealousy. "I have never witnessed any audience so moved, astonished and de-lighted," Philip Hone reported. "Her display of the strong feelings which belong to the part was great beyond description, and the expression of her wonderful face would have been a rich treat if her tongue had uttered no sound. The fifth act was such an exhibition of female powers as we have never before wit-nessed, and the curtain fell amidst the deafening shouts and plaudits of an astonished audience. . . . I am quite satisfied that we have never seen her equal on the American stage." Hone's opinion was borne out by the press. Fanny herself was astounded by the public's infatuation with her; by "the enormously expensive nosegays and huge baskets of forced flowers" that were passed across the footlights; by having in her hotel room "as many as a dozen huge baskets of camellias, violets, orange-flower and tuberose," and by receiving a table of magnificent hothouse flowers so large "that both sides of the street door had to be opened to admit it." And a group of adoring young men, with a band of musicians, came to serenade her, in the street, under her hotel window. Not knowing that this was a spontaneous demonstration of their devotion, she opened the window, rewarded the leader with a dollar, and was covered with confusion when he assured her that he would keep it forever.

Meanwhile, the engagement proceeded. Fanny played Juliet to her father's Romeo; the management had been forced to withdraw the inept Keppel. Thirty years earlier, Charles Kemble had been a celebrated Romeo; now, he was accounted an incomparable Mercutio; but though age disqualified him for the role of the young lover, he sustained the illusion of youth by the grace and eloquence of his acting. In its tenderness, passion and poetry, Fanny's Juliet was so profoundly moving that it became the standard for all other actresses. She displayed her talent for comedy as Lady Teazle in *The School for Scandal* to her father's Charles Surface; as Beatrice, in *Much Ado About Nothing,* to his Benedick; as Bisarre in Farquhar's *The Inconstant* to Charles's Young Mirabel, a role which he played with extraordinary elegance and subtlety. But audiences preferred Fanny in tragedy, and she agreed with them. For comedy was intellectual, not emotional; to play it beautifully, "tact, discretion, fine taste" were indispensable, in short, "a highly educated perfection" that was the fruit of long discipline and maturity. She was too young, too untrained, for comedy. But her Belvidera, in Otway's *Venice Preserved,* was a triumph. It was one of her aunt's most famous roles, but Fanny detested it, for the heroine, to her, seemed only a "lay figure in a tragic attitude." However, the last scene, in which Belvidera, having gone mad, digs in the earth for the body of her husband, finds it, and utters a blood-curdling shriek—this scene always froze audiences in horror, an effect that produced thunderous applause for which Fanny felt only contempt.

Fanny triumphed again as Julia, in Sheridan Knowles's *The Hunchback,* a role which she had created, the previous year, at Covent Garden; a role which every actress of note, during the next half-century, would undertake, striving to equal Fanny's performance of it. As Julia, Fanny brought to the stage a new type of girl; sprightly, impulsive, a natural coquette bewildered by the complexity of the fashionable world, yet always made enchanting by her youthful ardor. People said that Fanny's Julia represented the girl of the moment, that she was authentically "a modern." Anna Cora Ogden, the young daughter of a New York merchant, went with her father to one of Fanny's performances in *The Hunchback.* She had heard Fanny talked of, not only as a great actress, but "as a most devoted daughter and truly excellent woman." It was Fanny's high moral repute that persuaded Miss Ogden to defy the judgment of the rector of her church, who denounced theaters as "abodes of sin and wickedness." Although she had "a decided passion for plays and acting"

Fanny Kemble as Belvidera in
"Venice Preserved."
By Cruikshank

she had never before entered a theater. "I thought I had never beheld any creature so perfectly bewitching," she wrote of Fanny later. "The tones of her voice were richest music, and her dark, flashing eyes seemed to penetrate to my very soul. . . . The play was a reality from beginning to end, and I laughed and wept immoderately." All playgoers said the same thing, but for Anna Cora Ogden the experience of seeing Fanny play Julia proved to be decisive. It dissipated all her prejudices against the theater and, indirectly, later determined her to become an actress.

From New York, the Kembles went to Philadelphia, a ten-hour journey by steamer, coach, train drawn by horses, and another steamboat. The Philadelphia public, Fanny learned, "has high pretensions to considerable critical judgment and literary and dramatic taste, and scouts the idea of being led by the opinion of New York." Audiences in the eastern cities, though welcoming the stars sent them by Stephen Price, were beginning to resent the growing theatrical domination of New York. But Philadelphia, as a young man of the city described it, "went Kemble mad." Fanny preferred it to New York, because it had "an air of greater age." However, this relative antiquity was not the sole source of its appeal; there was also an "interesting youth." Pierce Butler came of a family regarded as socially distinguished. He was handsome, fond of music and the theater, a fine horseman. And he was very rich; he and his brother had inherited two Georgia plantations, with hundreds of slaves. Fanny was revolted by the institution of slavery, but young Butler, in his obvious infatuation, amused her. From Philadelphia, the Kembles went back to New York for a second engagement. Then they returned to Philadelphia, where Pierce Butler—always under the watchful and by no means approving eye of Fanny's Aunt Dall—pressed his suit. His cousin, the painter Thomas Sully, executed a portrait of Charles Kemble and made several attempts to paint Fanny, never to his satisfaction until, one night, seeing her as Beatrice and catching a fleeting, passionate expression, he hastily left the theater, returned to his studio, and painted her from memory; Fanny thought the portrait an excellent likeness. The Kembles played an engagement in Baltimore, went on to Washington, where Fanny and her father were received privately by President Jackson and paid homage by such dignitaries as ex-President John Quincy Adams and Daniel Webster. In Boston, the furor over the Kembles was so great that Fanny saw crowds rush the box office "to the imminent peril of life and limb, pushing and pummeling and belaboring one another like madmen" and learned that speculators "smear their clothes with treacle and sugar and other abominations, to secure, from the fear of their contact of all decently clad competitors, freer access to the box-keeper."

When the Kembles returned to New York, late in May, 1833, for a last engagement before the summer, everybody was talking about Pierce Butler's extraordinary pursuit of Fanny. Were they, or were they not, engaged to be married? Sitting beside Fanny at a dinner party, Washington Irving said that he had been told that she was engaged to Butler, intended to marry him and settle in the United States. An old friend of the family, Irving tried to warn Fanny discreetly; she would be happy in the United States only if she made the best of things as she found them. Other friends were more explicit; they warned her that Butler was "so infinitely inferior to her that the experiment of marriage might be dangerous." Charles Kemble planned a pleasant summer holiday. They would play a brief engagement in Albany, journey westward across the state by canal boat and private stage, visit Niagara, take the St. Lawrence steamer for Montreal and Quebec, play in both cities, then return to the United States for their final season of touring. Kemble invited Edward Trelawny, the buccaneering friend of Byron and Shelley, to accompany them; Pierce Butler, by this time a fixture in their lives, also went along. In the course of their summer's journey, Fanny fell in love with Pierce Butler, but she did not engage herself to him. The trip was marred by only one accident; near Rochester, the Kembles' driver had overturned their coach, and Fanny's Aunt Dall had sustained an injury. During the autumn she was taken ill, and the doctors told Fanny that her aunt would be a lifelong invalid. Miss De Camp had no money of her own; she had devoted her life to the Kembles; Fanny determined to make financial provision for her aunt's future. A Philadelphia publisher, Matthew Carey, had made repeated offers for the manuscript of Fanny's American journal. She had always refused them; now, to raise money for her aunt, she signed a contract and gave Carey the journal to publish; all names were to be left blank.

Everywhere the Kembles played, that autumn and winter, audiences were thrilled by Fanny's acting as never before; she transcended even the greatest of her earlier performances. "She certainly played this evening with the most affecting pathos and tenderness, and so the audience appear to think, for I never saw persons more attentive and more deeply affected," Philip Hone wrote. "This will probably be her last engagement, if the report is true that she is married already, or about to be, to Mr. Pierce Butler of Philadelphia." But the report was not true; Fanny was neither engaged nor married, though Butler was still persisting in his courtship. The tour continued. By now, Fanny's distaste for acting had become positive loathing, but contracts could not be broken, and it was necessary to earn sufficient money to provide for the old age of her father and mother. While the Kembles were playing an engagement in Boston, in April, 1834, Fanny's aunt took a turn for the worse. Night after night, Fanny hurried from the theater to the sick room, never certain that her aunt might not be dead when she arrived. Then her aunt died, and Fanny had her buried "in a lonely lovely place in Mt. Auburn Cemetery, where Pierce and I used to go and sit together last spring, in the early time of our intimacy. I wished her to lie there, for life and love and youth and death have their trysting place at the grave." There were more engagements to be played, in New York and Philadelphia, but Fanny wrote to a friend in England that she and her father would arrive there in July. In Philadelphia, she changed her mind and told Pierce Butler that she would marry him. She anticipated "no fairyland of enchantments within the mysterious precincts of matrimony," but "rest, quiet, leisure to study, to think, and to work, and legitimate channels for the affections of my nature."

Fanny Kemble and Pierce Butler were married in Philadelphia on June 7,

1834, and went to New York, where Fanny and her father were under contract for a final engagement. Her farewell to the theater, as she thought, was made as Julia in *The Hunchback,* after a series of performances that evoked the wildest enthusiasm. Fanny was the first actress to marry a gentleman of great fortune in the United States, and for a time Americans heatedly debated this social novelty. Then the excitement died down, only to be revived by the publication, in 1835, of the *Journal* of Frances Anne Butler. The two slim volumes caused an immense sensation. In general, Americans were infuriated by Fanny's account of their domestic manners and customs. A wave of indignation surged up in the press. In New York, Philadelphia and Boston "society" found it all too easy to supply the names that had been left blank. Drawing rooms buzzed with the annoyance of people who were convinced that Fanny had abused their hospitality. "There is all the light gossip, the childish prejudice, the hasty conclusions from erroneous first impressions, in which the diary of an imaginative youthful traveler in a country where all things are new and untried, may be supposed to abound," Philip Hone recorded. He copied into his diary Fanny's account of the dinner which he had given in her honor, making interpolated observations of his own to correct the record. Fanny had departed from the party "leaving no very favorable impressions behind her." Mr. Hone regretted that he had no liveried footmen, but his staff, he thought, were "rather smartish." As to the absence of water glasses, Fanny was mistaken; "we are never without them." As to the finger bowls, he scored a point. "With all submission, I disagree with my fastidious guest. We have them in the house but do not frequently use them. I think it unseemly to see a company at the dinner table, particularly the female part, washing their hands, rinsing their mouths, rubbing their gums with the finger, and squirting the polluted water back into the vessel, as was formerly the fashion in this country, a fashion which prevails yet in England in the higher circles." As to his piano, Hone agreed with Fanny—but the instrument, as he wished she knew, had cost him $700. Altogether, Philip Hone was not offended, and when, three years later, he met Fanny and her husband at a fashionable resort hotel, he touched her to tears by his courteous attentions.

Although the hullabaloo over Fanny's journal eventually died down, a certain feeling of rancor against her persisted. Americans did not foresee, any more than she did, that she was to return to the public as the foremost interpreter of Shakespeare's plays, or that the publication of another of her journals, during a conflict between North and South, would help to sway British sympathies to the cause of the North.

CHAPTER 3

Players on the Frontier

BEFORE Stephen Price had proceeded very far in his grand design, he discovered that life sometimes holds an irony in reserve for the exorbitantly ambitious. A daring project may succeed too well, and the unforeseen consequences of excess are apt to impose a heavy penalty. Price intended to develop an appetite for novelty in American playgoers, and gratify it by importing the most celebrated London stars. Yet who could have predicted that this appetite would quickly take the form of an obsessive craving? Or that the desire for novelty would become so morbidly exclusive as to dominate all theatrical affairs? But these were the first effects of Price's momentous project, and the first theater to suffer from them was his own. The Park Theater soon found that whenever it did not offer a visiting star, the stock company played to empty houses. The blight promptly spread to other cities. In Philadelphia, as Francis Wemyss indignantly noted, audiences demanded "novelty, new faces, strange faces," and failed to attend the theater when the demand was not met. In Boston, the same situation prevailed. "The favor of the public is lavished on *stars*," the *United States Gazette* complained, "while the deserving but less aspiring performer is neglected and disregarded."

Meanwhile, Price's concept of the theater as a field for speculative business enterprise had fired the imaginations of other promoters. Mostly, they were capitalists without any practical experience in the operation of theaters. But was this any disadvantage to men well versed in large affairs, capable of apply-

William B. Wood,
from a painting by J. Neagle

ing to a disorderly form of commerce the principles that assure financial profits? Not at all; besides, they could readily find managers willing to serve them. Unable, or perhaps not wishing to acquire control of the existing theaters, their plan was to build new ones. This program seemed to be justified by the booming times, which had brought about a rapid multiplication of urban factories, mills, banks, insurance companies and other enterprises. Commercial expansion was creating a new, fairly prosperous class of workers who, presumably, would be eager for the luxury of entertainment. For the first time, a formerly aristocratic diversion was to be made widely available to "the people," the "democracy"— with profit to the gentlemen who proposed to put dramatic art on a sound business basis.

Within a few years, the old Federal Street Theater in Boston was being challenged by the Washington and Tremont Theaters. In Philadelphia, the Chestnut Street Theater had to meet the competition of the Walnut Street and Arch Street Theaters. In New York, the monopoly of Price and Simpson's Park Theater was broken, and its fortunes seriously compromised. For three seasons, the Chatham Garden Theater was a formidable competitor, and very fashionable. The imposing Lafayette Theater was built on Laurens Street (now West Broadway) near Canal. Its stage was larger than any in England or the United States, and could be transformed into a tank of water during any performance. Stage illumination and machinery, for the first time, were controlled from the flies. But in splendor and size, these playhouses were far surpassed by another. This was the Bowery Theater, built by a group of wealthy New Yorkers on the Bowery just south of Canal Street, and opened with appropriate ceremonies in October, 1826, under the direction of Charles Gilfert. The Bowery, with its spacious portico, handsome lobbies, richly decorated auditorium that had four

William Warren

tiers of boxes and seated three thousand people, was incomparably the finest playhouse in the United States. It was illuminated, throughout, by gas jets shielded with ground-glass shades; a noteworthy innovation. There was another, even more significant. Gilfert hired a man to "write up," for the press, notices of his theater and accounts of the actors whom he wished to popularize; this anonymous publicist was the first theatrical press agent. Gilfert and his wealthy proprietors hoped that the Bowery would attract the most fashionable audiences in the city, as well as the metropolitan public. Initially, seats in the pit and boxes were sold at the same price: 50 cents. After a few nights, in order "to keep a portion of the house free from admixture with the vulgar and unrefined," the price of box seats was increased to 75 cents, and that of seats in the pit reduced to 37½ cents. But this measure failed to produce the desired result and, after a few years, the Bowery became the acknowledged citadel of "the democracy."

With the breaking up of theatrical monopoly in New York, Philadelphia and Boston, a period of savage competition began. Foreign stars were the only attraction that could be relied on to fill the theaters, and other managers determined to become independent of Price in importing them. The Chestnut Street Theater sent Francis Courtney Wemyss to England to recruit stars and stock actors; the Federal Street Theater sent Henry James Finn; Gilfert sent a representative. But even Price, with his superior facilities, could not obtain a sufficient number of stars of the first magnitude to satisfy the monstrous, incessant demand for novelty that he had conjured up. He and his competitors alike were compelled to send over, by the dozens, actors and actresses who, having failed to achieve stellar rank in London, arrived as stars in the United States. Many of these stars-by-necessity were less talented than the experienced stock actors who supported them, and their faint light soon went out. But some of Price's "discoveries" shone with remarkable brilliance, for he had a flair for the kind of novelty that would pay off in America. Miss Lydia Kelly, known to London only as the undistinguished sister of a successful actress, proved to be a gifted comedienne. In turn, she captivated New York, Philadelphia and Boston, played repeated engagements in each city, and eventually returned home richer by $25,000. The fortunes of Miss Clara Fisher were even more spectacular. She was a girl of sixteen, extremely pretty and extraordinarily versatile. In Great Britain, from her sixth year, she had tremendous success as a child prodigy, appearing in such roles as Richard III, Shylock, Sir Peter Teazle and Young Norval. To American audiences she personified novelty, astounding everybody by her unprecedented variety. She played protean roles in farce; enacted romping girls and mischievous boys in light comedy; sang English popular songs; undertook such operatic parts as Cherubino and Susanna in *The Marriage of Figaro;* gave spirited performances in high comedy like *The Belle's Stratagem* and *The Rivals;* and received praise as Shakespeare's Juliet, Ophelia and Beatrice. The furor over Clara Fisher swept the eastern seaboard. Ladies copied her gowns and style of hairdress. Her name was given to hotels, ships, stagecoaches, race horses, songs and dance music, even the juleps, flips and slings served in taverns.

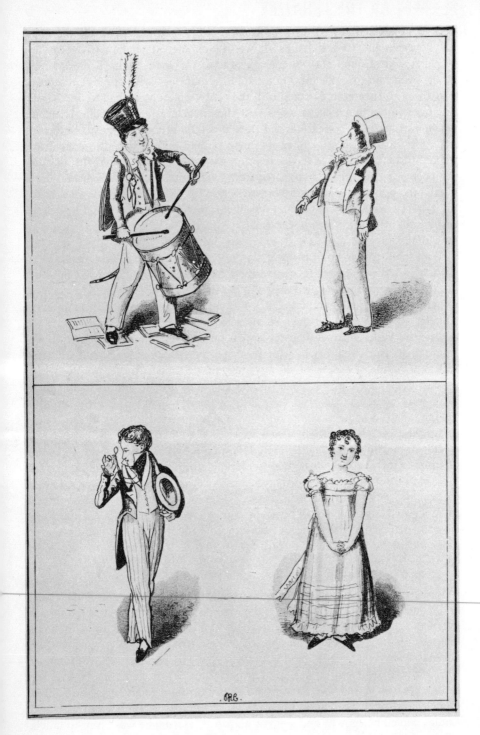

Miss Clara Fisher as The Four Mowbrays

Far more curious was the sensational success of Master Joseph Burke, who had achieved notoriety in Great Britain as "the Irish Roscius." He was a child prodigy, and American audiences went wild over him. Supported by adult stock actors, this diminutive star played Richard III, Hamlet, Shylock, Sir Giles Overreach and many other roles, not as a mimic, but according to his own peculiar interpretation. Young Master Burke's performances launched a strange fad for the playing of adult roles by precocious children, and an avalanche of infant stars presently lisped their way across the stages of American theaters, to the pleasure of audiences and the profit of managers. (One of them Louisa Lane, had preceded Burke, but achieved greater success in his wake. Later generations were to know her as Mrs. John Drew, a celebrated actress, manager, and founder of a theatrical dynasty.) Few people shared William B. Wood's contempt for the vogue of child stars. "I have ever held the baby-acting in infinite scorn, and finely have I been abused for laughing at the pretensions of Burke and Clara Fisher," the veteran Philadelphia manager wrote sourly to William Dunlap. But what were managers to do when the demand for novelty was so insistent? Worse things than Burke were in store for them. Lacking a stellar attraction for one week, the Chestnut Street Theater felt compelled to offer Calvin Edson, "the living skeleton," in the leading role of a play. In similar circumstances, the Arch Street Theater hastily negotiated for the services of Mlle. D'Jick, who could claim to be the most imposing feminine star yet seen, for she was a Siamese elephant. Managers knew better than to rely on the unaided efforts of their stock companies. At the Chestnut Street Theater,

Master Burke

for example, a performance of *The Rivals* with an excellent, though starless, cast had brought to the box office only $22.50.

Competition between rival theaters in New York, Philadelphia and Boston intensified their need for a ceaseless succession of stars. But the hostility prevailing among managers prevented them from combining to resist the exorbitant demands of stars who dictated their own terms. Thus James W. Wallack insisted upon receiving $200 a night, irrespective of the management's expenses or receipts at the box office. Miss Lydia Kelly demanded comparable fees, and required that she be paid in cash before the curtain rose on the final act of the play. Frequently the curtain was held while she sat on the stage in her costume, and her Irish maid carefully counted her stipend, the stock actors looking on in the dismal certainty that this drain on the treasury meant that their salaries would not be paid. For, under these conditions, full houses did not necessarily enable a manager to meet his expenses. And the situation was further complicated by a capricious public which, although star-hungry and clamorous for novelty, was inexplicably fickle. Managers were constantly faced by the swift decline of box-office appeal that overtook even the most popular stars without any apparent reason. Despite her phenomenal vogue, Miss Clara Fisher on a third round of engagements failed to draw large audiences, and the meteoric ascent of Master Burke soon reversed itself. The promoters who had determined to put dramatic art on a sound business basis were presently appalled by the results of their efforts. In New York, Henry Wallack, elder brother of James W. Wallack, found himself a bankrupt after one season as manager of the Chatham Garden Theater. Charles Gilfert met the same fate at the Bowery after three splendid seasons. In Boston, the first season of the Tremont Theater brought its manager, William Pelby, to insolvency. The proprietors of the theater themselves undertook a second season and lost $27,000. Eventually, to maintain the Tremont, they had to purchase the rival Federal Street Theater and close it. In Philadelphia, during the season of 1828–1829, five managements failed at the three theaters.

Francis C. Wemyss

For the actors in stock companies, the new "star system" held dire consequences. Accustomed to playing as an ensemble, to a carefully planned repertory designed to exploit their individual capabilities, they found themselves reduced to a condition of subserviency in which their sole function was to enhance
the attraction of a visiting star. And the new fickleness of the public hit them
hard. The case of Joseph Jefferson was one for which Philadelphia playgoers
long felt shame. Jefferson, whose father had been a colleague of David Garrick's, came to the United States at the age of twenty in 1796. After successful
engagements in Boston and New York, he joined the Chestnut Street Theater
stock company in 1803, becoming over the years so great a favorite that he
seemed almost to be a civic institution. Even in youth he was known as "Old
Jefferson" for, although a brilliant all-around comedian, he was at his best in
old men's roles. Two of his daughters and his son, Joseph II, followed him to
the stage. In 1829, he announced a benefit performance which very few people
attended. Heartbroken, Jefferson left the Philadelphia stage forever and set
out with his son to seek their fortune in minor theaters. Their luck soon ran out.
Eventually, they set up a company in Harrisburg, Pennsylvania, which—as
William B. Wood recorded—"must have been small and very imperfectly established in such a village." There, in 1832, "Old Jefferson" died in obscurity.

No story more eloquently illustrated the transiency of public favor than that
of Miss Emery, one of the recruits whom Francis Wemyss had brought from
England to Philadelphia. Tall, handsome, statuesque, she enjoyed outstanding
success in tragic and "heavy" roles, and was soon engaged by the Chatham
Garden Theater in New York as a star. After playing leading roles with Edwin
Forrest at the Bowery, her popularity began to wane. She joined the theater in
Albany, returned to New York, obtained occasional engagements. But these
became more and more infrequent; then, there were none. Miss Emery had to
sacrifice her home and sell her furniture at auction. Presently, her creditors took
possession of her fine theatrical wardrobe. Even had engagements offered, she
would not have been able to accept them. The stock actors at the Park Theater,
when they came to dress for the evening's play, frequently found her at the
stage door in Theater Alley, desperately ready to plead for small loans which
they knew could never be repaid. On their charity she managed to survive,
sharing with a poor family rooms in the Five Points, New York's worst slum,
where prostitutes and criminals congregated. One night, upon her return to this
miserable lodging, Miss Emery was brutally assaulted by a drunken neighbor.
She fled into the street, staggered a few blocks, collapsed and died.

By 1830, the bankruptcy of managers, the improbability of engagements, the
nonpayment of salaries when employed, made the plight of stock actors acute,
and the prospects for all but the greatest stars extremely uncertain. In Philadelphia, so well-known an actor as Francis Wemyss offered to play, for $5 a
night, payable in advance, roles which he had previously performed, asking
$10 if required to study a new part. But even on these terms, he could not
obtain enough work for a livelihood. He placed in the newspapers an advertise-
ment headed "Starved Out!" which announced that he had taken up the business of selling lottery tickets. In New York and Boston, as in Philadelphia,

"actors were to be seen walking the streets . . . with their toes protruding from their shoes, their elbows from their coats." Disaster had fallen on the theatrical profession in the cities of the eastern seaboard. For stars and stock actors alike there remained but one land of promise. This was the frontier.

When actors talked of the frontier, they referred to "the West" or "the South." The West denoted the land beyond the Alleghenies, as far as the Mississippi. The South meant the states of Georgia, Alabama, Mississippi, Louisiana and Tennessee. To the profession in general, these regions lay beyond the boundaries of civilization, a vast wilderness in which there were isolated primitive settlements and a few towns that boastfully claimed to be cities. In the South, New Orleans, where the Spanish and French population were said to resent Americans; a town plagued by yellow fever, infested by gamblers and gougers, seething with violence. In the West, Pittsburgh, steeped in coal smut and sin; Cincinnati, which prided itself on its culture. A year or two was to pass before Mrs. Frances Trollope, an Englishwoman residing there, would incense the nation with her book, *Domestic Manners of the Americans*. She reported that a cultivated resident of Cincinnati had told her, "Shakespeare, Madam, is obscene, and thank God we are sufficiently advanced to have found it out!" But even lacking the advantage of Mrs. Trollope's observations, actors surmised the worst. Rumor had it that money was to be made on the frontier. Yet nothing less than imminent destitution would have persuaded them to forsake the cities of the East to earn money in that immense, violent, semi-barbarous land of promise. Nearly seventy years later Clara Fisher, one of the first new stars to make the venture, recorded in a single sentence the feeling of all her colleagues: "I had a horror of going South."

Nevertheless, a warm welcome awaited them. Life in the booming frontier cities and towns had great areas of deprivation, and in the smaller settlements offered little more than continuous, grinding hardship. Many settlers, having come from seaboard cities, cherished nostalgic memories of the theater, and in nearly every town there flourished a "Thespian Society" which from time to time performed standard plays. Since respectable women could not take part in these performances, female roles were acted by men. One of the members of a Thespian Society in Cincinnati recalled, long afterwards, a production of *Douglas*—typical of such productions everywhere—in which "a Mr. Sweeney . . . was Lady Randolph, and he acted the character very well, considering that his voice was decidedly a baritone, and he had not shaved for a week. The 'meditating maid,' Anna, was personated by Mr. George Row, a tall, lank carpenter, who chewed tobacco and was obliged to turn aside every now and then to spit."

But meritorious as these amateur performances were, and eagerly attended whenever given, they merely increased the yearning of unhappy townsmen for the theater of the eastern cities, with its world of illusion which, if transplanted, would also become a world of brief, luxurious escape from reality. Sixteen years before hard times forced the theatrical profession in general to seek a livelihood on the frontier, the frontier sent East for professional actors.

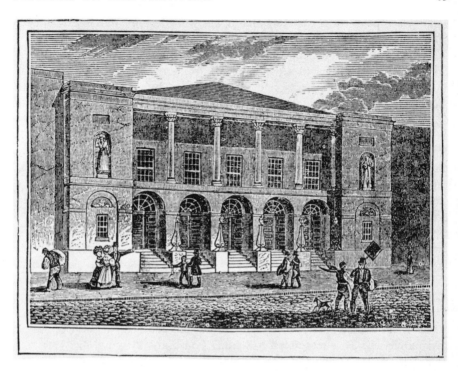

Second Chestnut Street Theater, Philadelphia

In the autumn of 1814, Noble Luke Usher, an actor earlier known in the theaters of New York, Philadelphia and Boston, applied for an engagement at the theater in Albany, New York, and was hired to play for a few nights. Samuel Drake, Sr., formerly a member of the Federal Street Theater stock company, was now, with several of his children, associated with the Albany theater, a notably unprosperous institution. To Drake, Usher stated that he had recently arrived from Kentucky, and that his main object in coming East was to engage a company of actors for that state—then regarded as "the far, far West"—where Usher claimed to own theaters in Frankfort, Lexington and Louisville. Drake agreed to form a small company with whom he would start for Kentucky the following spring, to play under Usher's management. But to form the company proved almost impossible. Experienced actors and actresses, profitably employed in the eastern theaters, refused to consider so wild a project—it meant a long journey by wagon, or on horseback, to the headwaters of a river, then another, even longer, by keelboat or flat-bottomed "broadhorn," drifting down treacherous waters through a wilderness where the few settlers were as likely as not to rob, or even murder, strangers. Drake offered to engage Noah Miller Ludlow, a twenty-year-old, stage-struck lad who had been playing small parts in the Albany Theater. "He told me very candidly that he was going on a voyage of adventure which possibly might result disastrously," Ludlow recalled sixty-five years later. But, at the time, Drake's offer represented an opportunity to play good roles and gain acting experience, and

Ludlow accepted it with alacrity. That it was going to bring him to a dominant position in the theatrical affairs of the West and South, Ludlow did not surmise.

For the rest, Drake depended chiefly on patriarchal authority to assemble the first theatrical company to set out for the frontier. It consisted of his sons, Samuel Drake, Jr., Alexander and James; his daughters, Martha, aged about thirty, and Julia, a girl of fifteen; Miss Fanny Denny, soon to become the wife of Alex Drake; Mrs. Lewis and her husband, who was to serve as stage-carpenter; Joe Tracy, hired as man of all work. Drake planned to have the company perform in towns along the way to Kentucky, not wishing to arrive there before the autumn, because a profitable engagement at Frankfort, the capital, was anticipated during the session of the state legislature. (It was a current delusion that legislators required entertainment when, actually, they provided it. Even the case of Washington, where the theater often played to empty houses during the sessions of the Congress, led no manager to the natural conclusion that the legislative chambers of the Capitol were, in fact, playhouses in which comedies were performed for audiences that paid no admission.)

In the summer of 1815, Drake's company, in two wagons and on horseback, moved westward across the state of New York from Albany to Canandaigua. There, they turned southwest to Olean, "a wild-looking place" on the Allegheny River, where horses and wagons were sold and a broadhorn, or "ark," was purchased. This resembled a floating house about twenty-five feet long and fifteen wide. At one end, there were two small rooms in which the women slept; the men "were expected to rough it." Navigated by "Old Sam" Drake, the ark drifted downstream only by daylight. From dusk to dawn it was always anchored, or tied up to shore if conditions were favorable, and the men of the company stood watches to detect possible marauders. One night, weary of the ark's discomforts, the company proposed to camp ashore. The younger men of the party, in a skiff, went to reconnoiter but returned in haste; they had come on a pack of wolves. The dismal howling of wolves became, to the company, the familiar night music of the river. At length they reached Pittsburgh, to find bad news awaiting them. Their impresario, Noble Luke Usher, had died on his way back to Kentucky. His theaters were now owned by his uncle, Luke Usher, who had no desire to assume responsibility for the company but was willing to give them the use of the buildings. Contrary to his expectations, "Old Sam" Drake was now entirely on his own—a penniless theatrical enterpriser who, with his company and costumes and scenery, had been abandoned to the hazards of the frontier.

In Pittsburgh, the company acquired a few professional recruits. The city already had a crude, frame theater used by its two Thespian Societies, organized by law students and by "respectable mechanics." The Drake company began its season in August, 1815, with a performance of John Tobin's comedy, *The Honeymoon*. The rousing success of this program inflated their ambitions, and they proposed to give Sheridan's *Pizarro, or the Virgins of the Sun*. This immensely popular play required elaborate scenery for the Temple of the Sun, and a procession of virgins, worshippers in the shrine. Since the company did not have enough women to make up a creditable procession, Drake was opposed

Walnut Street Theater, Philadelphia, 1811, The Oldest Existing Theater in America

to giving the play, but the actors finally won his reluctant consent. On the night of its performance, the first act went admirably. When the curtain rose on the Temple of the Sun, the delighted audience applauded enthusiastically. The local band struck up the processional hymn and, from each side of the stage, a virgin entered, veiled and robed in white. They met in the center of the stage, marched up to the altar of the god, knelt in reverence, then took positions at the sides of the altar and began chanting their hymn. The first pair of virgins, enacted by Mrs. Lewis and Miss Denny, were followed by a second, the Misses Drake. A third pair then entered, robed and veiled like the others. They were the property man, a short, corpulent figure, and a tall, scrawny old woman who had been hired to clean the theater. This pair concluded the procession, and also shattered the audience's illusion. As they met in the center of the stage, a roar of laughter broke from the spectators, and the actors, equally affected, gave up trying to play the scene with appropriate solemnity. Yet, despite this mischance, and many others, the Drake company played in Pittsburgh for nearly three months, and were able to collect enough money to permit their departure for Kentucky.

In November, 1815, they embarked on a broadhorn for the trip down the Ohio River. Arriving a week later at Maysville, they sold the ark, bought horses, a wagon for the actresses and one for the scenery, costumes and properties, and set out for Frankfort. There, other actors joined them briefly; these temporary recruits had been playing with a company recently taken to Cincinnati by William Turner and his wife, Sophia, English stock players who had appeared in several eastern cities. The Kentucky capital was not overwhelmed by the splendors of its first theatrical season, and many weeks passed before Drake took in enough money to move his company onward. Louisville, the next stand, proved unexpectedly profitable. Although the town had only three thousand inhabitants, "the people were prosperous, gay and fond of theatrical amusements," and the company played there for ten weeks. They then proceeded to Lexington, where the theater was located above a brewery, and there they terminated their season in the midsummer of 1816.

The year's record since their departure from Albany was not financially, reassuring. But "Old Sam" Drake had boundless confidence. He and his family decided to try a second season in Kentucky; if possible, to build up a permanent "circuit." Other members of the troupe, Ludlow among them, seceded and formed a company on the "commonwealth," or co-operative principle. This group made their way southwest, performing in every hamlet that they passed through, using as theaters the barrooms of taverns or any vacant shelter large enough to accommodate their few properties and small audiences. Barnstorming in this fashion, often hungry and desperate, they reached Nashville, Tennessee, early in the summer of 1817 and gave that remote capital its first experience of professional theater. After a season that lasted three weeks, Ludlow and another member of the company, Aaron Phillips, set out for Cincinnati on horseback to obtain replacements for those actors who, disheartened by hardships and lack of money, were abandoning the venture. In Cincinnati, Ludlow and Phillips found William Turner and his wife still in business. These indestructible optimists had, somehow, managed to keep a company playing. But that Ludlow was able to persuade actors to leave it for the more hazardous prospects of Tennessee indicates how little prosperous were the fortunes of Cincinnati's first professional theater.

Returning to Nashville with their recruits, Ludlow and Phillips and the "American Theatrical Commonwealth Company" began a second season. But since Nashville could not support a permanent theater, Ludlow soon proposed a far more reckless venture. New Orleans had a French theater, but no English-speaking company had ever performed there. Why not go to New Orleans? Phillips, frightened by the unsavory reputation of the city, opposed Ludlow's plan and resigned from the company when his objections were overruled by the others. Ludlow was appointed their manager. The first steamboats were already plying the Ohio and Mississippi, but there were none as yet on the Cumberland, so the company purchased a keelboat, named it the *Noah's Ark* for their leader, and prepared for the long voyage down the Cumberland, Ohio and Mississippi Rivers. A veteran river man offered welcome suggestions. They must always keep to the most rapid current. They must beware of sandbars, and the "sawyers," or uprooted trees, which—invisibly caught on the sandbars—were likely to stave in the keelboat. When approaching places known to be the haunts of river pirates, they must await the coming of another boat and travel with it. The river man enumerated other perils, and indicated the precautions to be taken.

But, inured to danger by their barnstorming tour through Kentucky and Tennessee, Ludlow's actors and actresses were not daunted by the perils of the rivers. Some of them recalled a night when, reaching an isolated inn very late, they had found it fully occupied by a band of evil-looking mule drivers. To obtain shelter, two actors quickly adapted the ghost scene from *Hamlet,* played it as if it were actually happening, and so thoroughly scared the supposed desperadoes that they fled from the inn. On their voyage down the rivers, actors and actresses often had to pole the boat around sandbars, and when passing the lairs of river pirates both men and women were armed with swords and spears taken from the company's stock of properties. Probably some performances were given on the keelboat at tiny settlements where it tied up overnight. In December, 1817, *Noah's Ark* arrived at Natchez, Mississippi. The reputable quarter of Natchez was situated on a bluff high above the river, but the river-bank district, known as Natchez-under-the-Hill, was notorious as a haven for gamblers, prostitutes and criminals. Everywhere along the Mississippi Ludlow had been warned that its residents "were safer to be encountered in the daylight than after dark." Performing for this raffish public would be extremely profitable, and the finances of the American Theatrical Commonwealth Company were in a bad way. But Ludlow was a stern moralist, and if any issue arose between profits and principles he knew only one way to decide it. The actresses of his troupe must not play in any depraved tavern or dance hall of Natchez-under-the-Hill. Fortunately, in the main town, on the bluff, there was a small theater used by amateurs. There, to a genteel audience, the company performed *The Honeymoon* and *The Lying Valet.* Either virtue or art was rewarded, for the receipts enabled Ludlow to take his troupe to New Orleans on the next steamboat.

In New Orleans, they opened at the St. Philippe Theater on Christmas Eve, 1817, with the inevitable *Honeymoon* and a farce, *The Hotel.* The theater "was crowded from bottom to top, half the audience being French and many of them not understanding one word in a hundred that was spoken. Nevertheless, the performance went off with great applause." This initial success launched Ludlow and his players on a prosperous season which continued into the spring of 1818, when the company returned to Natchez. There, Ludlow was stricken by illness, and the first theatrical troupe to play in the "deep South" was disbanded. However, New Orleans did not long lack an American theater. Rumors of Ludlow's success there drifted back to the East. James H. Caldwell, established as a manager in Richmond and Petersburg, Virginia, decided to risk an exploratory visit. Caldwell had come from England only a few years before, a young utility actor capable of playing any kind of role, who hoped to find wider opportunity for his talents in America. It came more quickly than he had dared to expect. Chance suddenly brought him the responsibilities of management, in which the avoidance of failure was almost the equivalent of outstanding success. In one respect, Caldwell was a precursor of the modern American theatrical enterpriser. His greatest gift was the ability to charm money from wealthy backers—as he first proved by persuading the rich men of Petersburg to build a theater for him. But, in another respect, Caldwell exemplified the stage of his own day. He wanted to be, not merely a successful manager like Price, but an actor-manager. Management, if he were lucky, might eventually make him rich. But it also had a more immediate attraction. It enabled Caldwell, as a businessman, to promote Caldwell, his favorite actor, to the star roles which talent alone would not have won for him so soon.

Caldwell was in his late twenties when, in the autumn of 1819, he and his Virginia company took ship from Norfolk for New Orleans. A company that had been brought from Paris was occupying the French Theater on Orleans Street. Caldwell arranged for his players to alternate with them and give performances three nights each week. His season lasted until April, 1820, so successfully that, after a summer season in Virginia, he returned the following autumn. The second season, also, proved profitable. When Caldwell brought his company to New Orleans in the autumn of 1821, it was with the intention of establishing himself there permanently. To this season he added luster by providing the novelty of two visiting stars. One was Junius Brutus Booth, who had performed *Richard III* the previous summer in Caldwell's Virginia theater. The other was Thomas Abthorpe Cooper, who was induced to take the long sea voyage from New York by Caldwell's promise to pay him $300 for every performance. Booth and Cooper aroused such great enthusiasm that Caldwell brought them back for annual engagements, and soon began casting his nets for other visiting stars to enhance the lure of his own continuous, but solitary, stellar light. Meanwhile, he had also put to work his uncanny gift for persuading men of wealth to finance his projects. This time, with a prophetic intuition of the methods of later American civic "boosters," he appealed to their civic pride. New Orleans had a French theater. But wasn't it an American metropolis? Shouldn't the American cotton factors, shippers, traders, be ashamed of the fact that, as yet, it had no American theater? They were, and Caldwell received enough money to build one. The Camp Street Theater was opened with great ceremony in 1824, staffed by a stock company of notable excellence. It was the first building in New Orleans to be illuminated throughout by gas; since no gas company yet existed in the city, the theater manufactured its own supply. (The lack of a municipal gas service was not lost on Caldwell. In 1833, he retired briefly from management and organized a company to provide the city with gaslight. The company prospered. Caldwell later organized similar enterprises in Mobile and Cincinnati and it was from these investments that he became wealthy after failure, in 1843, forced him to retire from the theatrical business.) Long afterwards Caldwell recalled that, when he built his theater, St. Charles Street was a marsh where boys went to shoot snipe; that Camp Street had only a few shanties, tobacco and cotton warehouses; that, for several years, to reach the theater, "people had to travel on gunwale sidewalks, and . . . carriages could not be used after a heavy rain in places so far out of the way as Camp Street."

Yet, from the outset, Caldwell's theater was successful and highly profitable. In some measure this was due to his monopolistic position, which remained unchallenged until 1840. Caldwell believed that the economic advantages of monopoly were mysteriously translated into an artistic benefit to the public. He argued that competition inflated the cost of everything connected with the stage and, as a result, often prevented managers from offering their audiences

James H. Caldwell

the finest talents available. Late in his career, Caldwell claimed that competition had brought the American theater to evil days by directly fostering "the most destructive system associated therewith—the starring system." The complaint that the theater was going to the dogs was, of course, a hardy perennial with a long history, and managers came to hold the star system responsible for the purported degeneration of the stage from its earlier, palmy days. But that Caldwell shared this view was somewhat remarkable, for few managers had more successfully exploited the star system; and he had, besides, made himself a star. Though Caldwell favored monopoly, he proved himself an expert in the tactics of ruthless competition. Wherever a pioneer manager opened up virgin territory, Caldwell soon followed and tried to supplant him. He annexed Natchez; he invaded the towns of Alabama; he contested with "Old Sam" Drake in Tennessee and Kentucky; for a time, he controlled theatrical affairs in Cincinnati; he made a daring attempt to include St. Louis in his orbit. Caldwell was the first theatrical enterpriser in the United States to conceive the project of creating an empire—and when, in 1835, he provided New Orleans with the St. Charles Theater, which surpassed all other American playhouses in luxury and splendor, it seemed an appropriately magnificent monument to his Napoleonic ambition. By that time, as he said, "I had one hundred and seventy-six thousand dollars, cash assets, in my grasp." He had developed his uncanny touch to almost absolute efficiency, for the cash assets, though in his grasp, were for the most part not his own.

Theatrical pioneers began hearing about St. Louis soon after "Old Sam" Drake took his band of actors out to the frontier. In this remote settlement, the first dramatic performance ever given west of the Mississippi had taken place on January 6, 1815, when the local Thespian Society produced *The School for Authors,* a comedy, and *The Budget of Blunders,* a farce, in the Courthouse. With a population of some two thousand, the town had the look of many another frontier village. Its three narrow streets were unpaved, unlighted and lay deep in filth. Most of its houses were primitive shelters built with logs or mud, though already there were several mansions in the New Orleans style, and some stone dwellings also. Two-thirds of the inhabitants spoke French only; the rest were Americans. St. Louis was the most isolated community of its size in the United States. There was, as yet, no comparable town within many hundred miles. To reach it from New York City by way of the Ohio River required a journey that took about three months. To reach it from New Orleans took almost as long, for until the first steamboat came in 1817 broadhorns had to be "cordelled" against the current of the Mississippi—a rope was tied to the boat, which was then pulled upstream by men on the bank, while a navigator steered the boat away from the shore with a long oar—and by this method progress seldom exceeded twenty miles a day. Life in St. Louis was as violent as in New Orleans. Murders and duels were frequent; so were manhunts for escaped slaves. Yet there existed a "refined and cultivated society" in the town, a cluster of wealthy French and American families that imported from the East fashionable, expensive attire and other luxuries, gave balls and parties, and had a fondness for diversion.

The entertainments of this social élite, and the dramatic performances staged by amateurs, were given in a one-story frame building originally erected for a blacksmith shop. So St. Louis, in a manner of speaking, had a theater ready for the first professional actors, whenever they should come. Early in January, 1818, the steamboat brought them—William Turner and his wife, with a company of fourteen. Incorrigibly hopeful though they were, the Turners may have surmised that this expedition was to be decisive. In Cincinnati, they had finally been forced to acknowledge utter defeat, and an effort to establish themselves in Lexington, Kentucky, had been crushed by "Old Sam" Drake and his family. But, if they had any doubts about the outcome of their venture, the Turners concealed them and offered the St. Louis public an ambitious repertory. For five months, the Turners and their troupe persisted, possibly because they lacked enough money to leave. Then they disappeared into the mists of frontier history. John H. Vos and his wife, members of the company, remained in St. Louis, where Vos took up his former trade of house and sign painting, an occupation no more remunerative than acting. But Vos stimulated an interest in the drama. A small theater, seating six hundred people in its single tier of boxes, pit and gallery, was built on Main Street, and amateur performances were given there, notably one for the benefit of Vos and his family, who were "in distress." It might have consoled the luckless sign painter to know that, eventually, he and his wife would earn their livelihood on the frontier stage, and that their daughter would become one of its favorite stars.

The next professional troupe to visit St. Louis arrived in March, 1820, and was led by Noah Ludlow. After the disbanding of his American Theatrical

Commonwealth Company in Natchez two years earlier, Ludlow had formed a small company, "half of it entire novices," and presented a summer season in Huntsville, Alabama, then a town with a population of little more than one thousand. He met with some success. The wealthy planters of the vicinity drove into town with their families to attend the performances; and "they soon began to consider theatrical amusements necessary to their pleasure." But since this necessity was not sufficiently urgent to assure Ludlow a livelihood, he abandoned the venture. The company which he brought to St. Louis was not greatly superior to the half-amateur troupe with which he had invaded Alabama. Besides Ludlow and his wife, it included nine men and four women, to whom Ludlow happily added Vos and his wife. He had every reason to consider them fortunate finds, for among his actors were a stage-struck tailor, a one-legged former sailor, and three printers, while one of the actresses was an aspiring amateur, and another a mere girl of fifteen. The company had been playing under Ludlow's management in Nashville, and had made the voyage to St. Louis by keelboat, drifting down the Cumberland and Ohio Rivers and cordelling up the Mississippi. "I confess I felt a little discouraged when I landed in St. Louis," Ludlow wrote; "it was not anything like as cleanly or as well built as any of the towns of the West or South that I had previously visited." Assuring the public that "no piece will be allowed to appear that shall be in any way indelicate or improper," Ludlow announced that performances would be given on Wednesday and Saturday nights, the curtain rising at six o'clock. Seats in the pit and boxes were priced at one dollar; in the gallery, at 75 cents; these were the charges then current in the East.

But soon after Ludlow's company gave their first performance, his former manager, "Old Sam" Drake, arrived from Louisville, Kentucky, on the steamboat *Rapide,* with a company that included his talented family, Palmer Fisher, his wife and two remarkable children. The Fishers were English players who had won some repute in the East, and their little daughters, Alexina and Oceana, already performing children's roles, were later to be among the first well-known actresses to follow the gold rush to California. Finding Ludlow in possession of the theater, Drake installed his company in the "ballroom" of the City Hotel. Its superiority to Ludlow's was all too obvious, and after three nights Ludlow gave up the hopeless contest and, with his wife, Vos, and some other members of his troupe, joined Drake's forces. "The talents of the two companies being thus combined, the expectations of the citizens cannot be raised too high," *The Enquirer* declared. "The females attached to the corps are all young and respectable performers, and it is a query whether there is a stage in the United States that can boast of a constellation of female beauty superior to that of St. Louis." Certainly few theaters in the East offered a larger repertory. During the month of April, more than twenty plays were produced; among them, *The School for Scandal, The Iron Chest, Othello* and *King Lear.* Yet neither this varied fare nor its vaunted constellation of female beauty enabled the company to prolong its season. After some weeks of diminishing business, Drake and his players departed.

Vos and Ludlow, with their families, remained in St. Louis and were soon in financial straits. Vos went into bankruptcy, but presently assembled a "Thespian Corps" and offered St. Louis another dramatic season in the Courthouse. Ludlow, after vainly advertising that he would undertake jobs of "framing and gilding" pictures and that his wife would "execute every description of painting in water colors," went off to act in Nashville, where the theater was being operated by the firm of Collins and Jones. Joshua Collins had been a member of the pioneer troupe brought to Cincinnati by William and Sophia Turner. When the Turners finally left the town, he remained there. Presently he formed a partnership with William Jones, an actor who had come West from the Park Theater in New York. For a time, they produced plays in a loft over a store, using such actors as they were able to find. By 1820, they had prospered sufficiently to build the Columbia Street Theater, which they opened with a company of actors from the East headed by Mrs. Groshon, who had played at the Park Theater. Collins and Jones hoped to build up a "circuit" in the West, and began by taking over the theater in Nashville. Ludlow may have persuaded them that St. Louis could be added to their territory. In any case, they decided to take their company there from Nashville.

Most of the troupe were sent by keelboat to the mouth of the Ohio River, there to take the first steamboat up the Mississippi. But Jones and his wife, Mrs. Groshon, her husband and their eight-months-old infant, with Ludlow, determined to make the journey overland. The Groshons and their infant traveled in a buggy; the others, on horseback. For weeks they fought their way through freezing cold; through the terrors of a tornado which sent trees crashing down along their course; they forded swollen streams, Ludlow holding the Groshon infant high above his head. Often they were without food and sometimes were refused shelter at isolated log cabins. When admitted to cabins, the men sat up all night, pistols in hand. Finally, they arrived in St. Louis, and

Sol Smith

the Collins and Jones season opened at the theater in December, 1820. Playing three nights each week, the company performed a wide range of dramas that included *Venice Preserved, Pizarro, Richard III, Macbeth, She Stoops to Conquer*. But when the season closed in April, 1821, the managers, after paying their bills, found that they had lost money on the venture. Concluding that St. Louis was not a "theater town," they took their company back to Cincinnati. Even Ludlow, however reluctantly, was forced to concur in this verdict. He and his wife left for New Orleans to join the Caldwell troupe, soon to depart for a summer in Virginia.

In Cincinnati, where his older brothers had established a store, young Sol Smith joined the Collins and Jones company as prompter. Already married at the age of twenty-three, he was earning his living by editing a newspaper, playing the organ in a church, and conducting singing classes; he was also studying law. But the theater had been his love ever since, as a boy of twelve in Albany, he had formed an acquaintance with the younger Drakes and stolen away at night to watch performances from the wings. During his travels on the frontier, he had done some acting also and when, in 1823, Collins and Jones offered to lease him their Cincinnati theater he seized the chance to establish himself as an actor-manager. His season was a failure, and left him heavily in debt. A barnstorming tour to Pittsburgh with a remnant of his company proved no more profitable, and a season in Pittsburgh, with excellent players recruited from the Drake company in Louisville, was so disastrous that Smith and his wife had to make their escape from the sheriffs by stealth. Nevertheless, Smith refused to give up the career he had chosen. The next years were filled with vicissitudes. Sometimes, like Noah Ludlow, he was employed by James Caldwell, acting in New Orleans or managing detachments of Caldwell's company that were sent to Natchez and Nashville. Sometimes, also like Ludlow, he tried his luck as an independent actor-manager, taking bands of strolling players to the little towns of Alabama, Georgia, Mississippi and Tennessee. The life was not easy. One season, having divided his company between Natchez and Port Gibson, fifty miles away, Smith had to make the journey every morning by horseback, for as the star of the troupe he had to play on alternate nights in the two towns. Another year, having taken his troupe from Montgomery, Alabama, across the lands of the Creek Indians to Columbus, Georgia, he found that there was no theater in the town and had one built in five days. He was not only a hard worker and resourceful, but he had an aptitude for business, and gradually his enterprises began to show a profit. In 1834, Smith was established in a theater in Montgomery, Alabama; Noah Ludlow in a theater in Mobile. Though they disliked one another personally, the two men formed a business partnership as actor-managers. Their plan was to conduct a winter season in Mobile, and take their company for a summer season to St. Louis, where an old salt warehouse had been rebuilt as a theater. Undismayed by the failure of James Caldwell, who twice had brought his company from New Orleans to play in this theater, the firm of Ludlow and Smith carried out their project successfully.

Two years later they persuaded wealthy citizens of St. Louis to build them a modern theater, seating one thousand people, at a cost of $65,000. It was opened with appropriate ceremonies in the summer of 1837. The partners, who disagreed about nearly everything else, were alike in their respect for the conventions and their rigorously puritanical code of morality. So they established a policy which made their theaters almost unique in the United States. "This was to refuse admittance to any female . . . who did not come attended by a gentleman, or someone having the appearance of a man of respectability, not even in the third tier," Ludlow recalled with pride; "and women notoriously of the *pave* were never, under any conditions, admitted." In 1840, Ludlow and Smith built a new theater in New Orleans, breaking Caldwell's long monopoly in that city. Three years later, after his splendid St. Charles Theater had been destroyed by fire, they rebuilt it, drove Caldwell from the field, and became the most important managers in the South and West, operating theaters in five states.

By the early 1830's, when financial disaster reigned in the theaters of the eastern cities, stars and stock actors found opportunity awaiting them on the frontier. Ludlow and Smith were each operating theaters in southern towns. Caldwell had an extensive circuit in the South. "Old Sam" Drake and his sons conducted a circuit in Kentucky. Other managers were established in the new theaters that had been built in Pittsburgh and Cincinnati. Such stars as ageing Thomas Abthorpe Cooper, Junius Brutus Booth, James W. Wallack, James H. Hackett, Clara Fisher, Charles Kean, and the celebrated Irish comedian Tyrone Power traveled over this immense area for months at a time. In New York, Charles Kean, returning from a tour of the South and West, warned Fanny Kemble that she and her father must "expect to meet strange co-adjutors in those lost lands beyond the world," should they decide to play there. But others were delighted by the enthusiasm with which they were received by audiences such as those in the deep South which, as Tyrone Power noted, came—men and women alike—on horseback "nightly to visit the theater, and this from very considerable distances," so that one saw "many fine horses, with their antique caparisons, piquetted about the theater," a peculiar anomaly in "this hackney-coach age." It was hard, of course, to pass so much of one's time in stagecoaches or on river steamers; to endure the discomforts of primitive theaters and drab hotels; to spend most of the day rehearsing, perform at night, and return wearily to one's room to study the next night's role—yet few stars failed to find their tours rewarding. Nearly all who traveled on the Ohio and Mississippi Rivers came back East with tales of "an original or singular speculation" that had been undertaken on these waters. This was the "floating theater" or "ark of the drama" operated by the Chapman family—the first of all the showboats that, for a century, were to ply the rivers of the West and South.

The family came from England to the United States in 1827: William Chapman and his wife; their twin sons William and Samuel; George, a younger son; Caroline and Therese. "Old William" Chapman—he was past sixty-five when he emigrated—had long been a member of the Covent Garden company, and the twin sons had also played there. He and William were engaged by the Bowery Theater in New York; Samuel went to the Chestnut Street Theater in

Philadelphia. Samuel, who was equally talented as an actor, playwright and producer, married Elizabeth Jefferson, daughter of "Old Joseph" Jefferson, and soon afterwards the rest of his family joined him in Philadelphia. In 1830, "Old William" Chapman and his twin sons took over the management of the Walnut Street Theater. This was the year in which many managers in the eastern cities were forced into bankruptcy, and, like others, the Chapmans also failed. Then they suffered another misfortune; Samuel was killed by a fall from his horse. In their bereavement, the family determined to remain together. They wished to leave Philadelphia, but no theater in any other eastern city was willing to engage "Old William" Chapman, William, Jr., George and Caroline. In the spring of 1831, the Chapman family set out for Pittsburgh.

Pittsburgh was prosperous; it had become the boat-building center for the traffic of the great rivers. But the city had no theater. With great difficulty, the Chapmans persuaded the landlord of a hotel to rent them lodgings—actors, and more particularly actresses, were not wanted in a reputable establishment. Eventually, he permitted them to perform plays in the hotel dining room on certain evenings every week. Financially, the results were not very satisfactory, and the Chapmans soon determined to move westward on the frontier. "Old William" Chapman had begun his career as an actor in England with a "traveling theater"—a troupe of strolling players who traveled, lived and performed in horse-drawn vans, stopping to give their shows wherever an audience could be collected. This method, he realized, was peculiarly applicable to the present case. But to reach that part of the frontier where no actors had ever played, and where the Chapmans would therefore find their most remunerative public, they would first have to make a long journey by river boat. And, once arrived, the lack of roads would prevent them from traveling by van. Their frontier lay along the rivers; its traffic and travel were carried by water; and Pittsburgh was busily building all kinds of river boats. The Chapman "van" must be a boat.

The boat which they ordered was a large broadhorn, about one hundred feet long by sixteen wide, with a crude, ridge-roofed house perched on it. Within the house, at the stern, was a shallow stage with draw-curtains and candles for footlights. The narrow auditorium was furnished with backless wooden benches, and was illuminated by a chandelier made from a hogshead hoop to which candles were affixed. In this floating theater, the Chapmans planned to drift down the Ohio and Mississippi Rivers, stopping to give a show at every settlement which seemed likely to provide an audience. Leaving Pittsburgh in July, 1831, they intended to arrive at New Orleans the following spring. There, they would sell their ark, return to Pittsburgh by steamboat with their costumes and simple scenery, have another ark built and, in the summer, set forth again.

Tyrone Power, on his first two-year tour in the United States, often heard about "Old William" Chapman's venture while traveling in the South. "At each village or large plantation," Power noted, "he hoists banner and blows trumpet and few who love a play suffer his ark to pass the door, since they know it is to return no more until the next year; for, however easy may prove the downward course of the drama's temple, to retrograde, upwards, is quite beyond its power. Sometimes a large steamer from Louisville, with a thousand souls on board,

Tyrone Power

will command a play whilst taking in fuel, when the profit must be famous." Touring without any fixed schedule, the Chapmans could remain for several days at any landing where there was a demand for more than a single performance—or where the fishing happened to be good. Fishing was not only their most available diversion, but the source of their cheapest food. Sol Smith recorded that, on one occasion, it "blew up" both the actors and their audience. The Chapmans were performing *The Stranger,* with "Old William" in the title role and William, Jr., in that of Francis, his servant. The Stranger called Francis; there was no reply, and Francis did not enter, as required. He called again, angrily. From afar, Francis answered, "Coming, Sir!" There was a long pause; "Old William," furious, strode up and down the stage. Eventually, Francis entered. "Why did you not come when I called?" the irate father demanded. To which the son replied, "Why, Sir, I was just hauling in one of the damnedest big catfish you ever saw!"

At the larger towns along the Mississippi—Memphis, Port Gibson, Vicksburg, Natchez—the Chapmans' showboat usually tied up for a week or more, and the family gave a series of performances. Their repertory was extensive. It included not only such tear-jerking "problem plays" as *The Stranger,* but many comedies and farces and, among other tragedies, *Hamlet.* Heavy roles and comic old men were the specialty of "Old William." The forte of William, Jr., who was in his early thirties, and Caroline, a girl still in her teens, was comedy. Caroline was tall, slender and plain-featured except for her beautiful dark eyes. But she was vivid, vivacious and versatile. She sang charmingly; she danced skillfully; she had a talent for mimicry and burlesque. Nearly twenty years after the Chapman showboat made its first tour of the rivers, William, Jr., and Caroline were to be leading players in New York's finest theaters and, still pioneers at heart, were to go on to San Francisco, where Caroline became the city's favorite comedienne. Meanwhile the Chapman "aquatic company," as Tyrone Power called it admiringly, prospered from the outset. In 1836, five years after their first courageous tour down the Mississippi, the family were able to buy a steamboat, built and equipped for them as a theater, having a stage twenty feet wide, an auditorium with comfortable appointments, and more homelike living quarters. Steampower made it possible for them to give performances on the upstream voyage from New Orleans to Pittsburgh. It also enabled them to carry the drama up most of the rivers that emptied into the Mississippi and Ohio. By means of this new "floating theater," one of the most remarkable cultural transfers in history was accomplished so quietly that later historians failed to record it. The acting traditions established at Covent Garden by Mrs. Siddons and John Philip Kemble, with whom "Old William" Chapman had played more than thirty years earlier, were brought by him to the remote backwoods communities of the American frontier, and were exemplified in a dramatic repertory of which no theater in any eastern city would have been ashamed.

In 1837 Joseph Jefferson II, son of "Old Joseph," was invited by his brother-in-law to join him in the management of the first theater built in the new town of Chicago. Jefferson had been acting and painting scenery for a theater in New York, but the East was in the throes of a financial panic, and he was without money or a job. With his wife, a capable singing actress, and his nine-year-old son, Joseph III, Jefferson set out for the frontier. Joseph III had already been put on the stage. Five years earlier, Thomas D. Rice, the first white actor to win fame as a "Negro minstrel," had brought the child out before an audience to imitate him as he sang and danced his celebrated "Jump Jim Crow" number, certainly not foreseeing that Joseph III was to become one of the most eminent of American actors, still playing as a star in the first decade of the twentieth century. The Jeffersons made their way to Albany, played there and in Schenectady; traveled along the Erie Canal, giving entertainments at Utica and Syracuse to earn money for their journey; played at a theater in Buffalo just opened by the firm of Dean and McKenny, and finally took a lake steamer to Chicago. There, as Joseph III recalled long afterwards, "I was the comic singer of the party; making myself useful in small parts and first villagers; now and then doing duty as a Roman senator at the back, wrapped in a clean hotel sheet, with my head peering over profiled banquet tables." It was the custom of the Chicago audience to throw money on the stage when pleased by a comic song or dance, and nine-year-old Joseph III added to the family livelihood by extemporizing verses and dance steps until donations stopped falling at his feet. But the season in Chicago soon ceased to be profitable and the Jeffersons, with the other members of the company, took to the road in an open prairie wagon, barnstorming as far west as Dubuque, Iowa, then embarking in a barge on the Mississippi—their scenery serving for sails—to play the small river settlements that soon would become cities. They performed in courthouses, in barns or even in the open air. Once they were reduced to playing Payne's *Clari* in a large "porkhouse" or pigsty, elevated from the prairie on poles, and Mrs. Jefferson's singing of "Home, Sweet Home" was accompanied by the squeals of the dislodged inhabitants of the theater, unhappily tethered under the stage. It was in similar circumstances that, for many years thereafter, strolling players would carry the drama westward, as the frontier moved across the continent.

CHAPTER 4

The People's Choice

THOUGH susceptible to the magnetic financial attraction of the frontier, the great stars who began touring the South and West seldom took a hopeful view of the audiences that awaited them. In Great Britain they had heard little to the credit of American culture, and they were pleasantly surprised to find that, in the cities of the East, the playing public was neither naive, lacking in taste, nor incapable of appreciating subtlety in the art of acting. The frontier, however, was quite another story. Cultivated Easterners who had never been there were scarcely less disdainful of its inhabitants than British travelers, like Mrs. Trollope, who had sojourned among them. The prospect of serving as missionaries of art in the wilderness, of acting for the ignorant, muddy democracy that inhabited its towns, was not alluring to stars who had enjoyed the acclaim of the East. Most of them undertook their first tours in a spirit of condescension which friendly Easterners warned them never to reveal. For one characteristic of the frontier had to be reckoned with by anyone intending to go there. The pioneers—as Judge James Hall of Vandalia, Illinois, reported in his popular *Letters from the West*—refused to be "patronized or high-hatted."

Their truculent independence, their hostility to the patrician, effete East, were not confined to politics and economic affairs, but extended to the life of

Edwin Forrest as Spartacus
(a caricature)

the mind and the arts. In these spheres Eastern approval was as likely to arouse prejudice as to confer prestige. The frontier defiantly asserted that it knew what it liked and would suffer no coercion. So the words "from the theaters of New York, Boston and Philadelphia" exercised no irresistible magic. As managers often found to their cost, these words acted as a powerful stimulus to curiosity, but nothing more. However famous they might be in the East, stars who toured in the South and West were required to prove their merits. The penalty for failing to meet this unexpected challenge was apt to be an empty house. Before long, the frontier carried its independence even further. Audiences on the southern and western circuits, recognizing the talents of young players unknown in the East, promoted their careers, established their repute in the theaters of the frontier, and sometimes elevated them to a position of regional stardom. As a result, there presently began a migration in reverse, for many favorites of the frontier longed for metropolitan success, dreamt of stellar engagements in New York.

It was not a baseless dream, but one already justified by glorious precedents. There was the case of Thomas D. Rice, the first frontier-made star. While playing small parts with the Drake company in Louisville, Rice picked up the queer song habitually crooned by an old, lame Negro stable hand who moved about with a lurching, shuffling gait. Making up in imitation of the Negro, Rice first tried his "Jim Crow" song and dance in Louisville between the acts of a play. The audience enjoyed it hugely, and he carried it to the other Kentucky towns on the Drake circuit, then to Cincinnati and Pittsburgh. So many repeated engagements were demanded that Rice was soon announced as a star, and presently managers in the East began to hear about him. In 1832, Rice appeared at the Bowery Theater in New York, met with sensational success, achieved immediate celebrity, and thereafter was able to command his own price from managers in other cities. Eventually, Rice performed in London and the provincial British theaters, and his reception was as enthusiastic as it had been at home. Meanwhile, he had collected many of the beautiful work songs sung by the Negroes. He wrote a libretto for these songs and brought them to the stage as an "Ethiopian opera," *Bone Squash*. Rice quickly became a wealthy man. A rumor reached the frontier that, in the East, he wore coats with five-dollar gold pieces for buttons, and waistcoats similarly adorned with quarter eagles, two-and-a-half-dollar gold pieces. But on his frequent tours of the West and South, he never displayed these trappings, probably realizing that they would cause no comment and bring him no publicity. Audiences there retained a warm affection for Rice; he was their "discovery," and his wider fame vindicated their judgment. They were even more proud of their share in the career of America's most illustrious tragedian. Although the frontier did not elevate Edwin Forrest to stardom, it schooled him in his profession and shaped his personality. It might well have claimed him as one of its products, for few public figures of the time so notably exemplified its intractable spirit, its characteristic ways of thinking and feeling, its distinctive aggressiveness, bravado and conceit.

Forrest was born in Philadelphia, the next-to-youngest of six children produced by parents who, as they sank in the economic scale, increased their progeny in the probable hope of future livelihood. Originally destined for the pulpit, his formal education ended at the age of ten, and soon afterwards his father's death plunged the family into destitution. An elder brother had entered the printing trade; two sisters became milliners; the mother added to their scanty income by binding shoes. Young Edwin was successively apprenticed to a printer, a cooper, a ship chandler and an importer. Later, he was to show exceptional astuteness in all matters of business, but his rapidly changing jobs did not suggest this aptitude. Physically well-developed and looking older than his actual years, he was tall, dark-haired, dark-eyed, and considered handsome. In the poverty-stricken neighborhood where the family lived, he acquired some reputation for pugnacity and skill with his fists. The compulsion to demonstrate his masculine prowess, and the belligerent temper that accompanied it, remained lifelong traits. Perhaps they were evoked by the hard discipline of a city slum, but they were probably intensified by an early humiliation.

Forrest's verbal memory was remarkable, and when scarcely more than an infant he had astonished his family with a talent for mimicry. By the age of eleven he had joined a "Thespian Society" in whose performances he was assigned female roles, and in one of these a peculiar incompatibility of costume and figure provoked such a storm of laughter that he was ignominiously hustled off the stage. But this humiliating failure apparently increased his determination to gain a foothold in the professional theater; he had already attended performances at the Chestnut Street establishment, almost certainly seeing Thomas Abthorpe Cooper, whom he took as his model. One summer night, at the Tivoli Garden, a showman who was exhibiting the effects of nitrous oxide gas asked young Forrest to become the medium of his experiment. After inhaling the gas, the boy wildly recited the soliloquy of Young Norval in *Douglas,* then dashed into the tent scene of *Richard III,* and was heartily applauded when he emerged from the brief anesthesia. A prominent lawyer, Colonel John Swift, was among the crowd. Impressed by Forrest's voice and declamation, he arranged to have the boy receive lessons in elocution and deportment, and he finally persuaded William Warren and William B. Wood, the managers of the Philadelphia company, to give his protégé one appearance at the Walnut Street Theater, where the company was then playing.

Forrest's début was set for the night of November 27, 1820. The piece was *Douglas,* in which Forrest was to play Young Norval. Presumably, he hoped to emulate John Howard Payne who, eleven years earlier, had made his debut in the same role at the age of seventeen and had achieved instant fame as "the American Roscius." Forrest, however, was only fourteen, although Warren and Wood believed him to be two years older. They were reluctant to give Forrest his opportunity; they had recently suffered numerous misfortunes with amateurs in "first appearances." "The usual arguments were strongly urged against embracing a profession at this time so especially unpromising," Wood recalled more than thirty years later. "The toils, dangers and sufferings of a young actor were represented with honest earnestness, but, as was soon discovered, in vain. Forrest was at this time a well-grown young man, with a noble figure, unusually developed for his age, his features powerfully expressive, and of a determination of purpose which discouraged all further objections." Undoubtedly his patron, Colonel Swift, argued ably in his behalf, for the play was cast to the full strength of the company, with Warren as Old Norval, Wood as Glenalvon, Frederick Wheatley as Lord Randolph, Mrs. Williams (later, Mrs. Maywood) as Lady Randolph, and the wife of "Old Jefferson" in the role of Anna, the maid. Billed as "Master Forrest, a young gentleman of this city," the novice acquitted himself so well that a second performance of the play was given, which brought him increased approbation. Soon afterwards, he was permitted to undertake the role of Frederick in *Lover's Vows,* William Dunlap's adaptation of a play by Kotzebue, and was granted a benefit performance in which he appeared as Octavian in George Colman's *The Mountaineers,* a role made famous by Edmund Kean who, as it chanced, was opening his first engagement in Philadelphia the following week.

According to Wood, Forrest's performances "were considered by all the principal actors as far beyond any they had ever witnessed from a novice." This was high praise, for the Philadelphia company was then the finest in the country. A local newspaper, commenting on Forrest's Young Norval, was surprised by "the excellence of his elocution, his self-possession in speech and gesture, and a voice that, without straining, was of such volume and fine tenor as to carry every tone and articulation to the remotest corner of the theater." At fourteen, he already revealed the specific merits that, in maturity, became his principal resources as an artist. But despite this recognition, his hope of emulating Payne's swift ascent to fame was frustrated. The largest receipts for any of his performances amounted to little more than $300, and this cool reception did not encourage the managers to engage him. They told him, instead, that their theater "presented no vacancy worthy his acceptance." Forrest's patron and friends conferred with the managers and, as Wood later recorded, a decision was reached "that he should abandon the young Roscius plan, and take a wide range through the Western theaters for the purpose of passing a regular apprenticeship to his profession." But banishment to the frontier was not easily effected. For more than a year Forrest vainly tried to obtain an engagement there. He succeeded only in the autumn of 1822 when, at a weekly salary of $8, he was hired by Collins and Jones who, that season, were operating a circuit that embraced Pittsburgh, Maysville and Lexington in Kentucky, and Cincinnati.

The troupe reached Cincinnati in February, 1823, by which time Forrest had played a varied series of roles that ran the gamut from broad farce to Shakespearian tragedy. In their opening performance of *The Soldier's Daughter*—a forgotten play highly popular on the frontier—Forrest took the small role of Young Malfort, a melancholy lover. Sol Smith, then editing *The Independent Press,* wrote a very favorable review of his acting, and later, when Forrest played *Richard III* for his benefit, Smith "prophesied his future greatness" and was ridiculed for doing so. Early in the summer, Collins and Jones took the troupe to Louisville, but soon sent a group of actors back to Cincinnati to open the Globe Theater. Forrest was one of the group, and during its brief season played *Othello* and other tragedies of Shakespeare, but, as Smith noted, "with scarcely any knowledge of the text, his taste generally leading him to prefer the low comedy characters." During the summer, the company produced a comedy, *Modern Fashions,* by Smith's brother, Martin, in which Forrest had the role of a dandy, and a farce by Sol Smith, *The Tailor in Distress,* in which Forrest took the role of a Negro. When the season failed, leaving the actors without any funds, Sol Smith rented the theater for one night, agreed to pay each of the performers $2, and put on the two plays with "the grand heroic pantomime of *Don Quixote.*" Thus, to earn a fee of $2, Forrest played the parts of a dandy, a Negro, Sancho Panza in the pantomime, and during an intermission also gave "mock imitations" of a well-known singer. Meanwhile Sol Smith, having concluded that Forrest was "trifling away his time," advised him to seek an engagement for the following winter with James H. Caldwell, in New Orleans, which Forrest secured at the weekly salary of $18. With this in prospect, he joined several other members of the company in a barnstorming tour through the small towns of Ohio. They met with disaster after disaster; in one town, Forrest's meager theatrical wardrobe was seized for debt; finally, penniless and hungry, he made his way back to Cincinnati on foot. Learning that Sol Smith was taking over the theater formerly operated by Collins and Jones, he pleaded to join Smith's company, offering to work for a salary of $10 a week, and somehow to obtain cancellation of his contract with Caldwell. Although Smith realized that this arrangement would be to his own advantage, his moral sense and a genuine concern for Forrest's future made him refuse the offer. In a fit of pique at this rejection, Forrest joined a circus troupe in the capacity of trick equestrian and tumbler. Sol Smith promptly intervened; "by dint of hard lecturing and strong argument" he prevailed on the headstrong youth to quit the circus and set out for New Orleans.

As a member of Caldwell's stock company, Forrest remained in New Orleans for two seasons. Again, he played a wide range of roles; among them, the inevitable Young Malfort, Octavian, and Jaffier in *Venice Preserved*. He was given the opportunity of playing Iago to the Othello of William Augustus Conway, a talented British star whose misfortunes in London had left him with a delusion of persecution and who, three years later, was to commit suicide while temporarily insane. Forrest also gave his first performance of Payne's *Brutus,* later to become one of his most popular vehicles, and a feature of his repertory for many years. In New Orleans, his fine physique, magnificent voice and effective declamation won praise. And his "robust style" for the first time commanded attention. His original model for the robust style had been Cooper, and Conway's acting provided him with another. But it was Forrest's natural, almost instinctive, form of expression. At eighteen, his character had been matured and his temperament fixed. He was still uneducated, and life on the frontier had done little to cultivate his taste. The robust style enabled him to overcome these deficiencies by sheer elocutionary force. Yet, for Forrest, this constituted a grave peril—and the facility with which he could make his superb declamatory technique serve as a substitute for poetic imagination and insight into character proved, throughout his career, a liability as well as an asset. This native tendency, moreover, was strengthened by the physical characteristics of the theaters on the frontier which, like those of Shakespeare's time, were ill equipped with scenery or costumes, so that the lack of visual illusion had to be compensated by the actor, with brilliance of delivery capable of firing the imaginations of his audience. Even at the end of his career, Forrest retained a prejudice against what he called "the scene-painter's drama," and insisted that in Shakespeare's time, as in his own youth, "it was absolutely necessary to be an *actor,* as no aid from without was known or dreamed of."

But in New Orleans, Forrest encountered conditions very unlike those he had met in the theaters of the West. Caldwell's stock company was remarkable for its excellence, and his theater was well equipped. Moreover part of its audience, also patronizing the French theater, were familiar with the classically restrained style of acting practiced by the company that had been imported from Paris. In general, the playgoing public was as "sophisticated" as that of Philadelphia or New York. These circumstances would have made it possible for Forrest to modify the crudity and provincialism of his robust style, but like many another self-made man he resented criticism, acknowledged no need for discipline and professed a hearty contempt for intellectualism and refinement. His conceit was already fully developed. It would afterwards take the form of haughty arrogance, but it would always remain the frontiersman's disguise of a profound sense of insecurity when confronted by the complexities of a cultivated society.

In New Orleans, this insecurity expressed itself in Forrest's secret admiration of the very qualities which he believed that he despised, and the ambivalence produced a stormy incident. His chosen intimates in the city define the nature of his taste. They were Colonel James Bowie, inventor of the bowie knife and a ferocious duelist; a steamboat captain named Graham, notorious as a fighter; and an Indian, Push-ma-ta-ha. By comparison with these, the girl with whom Forrest fell in love notably exemplified refinement, intellectuality and worldly elegance. She was Jane Placide, the talented leading actress of Caldwell's company and a member of a celebrated theatrical family. She was not attracted by Forrest, and he became convinced that Caldwell was his successful rival for her affection. This sufficed to strain the relations between actor and manager, and Caldwell put the finishing touch to an explosive situation by depriving Forrest of leading roles and confining him to humble ones. Forrest challenged Caldwell, who scornfully rejected the proposed duel. Infuriated by being dishonored, Forrest resorted to an expedient which, long afterwards, he was to use with more injurious effect. He published a "card" in the New Orleans newspapers which read, "Whereas James H. Caldwell has wronged and insulted me, and refused me the satisfaction of a gentleman, I hereby denounce him as a scoundrel and post him as a coward." This terminated his connection with Caldwell's theater. For several months Forrest took refuge in the tepee of his Indian crony, Push-ma-ta-ha. During the summer of 1825 he embarked for New York. But his ignominious departure from New Orleans was not final. Some years later he returned there, as the foremost American star, to play an engagement in Caldwell's theater; despite their hostility, neither was averse to using the other for purposes of financial profit.

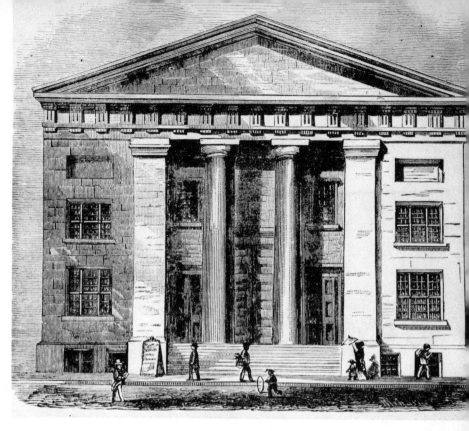

The First Bowery Theater, New York, 1826

Forrest had now served a hard three-year apprenticeship on the frontier, but he failed to obtain employment in any major theater of the East. The autumn of 1825 found him a member of Charles Gilfert's stock company in Albany, New York. Professionally, this engagement was far inferior to the one he had sacrificed but it drastically altered his fortunes. During its course, Forrest played with Edmund Kean, winning the great star's admiration and a subsequent public tribute in which Kean predicted his "rise to great eminence." The Albany season ended disastrously for Gilfert, but the New York capitalists who were building the Bowery Theater engaged him as its director. Forrest, meanwhile, contrived to make his first appearance in New York City, by playing a benefit performance for the actor Jacob Woodhull, on June 23, 1826, at the Park Theater. Kean had recently appeared there in the role of Othello; Forrest daringly undertook it, with such pronounced success that Gilfert, who was in the audience, promptly engaged him for the Bowery at a salary of $28 a week. A month earlier, in the role of Jaffier, Forrest had played a benefit performance at the Chestnut Street Theater in Philadelphia, but although a repetition had been called for, the two nights did not produce the offer of an engagement. In New York, however, Forrest's Othello was praised by the critics, one of them reporting that he was "highly original, and yet, except for a few mannerisms, without any disagreeable eccentricities of style," and judging his performance of the role "superior to any in this country except Kean's." This verdict gave Gilfert his cue. Having secured Forrest as a stock actor, Gilfert determined to promote him as a star of the first magnitude.

With considerable advance publicity, Gilfert brought Forrest forward as Othello a fortnight after the opening of the Bowery Theater. He made so brilliant an impression in the role that Gilfert immediately increased his salary to $40 a week. The British comedian Joe Cowell, who saw him play early during the season, recorded that, "He possessed a fine untaught face and good manly figure and, though unpolished in his deportment, his manners were frank and honest, and his uncultivated taste, speaking the language of truth and nature, could be readily understood." William Charles Macready, older by thirteen years and an established favorite in London, was then making his first American tour and, during the season, played five engagements at the Park Theater, his visit being the great theatrical event of the year. The Park continued to hold its fashionable following, which received Macready with acclaim. Enjoying great prestige with the critics, he performed to crowded houses and his earnings were large. To Forrest, they probably seemed tremendous, for Gilfert played him, as the Bowery's strong card, against the British tragedian, frequently in the same roles, and even in dramas which Macready had brought to the stage. There was thus some ground for envy on Forrest's part, and for resentment on Macready's.

The British actor went to see his young rival perform at the Bowery—the play was *Julius Caesar,* with Conway starring as Brutus, and Forrest in the role of Mark Antony—but he recorded his impressions only many years later, and they were probably colored by a dreadful retrospect. As he then recalled it, Macready had been struck by Forrest's remarkable qualifications. "His figure was good, though perhaps a little heavy; his face might be considered handsome, his voice excellent. He was gifted with extraordinary strength of limb, to which he omitted no opportunity of giving prominence. He had received only the commonest education, but in his reading of the text he showed the discernment and good sense of an intellect much upon a level with that of Conway; but he had more energy, and was altogether distinguished by powers that, under proper direction, might be productive of great effect." Macready went to see Forrest again in *William Tell,* in a role written for himself. "His performance was marked by vehemence and rude force that told upon his hearers; but of pathos in the affecting interview with his son there was not the slightest touch, and it was evident that he had not rightly understood some passages in his text. . . . My impression was that, possessed of natural requisites in no ordinary degree, he might, under careful discipline, confidently look forward to eminence in his profession. If he would give himself up to a severe study of his art, and improve himself by the practice he could obtain before the audiences of the principal theaters of Great Britain . . . he might make himself a first-rate actor." In his embittered retrospect, Macready continued, "But to such a course of self-denying training I was certain he would never submit, as its necessity would not be made apparent to him. The injudicious and ignorant flattery, and the factious applause of his supporters in low-priced theaters would fill his purse, would blind him to his deficiency in taste and judgment, confirming his self opinion of attained perfection. I spoke of him as a young man of unquestionable promise, but I doubted his submission to the inexorable conditions for reaching excellence."

During the season, in addition to Othello and Mark Antony, Forrest played King Lear, later to become one of his finest roles, and Shylock; Rolla in *Pizarro;* and, in direct rivalry with Macready, Jaffier, William Tell, the title role in Knowles's *Virginius,* and that of Damon in Banim's *Damon and Pythias.* The role of Damon was to remain in his repertory until the end of his career, and perhaps it was made significant for him by a parallel in his personal life. Forrest was soon to find his Pythias in a young Bostonian, James Oakes, and their sentimental, romantic friendship ended only with Forrest's death. But for audiences, Forrest's Damon was distinguished by its last scene, in which he leaped out of the arms of Pythias and, "with a gymnast's ability and perfect grace," sprang from the floor of the stage to the platform of a scaffold three feet above it. Forrest's popularity at the Bowery fulfilled Gilfert's hopes, and his performances, as the season went on, drew increasingly flattering reviews. On this rising wave of critical approval, Gilfert farmed out Forrest for brief engagements in Boston and Philadelphia, charging for his services a fee of $200 a performance. At the end of the season, when his contract expired, Gilfert sought to renew it for the following year. Forrest demanded the terms which Gilfert himself had set, and was instantly engaged, for eighty performances, at a salary of $200 a night. At the age of twenty-one he was not only an established star, but one of the most highly paid actors on the American stage.

And in one respect, Forrest was unique. He was the first native-born tragedian whose talent, in the first flush of its splendor, enabled Americans to claim for him a rank equal with that of Cooke and Kean and Macready; or, in their immense pride, to describe him as "the American John Kemble," however incorrectly. During his second season at the Bowery, as if to emphasize Forrest's pre-eminence, Gilfert co-starred him in a series of performances with Thomas Abthorpe Cooper, his earliest model and boyhood idol. Though Forrest could not know it, Cooper might have served him as a prophetic warning of the fate that, one day, would overtake him also. Cooper was fifty-two, and had been before the public as a star for twenty-five years. His once glorious powers had declined and his vogue had passed. In the eastern cities he attracted only meager audiences and received few engagements. He spent his time, now, wearily touring the frontier, and every season he was forced to venture into smaller and smaller towns, for even in the cities of the West and South his public was dwindling. Impotently, the old lion raged at the fickleness of the public, decried the new favorites by whom he had been superseded, and Forrest might have learned from him not to become a victim of the delusion that so often besets actors—the belief that a mystical, sentimental bond unites the admired artist and the public, and the conviction that this bond is proof against the ravages of time and the mutability of fashion.

But concerning himself and his destiny, Forrest was the least skeptical of men. His cresting fame and the nearly unanimous praise that came to him, he

Edwin Forrest as Rolla in "Pizarro,"
from a painting by J. Neagle

accepted as a personal tribute, his legitimate due. Yet, though he lacked humility, he was sensitive to the responsibilities of the prestige that he took for granted. He extended his repertory constantly, especially in Shakespearian roles. He also took active steps to foster a genuinely American drama. In part, his motives were practical; he wanted new roles that would not become available to any other actor. But, like other patriotic citizens, he deeply resented the current British belittling of all things American. This had been expressed most notoriously in the *Edinburgh Review* by a witty clergyman, Sydney Smith. "In the four quarters of the globe," Smith inquired, "who reads an American book? or goes to an American play? or looks at an American picture or statue?" Forrest may never have heard of Smith, or his scornful question. But he did not need to, for in the theatrical profession British condescension was peculiarly obvious; the great stars were British. In turning to native playwrights for new roles, Forrest was pledging his unique prestige to the service of a widely acknowledged patriotic cause.

In 1828, he offered a prize of $500, and half the receipts of the third performance, for "the best tragedy, in five acts, of which the hero, or principal character, shall be an original of this country." A committee headed by William Cullen Bryant read the plays submitted and awarded the prize to John Augustus Stone, an actor and playwright then living in Philadelphia, for his *Metamora,* the hero of which was the American Indian known to history as King Philip. The role was written to exploit Forrest's physique and his robust style, and in creating it he drew upon his intimacy with Push-ma-ta-ha. The play was an instant success, and Forrest's performance brought him a personal triumph. Although subsequently he became dissatisfied with it, and probably agreed with a later generation of critics in thinking it merely bombastic melodrama, unworthy of his talent, he continued playing *Metamora* to the very end of his career because it always made money for him. In Philadelphia, a group of writers were devoting themselves to the drama, and Forrest next turned to another, Richard Penn Smith, bringing to the stage his unproduced *Caius Marius,* a tragedy in verse. Immediately after its production, Forrest commissioned a tragedy from the most gifted of the Philadelphia playwrights, Dr. Richard Montgomery Bird. He and Bird were exactly the same age and, though in every respect unlike, became close friends. Bird had been brought up in a cultivated environment; he had read widely in ancient and modern literatures; his creative dramatic talent was supported by sound scholarship.

The first play that Bird wrote for Forrest, *The Gladiator,* was designed, not only to exploit the actor's personal aptitude for romantic tragedy, but to express the strongly "democratic" political views that Forrest and Bird both held. Spartacus, the character enacted by Forrest, is an enslaved freeman, a gladiator who leads an unsuccessful insurrection of his fellows against a tyrannous oligarchy—a situation that had current American parallels in the institution of slavery and in the dawning efforts of industrial workers to organize unions. The play had a powerful climax in a scene showing the rising of the gladiators in the arena, and Forrest mounted this with exceptional care for its stage effect. *The Gladiator* was an immediate, overwhelming success; Forrest played it for forty years, and after his death other actors kept it on the stage until the last decade of the century. Bird later wrote two more plays for Forrest. *Oralloossa,* a tragedy dealing with the Inca insurrection against Pizarro, served the actor only briefly. However, *The Broker of Bogota* was instantly successful and Forrest retained it in his repertory to the end of his acting career.

Forrest received great credit for his efforts to encourage the creation of a native dramatic literature. But his effect on the careers of the playwrights whom he patronized was the reverse of fortunate. Following current practice, he bought their works outright. He was both jealously tenacious of his legal rights and avaricious in his determination to acquire wealth. He began making money immediately from *Metamora, The Gladiator* and *The Broker of Bogota;* before the end of his career the three plays brought him hundreds of thousands of dollars. But he paid no royalties to either Stone or Bird. Stone, despairing at his inability to earn a livelihood, committed suicide four years after the production of his play. Forrest, who had not alleviated his financial distress, erected a costly monument over Stone's grave, an act widely publicized and praised. The case of Bird, who was far more talented than Stone, was even less creditable to Forrest. The men were close friends; their financial arrangements were only verbal, and Forrest failed to comply with the terms as Bird understood them. The actor's avarice not only ruptured their friendship, but caused Bird to cease writing plays. Furthermore, Forrest was bent on preventing other actors from performing the two plays Bird had written for him. To this end, he forbade their publication, thereby depriving Bird of a source of revenue and a means of enhancing his literary reputation. Long after Bird's death, when his son wished to publish the plays, Forrest reiterated his prohibition. The plays, he stated curtly, "are my exclusive property, by the right of purchase."

Yet, very probably, it was his association with Bird that stimulated Forrest to begin the serious study of dramatic literature which he was to carry on unflaggingly. And Bird also may have influenced his decision to make a two-year "grand tour" of Europe which, by enabling him to study the performances of the best French and British actors, brought about modifications of his own early style. Before Forrest sailed for Europe in 1834, he was universally acknowledged to be the most eminent figure on the American stage. Two years earlier, at a benefit for William Dunlap, he was starred with Fanny and Charles Kemble in a performance of *Venice Preserved*. And in a dramatic festival held the same year for the benefit of John Howard Payne, who had returned from a long absence in Europe, Forrest performed Payne's *Brutus;* James W. Wallack put on *Charles II,* a comedy by Payne and Washington Irving; and the Kembles played David Garrick's version of *The Taming of the Shrew*. It is notable that Forrest was the only American star whose services were solicited for both these important testimonials. And his prestige was further attested by a farewell banquet tendered to him in New York on the eve of his departure for Europe, for which a medal was struck, and at which William Cullen Bryant, Fitz-Greene Halleck and other distinguished men spoke in his praise.

Forrest returned from Europe in the autumn of 1836, to give six performances in Philadelphia and six in New York before sailing once more to make his first tour of Great Britain. He opened in London in *The Gladiator;* the play failed to duplicate its American success. But Forrest was acclaimed in *Macbeth, Othello* and *King Lear*. Perhaps as a propitiatory gesture to Americans in general, a group of eminent British actors, Macready among them, joined a number of equally eminent writers in honoring Forrest with a banquet at the Garrick Club. An international celebrity at the age of thirty, Forrest rejoiced at his reception and the financial profits of his tour. He recorded his delight in the "many delicate courtesies and attentions" which he received from Macready, "all showing the native kindness of his heart, and his great refinement and good breeding." It was perhaps through Macready, an old family friend, that he met Catherine Sinclair, the daughter of John Sinclair, a singer who had earlier toured the United States. They fell in love, were married, and in the autumn of 1837 Forrest brought his bride to the United States. Like Jane Placide, Catherine Sinclair was familiar with worldly society. She had a lively mind, and contact with her father's circle had developed her intellectual interests. That her spirit was independent later became abundantly evident; it was even alleged, to her discredit, that she held "advanced views" on the subject of women's rights.

Forrest's engagements, after his return, brought him a series of ovations. British acclaim intensified American pride in his achievement. In Philadelphia he performed many weeks to overflowing houses. A banquet in his honor, at the Merchants' Hotel, was sponsored by a committee of prominent citizens that included Chief Justice Gibson, Nicholas Biddle, and Mayor Swift. Francis Wemyss, who was one of the few actors invited to attend it, realized that the banquet was a great compliment to Forrest. Nevertheless, Wemyss regretted that Forrest had not been entertained in the homes of his distinguished hosts, since this would have given "the actor a claim to the position of a gentleman, in the society of gentlemen, upon terms of admitted equality—respected and respecting." Forrest was less sensitive to the implications. "This is the proudest

Edwin Forrest as Macbeth, by R. Thew

day of my life," he is reported to have told a friend, "for I have met on terms of social equality many of the conspicuous men of my native city whose names have been familiar to me from my boyhood, and whom I have never aspired to know."

Though Forrest's position as a "gentleman" may have been dubious, as an actor he was highly esteemed by the social élite of the East. It was the fashion to admire him. Philip Hone attended his first performance in New York, in the role of Othello. Hone recorded that, "The house was crammed in every part, and his reception was warm and enthusiastic. I think him improving; his acting is more quiet, and in person, deportment and voice the Senate in its most palmy state never had so magnificent a commander, black or white, nor had ever Desdemona so good an excuse for her misplaced affections." That Forrest everywhere played to crowded houses was remarkable, for the nation was in the throes of a severe financial depression. Hone, enumerating the theaters then open in New York—many of which were failing—considered it "almost incredible that in these times of distress, when the study of economy is so great an object, there should be nine of these money drains in operation." The prolonged depression neither diminished Forrest's audiences nor prevented him from rapidly amassing a fortune. It had resulted from President Andrew Jackson's successful war on the United States Bank, of which Forrest's admirer, Nicholas Biddle, was the president. The continued existence of the Bank had been an issue of the growing conflict between the economic interests of those whom Jackson termed "the rich and powerful," and those whom he described as "the humble members of society—farmers, mechanics and laborers." These constituted the Jacksonian democracy, and it was they who, in the presidential election of 1836, brought Jackson's hand-picked successor, Martin Van Buren, to the White House. Partisan feeling was bitter. Party lines represented sectional as well as economic interests. The defeated Whigs were the party of the eastern capitalists; the Democrats drew their strength from the mechanics and laborers of the East, the small farmers of the South and the inhabitants of the western frontier. In the continuing struggle between these interests, Forrest was soon to play a role that had unforeseen effects on his professional career.

Meanwhile, although Forrest enjoyed high repute among the wealthy élite of the East, he was the idol of "the people," the workingmen of the eastern cities and townsmen of the frontier. To their favor, very largely, he owed the fortune he was accumulating. Their dislike of the British was intense; they resented the predominance of British stars on the American stage and the fact that, in the cities of the East, many of the managers also were British. In these circumstances, Forrest became for them a focus, not only of patriotism, but of anti-British feeling. In several eastern cities, there had occurred riots very like those caused by Kean's second tour. In 1831, the rumor that a British singer had disparaged the United States incited a mob to prevent his appearance at the Park Theater in New York. The resulting riot continued for three nights, terrorizing the city, and subsided only when Edmund Simpson, manager of the Park, had the façade of the theater "covered with transparencies of patriotic subjects—flags and eagles in abundance." In 1833, Forrest, who previously had been playing engagements at the Park, returned to the Bowery Theater, largely because of the competition of the Kembles and other British stars at the more fashionable playhouse. The New York *Mirror* rebuked the Park's management for its "narrow, selfish and anti-American policy," and expressed satisfaction that Forrest had left it, and was "again treading the boards where his earliest laurels were acquired . . . and where he will have to deal with a manager not actuated by a desire 'to crush the infernal American humbug.' " The manager of the Bowery, Thomas S. Hamblin, was a British-born tragedian, and his public was by no means as confident of his American sympathies as was the *Mirror*. In the summer of 1834, before his departure on his "grand tour," Forrest volunteered to perform *Metamora* at the Bowery for the benefit of

George Percy Farren, a British actor and a member of the stock company. A report circulated that Farren had made "ill-natured reflections" on the United States, and one hour after the performance began it was interrupted by a riot against him in the theater, and on the Bowery. Hamblin came on the stage waving an American flag, but the rioters hissed and pelted him as a Briton, and called for "American Forrest." Forrest made a speech; the disturbance ceased and the performance proceeded.

It was at the Bowery that, in his youth, Walt Whitman first saw Forrest in Payne's *Brutus*. As an old man, he remembered that "it affected me for weeks; or rather, I might say, permanently filtered into my whole nature." He recalled that whenever Forrest played there, the Bowery was "packed from ceiling to pit with its audience mainly of alert, well-dressed, full-blooded young and middle-aged men, the best average of American-born mechanics," and that Forrest could evoke "one of those long-kept-up tempests of handclapping peculiar to the Bowery—no dainty kid-glove business, but electric force and muscle from perhaps two thousand full-sinewed men." Whitman remembered that "the young shipbuilders, cartmen, butchers, firemen . . . were always to be seen in those audiences, racy of the East River and the Dry Dock. Slang, wit, occasional shirt sleeves, a picturesque freedom of looks and manners, with a rude, good-natured, restless movement, were generally noticeable." Whitman's account of Forrest's shirt-sleeve adherents in New York sufficiently characterizes the four thousand people who, on July 4, 1838, crowded the Broadway Tabernacle for a rally of the Democratic Party. The featured speaker at this rally was Edwin Forrest, who held the audience spellbound by his eloquence for ninety minutes. A glowing account of his address appeared in the New York *Evening Post* next day; the dramatic critic of that paper, William Leggett, was one of Forrest's most enthusiastic admirers, and an intimate friend. Presently, there was talk of sending Forrest to Congress, and by mid-October the New York Democrats had offered to place him on their ticket.

The news of this offer aroused no enthusiasm in the wealthy élite. Philip Hone who, one year earlier, had extolled Forrest's acting, expressed their sentiments in his diary. Forrest, he asserted, had "no claim, that I have ever heard of, to the honor of representing the people of New York in Congress, but that of exciting, by dint of loud words and furious stamps, the pit of the Bowery Theater to raise their shirt sleeves high in the air and shout 'Hurrah for Forrest!' He may be a leader of the *Pitt* party, but no statesman. . . . I well remember how I was berated by some of my political friends when, as Mayor, I assisted in the ceremony of laying the cornerstone of the Bowery Theater and made a speech on the occasion. No act of my public life lost me so many friends, and here we have a regular-built actor presented to the people for their suffrages; and he will probably (if he should consent to serve) receive the greatest number of votes on their ticket." But Forrest declined the proffered nomination, in an elaborate letter written at Francis Wemyss' desk in Philadelphia. Wemyss asked him why he rejected a high honor conferred upon his profession. "I want no further honor," Forrest replied brusquely, "and can't afford to give my time for eight dollars a day, when I can make two hundred out of it. The day may come when I shall make the game of politics my study; and then it will be time enough to present myself to the suffrages of my fellow-citizens." But his speech to the Democratic rally, and the offered nomination, irreparably damaged Forrest's prestige with the wealthy classes. Gradually, they ceased to praise his art. In fashionable circles it became the fashion to depreciate Forrest's acting. In that portion of the press which catered to snobbery and made pretensions to "culture," there began to appear allegations that he "howled," that he "ranted," that he "overdid everything."

Meanwhile, the great popular public remained loyal to him. Forrest added new plays to his repertory, most notably Bulwer-Lytton's *Lady of Lyons,* in which he played the romantic role of Claude Melnotte, and *Richelieu,* in which he enacted the old Cardinal. His professional tours were long and highly profitable; his investments added to his income; he was already a wealthy man. He was the unchallenged leader of the American theatrical profession, but in the theater he was known for his arrogance, his ferocious temper, the outbreaks of violence that frequently occurred at rehearsals. Backstage he was given to being a bully, and actors found his abuse hard to take. But when the American Dramatic Fund was founded, for the relief of distressed actors and their families, Forrest was chosen as its first president. Tales of his "closeness" in money matters circulated in the profession. At the end of one short engagement in Boston, his share of the receipts amounted to $4,000, and although the managers had lost by their contract with him and temporarily were unable to pay their stock company, Forrest insisted on being paid in full. The money was handed to him, a few dollars being in rolls of 25-cent pieces. Presently he returned to the treasurer with one of these rolls, declaring that one of the quarters it contained had been refused by the bank because it was worn smooth. Forrest demanded another quarter in exchange, received it, and the story was added to those told against him. Tales of his generosity were more rare, but there were a few.

In New York, Forrest and his wife occupied a house on West Twenty-second Street. It had become certain that they could never have children, and when Forrest bought land in Westchester, on the Hudson, near Yonkers, and began building a castle there in Norman-Gothic style, it was with the intention of ultimately bequeathing it as an endowed home for indigent actors and actresses. In 1843, Macready returned to the United States for a second American tour, and was entertained by the Forrests. "Dined with Forrest," he recorded in his diary during October; "met a very large party, too large for comfort, but it was kindly intended. Bryant, with whom I talked very little, Halleck, and Inman, the artist, were of the party. Our day was very cheerful. I like all that I see of Forrest very much. He appears to be a clear-headed, honest, kind man; what can be better?" But although the two actors tried to maintain an illusion of friendship, they were in every way incompatible. Their relations were not improved by a prolonged and often acrimonious debate which broke out in the American press over their respective merits as actors. As on his earlier tour, Macready was favored by the intellectuals and fashionable people; perhaps with greater enthusiasm because of their growing distaste for Forrest's impassioned style. Forrest, however, had touched the height of his fame with the great public, and a large portion of the American press disparaged Macready in order more effectively to champion Forrest. Anti-British feeling entered largely into the discussion of two very different styles of acting, and when Macready sailed for home he was apparently convinced that Forrest was the instigator of a campaign against him.

Two years later, Forrest and his wife went to Great Britain, where the actor proposed to make a second professional tour. In London, he opened at the Princess' Theater with *Macbeth,* the American tragedienne, Charlotte Cushman, who had recently made a spectacularly successful debut there, playing Lady Macbeth. Forrest was greeted with a storm of hisses which increased in ferocity at the end of every act. Miss Cushman, however, was as loudly applauded. Surmising that she had entered into an intrigue against him, Forrest cherished a bitter enmity to her thereafter. The press attacked his performance so fiercely that he was compelled, after a few nights, to abandon his engagement. Forrest charged that the violence of his reception was due to Macready who, he alleged, had formed a cabal of critics to decry him, and had arranged for a claque to hiss him down. Disregarding her husband's charges, Mrs. Forrest received Macready socially, as an old family friend, though Forrest refused to speak to him. This gave rise to discord between husband and wife.

Despite the disaster that had fallen on him in London, Forrest set off for a tour of the provinces which eventually took him to Edinburgh. There, on the night of March 2, 1846, Macready was playing *Hamlet* and Forrest, with a friend, attended the performance, sitting in a box. To every British star, the Edinburgh public was known for its chilling lack of demonstrativeness; even Mrs. Siddons, in her day, had complained of this trait. As Macready recorded in his diary, the audience at first gave him less applause than he was accustomed to receiving. It was the eve of his fifty-third birthday; he was determined to win over the audience. He acted "with particular care, energy and discrimination," giving, as he thought, one of his best performances of the role, and soon felt that the sympathies of the audience "were cordially, indeed enthusiastically, with me." In the scene of the play within the play, after his instructions to the players, and just before the play commences, Hamlet observes to Horatio, "They are coming to the play—I must be idle—get you to a place." This line, Macready habitually delivered with a bit of stage business involving the repeated waving of a large handkerchief. Forrest, at this point, hissed him loudly.

Within a few days, the British press was boiling over the incident. Editorials appeared accusing Forrest of professional jealousy, and he was rightly excoriated for his ill-bred behavior and flagrant breach of the conventions of his profession. He retorted with a long letter published in the London *Times,* defending the right of an auditor to express his displeasure by hissing, and accusing Macready of desecrating *Hamlet* with a "fancy dance," or, as it was elsewhere described, a *pas de mouchoir.* The articles and correspondence that appeared in the British press were reprinted by American newspapers, and the private quarrel between Macready and Forrest quickly assumed the proportions

of an international issue. The American newspapers were by no means unanimous in supporting Forrest. There was enough controversy to impel James H. Hackett to enter the fray with a widely reprinted letter in which, although not explicitly justifying Forrest's conduct, he severely condemned Macready's *pas de mouchoir.* Hackett suffered from the comedian's legendary ambition to distinguish himself in tragedy. He had been exchanging letters with ex-President John Quincy Adams on the subject of *Hamlet,* and some of these had already been published, so his condemnation of Macready had an impressive air of authority. Its effect was to prolong the controversy. Forrest returned to the United States raging with hatred of Great Britain, of all things British, of Macready in particular. Among the democracy, his reception in the theater became an affair of patriotism. He had been hissed off the stage in London; his honor, and that of the American nation insulted in his person, must be vindicated. His engagements therefore produced a series of ovations that were, in fact, the partisan demonstrations of a political party. For Forrest had now become something more—or less—than America's foremost tragedian. In the economic, political and social cleavage between "the rich and powerful" and "the humbler members of society" he had come to represent, symbolically, the cause of the common man. There was a measure of irony in the fact that this spokesman of the underprivileged was also very nearly a millionaire.

The relations between Forrest and his wife did not improve after their return to the United States. At the end of May, 1848, they were in Cincinnati, where Forrest was playing an engagement. Returning unexpectedly, one afternoon, to the parlor of their hotel suite, Forrest found his wife in what he chose to consider a "compromising situation." George W. Jamieson, an actor, was seated on the sofa; Mrs. Forrest was standing between his knees; and Jamieson had "his hands upon her person." Jamieson fled and a stormy scene between husband and wife followed. Forrest apparently agreed to accept his wife's explanation that "Mr. Jamieson had been pointing out her phrenological developments."

When they returned to their home in New York, Mrs. Forrest resumed the normal tenor of their social life. Their circle included William Cullen Bryant, his daughter and son-in-law, Parke Godwin; Nathaniel P. Willis, editor of the *Home Journal,* and his wife; Willis' younger brother, Richard, well known as a man about town; and Captain Granby Calcraft, about whose marriage many years earlier there was an "ugly mystery," but who was nevertheless received in good society. Mrs. Forrest's hospitality seems to have extended to hours later than her husband approved, and to have been marked by a liberality with champagne which he considered unduly costly. The difficulties between them reached a head when Forrest, ransacking one of his wife's bureau drawers, found a letter written to her by Jamieson. Evidently Jamieson had been reading George Sand's novel, *Consuelo,* and he addressed Mrs. Forrest by the name of its heroine. To Forrest, the letter read like an avowal of love, which it probably was. But he certainly had not read *Consuelo,* or he would have realized that its heroine, far from being a "bad woman," is a figure of superhuman purity and moral virtue. To Forrest, the letter seemed deeply incriminating. He brooded over his supposed dishonor for four months. Then he insisted upon a separation. One afternoon, Forrest and his wife drove to the home of the Parke Godwins, with whom Mrs. Forrest was to live. With them in the carriage were his last gifts to her; a frostily inscribed copy of Shakespeare's plays, and a "manly portrait" of himself. The date of their separation is noteworthy. It was April 28, 1849, and in less than a fortnight Forrest would be held responsible for a catastrophe that permanently blackened his fame.

In the autumn of 1848, Macready had returned to the United States for a third tour. He opened at the new Astor Place Opera House in New York early in September; Forrest, at the same time, was playing an engagement at the Broadway Theater. But no disturbances occurred, and Macready's performances, during his three weeks' engagement, were not interfered with. However, a rumor reached him that a hostile demonstration had been planned and, unwisely, he alluded to this plan in a curtain speech. The rumor was true. A plan had been made and submitted to Forrest, who refused his consent. It was proposed by "Captain" Isaiah Rynders, an unsavory member of the Tammany Hall hierarchy. Rynders controlled the votes of the Irish immigrants who inhabited the Five Points, and also commanded the tough, dreaded Dead Rabbits gang which made that area its headquarters. On Macready's previous tour, the British star had made a curtain speech which Rynders, who was in the audience, found offensive. Rynders had leaped to his feet and berated Macready, whom thereafter he detested. That Rynders admired Forrest as an actor is probable; that he honored him as a political and social symbol is certain. And, as a practical politician, he was willing to make capital of the feud between the two stars.

Their feud soon came to a climax. In November, 1848, Macready was playing an engagement at the Arch Street Theater in Philadelphia. One night, a portion of the audience hissed him vigorously and long. Macready made a curtain speech in which he referred to the episode in Edinburgh, protesting that never before it had he entertained "a feeling of unkindness" to Forrest. To this, Forrest retorted with a "card" published in the Philadelphia *Pennsylvanian*. It was a long, abusive document which accused Macready of conspiring to drive Forrest from the London stage, and characterized him as a "superannuated driveller." Macready replied with a "card" dignified in tone, but spirited in defense of his cause. There were further exchanges, in which Forrest expressed himself with increasing violence and Macready firmly controlled his temper. Once again, the American press played up the quarrel sensationally. Throughout the country public excitement ran high.

During the next months Macready met with rude treatment nearly everywhere he played. Forrest, meanwhile, was overwhelmed by his marital difficulties. He had not ceased to love his wife, yet he had also come to hate her. To a man of his proud, imperious temper her supposed physical infidelity was an outrage not to be borne. It dishonored him; even worse, it undermined his colossal vanity. And hadn't she been spiritually unfaithful to him at the time of his humiliation in London, four years earlier, when she forced him to endure the presence of Macready as her guest? In every misfortune that had befallen him, personal as well as professional, Macready figured. Forrest had reason enough to detest the man. He had greater reason to detest the actor. For Forrest wished to believe himself the greatest of living tragedians, and unless this claim was universally acknowledged, he could not. Macready, his sole rival, had eclipsed him in the favor of fashionable and cultivated playgoers; in Boston, on this very tour, Macready had been ostentatiously lionized by Beacon Street, and feted by the nation's most famous men of letters. Much as Forrest affected to despise patricians and intellectuals, his vanity required their approval. But they derided his acting, they eulogized the "polished art" of Macready. Was his own art, then, tainted by crudity? Could it be true, as they asserted, that his heroic style was vulgar; that, having obstinately studied, he still remained ignorant? He could not ignore these charges, and they must have raised the self-doubt that, from childhood, had been the other face of his self-conceit. Maddened by the breakup of his marriage and the continuing contest with his rival, Forrest, given the opportunity, was unlikely to abstain from vengeance.

The opportunity soon became unavoidable. On April 23, 1849—five days before separating from his wife—Forrest began a three weeks' engagement at the Broadway Theater in New York. It was announced that on May 7th, at the Astor Place Opera House and under the management of James H. Hackett, Macready would begin a "farewell" New York engagement. The whole city seethed with excitement, and the press reflected a general sense of foreboding.

The New York *Herald* urged the rival stars to desist from their feud. It was absurd, *The Herald* asserted, that the public be in turmoil because of the quarrels of two "impertinent" actors. Presently, the bills were posted for the performance of May 7th. On that night, both Macready and Forrest would appear in *Macbeth*.

If Forrest, personally, did not incite his partisans to prevent Macready from performing and banish him from the American stage forever, he did nothing to dissuade them. Forrest's adherents filled the gallery of the Astor Place Opera House. Macready's entrance from the wings was greeted by catcalls and hisses. The storm continued with increasing fury, and the play proceeded in dumb show. Rotten eggs, copper pennies, apples, potatoes, lemons, blocks of wood and a bottle of asafoetida hurtled down on Macready. Three acts of *Macbeth* had been given when the star saw a man hurling four chairs from the gallery. He decided that he had discharged his obligation to the public and would endure no more. He ordered the curtain rung down. The victory was Forrest's.

Scheduled to play *Richelieu* on the following night, Macready refused to appear and announced the abandonment of his engagement. At the Broadway Theater, Forrest played *Richelieu;* at the Astor Place Opera House, *The Merry Wives of Windsor* was put on, with Hackett as Falstaff. Although as a critic of acting and a student of Shakespeare he had publicly agreed with Forrest's condemnation of Macready's Hamlet, Hackett never forgot his gentility. His sympathies, political and social, were with the patricians, and he had declared them in assuming managerial responsibility for Macready's engagement. At his instigation, a petition to Macready was drawn up and circulated for signatures on May 8th. It apologized to the British star for the outrage inflicted on him; requested him to continue his engagement; and pledged that he would be sustained by "the good sense and respect for order prevailing in this community." Forty-seven distinguished New Yorkers signed this document. Among them were Washington Irving, Herman Melville and other men of letters; Charles King, president of Columbia College; men of wealth like Moses H. Grinnell, a "merchant prince," and Samuel B. Ruggles, founder of Gramercy Park. To their appeal, Macready assented. The petition, with the names of its signers, was published by *The Herald* on the morning of May 9th. It was announced that, as originally planned, Macready would repeat *Macbeth* on the night of May 10th. On that night, Forrest was billed to play *The Gladiator* and, in the role of Spartacus, lead an insurrection against an oligarchy.

Publication of the appeal to Macready increased the fury of Forrest's adherents. As a contemporary pamphleteer stated, "The question became not only a national, but a social one. It was the rich against the poor—the aristocracy against the people; and this hatred of wealth and privilege is increasing over the world, and ready to burst out whenever there is the slightest occasion." (A wave of democratic revolutions had swept over Europe, the year before.) A rumor had been spread that the British crew of a Cunard liner intended to rally to the defense of Macready. It was also known that the municipal authorities were taking extraordinary precautions to prevent a riot at the "kid-glove opera house." In the event of a disturbance—so the rumor went—regiments of the militia were to be mustered to give the British star armed protection. On the morning of May 10th, New Yorkers found that an anonymous "American Committee" had affixed a poster to walls throughout the city. "Workingmen, shall Americans or English rule in this city?" it asked, asserting a threat had been made to the freedom of "all Americans who shall dare to express their opinion this night at the English Autocratic Opera House." It continued, "We advocate no violence, but a free expression of opinion to all public men. Washington forever! Stand by your Lawful Rights."

Had Forrest wished to prevent a riot, he could no longer have done so; the situation had passed beyond his control. It soon became clear that the initiative had been taken by such tribunes of the people as Isaiah Rynders, the accomplished demagogue Mike Walsh, and Edward Zane Carroll Judson, known as "Ned Buntline." Buntline was dabbling in politics as the publisher of a weekly dedicated to the violent affirmation of "nativistic," or anti-foreign, principles. His raffish career had already included one murder, and in ferocity he compared favorably with Forrest's former boon companion, Colonel Bowie. Forrest and Buntline might have been drawn together by their mutual hatred of the British, but there is no indication that they were personally acquainted.

On the night of May 10th, a sullen crowd gathered around the Astor Place Opera House before its doors were opened. The police had been stationed there in force; in the adjacent streets, at the entrances, in the lobbies and auditorium. They were able to exclude suspected partisans of Forrest, and the large audience was composed chiefly of Macready's supporters. He received a standing ovation when he came on stage. A few men who tried to make a hostile demonstration were spotted by the police and, after further interruptions of the performance, were gradually ejected. In the streets outside, the crowd kept increasing, and eventually numbered some twenty thousand men and youths; the Dead Rabbits, the Bowery Boys, men from the "Irish wards," mechanics and laborers, hoodlums from the slums. The mob were in an ugly mood. Presently, having surrounded the Opera House, they attacked the police. Policemen seized one of the leaders, Ned Buntline, overpowered him and confined him under the stage of the theater; there, unsuccessfully, he tried to set fire to the building. The arrest of Buntline goaded the mob to a more savage attack; they drove the police into the theater. Inside the playhouse, all doors were hastily barricaded. The mob tried to storm them, and shattered the windows of the building. A detachment of the Seventh Regiment, commanded by Colonel Duryea, arrived on the scene; more than two hundred infantrymen, and forty-two mounted soldiers. Ammunition had been issued to the soldiers, but Colonel Duryea had not been authorized to fire on the rioters. The jeering mob attacked the troops with paving stones and other missiles, preventing them from forming a cordon around the theater. Finally, Colonel Duryea obtained authorization for the troops to use their muskets. A first volley, fired above the heads of the rioters, failed to disperse them. Infuriated, they attacked the troops more fiercely. Two volleys were then discharged at them with terrible effect, and they fell back. A detachment of artillery arrived with two cannons. These were planted in front of the Opera House, loaded, and trained on the rioters. No further attack was made.

Riot at the Astor Place Opera House, May 10, 1849, by N. Currier

Meanwhile, inside the Opera House, an imprisoned and apprehensive audience saw *Macbeth* played out to the end—to the accompaniment of breaking windows, the raging clamor of the mob and the rattle of musketry. At the conclusion of the play, the audience, not waiting for the afterpiece, filed out into darkened, flooded streets; the rioters had smashed all street lamps in the neighborhood and opened all water hydrants. Macready left the theater among the audience, wearing a borrowed cap and overcoat, and escorted by his friend, Robert Emmet. Emmet succeeded in leading Macready, unrecognized, through the lingering remnant of the mob, to his own nearby home. There Macready remained until dawn, when he was driven to New Rochelle, in Westchester County, where he took a train for Boston, to sail home.

Next morning, the grim aftermath of the riot hung over New York like a pall. Twenty-two rioters had been killed; the wounded, soldiers and rioters, numbered several hundred. During the day, many of the distinguished signers of the petition to Macready received warnings that their homes would be attacked. Other citizens were alarmed by a new poster announcing a protest meeting in City Hall Park. The crowd that gathered there heard "exciting and inflammatory speeches" by Isaiah Rynders and Mike Walsh, but the meeting broke up without further disturbance. It was rumored that two gangs, the Plug-Uglies and Killers, were being imported from Philadelphia and Baltimore to renew the riot. The rumor proved to be false. That night, the battle-scarred Opera House continued to be guarded by troops with cannons. An eye witness recorded that a mob assembled there, "in a bitter bad humor but a good deal frightened, and the only overt acts that were committed, on the Bowery side, were met by prompt measures and with instant success. Some of the cavalry were badly hit with paving stones, but as soon as the Unwashed were informed that unless they forthwith took themselves off they'd be treated with a little artillery practice, they scampered." Gradually, the city quieted down. In September, 1849, Ned Buntline was convicted of having incited and fomented the riot, and was sentenced to one year's imprisonment and the payment of a fine. On his release from prison, Buntline was triumphantly escorted to his home by a parade of sympathizers.

To the so-called "upper classes," the Astor Place riot made Forrest an object of execration. But, as if to proclaim his defiance of them, he proceeded with headstrong obstinacy to another scandal by bringing suit for divorce from his wife. He charged that Mrs. Forrest had committed adultery not only with Jamieson, but with Captain Calcraft and Richard Willis, for whom she habitually kept "open house," detaining them in his home "until two or three in the morning," and on one occasion secreting Willis there for a period of three days. To vindicate her reputation, Mrs. Forrest filed a counter-suit. The affair became a nation-wide sensation when, before these suits had reached trial, Nathaniel P. Willis, in his influential *Home Journal,* publicly espoused Mrs. Forrest's cause. Forrest, Willis asserted, had overextended himself financially in building "Fonthill," his massive Norman-Gothic castle on the Hudson, and as a result wished to be saved the expense of his wife's support; he was also jealous of her intellectual superiority, and had enlisted "the kitchen and the brothel" in order to "throw her off like a mistress paid up to parting." The publication of Willis' article caused Forrest to add him to the now growing list of corespondents named in his divorce suit. Then, meeting Willis one day in Washington Square, Forrest knocked him down and horsewhipped him, an action which precipitated fresh lawsuits and further publicity.

The Forrest divorce case came to trial in New York City on December 18, 1851, and soon developed into a legal battle that was unprecedented both for its bitterness and the degree of excitement it aroused throughout the country. George Templeton Strong, a young attorney, member of the élite, the son-in-law of Samuel B. Ruggles, recorded its progress in his voluminous diary. Strong noted the case as "slowly dragging its dirty length along in the Supreme Court, like a wounded skunk." He expressed the attitude of good society in being "strongly prejudiced against that king of blackguards, Edwin Forrest," and—although not supposing Mrs. Forrest "utterly blameless" and characterizing her as "certainly a lady of little distinction and questionable taste"—in feeling that Mrs. Forrest was "helpless and oppressed by a powerful, unscrupulous and powerful man" who sought to "crush her by the worst means." During the course of the case, Parke Godwin, Nathaniel P. Willis and other distinguished friends appeared as witnesses for Mrs. Forrest, while servants in her former home appeared against her. Forrest's infidelity to his wife was established through the "reluctant testimony" of the "she-keeper of a house of assignation," and evidence was introduced that he had been guilty of misconduct with various leading ladies who had accompanied him on his professional tours, among them the young American actress Josephine Clifton, who had died four years previously. The trial reached its conclusion on January 24, 1852, with a verdict for Mrs. Forrest. The decree of divorce prohibited Forrest from marrying again, but left Mrs. Forrest free to do so. It awarded to her alimony of $3,000 a year—an award which Forrest appealed for fifteen years, until finally ordered to pay his former wife the sum of $64,000; of this, all but $5,000 was absorbed by the expenses of litigation.

On February 2, 1852, one week after her vindication by the Supreme Court, the former Mrs. Forrest, now calling herself Mrs. Catherine Sinclair, made her debut as an actress at the Lyceum Theater in New York. Untrained for the stage, but foreseeing that she would have to support herself, she had taken instruction in six roles from George Vandenhoff, a well-known British actor. Vandenhoff realized that "public curiosity would render her engagements highly profitable," and also agreed to perform with her "for an equal share of the profits which her temporary and factitious attraction would secure." With commendable sagacity, if not with fastidious taste, he insisted that she make her debut as Lady Teazle in *The School for Scandal,* a role which, in view of the immediate circumstances, she was reluctant to undertake. Squeamish New Yorkers deplored this choice, but among the playgoing public there was considerable desire to see the heroine of a scandal in real life enact its dramatic parallel. Another riot was anticipated on the night of her first performance for, as George Templeton Strong noted in his diary, "the chivalry of the Bowery is said to be in fierce wrath at the verdict against her husband." The police were therefore mustered in force to guard the theater, and a detachment of militia, veterans of the Astor Place riot, were "strongly posted in an adjacent groggery" as a reserve force. These precautions prevented any serious outbreak. The theater was crowded, and at the end of the performance Mrs. Sinclair received an ovation from the audience. Following this, a demonstration in behalf of Forrest, Isaiah Rynders and Ned Buntline was begun in the gallery, but no violence occurred. Mrs. Sinclair played the role for a fortnight, winning praise from certain critics for the elegance of her manner and gestures and the beauty of her attire. She continued in other roles until March 10th, then began a tour which took her to Philadelphia, to Boston and other New England cities, to Portland, Maine. The divorce trial had brought her country-wide notoriety and both her New York engagement and her tour proved highly profitable. Thus encouraged, Mrs. Forrest left the East and, the following season, resumed her theatrical career in San Francisco.

One week after his ex-wife's debut, Forrest also began a New York engagement at the Broadway Theater. His defeat in court had instantly raised him to even greater popularity with the masses than he had previously enjoyed, for they had seen their hero transformed, as they believed, into a martyr. At his opening performance, Forrest played the role of Damon and an audience that packed the theater greeted his first entrance with a thundering ovation. Bouquets and other floral tributes rained down on the stage. In the pit, Isaiah Rynders unfurled a huge banner bearing the legend, "This is the people's verdict!" At the close of the performance, Forrest came before the curtain and made a speech. He had already had the proceedings of the divorce trial published in book form by the New York *Herald* and the *Police Gazette.* In his speech, he spoke of his cause as that of "a deeply injured man." It was, he said, the cause of his audience also—"the cause of every man in the community, the cause of every human being, the cause of every honest wife, the cause of every virtuous woman, the cause of everyone who cherishes a home and the pure spirit which should abide there." This cause, he now submitted to "a tribunal uncorrupt and incorruptible . . . the sober second thought of the people." Another prolonged ovation began as he finished speaking.

For sixty-nine nights, audiences filled the Broadway Theater to see Forrest play a repertory of eighteen major tragic roles. In its duration, variety and tremendous profits, this engagement was until then unequaled on the American stage. Nearly every play that he performed offered Forrest some lines which were applicable to the divorce trial, and these he delivered with such malicious point that the audience often sprang to their feet and cheered him. And what could be more sensational than his performance of *Othello?* Night after night, responding to the demand for a speech, Forrest came before the curtain as an Othello in real life, heaping abuse on his enemies, eloquently defending his own course of action. It was as much for this titillating climax as for his acting that New Yorkers jammed the theater. The brilliant engagement was to be among the last of Forrest's great triumphs, and in it his dramatic powers reached their highest level. Many years later Lawrence Barrett, the most intellectual and scholarly of the next generation of American stars, tried to appraise Forrest's quality. "His obtrusive personality often destroyed the harmony of the portrait he was painting, but in his inspired moments, which were many, his touches were sublime. He passed over quiet scenes with little elaboration, and dwelt strongly upon the grand features of the characters he represented. His Lear, in the great scenes, rose to majestic heights, but fell in places almost to mediocrity. His art was unequal to his natural gifts."

But, during the following years, even Forrest's natural gifts suffered from the corrosive effects of his defeat in court. His former exuberance gave way to misanthropy. The hardness of his nature, his arrogance and despotism, became more pronounced. He gave up the New York home which he had shared with his wife, and sold "Fonthill" to the Roman Catholic Sisters of Notre Dame for a convent, insisting upon receiving his price of $100,000, but remitting, after the payment, $5,000 as a gift. He bought a large gloomy mansion on North Broad Street, in Philadelphia, and there lived in lonely state, for he deliberately cut himself off from many of his former associates. James Oakes, his closest friend, tried to persuade him to retire from the stage for a period of years. The decision was made easier for Forrest by a series of articles in which the critic of a New York newspaper attacked him as a "butcher," a "ranter" and a "stage ruffian." Embittered by the savagery of this denunciation Forrest, at the age of fifty, left the stage, as he thought, forever. When, some years later, he returned to his profession, it was to meet a changing public taste, a new era and a young, powerful rival.

CHAPTER 5

The First "First Ladies"

OLD-FASHIONED moralists were distressed when the scandalous Forrest divorce case launched the tragedian's wife on a prosperous stage career. True, a judge and jury had vindicated Mrs. Sinclair's honor. But their verdict was, so to speak, merely technical; though it declared her innocence, it could not restore her to respectability. Decorum obliged a woman in her position to go into retirement. Mrs. Sinclair not only defied decorum, but made money from her tarnished reputation. Obviously, the playgoing public had become cynically indifferent to standards of decency.

Among playgoers, especially among those who were both conventional and high-minded, the private morality of actresses was a touchy subject. Ideally, of course, virtue should be rewarded and sin discountenanced; the rule would have been easy to apply had an all-wise providence chosen to endow only the virtuous with talent. But, notoriously, the stage was an immoral environment. Of what actress could you believe, as was eventually to be said of one, that "in the might of her innocence she neither saw nor felt the fires that had scorched and

Lucia Elizabeth Vestris as Little Pickle in "The Spoiled Child"

Ellen Tree as Rosalind in "As You Like It."
By R. J. Lame

slain their thousands?" With characteristically American optimism, high-minded playgoers hoped that the unfavorable moral climate of the theater might yet produce a paragon of virtue. Meanwhile, conscience often put them in a dilemma, and their conduct showed little consistency.

When the lovely Ellen Tree made her first American tour, in 1836, she was heralded by an encomium. A respected British playwright, Thomas Noon Talfourd, certified that she represented "all that is more graceful and refined in English womanhood." Miss Tree proved to be a charming and talented actress, not a great one. However, her virtue was so impressive that ex-President John Quincy Adams wrote a poem in praise of her "fair perfection"; her tour lasted nearly three years; and she carried home with her, not only $60,000 in cash, but the reverential esteem of the American public. Her subsequent marriage to Charles Kean delighted everybody, and that Queen Victoria publicly honored this irreproachable couple seemed, to Americans, only just.

They took a very different view of another British theatrical couple. In 1838, Stephen Price offered Madame Vestris, the celebrated comedienne, $100,000 for a year's tour of the United States. Unlike Miss Tree, Eliza Lucy Vestris had no reputation for incorruptible virtue. Her love affairs had been numerous, spectacular and prodigally reported. She announced to Price that she would make the proposed American tour only if accompanied by her current lover and leading man, Charles James Mathews, son of the noted comedian. Price therefore insisted that they be married in London, and that accounts of the ceremony be published in the British press. "They say that before accepting him Vestris made a full confession to him of all her lovers. What touching confidence!" To this remark of an actress in her company, another retorted, "What needless trouble!" And a third added, "What a wonderful memory!" The marriage caused a sensation, but the American tour was a brief one, for it failed disastrously. Was its failure a punishment deliberately inflicted on flagrant sin, belatedly whitewashed? Though many people asserted that it was, outraged morality was less involved than they supposed. When she came to the United States, Vestris had passed her fortieth year, and although her talents were unspoiled, no vestige remained of her famed beauty. Americans could not be excited—even to moral indignation—by a siren so disappointingly passée. Their purported censure of Vestris would have seemed more plausible had they not, a year or so earlier, turned out in droves to see Miss Charlotte Watson. As everybody knew, Miss Watson's talents for the stage were imperceptible to the kindliest of critics. But—as everybody also knew—Miss Watson had conducted a long, tempestuous and ill-starred love affair with Nicolo Paganini, the world-famous violinist. Her appeal to American audiences was by no means exceptional. Youth, beauty and a reputation for sexual promiscuity seldom failed to attract gentlemen to the box office, and ladies often succumbed to curiosity about a "bad woman" whose rewards indicated that the law of compensation and the moral law were not, alas, identical.

Charlotte Watson as Celio in "Native Land."
By Stewart Watson

Conscience could not ignore this disturbing conflict between principle and practice. Clearly, the highest esthetic pleasure must preclude all moral anxiety. A simple distinction did away with the problem. Talent might find a lodging in the fair and frail; but genius, never. Genius would manifest itself only in a woman who led a pure and noble life. So high-minded playgoers, patriotically yearning to acclaim a native-born actress of the first rank, awaited the emergence of an improbable, permanently stainless cynosure. And presently there emerged, not one, but two. To Americans, their clearest title to fame was not founded on their artistic achievements, distinguished as these were. More exceptional, more gratifying and certainly more important was the fact that their private lives, like their public careers, were exemplary. One was an artist who made herself a lady; the other, a lady who made herself an artist. Both elevated their profession as well as their audiences, for both (as an eminent clergyman said of one of them) showed the world "how a vocation which is beset with peculiar difficulties and temptations may be filled with a lofty spirit."

Miss Charlotte Cushman never failed to impress her professional colleagues. They felt strongly, though variously, about her acting, but it was her personality that really challenged them. She was perturbing, perplexing. They argued about her interminably. Some of them, having speculated about her for years, in the end could do no more than record their conjectures. If she was animated by a lofty spirit, they oddly failed to detect it. Nearly all had been exposed to the powerful drive of her ambition, and the experience was not easily forgotten. Neither was her pronounced worldliness, so incompatible with the image of her cherished by the public. One of the most sensitive of her contemporaries, James E. Murdoch, first met Miss Cushman when she was a girl of nineteen and was struck by her air of "fixed and determined purpose." Long acquaintance with her merely confirmed this first impression. Murdoch admired her, but he came to feel that by nature she was "a lover of place and position," and he characterized her as "intensely prosaic, definitely practical." Her constant aims, he reflected, were "to be known in society, to possess and wield an influence." Observing her skillful management of people whom she considered useful to her personal interests or professional advancement, Murdoch thought her not unlike "a female Richelieu" and was convinced that "wealth had no more devoted worshipper." Murdoch's sense of Miss Cushman's "materialism" was widely shared by other actors. Men, on the whole, were put off by a streak of hardness in her character and were apt to say, disparagingly, that she not only thought like a man but looked like one. It was her lack of "feminine softness" that they assumed they resented. But Miss Cushman was the first actress on the American stage to evoke perpetual feminine adulation, and actors may also have been exasperated by her capacity, whether on the stage or off, for infatuating women.

Women probably understood Miss Cushman no better than men, but they accepted the accomplished fact in all its strangeness. Their devotion was a response to an element in her nature that few men perceived. They were not misled by the cast of her mind, her physique, or her manner, rugged and stalwart as these were. They recognized that her sensibility was not only unmistakably feminine, but that it was, even for a woman, excessive. To Miss Cushman herself, her sensibility was both a blessing and a curse. It was her principal resource as an artist. It was also the source of all her frustrations as a woman. She felt too deeply and too much, and every transient emotion was tormented by an awareness of its exorbitance. So the gift imparted a taint to its peculiar benefactions. Did it not, on the stage, force her to pitch every effect in too high a key so that, at her worst, she became "stagy" and strident, and at her best startling, weird and terrible? The gift brought her wealth as well as fame. But could the woman be proud that the actress had been victorious by force rather than by sweetness, as a woman should?

Her frustrations began in childhood. Her father, a merchant in Boston, failed in business. The family were plunged into extreme poverty and in 1829, at the age of thirteen, Charlotte was removed from school to start earning a livelihood. Serious enough in itself, the blow was made worse by the girl's conviction of superiority. Her father's ancestor, Robert Cushman, had been the financial agent of the Pilgrims at Leyden and, coming out to New Plymouth in the *Fortune,* had reputedly preached the first sermon delivered and printed in the colony. Her mother's ancestry was little less distinguished, in the distant past having been allied to such prominent Massachusetts dynasties as the Winthrops, Saunderses and Saltonstalls. Yet poverty and obscurity defrauded the pride of place instilled in her by parents whose only defense it was against humiliation. Life dealt her another blow by giving her the looks which would have made her a handsome boy, thereby the more injuring her sexual vanity as a girl who was not only undeniably plain, but plain after a fashion that people thought somewhat queer. She was too tall, too angular, too muscular. Her fine blue eyes, and the wavy golden hair that later darkened to chestnut, did not offset the square outline of her face, the strong protruding jaw, the blunt, manly features. Her character and temperament accorded with her looks. "I was born a tomboy," she acknowledged, ruefully, in later life; the word, in her youth, had an ugly note of opprobrium. At the age of ten a seafaring uncle with a fondness for the theater took her to see Macready and Thomas Abthorpe Cooper act. These performances fired her to distinguish herself in elocution at school, and to dragoon her playmates into theatricals in which, as one of them remembered, she showed her "penchant for a masculine masquerade." Meanwhile, she developed a remarkable singing voice, with a full contralto and almost full soprano register. Somehow, lessons for her were arranged, and she earned money by singing in the choir of a Boston church.

In 1834 the British opera singer Mary Anne Wood played an engagement at the Tremont Theater. At one of her concerts, Charlotte Cushman, then eighteen, was employed to sing duets with her, and Mrs. Wood was so impressed by Miss Cushman's voice that she urged her to give up the career of teaching for which she was preparing and, instead, study for the operatic stage. So Charlotte Cushman became an "articled pupil" of James G. Maeder, a composer and conductor who had married Clara Fisher. Under Maeder's direction, the following year, Miss Cushman made her operatic debut in *The Marriage of Figaro,* singing the role of Countess Almaviva to Clara Fisher's

Susanna. She appeared a second time as Lucy Bertram in an operatic version of Walter Scott's *Guy Mannering.* Then she accompanied the Maeders to New Orleans, where her teacher was to produce operas at the St. Charles Theater. There she sang several roles, including that of Patrick in the operatic farce *The Poor Soldier;* Murdoch, who heard this performance, always remembered that "in her soldier dress on the stage she challenged attention." But suddenly, at nineteen, her fine voice failed; she had ruined it by forcing the upper register. In her distress, she sought the advice of James H. Caldwell, who told her that she ought to study for the dramatic stage. Her contract with Maeder was annulled and she began taking lessons from Barton, the stage manager of the theater, who had acted with Mrs. Siddons and her brothers. Barton taught her the role of Lady Macbeth, which she enacted at the close of the season in his benefit performance. The result, Murdoch recalled, "was a brilliant audience and a triumph for Miss Cushman."

With this single triumph to her credit, Miss Cushman sought an engagement at the Park Theater in New York. Edmund Simpson, its manager, offered her a chance to "act on trial"—that is, without pay. Her vanity wounded by the fancied belittling of her talent, she accepted a contract to join the stock company of the Bowery Theater at a weekly salary of $25. She made her New York debut there as Lady Macbeth to the Macbeth of Thomas Hamblin, in the autumn of 1836. She appeared in several other roles; then the theater was destroyed by fire, and she found herself penniless and without prospects. By this time she had undertaken to support her mother and a younger sister and brother; she was a woman with a man's responsibilities in a man's world. She secured an engagement for five weeks at the theater in Albany, New York. She was soon advanced to the position of leading woman, and her engagement was extended for the full season. She enjoyed social as well as professional success in the capital. An Albany newspaper, reporting a great Fireman's Ball held at the theater, noted that Miss Cushman, "magnificently attired, her head adorned with an immense and beautiful Bird of Paradise . . . was the observed of all observers, the bright particular star of the evening." But the opulent, beautiful plumage quickly molted. There had been a love affair, and apparently she was jilted. Long afterwards, she confessed that she "had been called upon to bear the very hardest thing that can come to a woman." The experience resolved her to dedicate "my entire *self* to my work." She was now twenty-one; thereafter, as she said, "I actively pursued what became a passion—my art."

From Albany, she went on to brief engagements in Buffalo, Detroit and Boston. In her native city, she "astonished everyone" by her Lady Macbeth, enjoyed a second triumph as Portia, "announced her predilection for male roles" by playing the character of Henry in Thomas Morton's old comedy, *Speed the Plough,* and was "rapturously applauded" for her rendition of "Hail Columbia" at a benefit performance for Murdoch. Meanwhile, the active pursuit of her art had yielded more tangible results. She had a contract for three years with the Park Theater in New York as "walking lady"—or general utility actress—at a weekly salary of $20.

The long engagement gave Miss Cushman both a measure of economic se-

Charlotte Cushman,

from a drawing by Miss Teresa Kenney

curity and a rigorous discipline. Her position required her not only to play any role assigned to her, but to substitute on short notice for any other actress in the company who was unable to perform. Since there was a change of bill every night, and the customary schedule of two plays was sometimes expanded to three, she was obliged to acquire a list of roles formidable both in number and variety. Under this necessity, she developed the method of study which, during her later career as an international star, aroused such great interest among her colleagues. She learned her roles piecemeal. She would have a speech read over to her very slowly, and then repeat what she could remember of it. Another reading and repetition followed. A third was usually sufficient; then the same process was applied to the next speech. She experimented with the vocal expression of lines while learning them, and at rehearsals. But, as one of her close associates noted, after she became a star she left the *acting* of her parts "to the inspiration of the time and place"—a principle which, although it gave an illusion of spontaneity to her performances, also made them extremely uneven in quality. Miss Cushman's memory was exceptionally retentive and seldom played her false. It was said that "she never had to look over an old part, in the sense of study, before acting it, even after a very long interval."

An illustration of this was cited, in 1924, by the actor William Seymour who, fifty-two years earlier, had been a member of Lawrence Barrett's stock company at the Crescent Theater in New Orleans. In 1872, near the end of her career, Miss Cushman played a starring engagement with the company, and in *Henry VIII* enacted Queen Katharine to Barrett's Cardinal Wolsey. Barrett had never before performed the role, and at one of the rehearsals Miss Cushman asked whether he would like her to go through the famous trial scene for him. Fourteen years earlier she had played Wolsey at a number of performances, and then had dropped the role from her repertory. But she was still letter-perfect and, as Seymour recalled, "so poignant and so beautiful was her interpretation of the lines in which the Cardinal realizes that he has lost everything, that when she

finished there were tears in Barrett's eyes and the stage-people who were listening were all affected."

Rightly, Miss Cushman regarded her engagement at the Park Theater as an
apprenticeship. "I placed myself professionally," she noted long afterwards,
"where I found and knew all the mortifications in my profession." By the end
of her engagement in June, 1840, she had played some thirty leading roles and
a great number of minor ones, including parts in some farces which she must
have counted among her "mortifications." But, at the other end of the scale,
there were abundant compensations. With Edwin Forrest as star she played,
successively, Goneril and Cordelia in *King Lear;* Queen Gertrude in *Hamlet;*
Emilia in *Othello;* Volumnia in *Coriolanus.* With Forrest she also played the
Widow Melnotte in the first American performance of *The Lady of Lyons,* a
play in which she soon undertook Forrest's role of Claude, long to remain one
of her favorite male parts. She played Ophelia to Charles Kean's Hamlet. In
The School for Scandal, she played Lady Teazle to Murdoch's Charles Surface.
Her talent for comedy was not impressive, yet two seasons later she created the
role of Lady Gay Spanker in the first American performance of Dion Boucicault's celebrated *London Assurance,* and was acclaimed. But it was already
evident that Miss Cushman's forte was tragedy and melodrama; she had demonstrated this by the power of her Lady Macbeth, Belvidera in *Venice Preserved,* Elvira in *Pizarro,* Julia in *The Hunchback,* Mrs. Haller in *The Stranger.*
And, in addition to these standard roles, she had created two that were to rank
among her memorable achievements.

One of these roles was Nancy Sykes, in a dramatization of Charles Dickens's
Oliver Twist. She found it morally repugnant, yet morally justifiable by its
inculcation of "a dreadful lesson." Francis Wemyss was struck by the realism
of her acting: "As a portrait of female depravity it was painfully correct."
Lawrence Barrett, who appeared with her as Fagin many years later, asserted
that Miss Cushman's Nancy was as astonishing to the acting profession as it
was to the public. He considered her death scene magnificent; she dragged her-

self onto the stage and, keeping her face averted from the audience, produced a feeling of horror by the way she called for Bill Sykes and begged him to kiss her. Her voice, Barrett declared, "sounded as if she spoke through blood, and the whole effect was far greater than any other actress has ever made, with the sight of the face and all the horrors which can be added." But her playing of Meg Merrilies in Daniel Terry's dramatization of Sir Walter Scott's *Guy Mannering* was even more powerful and painful, and popular demand kept the role in her repertory to the very end of her career. She made of the demented old witch, as George Vandenhoff said, a character "half human, half demon—with the savage animal reality of passion, and the weird fascination of crime, redeemed by fitful flashes of womanly feeling." Her impersonation of Meg was luridly melodramatic, but it was also a masterpiece of what is technically called character acting. The actual text of her part was banal; she invested it with terror and a kind of wild poetry by her extraordinary vocal effects, her make-up, costume, gait and "business." Critics, like Miss Cushman herself, held that Meg was not her greatest role. It was, however, her most startling and effective one, and of all the parts she played, it came to be the one most intimately associated with her name. For this, her friend, the critic William Winter, offered a curious explanation. "Miss Cushman could give free rein to her frenzy in this part, and that was why she loved it and excelled in it, and was able by means of it to reveal herself so amply and distinctly to the public mind." In her acting of Meg, he asserted, "she obeyed the law of her own nature."

At the termination of her contract with the Park Theater, Miss Cushman, with her younger sister, Susan, went to Philadelphia as members of the stock company of the National Theater, directed by the British-born actor-manager William E. Burton. Susan Cushman, petite, pretty and distinctly feminine, had married and had been deserted by her husband. Charlotte, dominant as always, had taught her the rudiments of acting, secured an engagement for her at the Park, and thereafter stipulated that they be engaged together. Charlotte's association with Burton was notable chiefly for a performance which, after she became famous, she preferred to forget. In Philadelphia first, and later at the National Theater in New York, she enacted the title role of J. S. Dalrymple's *The Naiad Queen*. This "grand romantic spectacle in four acts" was, in fact, a musical extravaganza founded on the legend of the Lorelei, and the precursor of *The Black Crook* which, a generation later, was to shock and delight Americans by its unabashed sensuality. According to Francis Wemyss, who served as stage manager for the production when it was brought to New York, the great attraction of *The Naiad Queen* was its presentation of "fifty female warriors" led by Miss Cushman. "Such a display of ladies' legs no mortal man could resist the opportunity of seeing." In the first act, there occurred "an awful bath scene" in the nymphs' grotto at the bottom of the Rhine, "a most scandalous affair" in which the Naiads, and Miss Cushman as their queen, glided about attired in silk fleshings adorned with jeweled girdles, saved from purported nudity only by scanty gauze draperies. The even more dubious and exciting scene, in the third act, took place in "the Queen's crystal chamber beneath the Rhine," when Miss Cushman led her fifty nymphs, attired as Amazons, through a series of military evolutions and maneuvers, and "made the theater resound with applause." But, although *The Naiad Queen* played to crowded houses in both Philadelphia and New York, and the title role was said, by some competent judges, to brilliantly exploit Miss Cushman's "peculiar style," her excursion into the realm of the scandalous did not escape censure. "It is a sad pity," the critic of *The Spirit of the Times* asserted, "that a clever woman like Miss Cushman should be wasting time and a strong intellect in show pieces."

Her strong intellect took ascendancy during the next few seasons. She returned to the Park Theater for a year, and won recognition as one of the leading actresses of the American stage. She went back to Philadelphia and launched the innovation of "petticoat government" by becoming acting manager of the Walnut Street Theater. Yet petticoats were apparently a psychic as well as a physical encumbrance, for she systematically added to her repertory of "breeches parts." In the later days of her international fame, when she had acquired the immense dignity of being honored as a national institution, Miss Cushman explained her assumption of male roles as an expression of sisterly affection—she deliberately undertook them in order to cast Susan Cushman in principal female roles. George Vandenhoff, who played Mercutio to Miss Cushman's Romeo, considered her duels with Tybalt and Paris, executed in "masculine and effective style," the only good points in her performance. "She looks neither man nor woman in the part—or both," he observed sourly; "and her passion is equally epicene in form." He declared that in male roles she unsexed herself to no purpose. "There should be a law against such perversions," he fulminated. Many men were inclined to agree with him.

But women felt differently. Were not her Romeo, her Claude Melnotte, superbly impassioned precisely because as a woman she knew what love was, and as a woman knew how love should be made? The impetuousness, the fiery ardor of her lovemaking, thrilled her feminine audiences. Every woman present, identifying herself with Juliet, or with Pauline, felt that she was the object of Miss Cushman's so veritably real passion, and was ravished by it. Safely, of course, for Romeo, or Claude, was inaccessibly on the stage. And with perfect propriety, for Romeo or Claude was not, after all, a lustful male but a chaste and celibate woman. Yet, for those who had been kindled by her stage wooing, the good fortune of meeting Miss Cushman socially proved to be a heady experience. One lady recorded its effect: "Dearly as I loved my mother and my home, if Miss Cushman had asked me that day to go with her and be her slave, without even going back to say farewell to my friends, I should have consented. I would have given my life for her; and although I did not realize it, I was in such a state of excitement that, after leaving her, I burst into tears the moment another person addressed me and, so to speak, broke the spell under which she had laid me." And the lady added that it was not until years had passed, and she had known Miss Cushman very well, that she "could resist this peculiar influence" whenever she met the actress. To actresses who performed with her, however, Miss Cushman was sometimes irresistible in less enchanting fashion. Playing Effie Deans in *The Heart of Midlothian,* Miss Rosina Shaw had to cross

Charlotte and Susan Cushman as Romeo and Juliet

a bridge and scream loudly, in terror. At her first performance, her scream was so feeble that the audience laughed, ruining one of Miss Cushman's most effective scenes. When the play was next performed and the cue was given, Miss Shaw froze the audience by an agonized shriek. No wonder; Miss Cushman had jabbed her in the arm with a sharp darning needle. In her power to compel a willing service, an utter devotion, Miss Cushman was unusually versatile.

But nobody knew better than Miss Cushman herself that she was not yet the great actress she had determined to become. She might have agreed with George Vandenhoff, who thought that she "displayed a rude, strong, uncultivated talent," that her performances lacked "artistic study and finish." This was to be remedied when, on his second American tour in 1843, William Charles Macready came to Philadelphia, and Miss Cushman was cast to play leading roles with him. "The Miss Cushman who acted Lady Macbeth interested me much," he noted in his diary after their first performance. "She has to learn her art, but she showed mind and sympathy with me—a novelty so refreshing to me on the stage." She impressed him enough to make him undertake the always congenial office of mentor. He invited her to act with him during his next engagement in New York and, later, in Boston. Before he left the United States, Macready persuaded her to try her fortunes in Great Britain.

In the autumn of 1844, doubting the wisdom of her venture, suffering, as she said, from "miserable, frightful uncertainty," Miss Cushman sailed to seek an engagement in London. At the outset, she encountered difficulties. For a time, she lived on one mutton chop and a few stale muffins a day. But eventually she succeeded in obtaining a trial performance at the Princess' Theater, with the prospect of an engagement if she made a favorable impression. On February 14, 1845, she made her first appearance as Bianca in *Fazio*. The critic of the London *Times* hailed her performance as a great triumph, declaring that "for passion—real, impetuous, irresistible passion—she has not at present her superior." The critic of the London *Sun* asserted that, since the memorable first appearance of Edmund Kean nearly thirty years earlier, there had never been such a debut on the boards of an English theater. Not only did Miss Cushman surpass every English actress, but she possessed "the godlike gift" of absolute genius. She was immediately engaged for forty-seven performances, and then thirty-four more were added. "In my most ambitious moments I never dreamed of the success which has awaited me," she wrote to her mother. Social and literary London lionized her, and one of her English friends reported that "for the present she is the greatest creature in the greatest city in the civilized world!"

Her own hopes soared. "I have given myself five years more," she informed her family, "and I think that at the end of that time I will have fifty thousand dollars to retire upon; that will, if well invested, give us a comfortable home for the rest of our lives, and a quiet corner in some respectable graveyard." She sent for her mother and Susan. The sisters played *Romeo and Juliet,* causing a tremendous furor. In 1848, Susan Cushman married a wealthy man and retired from the stage. Charlotte went on to fresh triumphs. That summer, Queen Victoria commanded a performance of *Henry VIII* at Drury Lane. With royal approval, Miss Cushman was invited to play Queen Katherine to Macready's Wolsey. This was a signal professional honor for an American actress, and an equivalent social tribute followed immediately. Miss Cushman was entertained by the Duke of Devonshire at Bolton Woods, one of his estates. But in spite of critical acclaim, popular enthusiasm, financial rewards and social recognition, frustration still dogged her. She had been studying the acting of the

great French tragedienne, Rachel. "I used to look on in a perfect rapture of
wonder and admiration at her unapproachable art," Miss Cushman wrote soon
afterwards; "and often, as I left the theater, and compared my own acting with
hers, despair took possession of me, and a mad impulse to end life and effort
together."

In the autumn of 1849, after an absence of five years, Miss Cushman returned
to the United States. She had raised her sights; her financial goal was now
$150,000. On the massive foundation of her European celebrity, it seemed
probable that this goal could soon be reached. Yet even she may have been
surprised by her welcome. Americans were proud that, at long last, an American actress had been declared pre-eminent by the British press and public.
They were proud that her immaculate reputation had been publicly recognized
by Queen Victoria; that her ladyship of birth and breeding had been acknowledged by the aristocracy; that her intellectual distinction had brought her the
admiration and friendship of famous writers. With all these reasons for patriotic
satisfaction, it was inevitable that most Americans should consider her above
criticism. Great Britain had proclaimed her genius, but Americans knew that
Miss Cushman's entire dramatic education and experience had been acquired
in the United States. In a sense, therefore, she was something more than a
great woman and a great artist. She was a symbol of the new and high prestige
of American culture.

It was with this somewhat exalted status that Miss Cushman found herself
endowed when, in October, 1849, she began her American tour at the Broadway Theater in New York City. Among other roles, she played Mrs. Haller in
The Stranger; Rosalind, Lady Macbeth, Queen Katherine and Beatrice from
her Shakespearian repertory; Juliana in Tobin's old comedy, *The Honeymoon,*
Meg Merrilies, Julia in *The Hunchback.* In subsequent New York engage-

*Charlotte Cushman as Lady Mac-
beth*

ments, she appeared as Romeo and Claude Melnotte, Lady Gay Spanker in *London Assurance,* Bianca in *Fazio,* and Thisbe in *The Actress of Padua,* a tragedy by the Philadelphia playwright Richard Penn Smith. For three seasons, Miss Cushman toured the United States, playing repeated engagements in New York, Boston and Philadelphia; traveling south to New Orleans by way of Baltimore, Washington, Charleston, Savannah and Mobile; traveling as far west as St. Louis. Then, in the spring of 1852, at the age of thirty-six, she announced her decision to retire from the stage. After sixteen years of hard, often exhausting, work she had reached her financial goal; she was a rich woman. Did this determine her to retire? Was she persuaded that her genius had already attained its fullest development, so that she could cherish no hope of finer achievements and more enduring fame? Or, as William Winter surmised, was her decision prompted by "that element of feminine weakness, that unsatisfied and therefore forlorn tenderness of woman's heart" which formed the core of her nature? Miss Cushman took her purportedly final farewell of the stage at the Broadway Theater in New York in May, 1852, acting the role of Meg Merrilies, and soon afterwards sailed for England. For several years American newspapers and magazines reproached her for retiring, and expressed bitter resentment because, as one journalist put it, she had "renounced the land of her birth and avowed her determination of ending her days in a foreign clime." All this fuss was premature. During the next twenty years the same publications were to chide Miss Cushman for the frequency of her formal farewells to the stage. And while it was true that she resided abroad for most of that time, making her home first in London and later in Rome, she eventually returned to live in the United States.

Meanwhile, national pride was further gratified by the emergence of another actress of genius. Except for their attributed genius and the virtue which it connoted, Mrs. Anna Cora Mowatt and Miss Cushman were in every way unlike. Some critics, comparing them as actresses, declared Mrs. Mowatt to be the superior. Not only was her range wider but, within their common repertory, she excelled in those roles for which Miss Cushman was least capable. Miss Cushman, as James Murdoch put it, "grasped the intellectual body of the poet's conception without mastering its more subtle spirit"; but it was precisely in rendering the subtle spirit of a character that Mrs. Mowatt succeeded so notably. More significantly, she was, in her style of acting, an innovator, the precursor of a new school, whereas Miss Cushman was the representative of an old one. Barton, and perhaps Macready also, had inoculated her with the Siddons manner. Even her most ardent admirers could not deny that Miss Cushman, in the level scenes of any play, was apt to be "stagy"—that she resorted to the angular gestures, the stride and start and labored breathing, the stilted declamation employed by imitators of the "Tragic Muse." Mrs. Mowatt's method was very different, as was pointed out by so severe a critic of acting as Edgar Allan Poe. "The great charm of her acting," Poe asserted, "is its naturalness. She looks, speaks and moves with a well-controlled impulsiveness, as different as can be conceived from the customary rant and cant, the harsh conventionality of the stage." Reporting on her unprecedented debut—she made her first appearance on the stage as a star, after only three weeks of training and a single rehearsal with the company—Poe wrote, "We have to speak of her acting only in terms of enthusiastic admiration—let her trust proudly to her own grace of manner—her own sense of art—her own rich and natural elocution."

Undoubtedly, Mrs. Mowatt's immediate triumph was facilitated by her beauty, social position, prestige as a novelist and playwright and, most of all, by public knowledge of her "romantic" story and her motives for going on the stage. Slender to the point of frailty, golden-haired, blue-eyed, with features of a cameolike delicacy, she impressed one jaded critic as "an almost perfect combination of beauty, grace and refinement." Men who met her in society described her as "gorgeous" and marveled at her "splendor"; the adjective that most women applied to her was "fascinating." On the stage, she appealed equally to both sexes, enchanting them, as a contemporary remarked, by her physical loveliness and captivating them by the genuineness of her talent. But even had she lacked beauty and been less prodigally endowed with talent, American audiences would probably have received her with almost as fervent enthusiasm. "She carried with her the heart of every listener," an astute admirer observed, "for she exhibited the most beautiful moral spectacle of which human nature is capable, that of a wife turning her accomplishments to account to relieve the necessities of her husband."

Mrs. Mowatt was born and reared in circumstances of luxury. Her father, Samuel Ogden, was a wealthy New York merchant; her mother, a grand-daughter of Francis Lewis, a signer of the Declaration of Independence. One of a large family of sisters, Anna Cora Ogden as a child inaugurated the custom of celebrating their father's birthday with a theatrical performance in which they all took part. By the time she was ten she had read all of Shakespeare's plays and was already composing verse. In 1833, at the age of fourteen, she translated and produced Voltaire's *Alzire* at the annual birthday celebration. That year, she attended the theater for the first time, to see Fanny Kemble in *The Hunchback*. One year later there occurred her romantic marriage to James Mowatt, a wealthy New York attorney much older than herself. Mowatt was an intimate of the family circle and had been in love with her for two years. His suit was not disapproved by her parents, but they insisted that a formal engage-ment be postponed until she had reached the age of seventeen. However, she was about to be formally introduced to society, and Mowatt feared that, ab-sorbed by the gaieties of balls and parties, she would be lost to him. So he persuaded her to marry him secretly and inform her parents after the wedding. Remarkably enough, her parents forgave her promptly. The Mowatts made their home on an estate in Flatbush, Long Island; their pre-Revolutionary mansion was equipped with a fine ballroom which furnished an appropriate setting for the social exercise of young Mrs. Mowatt's talents. "We gave numer-ous fetes, but never mere dancing parties," she recorded in her autobiography. "They were always either of a poetic, musical or dramatic character." Threat-ened with tuberculosis at the age of eighteen, she was sent to Europe with an aunt to recover her health, and was presently followed there by her husband.

Anna Cora Mowatt,

from a painting by John James
Audubon

In Europe, Mowatt was overtaken by an ocular malady which permanently
impaired his vision, but his temporary recovery enabled Mrs. Mowatt to enter
Paris society in the era of Louis Philippe, and to analyze with clear insight the
American fashionable world's predilection for following the form of French
manners without conceiving the spirit which dictated them. She also studied
the acting of Rachel in all her major roles. "I never expect to see that acting
equaled," she wrote "—to surpass it, in impassioned force and grandeur, appears to me impossible." Before returning to the United States, Mrs. Mowatt
wrote her first play, *Gulzara, or the Persian Slave,* a verse-drama in six acts
intended for amateur production in her ballroom. For this fete the Mowatts
had elaborate scenery and costumes made in Paris. It was destined to be their
last one. Mowatt's failing vision forced him to abandon his legal practice; he
embarked on speculations in land and stocks; presently his fortune was swept
away.

In 1841, at the age of twenty-two, Mrs. Mowatt determined to earn a livelihood for her husband and herself. "I had talents for acting—I could go upon
the stage; but that thought only entered my mind to be instantly rejected. The
idea of becoming a professional actress was revolting." But giving public readings was less repugnant, although she foresaw that even this would cause her
to lose her position in society. She soon learned the penalty of incurring social
disapproval. Some beloved relatives and old friends turned from her. "They
were shocked at my temerity in appearing before the public. They even affected
not to believe in Mr. Mowatt's total loss of means. They tacitly proscribed me
from the circle of their acquaintance. When we passed in the street, instead of
the outstretched hand and loving greeting to which I had ever been accustomed,

I met the cold eye and averted face that shunned recognition." Fearing to embark on her career in New York, Mrs. Mowatt gave her first reading at the Masonic Temple in Boston, so successfully that two more were demanded. An appearance in Providence, and several series of readings in New York followed. These drew large audiences, but certain New York journalists condemned her "bold and novel" course of action, ignoring the motive that had prompted it. This public censure, following the sufferings inflicted by members of her circle, brought on a prolonged illness. When she recovered she turned to writing for a livelihood. Under the pseudonym "Helen Berkley," she contributed articles to the popular magazines; compiled a series of books on etiquette, cookery and similar subjects; finally wrote a novel in six weeks. This book, *The Fortune Hunter,* won a prize offered by *The New World* and, when published under Mrs. Mowatt's name, had a large sale. It was one of the earliest fictional satires of New York society, and its success led Epes Sargent, an influential Boston poet and dramatist, to suggest that Mrs. Mowatt write a comedy of manners and submit it to the management of the Park Theater.

Mrs. Mowatt wrote *Fashion* as an acting play, aiming at dramatic rather than literary success, avoiding, as she said, the temptation of "fine writing." "If it is a satire on American *parvenuism,* it was intended to be a good-humored one," she later explained. "No charge can be more untrue than that with which I have been taxed through the press and in private—the accusation of having held up to ridicule well-known personages." But this charge indicated the principal merits of her play; its authenticity as a study of fashionable life, its fidelity to contemporary manners and the impressive vitality of its characters as individuals, not mere types. The play was sent to Edmund Simpson, manager of the Park, who had known Mrs. Mowatt since her childhood. Possibly for this reason he read it at once and within a few days notified her that it was accepted for immediate production. "I was almost too much surprised to be elated," she confessed, and a subsequent interview about the casting of the comedy with Thomas Barry, the Park's stage manager, still found her in "a state of agreeable bewilderment." She attended only the last rehearsal and, instead of taking a playwright's customary place on the stage with the manager, she "preferred to overlook the mysterious doings from a private box, unseen by the actors." On the next night—March 24, 1845—*Fashion* was produced, and from the same box Mrs. Mowatt watched its "unequivocally brilliant success" with the audience. The play was announced for a run of three weeks and next day, at a "cutting rehearsal," Mrs. Mowatt, accompanied by her husband, crossed the stage of a theater for the first time. During the New York run of *Fashion,* the play was also produced at the Walnut Street Theater in Philadelphia where, at the first performance, Mrs. Mowatt received an ovation from the audience. Soon afterwards, the play was put on in nearly every other American city, and it continued to be revived well into the twentieth century.

The success of *Fashion* brought proposals from several managers that Mrs. Mowatt go on the stage. Her husband had founded a publishing firm; this now failed, and the earning of a livelihood became more necessary than ever. Meanwhile, her views about the stage and the theatrical profession "had undergone a total revolution." She had learned "how unfounded were the prejudices of the world against the profession as a body." She realized that, from her childhood, her tastes, studies and pursuits had combined to fit her for acting. The inevitable strong censure of "society" no longer dismayed her. She had discovered that, "in general, *success* sanctified all things; nothing was reprehensible but *failure*." She obtained her husband's and her father's reluctant consent to the momentous step. She wished to make her debut as an actress in a city where she was not personally known, but the juvenile lead of the Park Theater, W. H. Crisp, who was engaged to give her professional instruction and to act with her for one year, insisted that, for reasons of prestige, her first appearance must be made at the Park, in New York. She was announced to appear as Pauline in *The Lady of Lyons* on the closing night of the season, June 13, 1845. "The instant my projected appearance was announced," she recorded, "I had to encounter a flood of remonstrances from relatives and friends—opposition in every variety of form. But tears, entreaties, threats, supplicating letters could only occasion me much suffering—they could not shake my resolution."

With only three weeks to prepare for her debut, Mrs. Mowatt studied intensively. She exercised her voice four hours every day. She took fencing lessons and practiced with dumbbells. She wore a voluminous train for many hours daily, to acquire the graceful management of queenly or classic robes. Undoubtedly she also rehearsed her role at home with Crisp, who was to play Claude Melnotte. But the modern reader of her autobiography is amazed by a statement which Mrs. Mowatt considered in no way extraordinary. "The day before my debut, it was necessary that I should rehearse with the company. I found this a severer ordeal than performing before the public." While going through the third act, she was startled by a sudden burst of applause that came from members of the company who were standing in the wings—"an involuntary and most unusual tribute." This "first drop in the honeyed cup of success" was a prelude to the ovation she received the following night from an audience that filled every seat in the theater. At the conclusion of the play, she was called before the curtain. "The whole house rose, even the ladies—a compliment seldom paid. I think it *rained* flowers; for bouquets, wreaths of silver and wreaths of laurel fell in showers around us. Cheer followed cheer as they were gathered up and laid in my arms. The hats of gentlemen and handkerchiefs of ladies waved on every side. I curtsied my thanks, and the welcome green curtain once more shut out the brilliant assemblage. Then came the deeper, truer sense of thankfulness. The trial was over; the debutante had stood the test; she had not mistaken the career which had been clearly pointed out as the one for which she was destined." Yet Mrs. Mowatt apparently never realized that her achievement was unique in American theatrical annals. She was the first actress to become, and remain, a star without any prior professional experience.

Reviews of her performance in the press were highly commendatory, and offers of engagements presently poured in from all the principal theaters of the country. With her husband and Crisp she set out on a tour that began in Philadelphia; every night not consumed in traveling had been engaged in various theaters for a year in advance. Prepared only in one role when she made her

Anna Cora Mowatt as Beatrice in "Much Ado About Nothing"

debut, Mrs. Mowatt acted two hundred nights during her first season, playing "all the most popular characters in juvenile comedy and tragedy." Often, after a protracted rehearsal followed by a performance, she returned to her hotel exhausted only to have to study her next role for many hours, bathing her eyes and forehead with ice water and pacing her room to keep awake. Nearly everywhere she appeared, *Fashion* was produced to satisfy public demand, and she was compelled to play the role of Gertrude, for her "a severe punishment." Her other roles included Juliana in *The Honeymoon,* Mrs. Haller in *The Stranger,*

Lucy Ashton in *The Bride of Lammermoor,* Lady Teazle, and Juliet. She undertook Juliet with "timid reverence," disappointed herself during rehearsals, but on the night of her first performance—it occurred during the course of a long engagement at Niblo's Garden in New York—found that her "whole being merged itself into the impassioned existence" of the character. Of all her roles, she felt Juliet most intensely and it always remained, in the opinion of critics and audiences, one of her finest achievements. Her instant success in the part prompted her to think about, and then develop, a style of acting which previously had been merely instinctive. She was inclined to believe that the highest form of dramatic art was that in which the actor does not identify himself with his role, but "produces and controls, without sharing, the emotions of his audience." But this style of acting was alien to her nature. "No amount of study or discipline could have enabled me to belong to the grand and passionless school. I never succeeded in stirring the hearts of others unless I was deeply affected myself. The putting-off of *self-consciousness* was, with me, the first imperative element of success." Paradoxically, this subordination of her own personality to that of the character she was playing became the core of her personality as an actress—the trait that distinguished her from her most celebrated contemporaries and so, on playgoers and critics alike, produced an effect of inimitable individuality.

Mrs. Mowatt's technical training was greatly advanced by acting with a new leading man, Edward Loomis Davenport. Her senior by one year, Davenport had already had a varied experience of the stage, and he was soon to be accounted one of the most accomplished of American actors. He was exceptionally handsome; he had a fine voice; like Mrs. Mowatt, he was equally effective in romantic drama, tragedy and comedy. From the outset of their association, she was impressed by "his high moral character, his unassuming and gentlemanlike manners, his wonderful versatility and indisputable talents." Davenport's remarkable versatility stimulated her own, and the result was a rapid expansion of her repertory. Opening their tour at the Park Theater in New York and proceeding to Buffalo, they made "the whole circuit of the United States." On their journey through the South, when they came to towns where there were no theaters, Mrs. Mowatt gave readings and Davenport entertained the audience by singing ballads. They played a long engagement in New Orleans, where they met Henry Clay, who was to become a valuable friend to both. After an engagement in Vicksburg, Clay rejoined them on the "floating palace" which made the five-day river voyage to Louisville, during which Davenport delighted the statesman by his comic impersonations and, particularly, by disguising himself as a Yankee and carrying out the role so perfectly that none of the passengers recognized him. The long tour undertaken by Mrs. Mowatt and Davenport ended in Cincinnati, where they opened the new Athenaeum Theater, and became such favorites with the public that their engagement was repeatedly extended.

During the summer of 1847, Mrs. Mowatt wrote her second play, *Armand, a Child of the People,* a five-act romantic drama with leading roles designed especially to suit Davenport and herself. Mowatt, meanwhile, went to London to arrange for an engagement there. He consulted Macready, who recommended that Mrs. Mowatt and Davenport make their first appearance in a provincial theater, and an engagement was therefore arranged at the Theater Royal in Manchester. Before sailing, they played brief engagements at the Park Theater in New York, and in Boston, during which *Armand* was produced, meeting with success in both cities. Henry Clay provided them with letters of introduction to influential friends in Great Britain, and his sponsorship brought them unusual social advantages.

Professionally, however, they were at first resented. The company in Manchester received them inhospitably. "We were surrounded by an atmosphere of impenetrable frigidity," Mrs. Mowatt recalled. But their opening performance in *The Lady of Lyons* was favorably received by the audience and highly praised by *The Manchester Guardian,* and before concluding their engagement they obtained a contract to appear for six weeks at the Princess' Theater in London. Their London debut was to be made in *The Hunchback.* At rehearsal, "the stage aristocrats of the company made no effort to conceal their absolute contempt for the American aspirants," and on the evening of the performance a deliberate effort was made to so unnerve them that they would ignominiously fail. The attempt almost succeeded; only Mrs. Mowatt's indomitable will and Davenport's resourcefulness enabled them, in the final act of the play, to win the acclaim of their audience. By the end of their engagement, however, the new American stars had firmly established themselves with the London public and the principal critics. They subsequently played at the Olympic Theater, and for two seasons as "permanent stars" of the fashionable Theater Royal, Marylebone. Mrs. Mowatt achieved extraordinary success in a series of Shakespearian roles; Beatrice, Rosalind, Viola, Imogen, Desdemona, and especially Juliet, which she performed to Davenport's Mercutio, and the Romeo of Miss Fanny Vining, who was to become Davenport's wife. Her prestige was enhanced by the successful production of *Armand* and *Fashion.* Then, at the height of her success, her career was interrupted by an illness caused by worry over her husband's rapidly failing health. On her recovery, she learned that all her savings had been lost through the bankruptcy of her manager. In these dire circumstances, she bravely undertook a tour of the provinces, and during its progress received the news of her husband's death.

In August, 1851, after an absence of nearly five years, Mrs. Mowatt returned to the American stage, playing her first engagement at the new, magnificent Niblo's Garden in New York, which had replaced a theater destroyed by fire. It was the most fashionable theater in the city, and its audience, she knew, was "distinguished for purity of taste." This was the kind of audience that had acclaimed her in London, and the American public already knew its verdict, summed up in the statement of the British playwright, Bayle Bernard, that, although she was equaled by other actresses in art and surpassed in force by many, she was a true genius, unique in the quality of her poetic insight and poetic fervor. Miss Cushman, her sole rival for primacy, had been touring the country for two years, but Mrs. Mowatt was probably aware that she need not fear comparison. She had perfected her individual style of acting, she had ac-

Anna Cora Mowatt as Rosalind in
"As You Like It"

quired an extensive repertory of new roles, and her beauty was more radiant than ever. Every circumstance made it possible for her to consider herself in full command of her art and dispense with further study, especially since she had already fixed a time for her retirement from the stage. Instead, as she recorded with magnificent humility, "I determined, by close application to the study of my art, to win the highest distinction to which my abilities, in their full cultivation, would entitle me." Immediately after the ordeal of her first performance, she began daily study periods with Professor Hows of Columbia College, reading and analyzing her roles, and modifying her interpretation of them under his advice and criticism—and thereafter she resumed these study periods whenever she passed through the city.

After a New York engagement that drew overflowing audiences, Mrs. Mowatt set out on tour, playing in Boston, Providence, Philadelphia, Baltimore, Cincinnati and St. Louis. She had promised to return, by Christmas, to the home of one of her sisters in Philadelphia where, during the holidays, a ball was to be given and a revival of her play, *Gulzara,* was to be produced. The trip from St. Louis to Philadelphia normally took seven days, and after her last performance, on December 10th, Mrs. Mowatt boarded a steamer for Cincinnati. Three days later, the steamer was frozen fast in the Ohio River, eight miles from Evansville, Indiana. Escorted by two gentlemen who managed to secure an oxcart for the transport of her baggage, she tramped the eight miles to Evansville in order to proceed by stagecoach. Undismayed by having to abandon her baggage there, she traveled in rickety stages, through freezing weather and over snowbound roads, for four days and nights, eventually reaching Cleveland, Ohio. She changed to the railroad, but presently the train could make no headway, and once again she resumed the journey by stagecoach. On

Christmas Eve she reached Pittsburgh and the following morning boarded a train for Philadelphia. After an hour's travel, the train could get no further; she transferred to a stagecoach. Late that afternoon she boarded another train, which crept toward Philadelphia for more than twenty-four hours and finally stopped, snowbound, on the outskirts of the city. A long walk over icy roads to her sister's home completed the seventeen-day trip which Mrs. Mowatt considered one of the more unfortunate, but not exceptional, incidents of a theatrical tour. She had, after all, three days in which to produce her play and, to her relief, everybody understood that the grave realities of her professional life made her "unwilling to act in private for amusement."

For the next two seasons Mrs. Mowatt continued to tour the country, playing all the principal cities as far south as New Orleans and as far west as Cincinnati. From time to time she added new roles to her repertory, the most memorable being Parthenia, in a translation of the German drama *Ingomar,* a play which was to remain popular with audiences until the last years of the century. Parthenia became one of her favorite roles; she found it irresistibly attractive, she said, because it was pervaded by "an innate delicacy, an unconscious goodness, a depth of feeling, a high-toned sense of right." Her conception of the role indicates how finely it was suited to her talent, and critics considered her performance of it unequaled by any other actress. During the summer of 1853, fatigue and illness forced her to take a holiday of several months, and she spent it writing her vivacious *Autobiography of an Actress* which, published early in 1854, was widely read throughout the country. In it, she announced her approaching retirement from the stage. Did she have a love of the theater? She pondered the question and, perhaps with a memory of Fanny Kemble, acknowledged that "there is a species of aristocratic affectation existing among the members of the profession which induces many of them to declare that they detest their own vocation." Her own feeling was very different. "For my part, I answer frankly, I have received intense delight from the personation of some characters. The power of swaying the emotions of a crowd is one of the most thrilling sensations that I ever experienced. Yet I have *not* found in the profession the kind of absorbing fascination which I have often heard described as inseparable from the stage. There are too many incongruous elements mixed with every dramatic triumph for the charm, if any, to be complete."

On June 3, 1854, nine years after her debut, Mrs. Mowatt appeared for the last time on the stage at Niblo's Garden, before an audience that crowded even the aisles of the theater, playing Pauline in *The Lady of Lyons,* the role in which she had begun her career. A eulogistic testimonial signed by many prominent men and women throughout the country was presented to her. For Americans in general, proud as they were of her achievements as a playwright and an actress, were even prouder that she had "not bought these honors with the price of better things," but had "moved with simple dignity along the slippery paths of praise and success." She had, in fact, done what nobody believed possible. Entering a profession condemned by puritans and burdened by the imputation of loose morals, she had triumphantly demonstrated that a lady could rise to greatness in it without ceasing to be one.

CHAPTER 6

New York Takes the Lead

THE DEATH of Stephen Price in January, 1840, though little noticed by the theatrical profession, coincided with the end of an era. The star system which he imposed on the American theater had become one of its permanent features. But one of the remarkable developments of the new era already beginning was a reaction against it, a revival of the stock system which it had displaced. At the time of Price's death, New York had a population of some three hundred thousand. This would nearly double in ten years, and the bustling, roaring city—crowded by more than a half-million residents and throngs of visitors—would be recognized as the American theatrical metropolis. Before still another decade had passed, New York would become, like London and Paris, a theatrical world capital.

Price had made the Park Theater the ranking playhouse of the United States,

William Evans Burton as Mr. Timothy Toodle in "The Toodles"

the American "Old Drury." But when he died its supremacy had been effectively challenged and its prestige was declining. Price's partner, Edmund Simpson, continued a losing struggle for eight more years. Then, bankrupt and heart-broken, he gave up. He did not live to see the historic old Park destroyed by fire six months later; to learn that it would never be rebuilt; or to surmise that, a century after its destruction, people would wonder why a dingy byway between Ann and Beekman Streets was named Theater Alley.

There was irony in the end of the Park Theater, for it had been brought to failure chiefly by the star system that had elevated it to primacy. Ironically, also, its supremacy had been undermined by James W. Wallack, the first of Price's galaxy of foreign stars. In 1837, Wallack began the long career of management that was to make him a dominant influence on the American stage; and his first venture, brief as it was, signalized the opening of a new era. He leased the National Theater, then the finest playhouse in the city. It had been built, four years earlier, by a group of wealthy New Yorkers who were persuaded by old Lorenzo da Ponte—librettist for three of Mozart's operas and, in his remote youth, the friend of Casanova—that the city ought to have an opera house. Two seasons of opera in the splendid theater failed disastrously, and the wealthy promoters abandoned it. Although they had lavished $150,000 on the building, they had erected it on the corner of Church and Leonard Streets, in a neighborhood made disreputable by the city's most notorious brothels. Moreover, the National was one block west of Broadway and, as Philip Hone remarked, "New Yorkers are the strangest people in the world in their predilection for fashionable locations." If Wallack could succeed there, Hone asserted, "he is immortal."

But under Wallack's management, the National flourished. Bringing most of his players from London, he assembled a superior stock company. His remarkably varied repertory included standard dramas and classic comedies, many of Shakespeare's plays, the latest works of Sheridan Knowles and other popular British playwrights, extravaganzas sumptuously mounted, and opera sung in English. Although performances by the stock company were the central attraction at the National, Wallack also brought to its stage an impressive procession of stars: Junius Brutus Booth, Forrest, Hackett, T. D. Rice, "Yankee" Hill, Thomas Hamblin; William Vandenhoff, the British tragedian, and his celebrated daughter, Charlotte; Charles Kean, fresh from Drury Lane, in London. At the National, Wallack instituted the policies for which, subsequently, his theaters were to become celebrated. Probably to the dismay of his stars, and certainly to the astonishment of his audience, he insisted—not always successfully—on an absolute perfection of ensemble playing. This meant that no play was permitted to be merely the vehicle for a star, and have its values thereby distorted. To the contrary, it meant the achievement of a total, or collective, dramatic effect to which the individual performances of the actors were subordinated. Similarly, Wallack set an entirely new standard for stage production. At the Park, it was not considered singular for the leading lady to dress Lady Macbeth "in black velvet, point lace and pearl beads"; but Wallack tolerated no such anachronisms. Every detail of costume and scenery had not only to be accurate, but to contribute to the total effect of a stage picture.

William Mitchell

Early in Wallack's third season, at the very height of his success, fire broke out in the National Theater one afternoon. The building was soon in flames; the conflagration spread to four adjacent brothels and three churches; the theater itself was destroyed. Under the sponsorship of such prominent New Yorkers as Philip Hone, Samuel B. Ruggles, Robert Emmet and Samuel Ward, Jr., a meeting was held at the Astor House which resolved "that a metropolitan theater, corresponding with the wealth and population of this metropolis, should be erected on a suitable and convenient site" for Wallack and his company. Meanwhile, Wallack took his actors to the summer theater in Niblo's Garden, inconveniently "uptown" at Broadway and Prince Street. There, performances were given for six weeks until the onset of cold weather discouraged audiences from attending them. Since no progress had been made with plans for a "metropolitan theater," Wallace then disbanded his fine company and soon sailed for London.

The members of Wallack's company were thrown out of work just when theaters throughout the country were suffering from the economic depression that had followed the financial panic of 1837. A New York newspaper reported that the playhouses in Norfolk, Richmond and Buffalo had closed and were advertised for sale; in New Orleans, the Camp Street Theater had been converted to other uses; locally, "the Park is deserted and even the Bowery Theater is doing indifferently." Philip Hone noted in his diary that, "There are but few strangers in town, and the pockets of our citizens, for the most part, are too low to stand the united demands of Fulton Market and the theaters. Economy begins to follow reluctantly in the dirty footsteps of necessity." It was in these circumstances that William Mitchell, a British-born actor of low-comedy roles in Wallack's company, undertook a venture that popularized a new form of theatrical entertainment and made him, for the next ten years, the leading producer in the United States.

Mitchell adopted Wallack's policies of excellence in stagecraft and of having a strong stock company; since stars were too expensive, he determined to dispense with them. In the existing hard times, he believed that only the lightest theatrical fare, offered at the lowest possible prices, would attract a public beset by financial troubles. Mitchell had reliable evidence for his opinion. The genial Irishman, William Niblo, had drawn crowds to the little theater in his summer garden by producing Parisian "vaudevilles"—programs of short comedies and farces liberally peppered with songs. Taking his cue from Niblo's success, Mitchell rented the recently built Olympic Theater, a very small playhouse uptown on Broadway between Howard and Grand Streets. In December, 1839, he opened this establishment "for the production of burlettas, extravaganzas, farces . . ." with a superior company that included some of his former colleagues at Wallack's. He soon established the scale of prices at 12½ cents for the pit, 50 cents for the dress circle, and 25 cents for the two upper tiers. A barroom on the second tier augmented the box-office revenues, and Mitchell, by engaging his company for the entire season, was able to secure them at low salaries. Even after a prosperous first season, the highest salary paid was $25 a week, with one "benefit night" during the year. Some members of the company received $12; others were willing to join it for as little as $8; a few signed on for a weekly stipend of $5. During that season, the company worked hard for its salaries; eighty-six pieces figured on the bills, and sixty-four of these were novelties at the Olympic. Rumor had it that Mitchell's expenses did not exceed $80 a night, and his average annual profit for ten years was later reckoned at from ten to twelve thousand dollars.

Mitchell's Olympic quickly became the best-known theater in the country. Its extraordinary success resulted from the vivacious playing of a highly talented company, the hilarious nature of the pieces produced, and the irrepressible humor of Mitchell himself, which overflowed into his elaborately jocose playbills, announcements and speeches from the stage. In private life, as all New Yorkers knew, Mitchell illustrated the old legend that comedians are frequently tragic characters. He was a robust, handsome, florid man past his fortieth year, and his existence was made miserable by a vindictively jealous wife. She subjected him to so many public humiliations and scandals that he was forced, several times, to commit her to an asylum for treatment and, in the end, to seek a divorce. But Mitchell's personal tribulations never diminished his exuberant professional gaiety.

Nearly all topics of public interest, and currently fashionable fads and follies, were satirized on the stage of the Olympic. Any pretentious melodrama, or high-flown tragedy, or sentimental opera that was produced at another theater was sure to be ludicrously burlesqued by Mitchell's ebullient troupe. Mitchell himself scored as Crummles in a sketch founded on an episode in Dickens'

Nicholas Nickleby. He ridiculed the solemnities of eminent tragedians in a *Hamlet Travestie,* and in a burlesque *Macbeth* written for the Olympic by Dr. William Knight Northall, a dramatic critic who supplied the theater with some of its most successful pieces and, in effect, served as a house playwright. One of Mitchell's most memorable triumphs was his parody of the famous dancer, Fanny Ellsler, whose tour caused a tremendous furor throughout the country. One week after her first American performance at the Park Theater, Mitchell appeared on the stage of the Olympic in duplicates of her costumes, burlesquing her celebrated *pas seul, La Cracovienne,* as *La-Crack-a-Vein,* and her ballet about the effects of a spider-bite, *La Tarentule,* as *La Musquitoe.*

The audience at the Olympic was unique in New York. The pit was always crowded by newsboys, butcher boys from Center Market, members of the volunteer fire companies. Mitchell kept these boisterous playgoers under control. Whenever they became unruly, he would step to the front of the stage and blandly say, "Boys, if you misbehave yourselves, I shall raise the prices." This warning was sufficient to quell disorder. In spite of the rowdy element in the pit, the Olympic was also the most fashionable theater in the city. In the boxes, there were often present such representatives of "high society," as Washington Coster, the banker August Belmont, and the noted male fashion plate, "Dandy" Marks. Mitchell's comedians sometimes caricatured these personages on the

Mitchell's Olympic Theater, New York, 1840

stage, but this was never resented. Even Charles Dickens, who attended a performance of *Boz in America,* was sufficiently amused by finding himself the subject of mimicry to give his overcoat and hat to the actor who impersonated him. Any gentleman of prominence with whom Mitchell was acquainted—and there were few whom he failed to meet—had the privilege of entrée to the greenroom. Moralists deplored this practice. One of them, possibly a disgruntled Olympian, asserted that "it gives an opportunity or implied license for the exercise of immorality in different phases. The parties thus privileged to go behind the scenes generally do so for no legitimate or honorable purpose—a fact to which many can bear unequivocal testimony from personal observation and experience."

Nevertheless, the two most admired ladies in the Olympic company were as celebrated for their rectitude as for their beauty or their talents. Miss Mary Taylor and Miss Constantia Clarke were originally engaged by Mitchell at the weekly salary of $10. They evoked such extensive masculine adoration that they became civic institutions, ranking among the "sights" that all visitors to the city felt obliged to see. To New Yorkers, Miss Taylor was affectionately known as "Our Mary." Her worshippers among the town's gilded youth formed an organization called "the Taylor Guards," some of whose members occupied several boxes whenever she appeared. Miss Clarke's adorers were equally devoted in their attendance. When both ladies appeared on the same evening, a battle of bouquets between the rival factions always took place. These floral interruptions of the program became so troublesome that Mitchell finally forbade them. The two factions promptly found another means of expressing their enthusiasm. They showered their divinities with "diamond rings and gaudy trinkets."

Miss Taylor and Miss Clarke, so Dr. Northall reported, "had to be annual martyrs to popularity of the most excruciating kind. This occurred on New Year's Day, when all patrons of the Olympic made it a point of duty to call upon the ladies. Distinction of parties was on this day thrown aside, and Miss Taylor received the Clarkeites and Miss Clarke was at home to the Taylorites." There were rival factions in the pit as well as in the boxes and, since fire laddies and fashionables alike observed the ritual of paying calls, the "turmoil and confusion" in the homes of both favorites was appalling. Northall recorded that it was not unusual for Miss Taylor to receive six hundred visitors between ten in the morning and six, when she left her home for the Olympic. But that she inspired such extreme adulation was not surprising. People who saw her on the stage retained a lifelong memory of her beauty, her exquisite singing and dancing, and her accomplished art as an actress. As a small boy, Henry James attended a performance of *The First Night* at Burton's Theater, in which Miss Taylor took the role of a young actress making her professional debut. More than sixty years later, he still vividly recalled "the charming panting dark-haired creature, in flowing white relieved by a gold tiara and golden scarf" playing her principal scene. "Greater flights or more delicate shades the art of pathetic comedy was at that time held not to achieve," James declared.

During the eleven seasons that Mitchell managed the Olympic, he produced

Mary Taylor

for the first time in New York two hundred and thirty comedies, farces, burlesques and elaborately staged spectacles. He also presented many popular pieces that had been seen in other theaters. He established on the American stage two forms of entertainment—the intimate, satirical revue and the spectacular musical—which continued to flourish for more than a century. But none of his other productions achieved the fabulous success and fame of a play which came to the stage of the Olympic accidentally. A benefit performance for the Olympic's prompter, Ben A. Baker, was scheduled for February 15, 1848. One week before the event, illness took several leading members of the company out of the bills. As beneficiary, Baker was entitled to determine the composition of the evening's program, but lacking the services of Miss Taylor and other absentees, he was at a loss for an attraction capable of filling the house. In this emergency, he recalled that Frank S. Chanfrau, a new member of the company, had been badgering him to write a skit featuring the character of a "Bowery boy" volunteer fireman. Chanfrau was a native New Yorker, he had lived on the Bowery and served as a member of the "Old Maid" Engine Company. Although his ambition was to distinguish himself in serious drama— he was the dark-haired "romantic" type, and had acted in the support of Wallack—Chanfrau had a talent for mimicry and had specialized in dialects. Accepting Chanfrau's suggestion, Baker hastily set to work on a sketch for his benefit night.

A few days before the scheduled performance, Baker read *A Glance at New York in 1848* to Mitchell and the company. The central character, Mose, a tough Bowery fire laddie, was modeled on Mose Humphreys, one of the more obstreperous frequenters of the Olympic's pit. Dr. Northall, who attended the reading, observed that Mitchell and the company considered Baker's piece so outrageous that, "on any other than a benefit night," Mitchell "would never have permitted it to go on the stage." Northall's personal opinion of the piece was hardly complimentary; he found it "low in design, vulgar in language, and improbable in plot." In his play, Baker brought to the stage for the first time scenes from the slums, criminal haunts and tough quarters of New York. Even more daringly, he interpolated a jibe at "female emancipation" in high society. One scene was laid in a "ladies bowling saloon" that had a "bar at the back," where nine ladies, according to Baker's stage directions, appeared "dressed in plain white pants and blue blouses, and little black caps . . . all smoking cigars." During the scene, it developed that this dubious resort was a club formed by "fifty ladies of the first families of New York," and that men were debarred from participating in its pleasures. That Mitchell and his company may have been apprehensive about the public's reaction to this episode is easily understood. Apparently, this did not worry Baker. Long afterwards he recalled that he and Chanfrau had "felt very nervous as to how the Center Market boys would take the piece." Would the pit resent seeing itself represented on the stage as the New York underworld?

Chanfrau made his entrance wearing the characteristic "soap locks," red shirt, plug hat and trousers tucked in boots of the Bowery fire boy, smoking a cigar. From the moment he spat out Mose's first line—"I've made up my mind not to run wid der machine any more"—the pit loudly gave its approval. In a subsequent scene, Mose rescued a child from a burning building; thenceforward, as Baker noted, the play "was a triumph." After Miss Taylor and other absentees rejoined the company, Baker expanded his play, adding for Miss Taylor the character of Lize, a Bowery girl, and for James H. Seymour that of Syksey, Mose's boon companion. Before the season ended, *A Glance at New York* had seventy-four performances at the Olympic. But this was not all. Shortly after his first appearance in the role of Mose, Chanfrau took over the failing Chatham Theater, near Chatham Square, and there, in April, 1848, he staged *New York As It Is,* another play by Baker centering on the character of Mose. For a month thereafter, such was the public's excitement about Mose that Chanfrau acted the role on the same evenings in two theaters and in different plays.

During the following seasons, Chanfrau appeared in a cycle of "Mose plays" —*The Mysteries and Miseries of New York,* dramatized from a novel by Ned Buntline; *Three Years After; Mose in a Muss; Mose in California; Mose in China.* In conjunction with these, he perseveringly acted the leading roles in such serious dramas as *Richelieu, The Lady of Lyons* and *Don Caesar de Bazan.* But for nearly twenty years, both in New York and on his long tours, audiences were indifferent to Chanfrau as an actor of serious roles; they came to see him only as Mose. The role brought him fame and wealth, but he detested it as an inescapable, tedious burden that had thwarted his aspirations. The enormous success of Baker's hastily improvised sketch had an immediate effect on the drama. For nearly a decade, other playwrights industriously turned out melodramas in which the lives of the rich and poor in New York were contrasted. Melodrama had been the specialty of the Bowery Theater, but the new vogue brought it to the stages of the fashionable playhouses, where sophisticated audiences were treated to lurid pictures of the city's underworld, and to dramas in which virtuous seamstresses, milliners, printers, dry goods clerks and ship's carpenters demonstrated their moral superiority to corrupt men of wealth.

It was the success of Mitchell's Olympic that inspired the next memorable advance in the theater by bringing to New York, in 1848, a rival actor-manager who was also an outstanding public figure. At the age of forty-four William E. Burton had distinguished himself as a comedian, author, editor, playwright and successful businessman. He was short, very fat, very plain. A celebrated wit in private life, his gift for humor on the stage had an extraordinary range; he was equally effective in Shakespearian roles, classic English comedy, sentimental character parts and broad farce. Burton's elephantine figure and inveterate drollery suggested only one facet of his complex personality. Academic scholars were always impressed by his literary and historical erudition. The artists and writers who were his favorite companions praised his acute sensibility and fastidious taste. Yet his aptitude for practical affairs was exceptional. A few years after he had established himself in New York, Burton was rated as a millionaire —the first theatrical producer to become one. A precursor of later millionaires like J. P. Morgan and Henry Huntington, Burton assembled one of the most valuable collections of rare books in the United States and, adjoining his home on Hudson Street, built a fireproof library and art gallery where, for the first time in New York, the inner circle of society met actors, writers, artists and scholars on common ground.

Burton had come from London in 1834 to join the company of the Chestnut Street Theater in Philadelphia. Wallack brought him to New York for a starring engagement three years later. By then, Burton had already written several plays, acquired some reputation for his short stories and sketches, and founded *The Gentleman's Magazine,* the editing of which he shared, for a brief, unhappy period, with Edgar Allan Poe. In 1840 he began his career as a manager at the National Theater in Philadelphia. The following year he brought his company to the rebuilt National Theater in New York, producing *The Naiad Queen* with Charlotte Cushman; the venture ended disastrously, for the theater was again destroyed by fire. Burton returned to Philadelphia, took the Arch Street Theater, presently extended his operations to the Front Street Theater in Baltimore and, in addition to his activities as an actor-manager, played starring engagements in New York and other cities. When, in 1848, he decided to invade New York a second time, he leased a small theater on Chambers Street facing the north end of City Hall Park. It had been opened as an opera house, four years earlier, by Ferdinand Palmo, proprietor of a fashionable Broadway restaurant, who quickly failed as an impresario. Before Burton took it over, the pretty little theater had sheltered exhibitions of "model artists"—female, and deplorably unclad—whose "beautiful animated pictures" attracted an audience of "fashionable old rakes and ineffable scoundrels about town" armed with "pro-

Scene from "New York As It Is." Frank S. Chanfrau is in the center.
By James Brown

digious opera glasses and pocket telescopes." The police finally put an end to these proceedings. When the house reopened as Burton's Theater the new era approached its meridian.

Burton's plan was to form a permanent stock company composed of the finest players available, and train them to uniform excellence as an ensemble. He required, of every member, not only unusual versatility, but special proficiency in some particular line of acting. Their individual specialties would provide the foundation for building a large and varied repertory, and this would make it possible to feature every player in turn. Burton proposed to follow the current practice of a double or triple bill and nightly change of program. He was aware of the public's demand for dramatic novelty. He knew that rival managers invariably appropriated any successful piece—frequently, the same play was performed, simultaneously, in two or three New York theaters. In these circumstances, Burton recognized that a source of supply for new plays was indispensable.

Other managers had met this exigency by hiring a hack playwright. Burton had a better plan. He was a capable, prolific playwright and adapter; he determined to associate with his theater writers of equal competence and prestige. In addition to himself, Burton's initial writing staff included Dr. Northall and the Irish comedian John Brougham, a member of his company and the author of *Romance and Reality,* a recently successful comedy. Somewhat later, Burton also employed Dion Boucicault, already famous as the author of *London Assurance* and *Old Heads and Young Hearts* and the adapter of *Don Caesar de Bazan.* Burton intended to make his theater not only unique as an artistic institution, but entirely self-sufficient. "No good actor," he once told an apprentice in his company, "has a right to die until he has done something good for his art." This conviction dictated all his policies.

From year to year the personnel of Burton's company changed slightly, yet it always contained a brilliant constellation of talents. No other theater in the country had ever before assembled so remarkable a group of actresses as Miss Mary Taylor, Miss Caroline Chapman, Mrs. Josephine Shaw Russell, Miss Lizzie Weston and the incomparable leading "old woman," Mrs. Esther Hughes, who was as popular with audiences as her younger colleagues. Miss Chapman and her brother, William, had come to New York after the death of "Old William" Chapman, and critics were astonished that such gifted artists had learned their craft on a showboat. At Burton's, Miss Chapman was acclaimed as the foremost soubrette on the American stage. But it was her versatility that dazzled critics and audiences alike, for in comedy she was as fine as Burton himself, she was appealing in pathetic roles and uproariously funny in farce. Suddenly, after four triumphant seasons, her nostalgia for the frontier became irresistible. She withdrew from Burton's at the height of her metropolitan success to depart for California with her brother. Mrs. Russell had made her debut in *The Naiad Queen* with Miss Cushman. Blonde, very beautiful, she had a distinction, a grace, that enhanced her playing of the heroines of high comedy, and she quickly became the favorite leading lady of the New York stage. After two seasons at Burton's, having quietly divorced her actor husband, she amazed the city by announcing her retirement from the stage to marry a socially prominent, wealthy financier, John Hoey, who had recently formed the great Adams Express Company. No actress since Fanny Kemble had made a marriage like Mrs. Hoey's, but hers was soon followed by another. Miss Taylor—"Our Mary"—took her final farewell of the stage to marry W. Ogilvie Ewen, a member of the city's social aristocracy.

The retirement of Mrs. Russell and Miss Taylor elevated Miss Weston to the position of leading lady. She was slight, extremely pretty, a capable actress and adored by the public—until her brunette loveliness and her generous nature involved her in scandal. She married A. H. Davenport, a handsome young actor; they were unhappy and separated. (He was not related to the famous E. L. Davenport.) Shortly after their separation, Davenport went to the Broadway Theater and found his wife seated in a box with Edwin Forrest and another man. He waited in the lobby until the final curtain and, as the audience was leaving the theater, accosted Forrest and Mrs. Davenport, upbraided them furiously, and drew a revolver. An anxious bystander seized Davenport's arm and the pistol was discharged in the air. Some months later, Charles James Mathews —made a widower by the recent death of Madame Vestris—returned to the United States on a starring tour. During an engagement at Burton's, Mrs. Davenport constantly performed with him. Scandal broke out again when Davenport divorced his wife, and Mathews publicly asserted that Davenport had "sold her." One afternoon the two men met on crowded Broadway, and Davenport thrashed his elderly rival. Before the turmoil over this incident died down, New Yorkers were shocked by another. "Charles Mathews has just

Lester Wallack

married that showy little piece of harlotry Mrs. Lizzie Weston Davenport,"
George Templeton Strong recorded in his diary. "The marriage is a mere
nullity, but before it was solemnized, the lady had shown her lover, as she had
shown many others, that she cared little for forms and ceremonies. It's a pity,
but I suppose his first wife, Madame Vestris, was not much better."

The actors at Burton's were as remarkable a group as the actresses: Burton;
John Brougham; veteran, scholarly Henry Placide; William Rufus Blake, who
was unrivaled in old men's roles; the fine eccentric comedian Charles Fisher; and
Lester Wallack, James William Wallack's son who, refusing to trade on his
father's fame, called himself John Lester. Young Wallack had played in England
before coming to the United States in 1847, and had won praise from Miss
Cushman for his performance of Mercutio to her Romeo. "Young man," she
told him, "there is a great future before you, if you take care and do not let your
vanity run away with you." Forty years later, after Lester's death, Dion Boucicault added a footnote to Miss Cushman's prophecy. "Ah, if he had not the
misfortune to be so remarkably good looking," he wrote of Lester. "He provoked an admiration in which he innocently took a share. The looking glass
and the women did their best to make a fool of him." Young Wallack was thirty
when he joined Burton's company. He had played at the Broadway and Bowery
Theaters, had dramatized *The Three Musketeers* and made a great hit in it.
Tall, dark-haired, dark-eyed, debonair, Wallack on the stage was "the perfection of elegant extravagance." His grace and vivacity, and the refinement of
his acting style, quickly made him the most popular leading man in the American theater. His presence in the company enabled Burton to produce superb
revivals of such classic comedies as *The School for Scandal, The Rivals, She
Stoops to Conquer, The Road to Ruin,* and to stage modern comedies like
London Assurance and *Old Heads and Young Hearts* more perfectly than ever
before.

Comedy, farce and extravaganza were the staple fare at Burton's, but the actor-manager also produced a series of Shakespearian revivals noted for their constantly increasing excellence and splendor. In *The Winter's Tale* he took the role of the Clown, in *As You Like It,* that of Touchstone. In *Twelfth Night,* Burton played Sir Toby, Lester Wallack Sir Andrew, Blake was the Malvolio and Miss Weston the Viola. Joseph Jefferson saw the performance and, forty years later, asserted, "I do not believe that this play has been acted with greater skill since Shakespeare wrote it." But Burton's staging of *A Midsummer Night's Dream,* in its magnificence of scenery and costumes and its scholarly care for accuracy of detail, and a subsequent revival of *The Tempest* marked by a studious restoration of Shakespeare's text, established the new traditions that were to be followed, and further developed, thereafter.

Burton himself, however, was the greatest attraction at his theater. Critics, actors and audiences alike accounted him a supreme master of comedy; he was, as Jefferson remarked, "an actor to whom dramatic genius was universally accorded." Burton's repertory came to include no less than one hundred and eighty-five roles, but his fame rested most securely on three, and his performances in these were so insistently demanded that they figured almost weekly on the program. In a dramatization of Dickens's *Dombey and Son* made by John Brougham and himself, Burton's Captain Cuttle was remarkable for an ingenious elaboration of facial expression, stage business and by-play which invested the character with pathos as well as humor. In *The Toodles,* which he adapted from an old play, *The Broken Heart,* he played the perplexed husband of a wife addicted to the buying of preposterous bargains who, after years of endurance, finds a comic method for bringing her extravagance to an end. A companion characterization to his Timothy Toodles was offered by Morris Barnett's *The Serious Family,* in which, as the Reverend Aminadab Sleek, Burton gave an unforgettable portrait of a sanctimonious, lugubrious evangelical clergyman. It was on the basis of these three roles that, twenty-five years after his death, the critic Laurence Hutton declared that "Burton was probably the funniest man that ever lived." And Burton's Theater, Hutton recalled, "was better known throughout the United States than any other public building in the Union, not even excepting the Capitol at Washington."

There was, however, another theatrical enterprise quite as well known to the nation at large. This was the American Museum on Broadway at Ann Street conducted by Phineas T. Barnum. Fat, jovial Barnum was internationally famous, and his name had become a byword for a form of showmanship that combined new techniques of publicity with a strong element of fraud. In 1842, Barnum made the talented midget, General Tom Thumb, a national sensation. He then took the General to Europe, arranged to have him perform, by royal command, for Queen Victoria, and for King Louis Philippe in Paris, and returned home to make his Museum the Mecca of all rural visitors to New York. They were lured to the flag-decked building by his constantly changing exhibitions of freaks and prodigies. Could they be persuaded to patronize the drama also, and thereby bring greater profits to Barnum? He was fully aware of their strong moral prejudices against the stage, but in the summer of 1850 he announced the opening of a new "lecture room" capable of seating three thousand people. He shrewdly foresaw that the drama would be acceptable to puritans in the "lecture room" of a "museum," for these sanctifying words had the power of transforming any play, without loss of theatrical effect, into a program of moral edification.

For the opening attraction at his immense new auditorium, Barnum chose *The Drunkard,* a grim sermon on temperance that was destined to be one of the most long-lived of American plays. (In 1953, it began its twenty-first year of continuous nightly performances at the Theater Mart in Los Angeles.) The play was written by William H. Smith, a Boston actor who, having long been a "hard-drinking man," was persuaded to sign the pledge of total abstinence. With the author in the title role, "playing his own life," it had been produced at the Boston Museum, and for many months had brought to that decorous institution "a large class who do not frequent theaters"—chiefly to be horrified by a scene in which the drunkard writhed and raved through an attack of delirium tremens. Barnum's production of the play broke all previous records in New York by achieving an uninterrupted run of one hundred performances. The "lecture room" quickly became one of the most profitable theaters in the country. By guaranteeing year-round engagements and the payment of weekly salaries, Barnum was able to staff his playhouse with a competent stock company, sometimes headed by such well-known actresses as Alexina Fisher and Emily Mestayer, who previously had been featured at leading theaters. Two daily programs were offered: a bill of farces or light comedies in the afternoon, designed to attract mothers with their children; and a "strong" drama or melodrama at night, for the delectation of adult audiences. Nearly any play that had been successful at another theater was certain to enter the bills at Barnum's, and whatever its subject a note of moral uplift could be injected to maintain the pretense of edification. It was one of Barnum's most masterly insights to realize that the sensitive American conscience could be anesthetized by mere words, and that the most fanatical opponents of the theater would enthusiastically support it under another name.

Meanwhile, old stars continued to be seen, new stars appeared, certain young players emerged whose names, in the near future, were to be known throughout the country, and among the many new plays produced one became a landmark in the nation's history. Was James H. Hackett to be accounted fortunate or frustrated? In 1840, the noted comedian touched the goal of his aspirations. He played *King Lear* and, in an anxiety that, as he said, made him "frightfully nervous," *Hamlet,* suffering, during the performance, "a constant and violent palpitation of the heart." But this tremor of excitement did not communicate itself to his audience, which rewarded him chiefly "by mute applause"—a form of approbation not warmly encouraging. He repeated these performances in Philadelphia, with *The Kentuckian* as an afterpiece to *Lear* and *The Yankee in England* as an afterpiece to *Hamlet,* but with no greater success. "Without vexation or regret," he wrote bravely, "I struck them from my repertory." Yet he must have felt keenly the disappointment of this proof that his lifelong study, his analytical insight, his high purpose were not enough. And it must have hurt him that Forrest, whose acting he disliked and whose ignorance he despised, had succeeded as Lear when he had failed. Hackett returned to comedy, he undertook ventures in management, he made profitable investments and amassed a large fortune. As the years passed, New Yorkers saw him in brief engagements, always at the best theaters, always in the same plays. His roles were Falstaff, Rip Van Winkle, Monsieur Mallet, Nimrod Wildfire in *The Kentuckian,* Sir Pertinax McSycophant in Macklin's *Man of the World,* O'Callaghan in Bayle Bernard's farce *His Last Legs,* the title part of *The Yankee in England.* Elderly gentlemen, declaring him to be "the first gentleman of the theater," took their grandchildren to see Hackett in order to form their taste. For surely— though a few critics dissented—Hackett was the greatest of Falstaffs. This one Shakespearian character was exclusively his; the fat knight whom he considered a "philosophic compound of vice and sensuality," whose "moral deformity" he felt obliged to conceal with broad strokes of humor. Was it for Falstaff, or for himself, that Hackett's merriment in the role seemed always to be tinctured with scorn?

By Junius Brutus Booth, his contemporary, Hackett may have been envied. Booth was now "the elder Booth," for his oldest son, Junius Brutus, Jr., was on the stage and fairly well known. In New York, the erratic, ageing tragedian could obtain no engagements at the fashionable theaters. He played at the Chatham, renamed the National, a second-class house which catered to much the same public as the Bowery. There, he performed long familiar roles: Richard III, Iago, Lear; occasionally Hamlet, Macbeth and Shylock; Sir Giles Overreach, Sir Edward Mortimer, and one or two more. In the autumn of 1850, he permitted his son, Edwin, then a lad of seventeen, to appear for the first time in New York, playing the role of Wilford, the secretary, in *The Iron Chest.* Edwin Booth had made his stage debut in Boston, one year earlier, in the small role of Tressel, in *Richard III;* he played that role, and the important one of Hemeya in *The Apostate,* during his father's engagement at the National. In the following spring, the "little giant" returned to the Chatham for a week. On his benefit night, he was announced to play *Richard III,* but when it came time to leave for the theater, Booth declared that he was indisposed and would not appear. Instead, he ordered Edwin to substitute for him. Edwin knew the role—he had learned all of his father's roles during his years of service as dresser and guardian—and he obeyed the cruel order. At the National an audience long inured to the elder Booth's peculiar ways applauded the novice. Edwin Booth always believed that his father had used a ruse to test Edwin's mettle; he believed, too, that his father had come to the theater and watched the performance from some hiding place. One year later, in the spring of 1852, the elder Booth played a three-night stand at the National. It was destined to be his last engagement in New York. Almost immediately afterwards, he and Edwin took ship for California, summoned there by Junius Brutus, Jr., who had become stage manager of a theater in San Francisco. To the weary old tragedian, seldom noticed by the critics, forgotten by the fashionable public, and aware of his diminishing vogue in the cheaper theaters, an invitation to star in the golden Far West was a windfall.

Of the new stars, one astounded critics and playgoers by disproving a long-

Jean Davenport as Juliet,
  by H. B. Hall

standing axiom. In 1849, at the age of twenty, Miss Jean Davenport came before New York audiences under a heavy handicap. Eleven years earlier, as a child prodigy, she had come from London to tour the cities of the East and South under the management of her father, Thomas Donald. The melancholy maturity of child prodigies had been made abundantly evident; usually, they retained no vestige of their juvenile talents. Miss Davenport, moreover, was remembered as *the* child prodigy for, according to a widely credited rumor, Charles Dickens had taken her as his model for Ninetta Crummles, the "Infant Phenomenon" of *Nicholas Nickleby,* and had portrayed her father as Vincent Crummles in that novel. The rumor, industriously kept alive by Thomas Donald, made his child's tour extremely profitable, and had enabled him to give her an excellent education in Europe. Returning to the London stage at the age of sixteen, Miss Davenport quickly became a favorite with British audiences. New Yorkers, however, were skeptical until she won enthusiastic acclaim with her first performances.

Petite, dark-haired Miss Davenport had an exquisite figure, lovely brown eyes, a singularly expressive face. Critics rhapsodized about her silvery voice and beautiful diction. Surprisingly, in view of her exploited childhood, she had a native elegance, a quality of distinction, possessed by no other actress but Mrs. Mowatt. Miss Davenport was not only a fine artist, but unmistakably a lady, and people who met her were impressed by her superior intelligence. She triumphed as Juliet and Beatrice; as Pauline in *The Lady of Lyons;* as Julia in Knowles' *The Hunchback,* as Mariana in his *The Wife,* as the Countess in his *Love.* Having gained both celebrity and prestige, she decided to remain permanently in the United States. Who could foresee that, very soon, this refined young woman would provoke controversy by bringing to the American stage a sensationally immoral play, and becoming the earliest interpreter of a pathetic, perennial courtesan? Meanwhile, a young native-born star had met with comparable success in the same repertory. Miss Julia Dean—soon to marry and play under her husband's name as Julia Dean Hayne—was the granddaughter of "Old Sam" Drake, and had served her apprenticeship in the theaters of the West and South. Her golden hair, deep blue eyes and features of cameolike delicacy made her famous as a great beauty. Gilded youth adored her to a man, and despaired because their infatuated attentions were graciously rejected, but her extreme propriety compelled their respect. There was always, in her acting, a faint trace of melancholy, a minor note which, while it charmed, also perplexed. Long afterwards, playgoers who cherished a memory of her youthful radiance surmised that Miss Dean had a premonition of misfortune.

Remote from the fashionable theaters in which Miss Davenport and Miss Dean played their engagements, a young Irish-born actress gave no indication that, within a few years, she would take the city by storm. At the Bowery Theater, where handsome, stentorian Edward Eddy was idolized by the "boys" in such melodramas as *The Count of Monte Cristo* and *The Corsican Brothers,* Miss Matilda Heron joined the company as its leading woman. But her stay was brief. She failed to excite the shirt-sleeved Bowery audience. Her voice, low-pitched and soft, did not ring through the Bowery's vast auditorium; she refused to adopt Eddy's ranting style and flamboyant gestures; her acting was considered "too tame." Five years were to pass before Miss Heron again acted in New York—and startled audiences by a style that was the reverse of tame.

In the spring of 1852, the entire nation was reading—and hotly arguing about—Mrs. Harriet Beecher Stowe's *Uncle Tom's Cabin.* The celebrated, highly controversial novel had run its course as a serial in the *National Era,* and had also been published in book form. As a result of the public's demand for incessant dramatic novelty, nearly all successful novels were brought to the stage as quickly as possible, usually in adaptations hastily prepared by hack playwrights. But Mrs. Stowe's novel languished undramatized for nearly five months, probably because managers, always timid about presenting plays dealing with contentious issues, feared its explosive subject. However, in August, 1852, A. W. Purdy, manager of the National Theater, the formidable rival of the Bowery, decided to produce a version of *Uncle Tom,* and had one made by C. W. Taylor, an actor in his company who also served as house playwright. The piece, which omitted much of the novel's material and had been tricked out with a happy ending, was produced late in August with Taylor in the title role. Blasted by the *Herald* as "an insult to the South" and likely "to poison the minds of our youth with the pestilential principles of abolitionism," it ran for two weeks, supported by the added attraction of T. D. Rice who offered, as afterpieces, various items from his familiar repertory. The piece was twice revived before the year ran out; then it disappeared from the National's repertory, and no other New York theater took up the most widely read novel of the time, which had already sold more than three hundred thousand copies.

One month after the production of Uncle Tom at the National, another and more faithful dramatic rendering of the novel was staged at the Museum in

Julia Dean as Beatrice in "Much Ado About Nothing"

Troy, New York. It was this version, prepared mainly to provide fat roles for
a child prodigy and her parents, which became the standard one. The child
actress was four-year-old Cordelia Howard. Her father, George C. Howard,
was manager of the Troy Museum at the time; her mother, Caroline Fox Howard, had been a popular child star. She was the sister of George L. Fox, later
to become the most celebrated of American pantomimists, but then a favorite
comedian with Purdy's company at the National in New York. For his projected
version of *Uncle Tom,* Howard turned to his wife's cousin, George L. Aiken,
an actor in his company who occasionally did odd jobs of hack playwriting.

Aiken's piece was produced at the Troy Museum late in September 1852, with Cordelia Howard as Little Eva, her mother as Topsy and her father as St. Clair. After a run of one hundred performances, the play and its cast were transferred to Albany, with further success.

With this evidence of drawing power, overtures were made to Purdy to take over the production and stage it at the National in New York. Purdy was not immediately receptive, but finally yielded to the pressure brought by George Fox, whose services were indispensable to his theater and who, not unnaturally, was anxious to promote the interests of his sister, brother-in-law, niece and cousin. Aiken's dramatization of *Uncle Tom's Cabin*—announced as a new version "embracing the whole work" in six acts, eight tableaux and thirty scenes—opened at the National on July 18, 1853. Cordelia Howard played Little Eva; her mother, Topsy; her father, St. Clair; her uncle, George Fox, Phineas Fletcher. At various times, other members of the Fox family were present in the cast, notably Cordelia's maternal grandmother who, for a while, played the role of Aunt Ophelia. The original Uncle Tom was G. C. Germon; he was succeeded by James W. Lingard. N. B. Clarke took the role of Simon Legree, and the first Eliza to cross the ice was Mrs. W. G. Jones.

From the very outset, Aiken's *Uncle Tom* was a sensational success. Produced without an afterpiece—previously considered essential in every New York theater—it was the first play to offer scheduled matinée performances on Wednesday and Saturday afternoons. The press reported "a constant succession of crowded houses." Manager Purdy, delighted by this unexpected bonanza, advertised his production of a "religious drama" in out-of-town newspapers, decorated the lobby of the National with scriptural texts, and displayed a portrait of himself holding a Bible in one hand, and a copy of Mrs. Stowe's novel in the other. He also persuaded prominent clergymen to attend the matinée performances, among them Dr. Henry Ward Beecher, Mrs. Stowe's brother, who soon would be preaching thunderous sermons on the evils of the stage. Purdy celebrated the one hundredth performance of *Uncle Tom* with fireworks, a free band concert, and the presentation to little Cordelia Howard of a gold tea service. For it was the deeply moving performance given by this wonder child that, in the main, drew vast crowds to the National. Other dramatic versions of *Uncle Tom* were produced at Barnum's Museum and at the Bowery, where T. D. Rice played the title role; but these competing productions enjoyed no comparable success. Public enthusiasm about Cordelia Howard reached such intensity that Purdy soon presented her in other plays on Monday, Tuesday, Thursday and Friday afternoons, so that the five-year-old star appeared in twelve performances weekly. (The overworked child was still alive in 1930, a vigorous old lady of eighty-two.) After a run of three hundred and twenty-five consecutive performances at the National, the Aiken-Howard production of *Uncle Tom,* with little Cordelia as its star, went on tour, and was later taken to Great Britain, where it duplicated its American triumphs. In various dramatic adaptations, *Uncle Tom's Cabin* soon reached the theaters of every European country. The Aiken version was frequently seen in the principal cities of the United States throughout the nineteenth century, and was carried

Cordelia Howard as Eva in "Uncle Tom's Cabin," from a daguerreotype by Brady

even to rural hamlets by traveling "Tom companies." It was revived with an
all-star cast at the Academy of Music in New York in 1901, and the production
was sent on tour. New Yorkers were offered a serious revival as recently as
1933. One hundred years after its production at the National, Aiken's dramatization continued to be played "for laughs" in summer theaters, and a balletic
treatment of the story as "The Small House of Uncle Thomas" enchanted
audiences of *The King and I,* the musical play by Oscar Hammerstein 2d and
Richard Rodgers, then at the height of its phenomenal success in New York.

The slavery issue was also indirectly responsible for bringing back before
the public, after fifteen years of retirement, the first great actress whom Americans had ever been privileged to see. In her marriage to Pierce Butler, Fanny
Kemble had been miserably unhappy. His wealth derived from plantations in
Georgia; she detested the institution of slavery. With her two small daughters
and her husband, she had spent a winter on the Butler plantations, appalled by
conditions which she could do little to ameliorate. (Her journal of this experience, *A Residence on a Georgia Plantation,* she finally published in 1863.
It caused an immense furor in both Great Britain and the United States, weak-
ening British admiration for the Confederacy and thus helping to prevent a
loan that would have prolonged the War between the States.) Profound differences in taste and temperament between Fanny Kemble and her husband were
aggravated by their inflexibly opposed attitudes toward slavery. Butler soon
humiliated her by his public infidelities and systematic private cruelties; finally,
he compelled her to leave their home, forbidding her any contact with their
daughters. In 1846, driven by the need to earn her livelihood, she returned to
the stage in Great Britain under her husband's name. Two years later Butler
brought suit for a divorce, alleging that she had deserted him. The case was
bitterly contested, long drawn out, sensational and costly. Fanny Kemble ur-
gently required money, but her foray into the theater had only intensified her
distaste for acting. At the age of forty, she determined to embark on a new
professional career as a public reader of Shakespeare's plays. "I have passed
a large portion of my life with the greatest and best English mind and heart,"
she wrote, "living almost daily in that world, above the world, into which he
lifted me." Could she, while reading the plays, lift her audiences into that ideal
realm? Nothing less would satisfy her, but she did not underestimate the gravity
of the challenge. She had long been convinced that a "decline of the imaginative
faculties" had set in among cultivated playgoers. "They have forgotten what
human nature really is, and cannot even imagine it," she had remarked, much
earlier. "They require absolute reality on the stage, because their incapable
spirits scoff at poetical truth. . . ."

In the spring of 1849, she gave a first series of readings at the Stuyvesant
Institute on Broadway and Bond Street. Appearing three evenings and one
afternoon weekly for a month, she read fourteen plays; tragedies, comedies,
histories. "The fashionable world is agog again on a new impulse," old Philip
Hone noted in his diary; "the veritable Fanny Kemble has taken the city by
storm." The lecture hall was always filled; "delicate women, grave gentlemen,
belles, beaux and critics flock to the doors of entrance, and rush into such

places as they can find, two or three hours before the time of the lady's appearance." Amazedly, Hone reported that "she makes two thousand or three thousand dollars a week, and never was money so easily earned." But it was not earned as easily as he thought. To maintain her freshness and enthusiasm, to contrive that "illusion of the first time" essential to any dramatic performance, she invariably rehearsed every play before reading it to her audience, studying anew how to evoke its multitude of characters, endow them with their individual personalities and voices, make them so vividly present that her hearers would cease to be aware of her as she read. "I never consciously sacrificed my sense of what was due to my work, for the sake of what I could make by it," she asserted proudly.

No longer a radiant beauty, she was a woman of matronly figure and stately presence. In her gown of violet velvet trimmed with point lace she had an air of majesty as she came on the stage, bowed gravely, seated herself, arranged her billowing skirts, opened her book and began reading. Instantly, the audience was hers, captivated by the spell of her magnificent voice and perfect diction. "How our hearts glowed and trembled as she read," Henry Wadsworth Longfellow wrote in the sonnet which he dedicated to her. And Ralph Waldo Emerson, no lover of the theater, exclaimed, "What an abundance there is in her! She is Miranda, Queen Katharine and many more at the same time." Nathaniel Hawthorne, who knew her in Lenox, Massachusetts, where she bought a hillside farm, used her, and Margaret Fuller also, as models for his Zenobia in *The Blithedale Romance*. Herman Melville went twice to hear her read in Boston. "She makes a glorious Lady Macbeth," he wrote, but he thought that her Desdemona "seems like a boarding-school miss." Like Macready, who considered her "a woman of most extraordinary mind" but "quite like a man," Melville resented the fiery independence of spirit which made some men describe her as "a truculent Amazon." "She's so unfemininely masculine," he wrote waspishly, "that had she not, on unimpeachable authority, borne children, I should be curious to learn the result of a surgical examination of her person in private." Yet ten days after hearing her read, he was immersed in Shakespeare's plays. "Dolt and ass that I am," he acknowledged, "I have lived more than twenty-nine years, and until a few days ago, never made close acquaintance with the divine William." Thousands of Americans were, like Melville, inspired by Fanny Kemble to read the plays which they had heard her interpret. She toured the North, East and West, but refused to give readings in the South, for she would not accept money that had its source in the labor of slaves. For twenty years, as was said long afterwards, "Shakespeare and Fanny Kemble were bracketed in the public mind."

A farce entitled *Lola Montez, or Catching a Governor* had often been played in New York theaters when, in 1851, its notorious heroine arrived in the city from Europe to appear as a dancer. By any standard except that of virtue Lola was an extraordinary woman. She had enjoyed a career of conquest that, in a very few years, carried her from a Parisian *corps de ballet* to a royal palace. The elderly King of Bavaria, Ludwig I, made her his mistress, gave her the title of Countess Lansfeld, and permitted her to dictate government policy.

Europe rang with the scandal until the infatuated monarch was forced to abdicate and Lola was unceremoniously driven from Bavaria. This was in 1848, and a year later, in London, she was charged with having contracted a bigamous marriage with a wealthy young guardsman. Long before, she had deserted an earlier husband in India, without the formality of a divorce; his re-entry into her life by affidavit was inconvenient. To escape legal tribulations, Lola fled to the Continent, where news presently reached her that both her husbands had died. As a newspaper sedately reported, this left her "in the full enjoyment of that independence of all ties which was the most congenial to her nature." Though scarcely accurate with respect to her preference, the statement adequately described Lola's situation when she reached New York.

She was thirty-three, a woman of medium height with a fine figure. Journalists who interviewed her before her professional debut wrote glowingly of her magnolialike complexion, delicate features, bronze hair and large, deeply blue eyes veiled by long black lashes. They extolled her vivacity, her demure charm. A fashionable crinoline concealed the ultimate attractions that had lured a king to his downfall. Yet, although these were invisible, it could be easily understood that one lover, for her sake, had permitted himself to be killed in a duel; that she had inflamed such men of genius as Franz Liszt, the elder Alexandre Dumas, Théophile Gautier. During Lola's three-week engagement at the Broadway Theater prices for seats were doubled; the pit, except for its last two rows, was

"Lola Has Come"!   by D. C. Johnson. Broadway Theater, 1851. A cartoon showing the effect of the notorious dancer on New York.

James William Wallack
by Sir John E. Millais

converted into reserved seats; tickets for the opening night were put up at auction. The audiences were immense, but almost exclusively masculine. Even intense curiosity could not persuade ladies to attend the performances of so notorious a courtesan. Perhaps they were gratified when the critics ridiculed Lola's talents as a dancer. After a tour of the eastern cities, she returned to the Broadway as an actress, in "a new historical drama by a gentleman of this city" shamelessly entitled *Lola Montez in Bavaria*. The story was all too familiar to patrons of the fashionable Broadway, and the play was withdrawn after five performances. Lola then took this dramatization of her lurid past to the Bowery Theater, where the "boys" gave her a tumultuous welcome. Presently, she set off on another tour; this time, through the South and West. But this was merely preparatory. Her hopes were staked on the Gold Coast of California.

For New Yorkers, the autumn of 1852 was made memorable by the establishment of an institution which, during three decades, would be accounted the finest of all American playhouses. Persuaded by his son, Lester, James W. Wallack had come from London to undertake a second venture in management. At fifty-seven, the elder Wallack was still vigorous and handsome, and his popularity as an actor was undiminished. His ambition was to form a stock company superior even to Burton's, and to win the cultivated public with performances distinguished by such perfect acting, costuming and scenic investiture that no other management could hope to equal them. Wallack realized that a varied repertory was essential and he intended to offer one. Nevertheless, he hoped to specialize in the production of high comedy, modern as well as

Laura Keene and James W. Wallack as Beatrice and Benedick in "Much Ado About Nothing"

classic, not only because this was his own forte and Lester's, but because—since it reflects the play of intelligence on highly developed forms of social life—it would especially appeal to fashionable, sophisticated audiences. Wallack's real desire was to transplant in New York an ideal, rather than an existing, London theater; a playhouse which, celebrated for its elegance, would inevitably enjoy the greatest possible social prestige. This aristocratic aim was sincere, but Wallack was sufficiently familiar with America to be convinced of its fundamental practicality. The democratic republic had already evolved its own aristocracy of wealth, the "upper tendom" of New York, who set standards of fashion and manners for the rest of the country. If—so Wallack thought —he could identify his theater with this social élite, the patronage of the great, profitable middle-class public would be certain.

Wallack leased the Lyceum Theater, on Broadway near Broome Street, in the new "uptown" theatrical center. The company that he assembled included Lester Wallack (still playing under the name of John Lester) as leading man; John Brougham, William Rufus Blake and Charles Walcot. For his leading woman, Wallack brought from London Miss Laura Keene, an actress who was to have an extraordinary career in the United States. Miss Keene was in her twenty-sixth year; tall, slender, graceful, auburn-haired; not a beauty but, as the critics acknowledged, "passably pretty." In London, she had been associated with the company of Madame Vestris and Charles James Mathews, and had impressed Wallack by her unusual intelligence, her versatility and her marked talent as a comedienne. High comedy was Miss Keene's forte as an actress, but in private life she had already disclosed a propensity to misfortune that was to darken her later career. In London, she had been unhappily married and had separated from her husband, apparently without divorcing him. She arrived in New York with her mother and two little daughters who called her "Aunt Laura"—for the subject of her marriage was never referred to. (One of her daughters, long afterwards, remarked bitterly, "I never knew my father, I only know that he was a loafer.") Notwithstanding her somewhat equivocal situation, Miss Keene quickly won favor as an actress even with the most censorious of New York's élite. As Henry James recalled in his old age, she was "the original charmer of our parents, with a native grace at the start, a fresh and delicate inspiration." These qualities she revealed in a series of productions which made Wallack's first season notable: brilliant revivals of *The School for Scandal, The Road to Ruin,* Boucicault's *London Assurance* and *Old Heads and Young Hearts; The Lady of Lyons;* splendid stagings of *Much Ado About Nothing* (with Miss Keene as Beatrice, and the elder Wallack as Benedick), *The Merchant of Venice* and *As You Like It.*

Wallack's Lyceum began its second season with assured prestige; it already ranked as the equal of Burton's Theater in artistic excellence and fashionable distinction. One night late in November, 1853, when Miss Keene was to appear as Lydia Languish in a performance of *The Rivals,* Lester Wallack stepped before the curtain to announce that another actress would play the role. Without notifying the management of her intention, Miss Keene had departed for Baltimore with John Lutz, her business manager and lover, to assume the management of a theater in that city. When the details of her defection became public, the scandal was so great that Miss Keene found it inadvisable to reappear in New York until the reverberations died away. Her Baltimore venture quickly

Mrs. Hoey (Josephine Shaw)

failed and, like many another metropolitan favorite, she succumbed to the golden lure of California.

Miss Keene's desertion left Wallack's without a leading lady of first rank. But nothing more eloquently demonstrated the social luster that it had already acquired than the replacement effected for Miss Keene. On New Year's Day, 1854, Lester Wallack paid a call of ceremony on his former associate at Burton's Theater, Mrs. John Hoey. His hostess drew him to a window and quietly announced, "I am going back on the stage." "What!" Wallack cried in astonishment, "does not John object?" Said Mrs. Hoey, "He only makes the condition that, if I go on the stage again, it is to be at Mr. Wallack's theater, and nowhere else." Before the month ran out, Mrs. Hoey made her debut at Wallack's in Sheridan Knowles's *The Love Chase,* playing the role of Constance to Lester Wallack's Wildrake. She received an ovation from the audience; thereafter, until her final retirement ten years later, she was acknowledged to be *the* leading lady of the New York stage. Notable as was her talent, great as was her charm, her primacy did not rest on these alone. She was, after all, the first lady of fashion, the first member of "high society," to go on the stage not because she required a livelihood, but because she wished to enjoy that still unconventional luxury—an independent career.

CHAPTER 7

Troupers in El Dorado

GOLD was discovered at Sutter's Mill in January, 1848; but four months passed before the gold fever struck San Francisco. The lonely outpost of manifest destiny had an adult population of less than eight hundred. Including sheds and tents, it contained two hundred buildings clustered on the shore of Yerba Buena Cove. Its inhabitants boasted that the town "was becoming one of some consequence, and was assuming the pretensions and attractions of older, wealthier and more populous communities." Then, almost overnight, San Francisco took on the look of an abandoned village. Merchants, shopkeepers, clerks and workmen departed. Seamen deserted from their ships in the bay and soldiers from the barracks. Meetings of the town council were suspended for five months; its members had gone "to the diggings."

Late in 1848, when the news reached New York and other eastern cities, the gold rush to California began. "The frenzy continues to increase every day,"

James Stark

George Templeton Strong recorded at the end of January, 1849. "It seems as if the Atlantic Coast were to be depopulated, such swarms of people are leaving it for the new El Dorado. It is the most remarkable emigration on record in the history of man since the days of the Crusades. . . ." Nearly forty thousand immigrants poured through the Golden Gate, having made the voyage around Cape Horn or come by way of Panama; another thirty thousand made the perilous overland journey. By the end of 1849, the population of San Francisco was said to be twenty-five thousand, preponderantly male and notably cosmopolitan. It had become a city of rag mansions, with "a multitude of canvas, blanket and bough-covered tents" climbing its steep hills. Gambling saloons "glittering like fairy palaces" lined Portsmouth Square and the nearby streets. More than three hundred square-rigged ships stood idle in the bay, abandoned by their crews. (Some were soon hauled up on the mudflats and converted into warehouses and lodgings.) Everybody was making money, and the professional gamblers were making fortunes. Laborers demanded a wage of $20 a day. A good pair of boots cost $100. For plain washing, the charge was $20 per dozen articles. (Wealthy folk soon sent their fine linen to Hawaii or Canton for laundering; this took six months.) A pill or purge sold for $10 and the price of spirituous liquors seldom fell below $40 a quart. Coin was scarce and gold dust passed as currency. Loans carried interest of 15 per cent monthly, payable in advance. Rents were astronomical. The Parker House, a two-story frame building on Kearny Street facing Portsmouth Square, had an annual rent roll of $120,000, half of this sum being paid by gamblers who occupied part of the second floor. For many months, a gang of hoodlums known as "the hounds" terrorized the entire town. Murders and robberies occurred almost daily. Fire was a perpetual danger. (Six disastrous conflagrations were to destroy large portions of the city in a period of eighteen months, one of them causing losses estimated at twelve million dollars.) After exploring the life of this cardboard metropolis, a correspondent of the New York *Evening Post* reported, "The people of San Francisco are mad, stark mad."

The professional theater reached San Francisco by way of Sacramento, where the first playhouse in California was opened in October, 1849. The Eagle Theater was built as an adjunct to a saloon on the levee. A canvas-sided structure roofed with sheet iron, it was reputed to have cost $80,000. A company headed by J. B. Atwater as actor-manager—and including Mrs. Henry Ray, "of the Royal Theater, New Zealand"; her husband; "a gentleman who had been unfortunate at the diggings"; and several professional actors—inaugurated the Eagle with a performance of *The Bandit Chief; or, the Forest Spectre.* Patrons of the parquet entered the theater from the saloon, after "pouring out a quantity of gold dust in the treasurer's scales, who took down weight at twelve dollars to the ounce." There was also a dress circle, entered from the exterior of the theater by means of a stepladder the underside of which was covered with canvas "in deference to ladies." The *Placer Times,* in reviewing the opening performance, noted that the dress circle "was graced with quite a number of fine looking, well costumed ladies," and declared that "the sight was somewhat revivifying." Possibly more revivifying than the performance, which impressed

Interior View of Dramatic Museum, San Francisco

Bayard Taylor, who attended it, as "an infliction." Repeatedly inundated by the river, the Eagle finally closed. On January 16, 1850, Mrs. Ray and Atwater brought the drama to San Francisco, opening the city's first theater, an auditorium named Washington Hall which was located above a saloon. Performances of *The Wife* and *Charles II* were given on this historic night, and the company continued hopefully until it was discovered that their treasurer, succumbing to the prevailing mania for gambling, had lost the week's receipts. Tragedy in real life was repugnant to the New Zealand tragedienne; she and her husband promptly departed for Honolulu, and the company disbanded.

But the metropolis was not long deprived of the drama. "Its population of talent and education," a contemporary annalist noted, "ceased their menial occupations, emerged from their filthy lodgings, and doffed their coarse red shirts for Chesterfieldian apparel. All their wants now had to be of the same luxuriant kind." Realizing that "people like to go where they can see and be seen," Joseph Andrew Rowe added plays to the attractions of his circus at the Olympic Amphitheater on Kearny Street. For nearly two months, patrons of this establishment were offered—as a prelude to the feats of two celebrated trick horses, several equestrians and a team of slack-rope dancers—such fare as *Othello, Richard III, The Lady of Lyons, The Wife, William Tell* and other standard dramas.

Several theaters were meanwhile built, only to be destroyed by one or another of three conflagrations during the year, but two dauntless promoters of the drama emerged from these holocausts. Both were "forty-niners" who had come from the East; and although their previous connection with the stage was,

Thomas Maguire

at best, tenuous, in San Francisco they found their true vocations as impresarios. D. G. Robinson, a native of Maine, had set himself up as a druggist on Portsmouth Square and had thereby acquired the title of "Doctor" by which he was always to be known. An energetic, resourceful little man, he had a knack for improvising doggerel verse, topical in subject, satirical in tone, salty in flavor but slightly astringent in effect. He was also capable in Yankee impersonations, and since he enjoyed nothing more than exercising his talents he soon became a social favorite. Nobody questioned the degree of remoteness implied by his claim to be "late of the Boston theaters," and a rumor that he had toured the East in *The Reformed Drunkard* was generally believed. Presently he formed a partnership with James Evrard, who said that he had been a member of Mitchell's company at the Olympic in New York. The partners built a small theater, the Dramatic Museum, on California Street near Montgomery, and opened it on July 4, 1850. Dr. Robinson undertook the functions of director and dramatic author; Evrard those of stage manager and business executive. In addition, they were not only the theater's stars but, for some time, its entire company. The opening bill presented them in an old farce, *Seeing the Elephant,* which Dr. Robinson had cut down and adapted to the local scene. It also introduced "The Used-up Man," one of his most popular lyrical efforts. Eventually, Robinson and Evrard assembled a group of volunteers, male and female, and expanded their programs to include comedies and farces. But the chief attraction at the Museum was Dr. Robinson's topical doggerel in which, as a journalist asserted, "almost every municipal man of mark was hit off, and sometimes pretty hardly too." His pungent attacks on the corruption of politics had an unforeseen result; he was elected to fill a vacancy on the board of aldermen. The sprightly comedian discharged his official duties without interrupting his professional career, and there was soon talk of nominating him as candidate for the office of mayor. Fortunately, perhaps, nothing came of this project, for shortly afterwards Dr. Robinson reached the apex of his success as a showman.

The other emergent impresario, Thomas Maguire, was already well known as the proprietor of an elegant saloon and gambling establishment in the Parker House. A robust, floridly handsome man, he had been, in New York, a hack driver, bartender at the Park Theater, and part owner of a barroom near the City Hall. In the autumn of 1850 he transformed the upper story of the Parker House into a theater which he named the Jenny Lind after the famous singer whom Barnum had recently brought to the United States. As stars and managers of his theater, Maguire chose Mrs. J. Hudson Kirby and James Stark. They were the first actors from the East who came to California only to act and, perhaps because of their priority, they were enthusiastically acclaimed. Their local prestige must have surprised and delighted them. In the East—as San Franciscans were not aware—their talents had evoked little admiration. Stark was a tragedian of the robustious, declamatory school, addicted to ringing tones, stately gestures and fitful vehemence. With this style of acting Mrs. Kirby was especially familiar. Her late husband, whose name she retained for professional purposes, had been one of its leading exponents. J. Hudson Kirby had been idolized by the gallery gods of the Chatham Theater in New York, where the violence of his death scenes made him affectionately known as "Wake me up when Kirby dies." In private life, Sarah Kirby was now Mrs. Wingard.

Sarah Kirby

But Wingard was soon to be killed by a fall from his horse, and shortly thereafter she would marry James Stark and adopt his name. She appears to have
been destructive, matrimonially, though herself indestructible. Stark was to
have two successors, but Sarah Kirby would outlive all of her five husbands.
She was dark-haired, of medium height, thin, intense, intrepid. She lacked
beauty and might have been thought plain, but for the feminine charm, the
delicacy of nature, so widely imputed to her in a land of homeless men. Those
who were sensitive to these attributes probably failed to notice her incompatibly
resolute jaw.

Her spirit soon declared itself. Conditions in the city indicated the urgent
need for a cultural missionary. The innumerable saloons and gambling rooms,
the prostitutes who walked on fashionable Montgomery Street, the showy ad-
venturers, ruffians and rogues who were arriving in San Francisco on every
ship—surely these did not fairly represent the community. She was convinced
that among its residents there was a large proportion of men who were educated, refined, intellectual. This public must certainly crave entertainment
superior to that offered by the "model artists" imported from New York, or
the ebullient Dr. Robinson. Was it not, indeed, a public pining for art? Sarah
Kirby saw her opportunity and seized it. Her mission was to elevate the stage.
Maguire and his theater, Stark and the company at the Jenny Lind must be used
to serve that noble purpose. The company included John Hambleton and his
pretty wife, comedians from Australia, and Henry Coad, a personable juvenile
lead. Mrs. Kirby devised programs that challenged their talents and her own.
Every night, a tragedy or drama was followed by lighter fare; and Sarah Kirby
moved with dignity from the glories of Shakespeare to laughable nonsense.
For more than two months, she maneuvered her actors through a brilliant repertory: *Damon and Pythias, Virginius, A New Way to Pay Old Debts, The Wife,
Richelieu, The Rivals; Othello, Hamlet, Richard III, Macbeth, The Merchant
of Venice*. Then misfortune came suddenly.

Late one afternoon, in the boarding house where the Hambletons and Henry
Coad lodged, Mrs. Hambleton committed suicide by swallowing cyanide of
potassium. Next morning the *Alta California,* which had been lavish in its praise
of Mrs. Kirby, gave its readers an account of the melancholy event. An ugly
scene had taken place between Hambleton, his wife and young Coad. Hambleton had accused his wife and Coad of an illicit attachment, which they confessed. Both men had left the room; when Hambleton returned, his wife had
already taken the poison. Coad, too, had tried to commit suicide, but his attempt had been foiled. That the lovers had never consummated their guilty
passion was admitted by Hambleton. Nevertheless, everyone talked of the
scandal, and unpleasant rumors were afloat. Excitement mounted when, on
the afternoon of his wife's funeral, Hambleton published in the *Evening
Picayune* his version of the tragedy. His wife, he declared, had "gradually lost
all affection for me, riveting her attention on a female friend—who, like a
fascinating serpent, attracted her prey until within her toils." In vain, Hambleton had tried to separate his wife from Mrs. Kirby, "her female destroyer,"
who promoted the liaison with Coad. Mrs. Kirby was "the first and only cause

The Third Jenny Lind Theater, San Francisco

of the fatal occurrence." The moral issue raised by Hambleton's statement could not be ignored. However flagrantly they sinned, the men of San Francisco at heart were sentimentalists and puritans; they cherished the proprieties which they failed to observe, and exalted the virtues that they personally renounced. The *Pacific News* spoke for them in declaring that, if Mrs. Kirby had been guilty of the offense charged, "the indignation of an outraged community . . . should forever drive her from the stage of California"; but the editors hoped that she was guiltless.

In the *Alta California* Sarah Kirby published her denial of Hambleton's charges, and exposed the sordid tale of his cruelty to his wife. This was corroborated by a statement by Henry Coad and affidavits by other members of the Jenny Lind company. Meanwhile it was announced that the theater, closed since the suicide, would now reopen. Editorially, the *Alta California* declared: "When the deserving have been traduced, and an attempt made to ruin them in public estimation, it is the duty of the public to sustain them by its encouragement." Mrs. Kirby, the editors asserted, "has ever done her utmost to please and instruct the public," and they recommended that the community rally to her support. When the Jenny Lind reopened, every seat was occupied. Mrs. Kirby's first entrance on the stage was vigorously applauded. At the end of the play she was called before the curtain and made a speech which, "coming from her heart," evoked "a regular storm of cheers." Fully vindicated, and now established as the apostle of a purer morality and loftier art, Sarah Kirby surpassed all her previous efforts to please and instruct the public.

Two more "great fires" in the summer of 1851 wiped out large areas of the city, destroying the existing theaters, and an appalling rise in crime led to the organization of a Vigilance Committee of citizens which, by autumn, imposed order on the community. The city bravely rose from its ashes. New theaters were erected; in costliness and splendor two of them equaled the finest play-houses in the East. On Portsmouth Square, Tom Maguire built the imposing Jenny Lind. Its elaborate auditorium seated two thousand people, and the sand-stone for its façade had been imported from Australia. Construction of this vast building plunged the gambler-impresario into financial difficulties, and before a year ran out he used his political connections to sell it to the municipal authorities for conversion into a city hall. The deal brought him $200,000 and caused a major scandal but Maguire, always imperturbable, soon built the San Francisco Theater on Washington Street near Montgomery. His foremost rival, Dr. Robinson, had meanwhile opened the American Theater on Sansome Street, near California, a house as spacious as the Jenny Lind, richly decorated with gilt and red velvet. But he, too, encountered financial troubles and, after having been dislodged from his opulent new playhouse, eventually joined Tom Maguire.

With the opening of these great theaters, a tide of theatrical immigration from the East set in. On players of recognized merit who, in the East, had attained only secondary rank or even less, California exercised a powerful attraction. It offered the prospect of far greater earnings; even more beguilingly, it held the promise of a new, more illustrious career. These lures brought the first contingent, some of whom were to realize their hopes. Junius Brutus Booth, Jr., and his wife, Harriet, came to join Maguire's stock company at the Jenny Lind, where "June" Booth soon assumed the post of stage manager. Among the associates of the Booths were another couple from New York, both of whom would achieve conspicuous success in San Francisco. John Torrence, who had served as "machinist" in several New York theaters, occupied this post at the Jenny Lind; but he quickly rose from the humble position of stage carpenter to that of independent manager. His wife, known professionally as Mrs. Judah, was to become the most beloved actress on the San Francisco stage. More than thirty years later, after the close of her career, her scholarly colleague, Walter Leman, would record that "no Juliet ever played in San Francisco that was not overshadowed by the Nurse of Mrs. Judah, and her appearance even in a most insignificant role was always signalized by hearty applause." She was forty when she first appeared at the Jenny Lind, and for more than a decade had been playing character and comedy roles in the cheaper New York theaters. Even before this, life had dealt harshly with her; with her first husband and two small children, Marietta Starfield Judah had been shipwrecked in the Atlantic, had seen her husband drown and her children die of exposure and, after four days, had been rescued barely alive. In San Francisco, however, the middle-aged utility actress, stimulated by an appreciative and affectionate public, blossomed into an accomplished artist who sometimes outshone the stars she supported. Within a year of her debut at the Jenny Lind, she was honored by the presentation of a costly silver service, and still later she was to be described by a critic as "by far the most popular actress who ever appeared in California, and one whose private character renders her an ornament to society."

The case of Mrs. Judah illustrated the characteristic independence of the San Francisco public, which refused to take an actor's prior celebrity in the East as a proof of excellence, and often bestowed prodigal favor on actors and actresses who previously had enjoyed no such good fortune. As Lawrence Barrett was to note later, "San Francisco has proved the grave of many a great reputation, the starting-point and outset of many a prosperous career." Frank Chanfrau, the first star to visit the city, suffered an unexpected deflation of his eastern prestige. He appeared at the Jenny Lind Theater in October, 1851, soon after its opening, but his celebrated Mose, in *New York as It Is* and *Mose in California,* was only moderately successful. Chanfrau was more warmly received on a tour of the mining camps, during which he inaugurated the first primitive theater in Placerville, a community known to forty-niners as "Hangtown," because of a recent lynching which had occurred there.

The elder Booth—the second star to come to California—fared no better than Chanfrau. Supported by Edwin, Junius, Jr., and Harriet Booth, he began a two-week engagement at the Jenny Lind late in July, 1852, but although he played all his most famous roles and was said to "fairly wring the house with passion," the critic of the *Alta California* reported him to be "a splendid ruin, aged and crumbling, but majestic and magnificent even in its decay." Worse was in store for the old tragedian: he went to play in Sacramento, where he met so cool a reception from the miners that his projected tour was abandoned. A second brief engagement in San Francisco completed his disappointment, and he suddenly decided to return to "the States." Leaving Edwin in San Francisco with his older brother, Junius Brutus Booth departed alone. In November, 1852, he reached New Orleans and, after playing a successful engagement at the St. Charles Theater, boarded a Mississippi steamboat for Cincinnati. He fell ill during the journey and, quite alone, died in his cabin.

Yet to players far less renowned than Booth and Chanfrau the capricious city gave spectacular rewards. Who could have predicted either the honors or the fortune which came to Mrs. J. Lewis Baker, the former Alexina Fisher, and her husband? After her early days as a child prodigy on the old frontier and in the East, Miss Fisher had long been a favorite member of the stock company at the Walnut Street Theater in Philadelphia. More recently, she had played brief engagements in New York and had been featured as leading woman at both Barnum's Museum and Burton's. Talented, charming, pretty as she was, Mrs. Baker had not become a star, and her husband had achieved little success as an actor. Nevertheless, the Bakers inaugurated "a new era in the California drama." So asserted Frank Soulé, editor and critic of the *Chronicle* and part author of the contemporary *Annals of San Francisco.* To Alexina Fisher Baker he gave credit for "enriching the Pacific stage with the brightest gems of histrionic ability," while her husband, as manager and producer, "introduced a strict and severe discipline, had careful rehearsals and paid all needful attention to the necessary accessories of the stage." In short, the Bakers offered San

Francisco "entertainments of a refined character," presented in a style of excellence comparable to that "of the best theaters in New York or Philadelphia."

They foresaw no such ambitious undertakings when, in February, 1852, they began an engagement at the Jenny Lind Theater. Their first performance was *The Hunchback,* and Mrs. Baker's playing of Julia was acclaimed by the critics. A week later, when she took the role of Juliet, a rain of bouquets fell on the stage. To one of them was attached a costly diamond ring; the argonauts had a pleasant habit of expressing their admiration in tangible form. This practice was deplored by Mrs. Sarah Royce, a resident of the city and the mother of a future Harvard philosopher. "It must indeed be an obtuse moral sense," she reflected acidly, "that could not perceive the corrupting tendency of such customs." But this never occurred to the generous argonauts. Over the next two years their gallantry brought Mrs. Baker a diamond bracelet, another diamond ring, a handsome silver tea service and a diamond-studded watch. She and her husband played at the Jenny Lind for three weeks, "to crowded and enthusiastic audiences." An equally long engagement at Sacramento followed, after which they returned to San Francisco to play for thirty consecutive nights. By this time, the metropolis had seen Alexina Fisher Baker as Rosalind and Lady Teazle, as Pauline in *The Lady of Lyons,* as Bianca in *Fazio,* a play never before performed in San Francisco. Bianca was considered "in some respects her greatest part," though its "terrible emotions" taxed her physique, and this, in the last scene, made "the frightful writhings of her insane grief distressing to the audience." However, the poignancy of their distress did not reflect unfavorably on the actress. After a second engagement in Sacramento, Lewis Baker assembled a small company to support his wife on a tour of the mining camps. Traveling in wagons, they played in Nevada City, Grass Valley—where a saloon had been equipped with a stage, scenery, drop curtain and footlights—and Placerville. No doubt the miners frequently bestowed on Mrs. Baker the buckskin purses containing nuggets or gold dust which they regarded as "a proper testimonial of their appreciation."

Alexina Fisher Baker

The tour must have been highly successful, for when the Bakers returned to San Francisco, in August, 1852, Lewis Baker was able to set up as an independent manager. He took the small Adelphi Theater on Dupont Street (now Grant Avenue) near Clay, assembled a company, and exploited the talents of his popular wife as his only star. For a period of nine months this indefatigable actress performed on six nights every week. Her repertory included such Shakespearian roles as Katharine, Beatrice and Desdemona; such modern plays as *London Assurance, Fashion* and Bulwer's *Money;* dramatizations of Dickens' *Oliver Twist, Nicholas Nickleby, The Cricket on the Hearth* and *David Copperfield;* and several romantic melodramas new to the city. As a journalist observed, the Bakers were offering "a rare intellectual treat," and the public responded so appreciatively that they closed their season with a profit of $30,000. Their triumph, indeed, was all but complete. At the American Theater, Sarah Kirby Stark and her husband offered competition. But soon they were forced to add a circus troupe to their program—with the result that "tragedies and horses, melodramas and tumbling, farces and tricks with cannon balls, are shown up every night." To the cultural pioneers this must have been deeply humiliating, the more because their recourse to animals and tumblers did not offset the transcendent attractions of Alexina Fisher Baker. The contest was hopeless; the Starks realized that they would have to seek a new audience. In Australia, gold had been discovered and another worldwide gold rush had begun. They took ship for the distant frontier. There they prospered. After an absence of more than a year they returned to California with a fortune of $100,000.

But the Bakers could not impair the success of Tom Maguire's company at the San Francisco Theater. The jaunty impresario had assembled a troupe that included "June" Booth and his wife, young Edwin Booth, Dr. Robinson, Caroline Chapman and her brother William, whom the public had affectionately dubbed "Uncle Billy." The Chapmans had arrived in San Francisco shortly after the Bakers and, following a successful engagement at the Jenny Lind, had made a long tour of the mining camps. Their extraordinary versatility won them immediate acclaim. This was almost inevitable; as a local critic had pointed out, "In no place in the world do people require novelty more than in this country, and it needs more than ordinary exertion to cater successfully to the lovers of the drama in California." But to the Chapmans, more than to any other actors who had come from the East, protean ability was something merely to be taken for granted. They had acquired it on their father's showboat; they had developed it in the crude theaters of the old frontier; and Caroline, at Burton's in New York, had transmuted it into a perfected artistry.

Young Edwin Booth, darkly handsome, given to strange oscillations between melancholia and exuberant gaiety, was learning adaptability and versatility under the spur of urgent want. He had sometimes been penniless and often hungry. With a group of actors, he had made a tour of the mining camps as an entertainer and, for a time, was snowed in at Nevada City. Sharing with another actor a shack far out on the Mission Road, Edwin Booth listed himself in the San Francisco directory as a "comedian and ranchero." But he was ready to

Lola Montez

undertake any kind of role, from blackface singer in farce to Shakespeare. One of his most notable successes—it led a critic to predict that he would attain "a high rank in the profession"—was as the hero of a melodrama about volunteer firemen. In this, he rose to a tremendous climax: "Mother, let me go! The fire bells! . . . What is my death if I save the city? . . . A San Francisco fire boy is the noblest work of God!"

With Maguire's company, Caroline Chapman and young Booth appeared in Dr. Robinson's boisterous local farces; in a round of classic comedies; in melodrama; in Shakespeare. Miss Chapman played Katharina, Beatrice, Lady Anne, Desdemona, Ophelia, Juliet, with Booth as Petruchio, Benedick, Richard, Iago, Hamlet and Romeo. But Caroline Chapman's unique talents as a comedienne and soubrette were also highly esteemed; "in her particular line of characters," a critic declared, "she has never had an equal." This talent found an appropriate vehicle in *The Actress of All Work,* which gave her an opportunity to assume, in rapid succession, five sharply dissimilar roles, as interpreted by the actress who was the playlet's heroine. And again, her talent lifted above banality the farce, *Lola Montez,* new to San Francisco. But when she exploited it in Dr. Robinson's merciless satire, *Who's Got the Countess?*—to which "Uncle Billy" Chapman contributed an uproarious burlesque of Lola's spider-dance—Miss Chapman precipitated a controversy in the press.

The production of this piece was inspired by Lola's arrival in the city, and her engagement as a star by the enterprising Bakers, who had taken over the American Theater. The legend of her beauty and the saga of her sinful past had preceded her. Curiosity had been whetted by the rumor that she bathed in lavender water and dried her lovely body with rose leaves. And her fiery temperament was suggested by a published report that, on the day of her arrival, she quarreled with her agent and thrashed him soundly. San Francisco seethed with excitement about Countess Lansfeld, its first titled lady. Yet, could she be called a lady? Was she an artist, as she claimed, or only a creature of loose morals, as her legend implied? Or had she been greatly maligned? Perhaps appreciating the high comedy of her situation, Lola made her debut in the role of Lady Teazle at greatly enhanced prices. She was next seen in *Yelva,* a melodrama, and in her notorious spider-dance. She played *Lola Montez in Bavaria;* subsequently she appeared in other plays and dances. Business at the theater was tremendous. Critics, although not overwhelmed by her talents, found her personality, her effect of glamour, irresistible. She gave a benefit for the volunteer firemen and another for a local charity; these generous acts won the hearts of many argonauts. When Dr. Robinson, Miss Chapman and her brother held Lola up to ridicule, indignant protests appeared in the press. During the controversy that ensued the chivalrous rallied to Lola's support and the puritanical attacked her. The commotion subsided when, suddenly, she married a local journalist, Patrick Hull, and with him departed for Sacramento to play an engagement.

Lola's first appearance in Sacramento was greeted by a rain of decaying vegetables. She treated the audience to a vigorous tongue-lashing; there was a good deal of disorder; but eventually she danced. Later that night the miners gave Lola and her husband a shivaree. Always fearless, she appeared on the balcony of her hotel and shouted her defiant contempt of her tormentors, and

Caroline Chapman

an armed posse finally dispersed the mob. Her courage evoked the miners' reluctant admiration. When, unexpectedly, she gave a second performance, she received an ovation. After this gratifying victory, Lola and her husband retired to a cottage in Grass Valley. Their idyll in the mining town was brief; Lola presently drove her husband out of their home. Reports on her solitary existence frequently appeared in the press. She smoked cigars, kept an untamed bear cub as a pet, made long mountain journeys riding astride her black, ill-tempered stallion, and attempted to horsewhip an unfriendly editor. Her most significant activity was unnoticed by the press. She took an interest in the daughter of an unsuccessful miner and his wife. Little Lotta Crabtree was six years old, red-haired, black-eyed, vivacious. Detecting a talent for the stage, Lola gave the precocious child some training in singing and dancing. Two years later, managed by her shrewd mother, little Lotta would tour the mining camps as a child prodigy. She would then go on to perform in the saloons and "melodeons" of San Francisco. At the age of seventeen, having achieved a modest local celebrity, she would be taken by her mother to New York—to become, surprisingly, one of the most popular, durable and wealthy actresses of the century.

In engaging Lola to star at the American Theater, Lewis Baker had tried to meet some of the problems confronting managers in a city where theatrical conditions were rapidly changing. Novelty was increasingly demanded. Although the public remained loyal to Alexina Fisher Baker, her husband could no longer rely exclusively on her popularity to fill the house night after night. The annual rent of his theater was $30,000; its salary roll alone exceeded $3,500 weekly. To keep his enterprise solvent, Baker required the services of stars—and when these could be obtained he often had to pay them as much as a thousand dollars a performance.

When Mrs. Catherine Sinclair arrived in San Francisco, with the prestige of an eastern tour after her divorce from Edwin Forrest, Lewis Baker engaged her

Mrs. Catherine Norton Sinclair

Matilda Heron

for the American. Co-starring performances were unusual; Mrs. Baker and Mrs. Sinclair gave them an exciting novelty. They appeared together in *London Assurance,* Mrs. Baker taking the role of Lady Gay and Mrs. Sinclair that of Grace. In a second performance, they exchanged roles. In a third performance, they alternated in the two roles. This display of bravura delighted and thrilled the public. The *Alta California,* surmising that puritans might disapprove of Mrs. Sinclair because of her divorce, declared that she had won admiration not only by her art, but "by her most ladylike deportment, and by all those high and noble qualities and virtues that adorn woman." The Bakers had meanwhile persuaded an old friend, James E. Murdoch, to come out from "the States." Murdoch was an actor of the classical school, erudite, technically accomplished, equally proficient in high comedy and tragedy. He was extremely popular in Boston, but elsewhere in the East, although highly respected, he usually played to thin houses. In San Francisco, however, his elegance, his polished style, his repute as an "intellectual actor" received appropriate recognition. From his debut as Hamlet, Murdoch met with sensational success and his engagement—possibly to his own astonishment—was prolonged for many weeks.

Yet by the autumn of 1853, the Bakers foresaw the end of their ascendancy in theatrical affairs. A new theater, the Metropolitan, was being erected on Washington Street. This playhouse was the first in the city to be illuminated, throughout, by gas, and it was so extravagantly costly, so luxuriously appointed, as to warrant the assertion that it was "the most magnificent temple of histrionic art in America." The Metropolitan had been leased by Mrs. Sinclair, and her announced plans as a manager were fully as pretentious as her magnificent theater. Their prodigious efforts had yielded the Bakers a small fortune. Instead of risking it in a contest with Mrs. Sinclair, they wisely decided to retire from the field and return to the East. Their luck held to the very end. Two nights after Mrs. Sinclair opened the Metropolitan, and little more than a week before closing their California adventure, the Bakers gave San Francisco a spectacular surprise.

Enthusiastic letters from Murdoch, with whom she had acted in Boston, determined Miss Matilda Heron to try her luck in California. She arrived in San Francisco under peculiarly distressing circumstances; her agent, with whom she was traveling, had died on the voyage up from Panama. Unheralded, virtually unknown, she made her debut on December 26, 1853, as Bianca in *Fazio,* supported by Lewis Baker, and was received with "an enthusiasm that knew no bounds." The next morning, the newspapers gave her unstinted praise—"all placing her in the topmost rank of the profession, and some claiming that no performance of equal excellence was within the powers of any actress on the stage." The actress who had failed at the Bowery in New York because she was "too tame" was hailed as a genius; the theater immediately sold out for her engagement. Word leaked out that Miss Heron had decided to donate the proceeds of her benefit to the widow of her agent; that, in order to expedite the gift, she had advanced the performance to the eve of "steamer day." Before the curtain rang up, "a number of gentlemen spontaneously contributed to the purchase of a diamond cross for the generous girl, as an appropriate reward of an act of such pious and munificent charity." In rapid succession, Miss Heron appeared as the Countess in *Love,* Mrs. Haller in *The Stranger,* Juliana in *The Honeymoon,* Mariana in *The Wife,* Margaret Elmore in *Love's Sacrifice.* She was commended for offering these domestic dramas, because "our people are, many of them, long separated from their families and friends, and the scenes of domestic trials and sufferings, joys and surprises, are those which recall their homes, and appeal most forcibly to their better nature." Yet it was her Juliet, to the Romeo of Alexina Fisher Baker, at that lady's farewell benefit on New Year's night, which entranced and fascinated not only a "walnut-cracking holiday audience" but the critics also, and sealed Miss Heron's triumph. "Her chief merit," Frank Soulé later recorded, "was found in her perfect naturalness of manner; the total absence of those screamings, rantings and gesticulations which have grown up rank and deep-rooted weeds on the dramatic field. . . . Miss Heron has thus been an eminent reformer of the California stage. Actors and actresses have subdued their rantings under her influence, and adopted a more lifelike style of performing. Hence the vast improvement in theatrical representations in this city, even in mediocre players."

With the departure of the Bakers and the closing of the American, Miss Heron joined Mrs. Sinclair at the new, splendid Metropolitan, where Murdoch was also starring after a successful tour of the mining towns. There Edwin Booth, although listed only as a stock actor, was performing star roles, and Miss Heron played Ophelia to his Hamlet and Juliet to his Romeo. In other roles, she justified Soulé's description of her as "a dazzling star, whose radiance will always shine pre-eminent, by whatever constellation it may be surrounded." So brilliant was her radiance that when, after much advance publicity, Miss Laura Keene arrived in San Francisco and made her debut at the Metropolitan, she was compared with Miss Heron and found wanting. "Californians," one critic declared, with an obvious reference to the reigning favorite, "have been educated in too high a school of taste." And another asserted that, "Although Miss Keene has by no means made a failure, it would be useless to deny that she has not made a 'hit.' " Miss Heron, moreover, had scored a social conquest also; "the devotion of half the *jeunesse dorée* of San Francisco was at her feet, and her admirers were numbered by the score." Her choice fell upon Henry Herbert Byrne, a wealthy young lawyer, and they were secretly married in June,

1854. After a honeymoon of only five days, Miss Heron sailed from San Francisco for the East, prepared to take her farewell of the stage. Early in the autumn, her husband followed her. He joined Miss Heron in Pittsburgh and, as one of their friends recorded, "remained in her society but a single night, then left her, never more to meet her on earth, and returned to San Francisco a wretched and broken man."

More fortunate than Miss Heron, Miss Keene was attended by a gentleman who, although not yet her husband, devotedly promoted her interests. Following her unsuccessful debut, John Lutz took Miss Keene on a short tour of the mining towns, and on her return to San Francisco launched her, once again, as an actress-manager. Late in June, 1854, she opened the Union Theater on Commercial Street, near Kearny, with a company that included Caroline Chapman, Dr. Robinson, Henry Coad, and other local favorites. The first bill introduced *The Sea of Ice,* an elaborately scenic melodrama with which, three years later, she would achieve an outstanding success at her own theater in New York. It did not please the public, and subsequent productions did little better. Even the triple attraction of Miss Keene, Miss Chapman, and comedies new to the city failed to nourish the box office. After a little more than a month, Miss Keene closed her theater and disbanded her company. Perhaps she had heard reports of the success of the Starks in Australia. Presently, accompanied by her manager and by Edwin Booth as her leading man, she sailed to make a tour of the Australian cities, the first accredited eastern star to undertake that hazardous venture.

The fact was that Miss Keene's managerial experiment had been doomed from the outset; the supremacy of the Metropolitan could not be challenged. Whatever her deficiencies as an actress, Mrs. Sinclair was a brilliant, resource-

Interior of the Metropolitan Theater, San Francisco

ful manager who not only gratified the community by anticipating its changing preferences, but who also undertook to elevate its taste. Her own taste was impeccable. She knew the best that London and New York could offer; she determined to make her theater the equal of any in those capitals; she achieved her ambition. In San Francisco, a city still proud of "all its wickedness and splendid folly," there was probably no folly more splendid than hers. During the eighteen months of her direction of the Metropolitan, she introduced grand opera with famous singers brought from the East. She produced musical extravaganzas, ballets, pantomimes and spectacles. Her dramatic bills offered a repertory of Shakespeare, standard tragedy, classic comedies, new romantic plays, farces. The public demanded stars, and Mrs. Sinclair provided them: the celebrated Bateman sisters, child prodigies; Barney Williams and his wife, comedians who took the roles of a roistering Irishman and a Yankee girl in pieces tailored for their ebullient talents; Miss Jean Davenport, who became a great favorite. It was said that several of Mrs. Sinclair's stars, musical and dramatic, earned as much as $30,000 in an engagement of several weeks at the Metropolitan, and the receipts of the theater during her first season were reported to be $400,000—far more than was taken in by Wallack's, Burton's, or Niblo's in New York.

But this glittering prosperity was brought to an end by a sudden, ruinous financial depression. In the autumn of 1854, one of San Francisco's most prominent and respected citizens secretly took ship for South America. Henry Meiggs was a wealthy lumber merchant, a pillar of the church, builder of the city's first concert hall and a member of its board of aldermen. After his flight, it was discovered that he had forged municipal securities to the amount of several millions as collateral for loans used in his speculations. In the wake of this disaster, hundreds of business houses and two leading banks failed. People in the city said that Meiggs might have been forgiven had he been content only to cheat his bankers; but he had also cheated his washerwoman, and this, even for California, was carrying rascality too far. Indirectly, Mrs. Sinclair was as much a victim of his swindling as the washerwoman. She struggled valiantly against financial troubles and diminishing attendance until June, 1855, when she relinquished her management of the Metropolitan. She continued to act in San Francisco for one more year. Then, like the Starks, Miss Keene, Lola Montez and many another star, she departed to seek her fortune in distant Australia.

Meanwhile, hardy players were carrying the drama beyond Stockton, Sacramento and Marysville—the established circuit for stars—to the most remote mountain mining camps. There was, for example, the picturesque Dan Virgil Gates, a forty-niner who had come from the New York theaters to make a strike in the gold fields. Instead, he had turned to acting, playing with both the Starks and the Bakers before conceiving his project of a touring one-man theater. Gates traveled everywhere astride a mule, ringing a clattering bell as he entered each town or camp. Then, according to Walter Leman, who knew him well, he "posted his own bills, beat his own drum, fiddled, sang, danced and recited, and gave a ball after the dramatic performance to the intense satisfaction of his patrons." Where Gates led, others soon followed. A typical expedition set out from Sacramento in the summer of 1856. It was organized by McKean Buchanan, a self-styled tragedian whose nerve greatly exceeded his talent. Leman, a talented, scholarly middle-aged actor and playwright, was a member of the small company. Well known in the theaters of the East, Leman had played with Mrs. Sinclair and Laura Keene in San Francisco, and was to remain prominent in California theatricals for two decades.

An advance agent preceded Buchanan's company in a light buggy, to make arrangements for halls and lodgings and "bill" the camps. The company traveled in a Concord wagon; it held ten people, costumes and other baggage, and was drawn by a four-horse team. Where the grades of the roads were too steep, the actors and actresses had to leave the wagon and make their way on foot. A tour lasting six weeks took them over a distance of seven hundred miles to forty towns and mining camps, during which they brought "the drama as it had never been seen before" to such settlements as Cherokee Flat, Rough and Ready, Rattlesnake, Mud Springs and Indian Diggings. If business was bad, and the box-office receipts were meager, Buchanan went out "after playing Hamlet and won enough at poker to square the salary bill the next morning." Frequently, when they entered a town, Buchanan himself would thump the drum all the way to their lodgings. Leman tried to discourage this unnecessary lowering of the star's dignity, but Buchanan had a sound argument in its favor. "It makes capital," he asserted. "They say I'm eccentric; and when the miners see me beating the drum they'll say, 'See, there's Buchanan, the great tragedian, beating the drum; how odd! It shows that, great actor as he is, he can descend from his pedestal. Let's all go and see him tonight.'"

The following summer Leman made another tour, this time with lovely Mrs. Julia Dean Hayne, whose brilliant success in San Francisco had aroused curiosity throughout the state. The tour lasted for nearly three months, beginning with an engagement of ten nights in Placerville, where "a new and pretty theater had been built," and took the company as far up in the mountain region as Downieville, "which in those days was the *ultima thule* of actors." It was a town notorious throughout the country; only six years earlier, under lynch law, its citizens had hanged a woman. At Downieville, or some other camp high in the Sierras, the company performed in the upper story of a cloth-and-paper house. Since this hall had no stage, the actors had to improvise one from two billiard tables covered with boards. "There being no room for exit or entrance, excepting by a narrow door on one side, and two narrow windows leading to the roof of a shed on the other, a heroic exit or entrance was out of the question, and in getting before the audience Master Walter had to push Julia up through the window, the frame being taken out, and in getting off let her down in advance." But the spectators seemed to enjoy this performance of *The Hunchback* as much as the players, "and there was a deal of fun, if not of tragic fitness." Even in the roughest mining camps, the company seldom played to less than $300 a night. But, aside from the fact that mountain tours were profitable, stars like Mrs. Hayne were willing to endure "the discomforts of travel, and the inconveniences of ill-lighted halls and meager appointments," for a curious reason. "There was an amount of intelligence in the audiences of those mining regions," Leman recalled, "fully equal to that which gathered in the pit and boxes in San Francisco or Sacramento. College graduates and accomplished scholars, as well as merchants and artisans, were hunting gold in every gulch and ravine, and rough though their attire might be, they were as well qualified to judge of the merits or demerits of author or actor as a New York or Boston auditor." Indeed, Californians took the drama perhaps more seriously than it was taken in the East. In the Spring of 1857, the Governor of the state sent to Edwin Forrest an official invitation to honor its citizens by making a professional tour; the document was signed by four other high officials and seventy-five members of the legislature. Quite correctly, Forrest accounted it an honor "never before conferred on one of my profession," but he did not visit California until nine years later.

During the troubled period that followed the failure and flight of Alderman Meiggs, the theater in San Francisco languished. Returning from an unprosperous tour of Australia in the spring of 1855, Miss Laura Keene took the American Theater and bravely made another venture in management. But, although she staged costly productions of *Twelfth Night, A Midsummer Night's Dream* and *The Tempest,* she succeeded no better than before, and after three months she departed for New York. The times were against her; the public wanted only light fare. Minstrel shows flourished, and the efforts of pantomimists and dancers drew large audiences. It was at an entertainment of this kind that there occurred the incident which first set prominent citizens to thinking of the "businessman's revolution" that took form in the second Committee of Vigilance. On the night of November 15, 1855, two troupes of pantomimists were performing at the American Theater. The performance was attended by General William H. Richardson, the United States Marshal, with his wife and another lady. General Richardson became indignant when he found, seated immediately behind his party, Charles Cora, a professional gambler, and his mistress, Belle Cora, a noted personage of the city's underworld. Affronted by her proximity to his ladies, General Richardson complained to the management and asked that she be ejected. His request was refused, and the General with his ladies left the theater. Three days later, meeting General Richardson on Sansome Street, Charles Cora shot him through the heart. The community was incensed, not because the gambler had chosen to avenge an insult, but because, in defiance of the traditional code of etiquette, he had killed an unarmed man without uttering the essential preliminary warning. Cora was committed to jail, but the authorities took no steps to bring him to trial.

Their negligence exasperated the editor of the *Bulletin,* a new crusading newspaper. James King of William, as he called himself—adding the patronymic "William" to distinguish himself from other James Kings—was daily assailing official and social corruption in the city. Particularly, King denounced the existing alliance between politicians, gamblers and criminals. On May 14, 1856, King was shot down in the street, but not killed, by James Casey, a city official whose criminal record he had exposed. Casey was confined to the same jail in which Cora was comfortably lodged. King lingered for six days, during which public excitement constantly mounted. A second Committee of Vigilance was organized by prominent businessmen. Soon afterwards, this Committee, having possessed itself of most of the arms in the city, went to the jail, obtained the surrender of Casey and Cora, and took them to its headquarters. After King's death, the two men were tried and found guilty. They were permitted to see spiritual advisers, and Cora was married to his mistress. On May 22nd, as King's funeral was taking place, Casey and Cora were hanged from a second-story window of the Committee's headquarters before a vast crowd. The activities of the Committee caused deep and bitter divisions in the community; for some weeks it appeared that armed conflict might occur between its volunteer forces and those of the state militia or federal troops. But order prevailed, for the Committee had mounted cannon at its headquarters, "Fort Gunnybags," on Sacramento Street. Startling rumors circulated in the city. There was an awareness of imminent danger and an atmosphere of grave anxiety while the Committee proceeded with its work, until its final parade and retirement from activity in August, 1856.

Yet it was characteristic of San Francisco that, during this dark period of crisis, great events in the theater were appropriately celebrated. One was the first engagement of Mrs. Julia Dean Hayne at the Metropolitan Theater, which began late in June and, recognized as a gala occasion, drew "not only remunerative but crowded houses." Crowds also flocked to the American, where the Chapmans presented a new star, Miss Mary Provost, in exactly the same plays which Mrs. Hayne was performing. And during the month of July—in which the Committee of Vigilance hanged two more murderers—the whole town turned out for the farewell engagement, at the American Theater, of the Misses Adelaide and Joey Gougenheim, exquisite comediennes adored by playgoers. The celebrated sisters were making an Australian tour after a year's stay in California. Neither the antecedent economic depression nor the social crisis diminished the enchantment of their gaiety. They had, indeed, come to San Francisco at the worst of times. Yet they took to Australia, as souvenirs of the city, "two magnificent watches, richly adorned with brilliants; one costly and very splendid diamond necklace; two exquisitely wrought and valuable bracelets, highly embellished with diamonds and emeralds; two diamond rings of much value, and a massive gold bouquet holder, splendidly chased." In spite of its gamblers, prostitutes and murders, its shanties and unpaved streets, its air of hasty improvisation, San Francisco—so far as the theater was concerned—gave precedence to no metropolis in the world.

CHAPTER 8

The Old Order Passes

IN New York, toward evening on September 3, 1855, a crowd gathered in front of the Metropolitan Theater. This handsome new playhouse, on Broadway facing fashionable Bond Street, was offering an unusual attraction—the American debut of a world-famous tragedienne. For days past the newspapers had been publishing long articles about Mlle. Rachel. Broadway restaurants were featuring puddings and ice creams *à la Rachel;* hairdressers had put cards in their windows announcing coiffures *à la Rachel;* several shops advertised gaiters *à la Rachel,* "just arrived from Paris." Soon after the doors of the theater opened, at half past six, every seat in the house was occupied, although the performance was not to begin until quarter past seven. A critic noticed that the audience included "most of the distinguished men of the country." It was clearly a gala occasion, for ladies in the boxes and orchestra seats wore ball dresses, and were adorned with "diamonds by the shovelful, flowers as if it rained flowers." No actress since Fanny Kemble in her girlhood had aroused such intense curiosity among cultivated playgoers.

Rachel enjoyed a unique prestige. The French people cherished her as a national possession, and the government of Napoleon III, responding to a wave of protest, had tried to dissuade her from making an American tour. London, Berlin, Vienna and St. Petersburg had acclaimed her genius. Such diverse but expert judges of acting as Fanny Kemble, Charlotte Cushman and Mrs. Mowatt had testified to the overwhelming effect of her art. After seeing her play *Phèdre* at the Comédie Française, Ralph Waldo Emerson wrote, "She deserves all her

Matilda Heron as Camille

fame and is the only good actress I have ever seen." Her fame had preceded her to the United States, and so had the story of her swift ascent to it. Rachel was the second of five children of an itinerant peddler named Félix, and as a little girl had been forced to sing in the streets of Paris and beg coins from passers-by. A teacher of music, impressed by her voice, gave her some lessons. Mlle. Mars of the Comédie Française, so the story went, obtained a place for the young girl at the Conservatoire. Edwin Forrest saw her there, in a student performance, was struck by the "demoniacal power" of "that little bag of bones with the marble face and flaming eyes," and predicted for her a magnificent future.

After playing briefly at another theater, Rachel appeared at the Comédie Française in 1838, at the age of seventeen. Jules Janin, the Parisian critic of greatest influence, immediately hailed her as "the most marvelous actress that this generation has seen on the stage." He, too, was astonished by her extraordinary power. She was dark, small, extremely frail. She lacked beauty to the point of plainness. Janin thought her an "uneducated child." Nevertheless, he wrote, "She has that which is better than knowledge. She has that sudden illumination which she throws about her; she grows ten inches taller on the stage; she raises her voice and extends her chest; her eyes brighten; she treads like a sovereign; her voice vibrates, instinct with the passion that agitates her." Three years later Rachel conquered London as easily as she had triumphed in Paris. "She is completely the rage in London now," Fanny Kemble Butler noted in 1841; "all the fine ladies and gentlemen crazy after her, the Queen throwing her roses on the stage out of her own bouquet, and viscountesses and marchionesses driving her about . . ." The ignorant, ugly beggar girl had become not only a great artist but a great personage; and Mrs. Butler, who thought her as an actress supreme, met her in society and was also "very much pleased with her quiet grace and dignity, the excellent *bon ton* of her manners."

The audience at the Metropolitan waited in polite boredom while the company that Rachel had brought from Paris played a two-act comedy. This was to be followed by Corneille's tragedy, *Horace,* in which Rachel had made her debut at the Comédie Française. The interval between the two plays was brief. Behind the scenes Rachel was impatient, excited, very nervous; her hands were icy cold. The curtain rose on *Horace,* and the audience was slightly disconcerted by the traditionally simple setting of French tragedy; a grim array of columns and two chairs. Presently a severely classic figure glided past the columns, to the accompaniment of salvos of applause and shouts. Declaiming poetry in a golden voice, Rachel thrilled the audience by her magnificent diction, the expressiveness of her face and posture and gestures, and the way she moved about the stage "with a panther's terrible and undulating grace." As the critic for the *Tribune* reported, there was but one feeling in the theater; "she surpassed expectation."

Rachel appeared next in Racine's *Phèdre,* and in her most celebrated role. The character of Phèdre, torn by the conflict of incestuous passion and tortured conscience, exhibited the full range of her art. The pathos and eloquence of her acting seemed, to the critic of *The Albion,* "almost intolerably exciting." In appearance, she reminded him of the polychromatic statues of ancient

Rachel as Phèdre,
from a painting by E. Dubufe

Greece, and she was like "a goddess chiselled by Phidias in ivory and gold." But only the visual image suggested antiquity. Rachel's portrayal of passion and woe was wholly modern in its conception. During the great scene of Phedre's avowal to Hippolyte of her guilty love, she held the audience breathless by her evocation of humiliated and despairing womanhood. This momentary silence of the spectators probably came as a relief to the tragedienne. Most of the audience knew no French and were unfamiliar with the texts of her plays. They attempted to follow the performances from pamphlet translations, noisily rustling the pages as they turned them in unison. "You would say that a regiment in black uniform was executing a military order," Léon Beauvallet, one of the actors, noted. Rachel herself was puzzled by the deluge of sound from the "accursed pamphlets" which often drowned the voices of the actors and sometimes spoiled her own finest scenes.

From classic tragedy she passed to modern drama, presenting *Adrienne Lecouvreur* at her third performance. The play had been written for her, six years earlier, by Legouvé and Scribe. It gave her a flamboyant and varied role as the famous eighteenth-century tragedienne who had been involved in a love affair with the Maréchal de Saxe. An adaptation of the play had already been performed in New York by Miss Jean Davenport. Partly because some of the public were familiar with it, partly because, being a contemporary play, it provided for changes of scene and costume, *Adrienne Lecouvreur* became the most popular piece in Rachel's repertory. Audiences were deeply impressed by the splendor of her costumes and jewels. The critic of the *Tribune* declared that her jewels were valued at very nearly a quarter of a million dollars and "throw such a luster over the stage when she enters as Adrienne that you can almost fancy you see one of the heroines, clad in precious stones, who are pictured around the court of Solomon." He also announced that certain of these jewels had been presented to the actress by "the pious and good Queen Amelia, the widow of Louis Philippe. It speaks the noblest answer to lying canards which small curs bark after Rachel, that she has retained through life the love and regard of this model Queen . . ."

Rumors were already circulating about Rachel's private life. She had come to the United States under the management of her brother, Raphael Félix. Her three sisters were members of her company, and her father, also, had accompanied them. On arriving in New York, the whole family took quarters in the luxurious new St. Nicholas Hotel. But soon afterwards Rachel with two of her sisters moved into a private house on Clinton Place (now Eighth Street) just east of Fifth Avenue. The third sister took a separate lodging. Raphael Félix and his father went to live in rooms on Broadway. This dispersal of the family, as Beauvallet recorded, "did not fail to excite the inquisitiveness of all the New York tattlers," and it caused widespread speculation. This, he remarked, was "a much ado about nothing," for the family "lived separately because they lived separately, and that was all." Yet New York thought it peculiar, and when Rachel appeared as Phèdre the gossips began spreading a more destructive story. She had first undertaken this role twelve years earlier, shortly after being discarded by her lover, Count Walewski, the illegitimate son of Napoleon I, to whom she had borne a son. Parisians said that it was the bitter experience of being repudiated by a man she adored that taught her to play Phèdre. Later, she took another lover and became the mother of a second illegitimate son. The tale of her flagrant immorality was not offset by the widely publicized fact that, just before coming to the United States, she had performed at Drury Lane under the august patronage of Queen Victoria, for the benefit of a charity.

Polite society in New York was captivated by Rachel, as George Templeton Strong noted in his diary. Many of its members attended all her performances and their praise sounded like "the ecstatic exaggerations of very green schoolgirls." However, he remarked that Rachel's "moral repute . . . is certainly low, for though she's so prodigious a lion, she has been asked, I believe, to meet ladies but once. . . . People whisper very black things of her." It was because of these whisperings, primarily, that in spite of the eulogies of critics the circumspect middle classes failed to attend her performances. During an engagement that lasted six weeks, Rachel appeared in plays by Victor Hugo, Schiller and other modern dramatists, in addition to her repertory of classic French tragedies. The nightly receipts were never less than $3,000, and reached the impressive total of approximately $87,000, of which Rachel's share was about $30,000. But her brother complained that the engagement had not yielded the profits he anticipated.

Misfortune dogged the tragedienne. Long subject to pulmonary hemorrhages,

she caught cold in New York and illness forced her to cancel several performances in Boston, where she played in the new, ornate Boston Theater on Washington Street. The scandal which had alienated the middle classes in New York
did not have the same effect in Boston. But, foreseeing a great demand for
tickets, speculators bought most of them, and resulting high prices provoked
indignation. Yet the excitement about Rachel was so extreme that she had to
give an unprecedented Saturday matinée. At one performance, a large contingent of Harvard students volunteered as supers in order to obtain a closer view
of her. Beauvallet found it odd "to see these young men, of the best American
families, serving as supernumeraries in a French tragedy" and hastening, half-
clad, from their dressing room to applaud Rachel from the wings. He was also
puzzled by a performance of *Adrienne Lecouvreur* which he saw at the Boston
Museum. To satisfy American moral scruples, he surmised, the translator had
deleted from the play the illicit love affair of a married woman. "In this country," he reflected, "they have a queer way of explaining morals." But he was
pleased by the unexpectedly elevated taste of Boston, "where everything is
exactly the opposite of New York," and where playgoers "like tragedy better
than drama." On the cultivated, appreciative Boston public, the effect produced
by Rachel "was very great, and the success immense."

Her pleasure in this triumph was dispelled soon after her return to New York
for a second engagement. Performances were first given in the Academy of
Music on Fourteenth Street, but the cavernous opera house was too large, and
the company was transferred to Niblo's Garden, where attendance improved.
Presently, there was received in New York a copy of the *Journal des Débats* of
Paris. It contained an article by Jules Janin on Rachel's American tour—
a savage attack on the barbarous American people, "shopkeepers, fathers and
sons of shopkeepers." They were "insensible to the charms of accent, voice,
gesture; insensible to learned speech, to the soul and spirit of ancient genius."
They liked only "cigars and whiskey, Uncle Tom and whittling, dirty boots and
Bloomerism," and among them, Janin said, though she enjoyed the favor of
Queen Victoria, Rachel "is the barbarian, because she is not understood." The
article was promptly translated and published in the *Times,* causing an explosive tempest in the press. Beauvallet noted that Rachel herself was vastly
displeased, because the article proclaimed to the whole world "that her campaign in America is, after all, only an immense defeat." But her final performance drew a large, cheering, stamping audience. The *Tribune,* reporting that
her receipts in New York far exceeded those in European capitals, regarded
this as proof of "the fact which the experience of every really great artist who
has visited this country attests, that in no other is genius so highly appreciated
or magnificently rewarded."

Rachel had not recovered from her racking cough and cold. In Philadelphia,
where she went to play at the Walnut Street Theater, a spell of freezing weather
had set in. Her parsimonious brother refused to pay the costs of heating the
backstage area of the theater. On the morning after her first performance
Rachel was stricken by pneumonia. It was soon obvious that she would not
be able to act again in Philadelphia. Her company therefore appeared in

double bills with the local stock company, to thin houses. Lucrative engagements in Baltimore, Washington and Richmond were hastily canceled. Physicians recommended the climate of Charleston, and when Rachel was thought capable of the journey she followed her troupe there. At first they played without her. But, in spite of her illness, her spasms of coughing, her frightening hoarseness, she insisted on giving one performance. The performance of *Adrienne Lecouvreur* on December 17, 1855, was announced as Rachel's last appearance in the United States. It was her last performance on any stage. A visit to Cuba failed to improve her health. She returned to France ravaged by pulmonary tuberculosis; three years later she died.

Only then did Americans learn that their moral condemnation had been ironically misguided. It was generally understood that Rachel had come to the United States in a fit of pique at the sensational success in Paris of a rival actress, the Italian tragedienne Adelaide Ristori, who was to follow her to America eleven years later. But this was only partly true. From childhood, she had permitted her parasitic family to exploit her. Like Fanny Kemble, she was a self-sacrificing daughter and sister, and she idolized her children. When Raphael Félix, beguiled by the immense fortune which Jenny Lind had made in the United States, first proposed an American tour, Rachel rejected the project. Why should she undertake the quest of probable millions when she was already a very wealthy woman? But her brother pleaded the interests of her family; the promised golden harvest would be shared by her parents, her sisters and himself; he had managed her triumphal European tours. And was it not her duty to provide, as generously as possible, for the future of her adored sons? His arguments prevailed. "My brother, you see," she gently told Léon Beauvallet in New York, "is the Wandering Jew, and I am his five sous."

Rachel's visit, which posed a moral problem for many American playgoers, had an indirect influence on their moral attitudes. It prepared sophisticated audiences to accept the current Parisian drama. French plays—adapted in such fashion as to suppress their reprehensible levity concerning sexual relations—already dominated the London stage. American managers were keenly aware that the patronage of the sophisticated would not fill their theaters. The difference between profit and loss was made by the middle classes, and experience indicated that their prejudices could not be disregarded. There was the case of *Mlle. de Belle Isle,* a drama by the elder Alexandre Dumas, adapted by Fanny Kemble as *The Duke's Wager.* Miss Julia Dean had produced it in St. Louis and New Orleans. In both cities it was rejected as "too broadly French for the American stage," and when Miss Dean presented it in New York it had only two performances. Miss Jean Davenport met the same discouraging reception in December, 1853, when she produced an adaptation of *Adrienne Lecouvreur* from which objectionable elements had been eliminated. Mrs. Mowatt, during her farewell engagement at Niblo's Garden the following spring, gave one performance of the play with no greater success. But the splendor of Rachel's costumes and jewels in the role of Adrienne received widespread publicity. This stimulated popular interest in the play and launched it on its long career as a vehicle for "emotional" actresses.

It was another French drama, however, that in successive versions made by three actresses most seriously challenged the moral prejudices of audiences. Very probably it was the initial production of this play by Miss Jean Davenport which led Dr. Henry Ward Beecher, some months later, to publish in *The Independent* a denunciation of the theater as "an unmitigated evil." In 1852 the younger Alexandre Dumas' drama, *La Dame aux Camélias,* achieved a sensational success in Paris, and Miss Davenport determined to adapt it for her own use. As Henry James pointed out long afterwards, the play "is all champagne and tears—fresh perversity, fresh credulity, fresh passion, fresh pain." Moreover, it was the work of a playwright who, conceiving his function to be that of a didactic moralist, studied sexual passion from the standpoint of current social ethics. To French audiences Dumas' drama seemed highly edifying, but Miss Davenport was aware that a play about the ill-starred love of a cocotte and a young man of good family was unsuited to the American stage. American conventions would have to be substituted for French ones, and Dumas' rigorous moral lesson would have to be transposed into other terms. Accordingly, Miss Davenport transformed the Parisian lady of the camellias from a cocotte into a flirt. The young lovers were vaguely represented as being engaged; the moral question raised by the play concerned the propriety of their marriage.

In September, 1853, Miss Davenport produced her *Camille, or, the Fate of a Coquette* in Philadelphia. One critic acknowledged that the play had been "divested of all the immoral, objectionable features of the French drama," and that it was "an entertainment of virtuous instruction." On December 9th, she performed *Camille* at the Broadway Theater in New York. Although her acting of the role was praised as being exquisitely chaste and refined, audiences were repelled by the story, and the play was withdrawn after two performances. But Miss Davenport was not to be vanquished so easily. In August, 1854, she returned to the Broadway and again performed *Camille*. This time its reception was gratifyingly different. The audience first endured, then pitied, finally wept over the unfortunate heroine. Laurence Hutton, who attended the performance, recorded that Miss Davenport's acting of the role was "painfully realistic and harrowingly true to the life she portrayed." The play ran twelve nights and the actress, always a popular favorite, "became at once the great dramatic sensation of the day." The success of the play having been demonstrated, Miss Davenport was brought back for another engagement later in the season, during which she presented it for a week's run. On tour, however, *Camille* encountered vigorous moral opposition. In San Francisco, the following spring, Miss Davenport played her unhappy coquette to the Armand of Edwin Booth. Many playgoers there found the drama objectionable; and when she revived it two years later, the *Evening Bulletin* rebuked her for "pandering to the grosser passions of human nature."

Meanwhile, Miss Laura Keene had returned to New York, and had established herself as an actress-manager. Considering herself equally capable in comedy and tragedy, she decided that the role of Camille was peculiarly adapted to her talents. She was less fastidious than Miss Davenport, but more astute.

She saw that her predecessor's version of the play, in its concessions to moral sensibility, sacrificed dramatic values that ought to be retained. Pruning and purification of the original text were essential. Could not Camille be presented as a French courtesan? One major change would make this possible. A prologue and epilogue could be added to the play, indicating that her sinful profession, her redemption through love, her sacrifice of her lover, her illness and death, were only a dream. Camille would thus become a virtuous woman tempted, and rescued from temptation by a premonitory vision. Miss Keene, so to speak, determined to have her moral cake and also eat it. She would neither relinquish the sensational subject of the life of a cocotte, nor offend censorious playgoers by transgressing American proprieties. She produced her version of the play, *Camille, or, a Moral of Life,* in March, 1856, and was well rewarded for its expedient evasions. It ran for three weeks to crowded houses.

But the virginal Camille of Miss Davenport and the virtuous Camille of Miss Keene soon met formidable competition. Neither star had seen the play in Paris, with Mme. Doche as the heroine, and handsome young Charles Fechter as Armand. Another actress was more fortunate. After the breakup of her marriage, Miss Matilda Heron went abroad. In Paris, she and her brother attended a performances of *La Dame aux Camélias.* "Tilly, if you translate this and introduce it at home," her brother said, "you will make your fortune." Miss Heron made a translation of the play which adhered closely to Dumas' text. She staged *Camille* on tour in October, 1855, and during the next year accounts of her performance probably reached the New York managers. Wallack's Theater, with its splendid company, had been taken over temporarily by William Stuart, a manager who was experimenting with stars. Although Miss Heron was known to him only as a "western actress," he engaged her to play for a period of three weeks. She arrived in New York after an arduous trip from New Orleans during which blizzards had forced her to abandon her trunks. Harry Watkins, an actor, called on her, learned that she had spent $500 on "an entire new set of dresses" for *Camille,* her opening play, and helpfully "loaned her quite a lot of stage jewelry." Conditions at Wallack's Theater were scarcely encouraging. The company was convinced that the fastidious Wallack audience would be horrified by the play as Miss Heron intended to present it. Three days before the performance Lester Wallack, who was cast as Armand, flatly refused to play the part and asked young Edward A. Sothern whether he could learn it in time to substitute. To Wallack's astonishment, Sothern said that he was already "up" in the role, and next day came to rehearsal letter perfect.

On the night of January 22, 1857, Miss Heron presented *Camille.* Because of a heavy snowfall, the theater was half-empty. In the audience a young man named Adam Badeau (he would later become General Grant's military secretary) suffered "such a wrenching and tightening of emotions, such a whirlwind of feeling as made criticism impossible." He was overwhelmed by the unrelieved realism of Miss Heron's acting. She did not in any way idealize the character of the cocotte; she eliminated nothing "coarse or displeasing"; she was "not only terrible in her lifelikeness, but at times offensive." Nearly sixty years later the critic William Winter, a stern moralist, would remember that Miss Heron "could, and did, so deeply affect the feelings and so entirely beguile the sympathies as to confuse, if not destroy, perception of the difference between right and wrong." She seemed to Winter "an exponent of the elemental passions, in their universal flow and ebb; she was the whirlwind, not the zephyr." She electrified the sparse audience at Wallack's. At the end of each act, they shouted and stamped until she came before the curtain; Sothern, also, was called out; at the end of the play the audience "rose in tumultuous applause." Harry Watkins noted in his diary that night that Miss Heron "achieved a greater success than was ever accomplished by any actor or actress that has preceded her." The reviews, next day, confirmed this opinion. The critic of the *Herald* described her as "a great tragedienne." The critic of the *Tribune,* hailing her as a genius, declared that she surpassed Rachel in expressing "feminine intensity of love." Miss Heron's engagement was prolonged to seven weeks, and although she appeared in other plays, she performed *Camille* forty-six times, always selling out the theater.

When she came back to Wallack's the following autumn, Miss Heron had performed *Camille* more than two hundred times on tour. While she was appearing in New York, Miss Cushman returned to the United States after an absence of five years and began an engagement at Burton's New Theater, the former Metropolitan. The critic of the *Tribune* felt obliged to chide the public for comparing the two actresses. Only "the foolishness of ignorance," he asserted, would compare an "artist of intellect and experience" like Miss Cushman with Miss Heron, who was "an extraordinary and eccentric genius, blinding judgment by the blaze of her passion." Yet the fact that a leading New York critic asserted her superiority to Rachel, and contrasted her art with that of the incomparable Miss Cushman, indicated the nature of Miss Heron's triumph. With respect to her two predecessors in the role of Camille, her triumph was complete. Miss Keene made one ill-fated attempt to revive her version of the play in competition with Miss Heron's. She then discarded it and gave up the role. Although Miss Davenport retained her version of the play in her repertory, she was seldom able to revive it for more than a few performances. Miss Heron's version of *Camille* became the standard one, and her playing of the role, soon imitated by every actress who wished to be identified with "emotional" parts, established a stage tradition that was to be followed for nearly a century. She introduced to the American theater not only a new, startling realism in acting, but a new form of drama—the sensational problem play of contemporary "real life."

Yet this new type of drama aroused the moral indignation of a large, important segment of the public. William Winter, then reviewing plays for the *Saturday Press* and soon to begin his forty-four years of service as dramatic critic of the New York *Tribune,* expressed their judgment of *Camille.* He never ceased denouncing its "pernicious influence" on the drama. He described it as "diseased" and "sophistical." Dumas' moralistic play, he declared, merely proved "that the courtesan and the virtuous woman are alike pure—that chastity is immaterial."

The vehemence of such attacks on the stage indicated that moral attitudes and tastes were changing radically. A generation of Americans had reached maturity in a social environment that was being transformed with unprecedented rapidity, and in a period of accelerating crisis that was soon to result in the Civil War. Preoccupied by the present and the future, it had little respect for the authority of the past. Its impatience with tradition applied with special force to the theater. It thought the old drama irrelevant, the old school of acting pompous and artificial. Miss Heron and her *Camille,* as Harry Watkins shrewdly noted, "just hit the time." On the stage, the new generation required realism of effect, timeliness of subject and theme. Nobody understood the implications of this demand more thoroughly than Dion Boucicault, who for twenty-five years was to occupy a unique position in the American theater. He exercised a powerful influence as a playwright, producer, director and occasional actor. He was a theatrical craftsman of extraordinary ingenuity, and he lifted the craft of the dramatist to the status of a recognized, lucrative profession. His flair for anticipating what the public wanted, and his fecundity in providing it, were equally remarkable. During a writing career of some fifty years, he wrote and adapted more than four hundred plays; of these, he acknowledged the authorship of one hundred and twenty-five. At the height of his fame, in 1875, it was said that playgoers in the United States and Great Britain had paid twenty-five million dollars to see his plays. But fifteen years later, and two weeks before his death, he summed up his career in a letter to a friend: "It has been a long jig, my boy, and I am just beginning to see the pathos of it. I have written for a monster who forgets."

When Boucicault arrived in New York in 1853, he was already famous as the author of *London Assurance* and *Old Heads and Young Hearts,* and the adapter of such popular plays as *Don Caesar de Bazan* and *The Corsican Brothers.* Then in his early thirties, he was slender, rather handsome and prematurely bald. He had the air of "an elegant theatrical beau and man of fashion." Reputedly the son of a Dublin wine merchant named Boursiquot, he was in reality the illegitimate child of Dr. Dionysius Lardner, an eccentric scientist who provided for his education. At the age of seventeen, he began acting in the British provincial theaters and also writing plays. He became a celebrity at twenty-one, when *London Assurance* was produced at Covent Garden. This play and several others proved his mastery of literary form and the high level of his dramatic talent. He wished to become a creative artist, but he was also eager for wealth. When a manager refused to pay his price for a play, asserting that a successful French comedy could be pirated more cheaply, Boucicault put aside his creative ambitions and his literary conscience. He resolved to be a popular, well-paid playwright and to follow the prevailing custom of drawing his material from the works of other writers. "I am an emperor," he boasted long afterwards, "and take what I think best for Art, whether it be a story from a book, a play from the French, an actor from a rival company."

This was, in fact, his practice. He spent some years in France, writing and adapting plays. While there, he married a woman of means who died in mysterious circumstances. He returned to London and joined the Charles Keans

Agnes Robertson (Mrs. Dion Boucicault)

at the Princess' Theater as house playwright, literary adviser and actor. Among the members of their company was their ward, Miss Agnes Robertson, a dark-haired, beautiful young actress equally adept in comedy and pathetic roles. Boucicault wrote a play for her and they fell in love. Because of her infatuation with him, Miss Robertson refused a proposal of marriage by the Earl of Hopetown. Apparently this exasperated the Keans. Miss Robertson sailed to act in

Canada and the United States. Boucicault joined her in New York. Were they, or were they not, man and wife? More than thirty years later, this question would flare up in an international scandal. But in 1853, when the actress and the playwright were first delighting New York, their constant, intimate association provoked much scandalous gossip. This, Boucicault finally stilled during a repeatedly extended engagement which Miss Robertson played at the Boston Museum. One night, in a speech from the stage, he announced that he was Miss Robertson's husband.

Miss Robertson took New York by storm on the night of her debut. Quickly dubbed "the fairy star," her engagement at Burton's Theater was prolonged to three months. Working rapidly as a house playwright, Boucicault provided her with a number of new vehicles. He accompanied her on a tour that was prodigiously successful. In Boston, where she played for nine weeks, special trains were run from outlying towns to bring people to her performances, and Moses Kimball, manager of the Museum, made a profit of $20,000 on her engagement. The tour took the couple to Philadelphia, Washington, Baltimore, Chicago, New Orleans and many other cities, with frequent engagements in New York. Boucicault turned out new plays for Miss Robertson, carefully exploiting her special capabilities as an actress, and with equal care concealing her limitations. Her triumph was in great part due to his expert craftsmanship, but the fact that she did triumph initiated a demand for his plays that, in effect, launched his American career. His practice in tailoring roles for Miss Robertson and, occasionally, for himself, soon enabled him to devise plays especially fitted to the individual talents of any major company—a technical resource which increased his market, his earnings and his prestige.

One of the pieces which he wrote for Miss Robertson and himself, *The Life of an Actress,* first performed in New Orleans in 1855, was in substance an eloquent defense of the reputability of the acting profession and the theater. Allegedly founded on "events in the early career of Mlle. Rachel," it appears to have been prompted, not only by American moral condemnation of the tragedienne, but by Boucicault's resentful discovery of American social prejudices against theatrical folk. He also discovered—presumably with equal resentment—that the rights of American dramatists in their work were not protected by a copyright law. Attempts to secure the enactment of a law by Congress had been made, without success, by Dr. R. M. Bird and George H. Boker, author of the poetic tragedy *Francesca da Rimini.* But in 1856, largely as a result of Boucicault's persistent effort, Congress passed the first copyright law, giving the author of a play "along with the sole right to print and publish the said composition, the sole right also to act, perform, or represent the same." Although frequently violated, this law protected the property right of a dramatist in his plays. It afforded legal basis for the collection of royalties on performances in other theaters than that in which a play was originally produced. It also tended to give dramatists social respectability.

Naturally, Boucicault did not argue that the law should protect foreign playwrights, whose works he considered himself imperially privileged to pillage. It was with one of these exercises in "adaptation" that his era of great success

began. A French melodrama served as the basis for *The Poor of New York*
(afterwards known as *The Streets of New York,* and still to be seen in summer
theaters in 1952). This was produced at Wallack's Theater, then under the
management of William Stuart, in December, 1857, with Mrs. John Hoey,
Lester Wallack, E. A. Sothern, A. H. Davenport and other members of the
Wallack company in the cast. The play brilliantly illustrated Boucicault's genius
for timeliness of subject and realism of effect. Its action opened during the
panic of 1837, and quickly progressed to the panic that began only a month
before the production of the play. Contemporaneousness could hardly be carried further, and Boucicault invested the action with a realistic atmosphere by
providing scenes in Madison Square, the Academy of Music, the Five Points
and other familiar places. He also devised a lurid fire scene in which the
villain's lodgings are set aflame. This novel effect of stagecraft never failed to
thrill the audience, and whenever possible thereafter he incorporated some
equivalent "sensation" in his plays. The success of the play demonstrated that
Boucicault's sense of theatrical values and effect surpassed that of any other
contemporary dramatist, British or American. Nevertheless, it brought him a
rebuke from James W. Wallack. As they strolled up Broadway one night from
the theater, the old actor-manager put his hand on Boucicault's shoulder "with
tender reproach" and asked sadly, "Ah, why don't you give us another *London
Assurance?*" Boucicault long afterwards remembered that Wallack's "heart was
always aspiring to better things, while I was groveling after the lucre."

An even greater success, of very much the same kind, followed quickly.
During the autumn of 1857, the civilized world had been horrified by the Sepoy
Rebellion in India. The apparently hopeless defense of the besieged city of
Lucknow by a small garrison of British troops was still fresh in the public mind,
and everyone remembered Jessie Brown, the young Scottish girl who had pre-
vented the garrison from surrendering by declaring that the pibroch of a
Scottish regiment coming to their relief was ringing in her ears. Lucknow was
relieved on September 25, 1857. On February 22, 1858, Boucicault brought
the story to the stage of Wallack's in his three-act drama, *Jessie Brown, or, The
Relief of Lucknow,* with Miss Robertson, herself a Scottish girl, in the title role.
So detested was Nana Sahib, the Sepoy leader, that no member of Wallack's
company would play the role, and Boucicault audaciously braved the hostility
of the gallery gods by playing the "demon of Cawnpore." The play ran for six
weeks and was constantly revived throughout the country. Writing about it
many years later, Lawrence Barrett asserted that "the situation, the dialogue
and the superb acting at once changed the indifferent spectator into an eager
and enthusiastic listener." The production of *Jessie Brown* at Wallack's, he
declared, "marks the line which separates the theater of the past from that of
the present in America."

Boucicault presently embarked on management with William Stuart, who
ceased to be associated with Wallack's Theater when the elder Wallack resumed
its management. Like Boucicault, Stuart was a native of Ireland; his real name
was Edmund O'Flaherty. He had made "an unfortunate error" in London
which caused him to emigrate to the United States, where he adopted a new

name. He drifted into the theater by way of journalism. (Long afterwards he was identified as the author of the venomous attacks on Forrest that sent the star into retirement.) Stuart was an adventurer who, willing to live by the theater, despised it and held all actors in contempt. The ill-suited partners took the former Metropolitan Theater, which William Burton had relinquished after two unsuccessful seasons, and renamed it the Winter Garden. The company which they assembled included Miss Robertson, the comedian Joseph Jefferson, A. H. Davenport and Mrs. John Wood. Mrs. Wood, a dazzling beauty and spirited comedienne, håd come with her husband from London and, two years earlier, had captivated male playgoers in a musical burlesque of *Hiawatha*. She toured the country with success and played a long engagement in San Francisco, where at every performance Judge John S. Hager, from a stage box, dropped a white japonica flower at her feet which, in the next scene, she wore in her hair. This gallant episode never failed to delight the audience, but presumably it encouraged Mrs. Wood to bring suit for divorce against her husband. The suit was tried in Judge Hager's court. To the profound surprise of the San Francisco public, he gave a verdict for Mrs. Wood's husband. The japonica flowers no longer fell at her feet, and Mrs. Wood returned to New York, where gallantry was less likely to be blemished by the fear of its consequences.

For the Winter Garden company, Boucicault dramatized Dickens' *The Cricket on the Hearth* as *Dot,* casting Miss Robertson in the title role, Mrs. Wood as Tilly Slowboy, and Jefferson as Caleb Plummer, a role which he retained in his repertory to the end of his career, and in which he made his final appearance on the stage in 1904. Having established his reputation as a comedian, Jefferson was dubious about a role requiring pathos. At the dress rehearsal he disappointed Boucicault, who gave him a lesson in acting which he never forgot. "You have acted your last scene first," the playwright told him; "if you begin in that solemn strain you have nothing left for the end of the play." For the performance that evening, Jefferson entirely revised his playing; the piece was an enormous success. A flare-up—perhaps inevitable with two such radiant stage beauties—occurred between Miss Robertson and Mrs. Wood, who left the company. In this emergency, Boucicault quickly dramatized *Nicholas Nickleby* under the title of *Smike*. With Miss Robertson in the title role, Jefferson as Newman Noggs and Boucicault as Mantalini, this also was an immediate success.

Meanwhile, the long struggle over slavery touched a climax in the raid made by John Brown on Harper's Ferry, and tension between North and South became acute when he was sentenced to death. Brown's execution took place on December 2, 1859, and three days later Boucicault produced the most daring of his original plays. He could not have chosen a more inflammatory theme than slavery, which dominated *The Octoroon, or, Life in Louisiana*. The play dealt with the love of a ruined planter for the illegitimate daughter of his uncle, a slave by virtue of her strain of Negro blood, revealed by the plot, which eventually brought her, with the other slaves, to the auction block. Boucicault embroidered his plot with novel stagecraft. A murder by the villain was photographed by a self-acting camera, thus trapping him. A Mississippi steamer was

Edward A. Sothern as Lord Dundreary in "Our American Cousin"

destroyed by fire in view of the audience. But the enduring appeal of *The Octoroon* derived from its characters, and from the plight in which many of them were placed by the institution of slavery. Jefferson, a member of the cast, recorded that audiences were deeply affected, and that Southerners and Northerners alike approved it. "The dialogue and characters of the play made one feel for the South," he explained, "but the action proclaimed against slavery and called loudly for its abolition." This effect, deliberately contrived by Boucicault, assured the success of a dangerous controversial drama, and also accounted for the frequency of its revivals during a period of more than forty years. But within a week of its first performance, a quarrel occurred between Boucicault and Stuart. With Miss Robertson, Boucicault unceremoniously left the Winter Garden and joined Miss Laura Keene at her theater, across Broadway near Houston Street.

After many difficulties, Miss Keene had established her playhouse in public esteem. During the previous season she had scored, almost by accident, the longest run thus far achieved by any first-class New York theater. Her company then included Jefferson, C. W. Couldock and E. A. Sothern, among a fine galaxy of players. A comedy by the British dramatist, Tom Taylor, *Our American Cousin,* was offered to her because it provided an excellent role for Jefferson, and good ones for herself and Couldock. She was not impressed by the play and laid it aside. In the circumstances, it appeared that nothing could be done. Miss Keene was high-tempered, imperious; she "looked like an angel, but was, in fact, a martinet"; the company privately called her "the Duchess." Taylor's manuscript was read by John Lutz who, though he knew little about the stage, discovered the play's effectiveness. Jefferson also read it, saw great opportunities for himself in the role of Asa Trenchard, and "was quite selfish enough to recommend the play for production." Lutz and Jefferson convinced Miss Keene. When the play was read to the company, few were pleased. Miss Keene as Florence Trenchard, Couldock as Abel Murcott, and Jefferson as Asa Trenchard, had the only good parts. Sothern, especially, was incensed by being cast as Lord Dundreary, "a fourth-rate old man" having only forty-seven lines. He refused to take the role unless he was permitted to rewrite and amplify it. Miss Keene objected, but was compelled to consent. "In rewriting the part," Sothern recalled later, "I threw into it everything that struck me as wildly absurd." One cold morning at rehearsal, he began hopping about at the back of the stage. Miss Keene sarcastically inquired whether he intended to incorporate that bit of business in his performance. The actors and actresses laughed; nettled, Sothern replied, "Yes, Miss Keene, that's my view of the character." Having said it, he felt bound to stick to it; this was the origin of a famous element of characterization. Sothern did not foresee that the role of the "silly ass" would carry him to stardom and fortune. He detested it, and was striving only to "guy" it. But as rehearsals proceeded, he found that the company, scene shifters and property men were "roaring with laughter at my infernal nonsense." After the play opened, he continued to add antics to his performance, to the delight of audiences. Before long, his outstanding talent as an eccentric comedian made Dundreary the central feature of *Our American Cousin,* which ran for more than five months. But at the end of the season, "the Duchess" lost the services of Sothern, Jefferson and Couldock.

The absence of these popular actors, and the lack of a play as promising as *Our American Cousin* made the acquisition of Boucicault peculiarly valuable to Miss Keene. Early in January, 1860, he provided her with a success by dramatizing Scott's novel *The Heart of Midlothian.* But he followed this with a failure, which had to be hastily withdrawn. Faced with the loss of all her profits from the season, Miss Keene pleaded with Boucicault to provide a replacement. He had already written six plays in six months; he declared that he had dried up. According to the story which he told later he went to a bookstore, picked up a dozen novels at random and went home to spend the night searching them for a potential play. One of the novels was *The Collegians,* by the Irish writer Gerald Griffin, founded on a sensational murder. Next morning, he wrote to Miss Keene: "I have it! I send you seven steel engravings of scenes around Killarney. Get your scene-painter to work on them at once. I also send a book of Irish melodies, with those marked I desire Baker to score for the orchestra. I shall read act one of my new Irish play on Friday; we rehearse that while I am writing the second, which will be ready on Monday; and we rehearse the second while I am doing the third. We can get the play out within a fortnight." But the play, according to the program, was "written in five days," and it was produced exactly five days after the withdrawal of the failure. The record suggests necromancy beyond even Boucicault's capacity. The fact was that he had already written two acts of the play, which had been commissioned by the Irish comedian Barney Williams for the use of himself and his wife the following season.

Boucicault's *The Colleen Bawn,* the first of the series of romantic Irish dramas on which his fame was to rest most securely, made an immediate success. It dealt, not with the stereotyped stage Irishmen of popular farces, but with the life of gentlefolk and villagers as Boucicault knew them. Romantic in theme, it was realistic in its portrayal of character. Boucicault provided magnificent acting roles for Miss Robertson as the pathetic heroine, Eily; for Miss Keene as the lovable gentlewoman, Anne Chute; for himself as the loyal, heroic, but hopeless lover, Myles na-Coppaleen. But was the major attraction the stars who played it, or the play itself? During a long and prosperous run, Boucicault pondered this question. He had already decided to take the play to London at the end of the season, and produce it there with Miss Robertson and himself in their original roles. But before his departure he reached a decision that was to have profound consequences for the American stage. A decade earlier, there had been less than six thousand miles of railroad in the United States. Now, there were more than thirty thousand miles, and continuous railroad lines stretched from New York west of the Mississippi. In these circumstances, Boucicault surmised that a touring company, appearing in a play that had been overwhelmingly successful in New York, would draw larger audiences in inland cities than traveling stars supported by local stock companies in standard repertory. He therefore assembled, for *The Colleen Bawn,* the first "road company" to take a play on tour. Among its members was Sarah Kirby Stark, who had appeared unsuccessfully in New York with her husband, and afterwards had reappeared as Mrs. J. Hudson Kirby; John Drew, husband of the former Louisa Lane Hunt; Mrs. John Sloan and her husband. Boucicault offered *The Colleen Bawn* to managers, with its own company, as a star attraction. At first there was resistance to the project, but the scheme was tried and proved to be financially successful. From London, Boucicault made similar arrangements for his subsequent plays. In time, the innovation led to the abandonment of local stock companies except in such cities as New York, Boston, Philadelphia and San Francisco.

In the tragic drama, there also appeared the exponent of a new, eloquent realism. Edwin Booth came to New York as a star in 1857, after a tour of the South and an engagement in Boston that had won him laudatory notices from the critics. An overzealous agent, to his extreme mortification, advertised him in the press as "the hope of the living drama." "The height of my expectation," he noted later, "was to become a leading actor in a New York theater after my starring tour—which I supposed would last a season or two." Conditions were propitious for him. The retirement of Forrest left, as the most accomplished Shakespearian actors, Edward L. Davenport, a polished, versatile artist, and James W. Wallack, Jr., nephew of the elder Wallack. But Davenport and Wallack were already middle-aged; they exemplified the traditional school of acting. Booth was twenty-four, and although he professed respect for the acting tradition represented by his father and Edmund Kean, he was by temperament a daring innovator. He was already developing his own style, eventually to be made distinctive by imaginative power and seemingly spontaneous passion. Unlike Forrest, he refused merely to stand and declaim his great speeches. This

Scene from "Colleen Bawn" by Dion Boucicault

was the established method, and he discarded it. He dramatized every line of his roles, in intonation, gesture and posture; he introduced, as Lawrence Barrett, who was in his support, observed, "a rapidly moving, nervous embodiment of all the passions." During his first New York starring engagement Booth appeared as Richard III, Shylock, Lear, Romeo, Iago, Hamlet; as Richelieu, Claude Melnotte, Sir Giles Overreach, Sir Edward Mortimer, and in several other roles associated with his father. His "rich, sonorous voice of unusual compass and flexibility"; his "fine personal endowments"; his capacity for "great power and grandeur"—all these won critical eulogy. But especially notable in his acting was "a vigorous truthfulness which startles his audience into wild enthusiasm, and brings down a perfect storm of applause."

Booth's triumphs in Boston and New York were the turning point in his career. As a traveling star he toured widely, but he played frequent engagements in New York, where the critics, acknowledging that he possessed "the true fire of genius," usually bestowed lavish praise. But not invariably. There were inferior performances, and for these he was severely rebuked. Like his father, Booth was always to be an uneven actor, even in his greatest roles. His mood continually varied. He could not at will command his inspiration; when it was absent, his performance was likely to seem, in his youth, stagy, and in his later years, cold. Then, too, there was a personal infirmity of which he was to say, afterwards, "I had not yet got the control of my devil." It was his father's devil—an intermittent craving for drink. He had learned to resist it, but had not yet conquered it. However, he was perfecting the style of acting that he

Edwin Booth as Iago

had conceived. His following constantly increased and the younger generation, particularly, acclaimed him. It was probably Booth's growing fame that caused Edwin Forrest to announce, through his friend James Rees, his intention of returning to the stage because "thousands are so sickened, and in some instances disgusted, at the present state of the drama and the paucity of genuine talent in our midst." Booth was Forrest's namesake, but Forrest detested him because, in San Francisco, Booth had been associated with the former Mrs. Forrest, Catherine Sinclair. In July, 1860, Edwin Booth was married in New York to Miss Mary Devlin, a pretty actress who, on one occasion, had played Juliet to the Romeo of Charlotte Cushman. One of the witnesses was the groom's younger brother, John Wilkes Booth.

In the autumn of 1860, Forrest made his promised return in an engagement at Niblo's Garden that lasted for six months, during which he acted three nights weekly, appearing in all his most celebrated roles. Though nearing sixty, his vigor seemed unimpaired and his voice retained its resonance and power. That portion of the public which had always admired him declared that he was acting better than ever before. Vanity must have driven him to draw on his resources to their utmost limit, for he was seriously challenged. Miss Cushman, whom he hated as his enemy, returned from an absence of three years in Europe and played against him at the Winter Garden. She, too, appeared in her familiar repertory for two months during which, in performances of *Henry VIII,* she alternated in the roles of Queen Katharine and Cardinal Wolsey, muffling her Cardinal with a full beard. At forty-four, matronly in figure, she also offered a Romeo no longer youthful in what an eminent singer described as "a fine *baritone* contralto voice." Still more difficult for Forrest was the challenge of Edwin Booth who, in three engagements at the Winter Garden, contested with him as Hamlet, Shylock, Macbeth, Othello, Richard III and—with even greater daring—Richelieu, a role which Forrest had made peculiarly his own, but in which his young rival already excelled him. It could not have pleased him that Booth and Miss Cushman played a joint-starring engagement in Philadelphia, appearing in *Macbeth, Henry VIII* and other Shakespearian plays. New York saw their *Macbeth,* during Forrest's long engagement, when they gave a single performance at the Academy of Music for the benefit of the American Dramatic Fund. But it might have consoled the veteran to hear Miss Cushman's comment on Booth's conception of the role: "Your performance is exceedingly interesting, but Macbeth was the great-grandfather of all the Bowery ruffians." She adhered to the old style of acting, rejecting all subtle interpretations, imparting the obvious meaning always, and she thought Booth's Macbeth insufficiently simple and massive.

The outbreak of the Civil War, temporarily disrupting the revived prosperity of the theater, sent Booth to Great Britain on a professional tour. He met with scant success in either London, Liverpool, or Manchester (where a young actor named Henry Irving was a member of the stock company that supported him). Abandoning the venture, he made a visit to Paris, studied the theater there, and returned to the United States. The contest with Forrest was immediately resumed. Forrest added to his support John McCullough, a handsome, physically powerful young actor who eventually was to perpetuate his style. McCullough had come to the United States from Ireland as a poor farmer's boy who had been taught to read, but had never learned to write. He managed to acquire the rudiments of an education and, after four years of playing minor roles in stock companies, attracted Forrest's attention by a remarkable feat of quick study.

Booth added to his support Lawrence Barrett, his junior by five years. Barrett, a native of Paterson, New Jersey, had suffered the same early disadvantages as McCullough. He had gone on the stage at the age of fifteen, and at twenty was playing juvenile leads at the Boston Museum. Studious by temperament and scholarly in his tastes, Barrett was to become known as the most intellectual actor on the American stage. In February, 1863, unnerved and obsessed by a presentiment of disaster, Booth was playing an engagement at the Winter Garden in New York. He had been on a long tour, and his wife and small daughter were at their home near Boston. Mrs. Booth's health had been failing, but she prevented her husband from learning the truth. Working under great anxiety, Booth succumbed to his devil. He was finally summoned by telegraph to his home, but his wife died before his arrival. He seldom thereafter touched liquor, even as a medicine. Shortly after his wife's death he wrote to the clergyman who had married them: "The beauty of my art is gone—it is hateful to me—it has become a trade."

But Booth could not endure the long retirement that he had planned. In the autumn of 1863 he returned to the stage as an actor and also, for the first time, embarked on management. With his brother-in-law, the comedian John Sleeper Clarke, he bought the Walnut Street Theater in Philadelphia, and in partnership with Clarke and William Stuart leased the Winter Garden in New York. As in past seasons, Booth and Forrest played simultaneous engagements in New York. The tide of critical and popular favor abruptly began to run against the veteran. One reviewer quoted an English critic to the effect that Forrest was "the best melodramatic actor and the worst tragedian in the world." Even in an elaborately designed revival of *Coriolanus* he did not excite the enthusiasm of earlier years, although this, Lear and Othello were his greatest Shakespearian roles. His most successful roles, now, were Metamora, Damon, Spartacus and Virginius, and most of these had become odious to him. But Booth was rising to ascendancy. In the spring of 1864, at Niblo's Garden, he undertook a new role that displayed the full intensity of his dramatic power, causing the critic of the *Herald* to acclaim him as "the greatest actor of his time." The play was Tom Taylor's *The Fool's Revenge*, an adaptation of Victor Hugo's *Le Roi S'amuse,* and in it Booth enacted the deformed jester, Bertuccio, who, in procuring his revenge on the libertine who had despoiled him of his wife, unwittingly assists in the abduction of his beloved daughter. Booth's sardonic humor, his fiendish vindictiveness, and his scene of pitiable agony as he danced before the courtiers, scoffing at him while his daughter was supposedly being ravished in the adjoining chamber, his frantic grief and terror breaking through at last— these ranked his performance among the most effective ever achieved by an actor.

Embittered by his declining fame, Forrest obstinately persisted in remaining before the public; he was more eager than ever for applause. In 1865, while playing the role of Damon at the Holliday Street Theater in Baltimore, he suffered a spasm of excruciating pain. He forced himself to continue to the end of the play. Then physicians told him, to his horror, that the right side of his body was partially paralyzed. From that day, his sturdy gait and proud tread were gone forever. He could no longer brandish a sword, his stride was hampered by a perceptible hobble and jerk. Early the following season he set out on a tour of the Middle West and, for the first time in eighteen years, played in Chicago, at Crosby's Opera House. "The applause I have received here has been as enthusiastic as I have ever known," he wrote to James Oakes. "Give me joy, my dear and steadfast friend, that the veteran does *not* lag superfluous on the stage." But he had already endured the mortification of meager audiences in the East, and he determined to go, at last, to California, taking John McCullough with him as his support. An engagement of one hundred nights was arranged with Tom Maguire at his Opera House in San Francisco. Seats for Forrest's opening night were sold at auction; one was bought for $500. On May 14, 1866, he appeared in *Richelieu,* and when he came on the stage the audience rose and cheered him. But before the performance had ended, the audience was aware of Forrest's diminished powers, and from the outset critical comment was not only adverse, but often scathing. Receipts at the box office dwindled, and after thirty-five performances he acknowledged defeat and abandoned his engagement. When Forrest returned East, McCullough remained in San Francisco with Tom Maguire.

After forty years of fame, Forrest resumed the life of a strolling player, at the head of inferior companies, venturing only into the smaller cities and towns. The younger generation, who had never seen him, compared the broken actor with his herculean legend and were derisive. In many places where he played, his name was scarcely even known, and the box office told a humiliating story of his failure to attract. The hardships of travel wore him down. One night, shivering in the wings of a small-town "opera house," he complained, "I am worth three hundred thousand pounds sterling, and I can't purchase five cents worth of heat for my body!" As his tread became more and more feeble, he tried to disguise his infirmity by artifice. Whenever he played *Damon and Pythias,* he worried about the last scene, with its climactic leap to the scaffold; before permitting the curtain to rise, he inspected the platform and tried the jump. The elevation of the platform, which once had been three feet, was gradually diminished. One night, Forrest found that he could not take the leap until the height of the platform had been cut down to three inches. Asked whether this was satisfactory, he nodded sadly and turned away to hide his tears. After a performance of *King Lear* in St. Louis, he had supper with an old friend who, thinking to cheer him, said, "Mr. Forrest, I never before saw you play Lear as well as you did tonight." The tragedian laboriously rose from his chair and drew himself to his full height. *"Play* Lear? What do you mean, sir? I *play* Hamlet, Richard, Shylock, Virginius, if you please. But, by God, sir, I *am* Lear!"

The reply was neither arrogant nor fanciful. Better than anyone, Forrest knew that his spirit had been broken, that he was deserted and forgotten, and that his crown was only a mockery.

Clearly, the old order was passing. Burton had been the first to recognize it. After two unsuccessful seasons at his new theater uptown, the former Metropolitan, he disbanded his company, retired from management, and took up the career of a touring star. Less than two years later he fell ill while traveling, returned to New York, and died. Burton's theatrical wardrobe was purchased by the Irish comedian William J. Florence, and nobody was shocked when, soon after Burton's funeral, Florence appeared in the old master's celebrated roles of Toodle and Captain Cuttle, wearing his costumes. The elder Wallack, however, seemed to have defeated time and change. He had achieved his ambition of making Wallack's Theater the premier playhouse of the country, to which cultivated people from other cities went whenever they were in New York, seldom asking what play was being given, for it was the company and not the play that attracted them. Every season, James Wallack insisted on producing magnificent revivals of classic comedies. He still considered these the proper central feature of the theater's repertory; its reason for existence, and the foundation of its pre-eminence. But gradually the management of the theater slipped from his hands into those of Lester Wallack. Keenly responsive to changing taste, Lester introduced more and more contemporary plays; adaptations from the French, like Octave Feuillet's *The Romance of a Poor Young Man,* or current London successes, like Tom Taylor's *The Overland Route,* or pieces specially written for the company, like his own melodrama, *The Veteran,* and local comedy, *Central Park.* In 1859, forty-one years after his American debut at the Park Theater, the elder Wallack played a long engagement in his favorite roles. At sixty-four, he was still capable of enchanting audiences in such youthful parts as Benedick and Don Caesar de Bazan. The following year, Lester Wallack completed negotiations for the building of a new, elegant Wallack's Theater on the northeast corner of Broadway and Thirteenth Street, just below Union Square. The theater was opened in the autumn of 1861, and the elder Wallack addressed the audience from the stage. It was his last public appearance. On Christmas Day, 1864, he died at his home. The newspapers were full of eulogy, and a sense of mourning, a feeling of civic loss, pervaded New York.

Like Lester Wallack, Miss Laura Keene tried to gauge the change in public taste. When her husband, John Taylor, died in 1860, she was married to John Lutz. Possibly he took a more active hand in forming the policy of her theater. Although, as an actress, her forte was classic comedy, she abandoned her attempt to compete with Wallack's in that department of the drama. Gradually, she gave up the repertory principle entirely. Her effort centered on finding pieces that promised long and profitable runs, and she turned more and more to melodrama and extravaganza. One of these musical spectacles, *The Seven Sisters,* achieved the phenomenal run of two hundred and fifty-three consecutive performances, and became so celebrated throughout the country that its name was adopted by New York's costliest, most luxurious brothel. But al-

Adah Isaacs Menken as Mazeppa

though productions of this type were financially remunerative, they cost her theater a heavy loss in prestige. Perhaps this made her unhappy. Perhaps she could not reconcile herself to the waste of her talent and her narrowing opportunity. In the spring of 1863, she appeared once again in three of her finest roles: Peg Woffington in *Masks and Faces*, Lady Alice Hawthorne in *Old Heads and Young Hearts*, Miss Hardcastle in *She Stoops to Conquer*. Soon afterwards she surrendered her theater, disbanded her company and joined the ranks of touring stars.

The touring stars made money, especially "emotional" actresses who were fortunate enough to find an appropriately tear-provoking vehicle. Miss Heron played *Camille* up and down the country and was said to have profited by more than $100,000. Miss Lucille Western, whose acting seldom pleased the critics, paid Clifton W. Tayleure, an actor, manager and occasional playwright, $100 to dramatize Mrs. Henry Woods's popular novel *East Lynne,* and in a single season performed that long-lived tale of woe more than nine hundred times. Miss Kate Bateman, formerly celebrated as a child prodigy but now a handsome young woman, scored an enormous success in *Leah, the Forsaken,* adapted from the German by young Augustin Daly, then dramatic critic for the *Sunday Courier,* but soon to begin his brilliant career as a manager. Cultivated New Yorkers failed to notice the first appearance of Adah Isaacs Menken in the role that was to carry her to European, as well as American, celebrity. She was already notorious, a figure of mystery perpetually involved in lurid scandals, a *femme fatale*. New Yorkers first heard of her as a member of the dubious "bohemian" group that congregated about Walt Whitman in Pfaff's cellar restaurant on Broadway, near Bleeker Street. She wrote an essay in defense of his *Leaves of Grass,* promptly appropriated his form of free verse, and published poems that were far too fleshly to please the well bred. At the

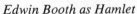
Edwin Booth as Hamlet

New Bowery Theater, in the spring of 1862, she appeared as the Prince of Tartary in *Mazeppa,* an old romantic melodrama, during the course of which, clad in flesh-colored tights and bound to the back of a white horse, she rode up a series of perilous inclined planes to the flies above the stage. Her beautiful unclothed body, her exquisite face, her lovely auburn-gold hair made this sensational "ride of death" a thrilling spectacle. "The Menken" took her beauty and her steed on a prolonged tour of the country. In San Francisco, where she played two engagements, she became the toast of the city. Eventually she reached Virginia City in Nevada, the wild boom town of the Comstock Lode, where Tom Maguire had built an ornate Opera House. There, to the delight of the miners, she not only played *Mazeppa* but, with equal skill and success, the game of faro, and after her performances joined them in a saloon where she sat out the night happily smoking cigarettes and gambling.

During the commemoration of Shakespeare's tercentenary, eminent New Yorkers established a fund to erect a statue of the poet in Central Park. For the benefit of this fund, on November 25, 1864, Edwin Booth arranged a performance of *Julius Caesar* at the Winter Garden, in which he played the role of Brutus, Junius Brutus Booth, Jr., that of Cassius, and John Wilkes Booth that of Mark Antony. The three brothers had never before acted together and, since it was known that the play would not be given again, the Winter Garden was sold out at increased prices, $5 being charged for orchestra seats. From the first entrance of the brothers side by side, the performance was enthusiastically received and it ended with an ovation. On the following night, Edwin Booth began a revival of *Hamlet.* Three months had been given to preparing the production, with which Booth planned to inaugurate a new policy. He intended, in the future, to treat his Shakespearian productions as dramatic pageants, investing them with a pictorial beauty that had not previously been attempted on the American stage. He had restudied the role of Hamlet, and had considerably altered his interpretation of it. He presented Hamlet, now, as a forlorn, desolate dreamer. Hamlet was tender to Ophelia, but sadly aware that his former love for her had been wasted, and convinced that love could find no security or real fulfillment. Hamlet was not mad, but sane; distracted and irresolute, yet capable of feigning madness as a shield for his sensibility and his purposes. Booth gave greater emphasis to the poetic, contemplative dreamer than to the anguished sufferer. His new Hamlet was immediately hailed as "one of the noblest pieces of dramatic art ever seen in any land or any age," and it was generally acknowledged that, for intellectual clarity and emotional power, he had no living equal in the role. The revival drew capacity audiences. "I was heartily sick and wearied of the monotonous work," he wrote, nine years later, "and several times during it suggested a change of bill, for I felt that the incessant repetition was seriously affecting my acting, as at that time I was unused to such a thing." But his partner, Stuart, was implacable and insisted that Booth "keep it up, if it goes a year." *Hamlet* ran for an unprecedented consecutive one hundred performances. It was announced that on the last night of the engagement, a committee of prominent New Yorkers would present Booth with a gold medal. (The medal was not delivered in time; its presentation was deferred.) At the age of thirty-one, he took rank as the foremost artist on the American stage. After the New York run, he began an engagement in *Hamlet* at the Boston Theater.

On the night of April 14, 1865, five days after General Lee's surrender to General Grant, President Lincoln attended a performance at Ford's Theater in Washington. The play was *Our American Cousin;* the star Miss Laura Keene. The presidential party included Mrs. Lincoln, Miss Clara Harris and Major H. R. Rathbone, the engaged daughter and stepson of Senator Ira Harris of New York. The party arrived late; the play was already in progress. Miss Keene was standing in the wing opposite the President's box, waiting to make an entrance on the stage, when John Wilkes Booth shot Mr. Lincoln, stabbed Major Rathbone, and leaped to the stage. In making his escape, he brushed past Miss Keene. On the following day, the New York *Herald* published an account of the event, purportedly founded on a statement by the actress. She had gone to the front of the stage and asked the panic-stricken audience to keep their places. Then, from the box, Miss Harris had called to her to bring some water, and she had done so, making her way "which was rather circuitous," to the box. There she remained until the President was removed from the theater. In the aftermath, Miss Keene's movements were much disputed. Some persons in the theater denied that she had gone to the President's box; members of the company, from the stage, saw her there. Seaton Monroe, a Washington lawyer who was walking on a nearby street, heard the report of the assassination and forced his way into the theater. Thirty-one years later, he published an account in the *North American Review.* He had met Miss Keene as she came down the staircase from the presidential box: "her hair and dress were in disorder, and not only was her gown soaked in Lincoln's blood, but her hands, and even her cheeks, where her fingers had strayed, were bedaubed with the gory stains."

At about the same time Mrs. Louisa Eldridge, an old actress affectionately known to the profession as "Aunt Louisa," corroborated this story. She had been a member of the stock company at Wood's Museum in Cincinnati, where Miss Keene went to play directly afterwards. Miss Keene told her that she had held the martyred President's head in her lap, and had given Mrs. Eldridge a piece of her blood-stained costume. (Historians have since established that any blood on Miss Keene's costume was not that of President Lincoln, but of Major Rathbone, who was bleeding profusely from his wounded hand.) Whether or not Miss Keene ministered to the dying President, whether or not she was present in the box, the story of her errand of mercy became a dramatic legend in the annals of the American stage.

The news of the assassination reached Edwin Booth in Boston. His engagement was immediately canceled by Henry C. Jarrett, manager of the Boston Theater. "While mourning, in common with other loyal hearts, the death of the President, I am oppressed by a private woe not to be expressed in words," Booth wrote in reply. "But whatever calamity may befall me and mine, my country, one and indivisible, has my warmest devotion." In the prevalent excitement, the whole Booth family fell under suspicion and popular resentment. Edwin Booth went into retirement in his New York home, declaring that he would never act again. In these difficult days his worst enemy was William Stuart, who "habitually spoke of Booth with ridicule and aspersion"; much disparagement of Booth that later drifted through the American press originated with him. The assassination left permanent traces on Booth's character, intensifying his predisposition to melancholia. Public sympathy gradually veered to him, and the pressure of financial obligations forced him to return to the stage. In January, 1866, he reappeared at the Winter Garden, in New York, as Hamlet. One newspaper attempted to incite hostility to him because of his brother's crime, but failed to do so. The public had determined to convince him of its esteem; the audience rose and cheered him as he came on the stage. Booth was so much affected that he could hardly control himself sufficiently to begin his performance, and William Winter, present as critic of the *Tribune,* stated that "he never acted better than he did on that memorable occasion."

But Booth was haunted and distressed by the memory of his brother John. Eventually, at his mother's insistence, he prevailed on President Andrew Johnson to turn over the body of the assassin to his family, for burial in an unmarked grave in the family plot in a Baltimore cemetery. Edwin Booth always avoided any mention of the assassination; and he seldom mentioned John Wilkes Booth's name. Years afterward, in enumerating the members of his father's family to a young actress in his company, he omitted John Wilkes Booth, and to one correspondent he even wrote, "I seldom saw him since his early boyhood in Baltimore"—which was somewhat less than truthful. In 1873, he recovered his brother's trunks and theatrical wardrobe. At three o'clock one morning, he and a young employee secretly burned them in the furnace of Booth's Theater. Never, after the assassination, would Booth consent to act in Washington. Residents of the capital who wished to see him play had to journey to Baltimore. His manager was instructed to refuse any floral tributes that were sent from Washington. On one occasion when plans had been made to honor him in this fashion, Booth "turned pale when he heard of it." Perhaps equally characteristic of his secret mourning for his brother was the fact that "to the last he kept a framed picture of him in his bedroom."

CHAPTER 9

The Palmy Days

AT THE END of the Civil War, Charles Kean and his wife were making a farewell tour of the United States. To the newly mature generation of play-goers, they were known only by name. They seemed to be legendary figures, emerging from a past already remote, far back in the half-forgotten world of "before the war." Charles Kean was a shriveled, sad, old man. His memory had begun to fail, and he was accompanied by two London actors who knew every line of all his roles; one of them was always present to prompt him at the first sign of hesitancy. Mrs. Kean—whom elderly folk remembered as the beautiful Ellen Tree—was a stout, stately old lady. A young stock actress who performed with the Keans in Cleveland was impressed by the grandeur of their acting in *Henry VIII*. On the stage, they could still rise to noble eloquence. Off it, they were quaintly funny, like "a pair of old, old lovebirds—a little dull of eye, nor quite perfect in the preening of their somewhat rumpled plumage, but billing and cooing with all the persistence and satisfaction of their first caging." The critics were kind, their reviews of the august stars blended eulogy with elegy. The Keans were the last surviving exemplars of the old school of English tragedy. During their final tour, the stage of the Kembles and Edmund Kean was briefly touching the stage of a swiftly changing America, and when the Keans departed ancient splendors would vanish forever.

But these splendors had only an antiquarian interest, for acting of the old

Poster for "Article 47"

school was being made obsolete by the methods of a new one. When he came out of retirement, Edwin Booth resumed his program of staging elaborate pictorial productions of the plays in his repertory. To his superb *Hamlet* he added equally beautiful productions of *Richelieu, The Merchant of Venice* and *Othello.* In spite of their magnificence, in spite of the fact that Booth had now perfected his acting style to a sustained, controlled naturalness, certain critics deplored the inferiority of his company. The complaint was justified; it always would be. Like his father, Booth disliked the drudgery of the theater. He was impatient of detail, exasperated by rehearsals and "annoyed by the ignorance and vanity of the lower order of actors, whom he commonly designated as 'dogans.' " His genius was for acting; he had little talent for management. The gold medal commemorating his hundred performances of *Hamlet* was presented to him at the Winter Garden in January, 1867. "You have won a position in your profession such as few men have attained," Judge William Fullerton assured Booth in an address. This was an understatement; Americans believed that, in his best roles, Booth had never had an equal. Two months later, he concluded his New York engagement. Early the following morning, the Winter Garden was destroyed by fire and with it Booth's wardrobe, as well as the scenery, costumes and properties of his four costly productions. Soon afterwards, it was announced that Booth intended to build his own playhouse in New York—"a theater of the highest order, to be devoted to plays and actors of the best kind."

The new school of acting was exemplified in comedy as well as tragedy. Joseph Jefferson returned to New York after a prolonged absence, during which he had visited California, then acted for four years in Australia, then gone to London. There, he persuaded Dion Boucicault to provide him with a new version of *Rip Van Winkle.* Against Jefferson's wishes, Boucicault insisted on beginning the play with an act showing Rip as a young, romantic scamp. Only if this were done, he declared, could the character be made sympathetic. If it were not done, audiences would see no more in Rip than a repellent old sot. Reluctantly, Jefferson yielded the point, which proved to be decisive. But when Boucicault finished the play he had no confidence in it, and on the night of the opening told Jefferson that it would surely fail. Instead, play and actor were extolled by the critics. In London, *Rip Van Winkle* ran for one hundred and seventy performances, and Jefferson scored a success with it in New York also. He invested the character with poetry, as well as humor and pathos; the young scamp who ended as an American King Lear attained the stature of a symbolic figure. Jefferson was neither learned nor scholarly, but from the day of David Garrick four generations of his family had been on the stage, and he inherited a massive technical knowledge of acting. This he was expert in applying. Every detail of his performance was governed by a design that he had worked out minutely. But he had mastered the art of concealing his art. His playing of *Rip Van Winkle* produced the illusion of spontaneity, of casual, even careless, fluency. In "costume" comedy, it established the standard of the new school of naturalness. Within a few years Jefferson's Rip became, like Booth's Hamlet, a national tradition.

To older playgoers, to many actors and actresses, the swift obsolescence of the "old school" was incomprehensible. Exceptionally, it did not diminish the immense prestige of Miss Cushman; nevertheless, it puzzled and affronted her. When she returned to make her home in the United States, at Newport, she had been stricken by cancer but her physicians had ordered her to continue acting. In her hours of leisure, she frequently went to the theater—a conspicuous figure, a tall, elderly, gray-haired woman wearing an old-fashioned gray silk gown and stout shoes. She liked neither the plays nor the acting that she saw. Shakespeare, she declared bitterly, was being perverted by actors to exploit their individual idiosyncrasies. If the methods of the new school, approved by the public, were correct, she and others of her generation must acknowledge that they had never been artists; they had merely wasted their lives. Of Edwin Booth, she remarked that he "had pampered the popular taste with jellies, instead of feeding it with strong meat." Forrest, going with Lawrence Barrett to see one of Booth's ornate productions, contemptuously dismissed it as "scene-painter's drama." The veteran Edward L. Davenport, asked by a friend what he thought of Booth's Hamlet, replied that Booth "is not a great actor; but his reading of the text is divine." In the role of Hamlet, Davenport himself had been Booth's most illustrious predecessor. He had tried to adapt himself to the new conditions, forming with James W. Wallack, Jr., the "Wallack-Davenport combination" which, with various leading ladies, toured the East and Middle West in a repertory of standard and modern plays. But as the years passed, he felt himself displaced and outmoded. In acting, he told one friend, "much has to be sacrificed to upholstery and furniture." And in an outburst of indignation to another friend, he expressed the bewilderment of his generation. "There are no actors any more. There are pantomimists, and walking gentlemen, and juveniles, and whatnots, but no *actors*. . . . No nine changes of bill a week; no mastery of a new part in forty-eight hours; no rehearsals every day; no bills to show a man's versatility. Why, I've played an act from *Hamlet,* one from *Black-Eyed Susan,* and sung 'A Yankee Ship and a Yankee Crew' and danced a hornpipe, and wound up with a 'nigger' part, all in one night. Is there any one you know of today who can do that?"

Stars even younger than Davenport found that, inexplicably, they had lost their appeal. After acting in California and the West for twelve years, Mrs. Julia Dean Hayne came back to the New York stage which she had left as a reigning favorite. Her unhappy marriage had ended in divorce. Her radiant beauty was fading. Some critics asserted that playing to audiences in mining camps had vulgarized and coarsened her art. Former admirers were surprised to find that her acting now seemed somewhat stilted and old-fashioned. The public did not patronize her performances. Disheartened by this unexpected failure, Mrs. Hayne ended her engagement and played no more in New York. In the years after the war Miss Matilda Heron, so lately a sensation, faced diminishing audiences. The novelty of her Camille wore off, and though she tried other roles none of them excited the public. In private life, also, misfortune overtook her. She had married Robert Stoepel, a musician; the marriage turned out badly. The fortune made from *Camille* gradually slipped away. She put her daughter, Bijou, on the stage as a child actress. Eventually she was reduced to dire poverty, and a benefit was given for her by the profession. A few years later her mind clouded. Forgotten by the public, prematurely old, she died at the age of forty-seven, murmuring at the end, "Tilly never harmed anybody. Poor Tilly is so happy."

Miss Laura Keene, too, failed when after many years of absence she returned to New York for a starring engagement. Her last performances, melancholy and played to almost empty houses, later seemed noteworthy because, in her company, there was a child actress named Minnie Maddern who would become famous as Mrs. Fiske. Of prewar stars, Miss Jean Davenport was the most successful in trying to meet the challenge of new times. Before the outbreak of war she had married Frederick Lander, a poet and explorer. He entered the Union army, rose to the rank of brigadier general, and died from the effects of wounds received in battle. Mrs. Lander immediately volunteered for hospital duty and was sent to the front as a nurse. When she returned to the stage after the war, she wisely discarded her old repertory and appeared in adaptations of foreign plays with roles that were suited to her age. The critic of the New York *Herald* rewarded this decision by declaring that Mrs. Lander "carries us back to those delightful days when it required brains, not brass, to be a star."

Certainly the new popular favorites were very unlike their immediate predecessors. The public was enchanted by Miss Maggie Mitchell, a sparkling comedienne. She toured widely and successfully every year in *Fanchon,* a piece skillfully tailored to her personality. She added few other plays to her reper-

Joseph Jefferson in "Rip Van Winkle," 1869

tory; it was obvious that audiences came not to see a play but to see Miss Mitchell. Lotta Crabtree earned a fortune by following the same policy. "Art, acting, actress? What are you thinking of?" John Brougham exploded, at one of Lotta's early performances. "She's no actress. She's—a little dramatic cocktail." An actor and playwright of the old school, Brougham dramatized Dickens' *The Old Curiosity Shop* for Lotta. In this piece, *Little Nell and the Marchioness,* the red-headed diminutive star delighted audiences throughout the country for more than twenty years. (In 1875, after one of several triumphant engagements in San Francisco, she presented the city with an ornate drinking fountain, erected at the intersection of Market and Kearny Streets, where it remains to testify to her former celebrity.) Lotta's banjo-playing and singing, her clog dances and jigs, her impudent deviltries and unflagging high spirits, could always be relied on to fill a theater. When required to take a "call," she would thrust her foot and ankle out beyond the curtain and wriggle them at the audience. Invariably, the applause doubled. An elderly actress, watching this bit of business, and hearing the audience respond, exclaimed perplexedly, "But—I don't understand!"

In the larger cities, people took to dining later. As a result, performances now began at eight o'clock or shortly after; the old custom of providing a farce as an "afterpiece" was discarded. But actors and actresses complained that they were being forced to work too hard, for Saturday matinées began to be scheduled. (An additional matinée on Wednesday eventually followed.) In many theaters the most overworked employee was the "basket boy." It was his job to call for and deliver at the lodgings of the cast the champagne baskets in which they packed their costumes; changing bills and numerous rehearsals kept him constantly on the move. Actresses of prominence, stars especially, tried to surround themselves with "an atmosphere of exclusiveness and mystery." Lotta seldom permitted the public to see her outside the theater; she lived practically in seclusion with her mother. Glamour was a star's most valuable asset, and some stars therefore took extreme precautions to avoid casual observation. Miss Lucille Western protected the legend of her opulent beauty. She never set foot in the public rooms of the hotels where she stayed when on tour. Her meals were always served in her suite, and when entering or leaving her hotel she wore a heavy, shoulder-length, black lace veil that concealed her features. Even in her suite she kept this veil at hand and, if anyone knocked at her door, invariably covered her face with it before answering the summons. But with the increasing use of colored lithographed posters for publicity, pictures of actresses were everywhere exposed to public view, sometimes to their disconcertment. Handsome Miss Rose Eytinge, when playing an engagement at Mrs. John Drew's Arch Street Theater in Philadelphia, was made indignant by finding her portrait displayed in the window of a low saloon. That evening in the theater, she stormed at her agent. Mrs. Drew came to her dressing room, looked at her quizzically and said, "My dear, don't be a fool. We will all be obliged to come to it, and God knows where we will next see ourselves pictured. But wherever it may be, we will have to submit."

In the rapidly changing theatrical scene, Wallack's Theater seemed im-

John Lester Wallack in "She Stoops to Conquer," 1884

mutable. As the New York *Times* asserted, it was "justly and properly regarded as the leading theater of America." First nights there drew the most distinguished audiences to be found in the city: the world of fashionable society, members of the best clubs, celebrities of the stage, beautiful *demi-mondaines,* all attended them as much to be seen as to see. Charming Mrs. John Hoey had retired from the company, bequeathing to younger actresses the legacy of a troublesome innovation. Enabled by her husband's wealth to spend extravagantly on her stage attire, she had set a standard of elegance and costliness in costumes which ambitious actresses felt compelled to approximate, in spite of the heavy inroads on their salaries. As a result, feminine fashions were soon being launched, not by "society," but by the stage. This gratified Lester Wallack, who was as proud of his theater's social tone as of its artistic primacy. Having a reverence for his profession, he was also proud of the tribute to it implied by his association, in private life, with New York's exclusive aristocracy.

Wallack was nearing his fiftieth year, and he did not take this easily. He had won his fame as a light comedian in roles of dashing young men and beaus; he could not endure the prospect of giving up the romantic line. He strove desperately, pathetically, to retain the look of youth. His increasing portliness could be partly disguised, on the stage. When his hair and walrus mustache began to turn gray, he had them dyed coal black. He tried to contend against the calendar, but his real enemy was the memory of the public. Young playgoers knew all about his early career from their grandparents, his contemporaries, and even the simulated appearance and spirit of youth could not prevail over their dire knowledge. For some years Wallack's vanity as an actor was in conflict with his intelligence as a manager. Then he could no longer ignore the obvious fact that his company needed a leading man younger than himself, and his vanity capitulated. Thereafter, he toured for a part of every year and, as a star, played occasional engagements at his own theater, most frequently in the old comedies. One role—that of Young Marlow in *She Stoops to Conquer*—he retained as his personal property, continuing to play it until his sixty-sixth year. It was the last role in which he appeared.

Productions of the old comedies were a staple of every season. But Lester Wallack also introduced to the American stage, with the comedies of the British playwright T. W. Robertson—*Society, Ours, School, Caste, Progress, Home*—a new form of drama; the quiet, "natural" play of contemporary life, usually enacted in an elegant drawing room. Drawing-room comedies proved to be enduringly popular with sophisticated audiences, and Robertson's plays initiated a trend in the drama. They also had an influence on acting, for they required, instead of the old stilted style of playing, an effect of extreme naturalness combined with high polish; their "points" had to be scored by understatement rather than emphasis. The new style dispensed with emotional intensity. Its primary requisites were grace, elegance, suavity of manner and an ability to handle romantic situations with an air that blended banter and sentiment. As they left Wallack's to join other companies, or to become stars, actors and actresses trained in the new style carried it to the entire American stage.

But Wallack's continued to be, as the elder Wallack had planned, virtually a London theater in the United States. Notwithstanding his long American residence, Lester Wallack was at heart an Englishman. (On one occasion when the relations between Great Britain and the United States were dangerously strained, he incurred severe censure for flying the British flag over his home.) It did not occur to him to produce plays by American playwrights; he felt that there were no playwrights whose work merited his consideration. Instinctively, he turned to the major London playhouses for new plays and leading players. (He sedulously cultivated his professional and social connections there and

Rose Coghlan in "The School for Scandal"

his wife, elder sister of the painter Sir John Millais, sometimes represented him on frequent visits.) Although the personnel of his company, over the years, was predominantly British, there were a few notable exceptions. John Gilbert, a pillar of the company for twenty-five years, was an American. Gilbert, who specialized in old men's roles, was a superb player of old comedy; critics afterwards said that he was the last representative of the classic tradition. Mme. Elizabeth Ponisi, who long took the dowager roles, was British by birth, but her entire career was identified with the American stage. Miss Eytinge, a member of the company for several seasons, and Miss Madeline Henriques, who succeeded Mrs. Hoey as its leading woman, were Americans. But when Miss Henriques retired, after her marriage to Louis J. Jennings, editor of the *Times,* Wallack chose London actresses as his leading women. Of these, the most distinguished was Miss Rose Coghlan. She was an Irish beauty, blonde, blue-eyed; her figure was exquisite, and her stage presence commanding. An actress of remarkable versatility, she played with equal brilliance Shakespearian roles, the heroines of classic comedy and those of the modern serious dramas and melodramas which, because of changing taste and vigorous competition by rival managers, Lester Wallack was eventually forced to make the mainstay of his theater. Miss Coghlan's Lady Teazle was considered peerless; her Rosalind was highly praised; and she was widely acclaimed for her Countess Zicka in *Diplomacy,* an adaptation of Victorien Sardou's *Dora.* For many years she was accounted one of the finest actresses on the American stage. Early in the twentieth century she toured in Bernard Shaw's *Mrs. Warren's Profession,* and before her retirement in 1920, at the age of seventy, achieved a final triumph as the elderly, wicked Duchesse de Surennes in Somerset Maugham's *Our Betters.*

Miss Coghlan's illustrious career, spanning nearly a half-century, indicated the enduring influence that "Wallack schooling" was to have on the American stage. This was also illustrated in the careers of his procession of leading men, all British, who fixed a general pattern of acting style that survived well into the twentieth century. The first, Charles Wyndham, had served as a surgeon in the Union army during the war. After an unsuccessful debut on the New York stage, he returned to London to gain acting experience. Following his engagement at Wallack's, he had a long career as an actor-manager in London, made frequent American starring tours, and was knighted in 1902. His successor, Harry J. Montague, became the first "matinée idol."

"He was charming in trouser and coat and 'cigarette parts,'" Wallack recorded, "and wore the dress of our day with the ease of a thorough gentleman; but put him in costume and he was gone, miserably conscious that he was awkward and out of place." From Wallack's standpoint, this was a lamentable deficiency. That the feminine audience did not agree was soon made obvious. Montague wore his thick brown hair parted at one side and brushed back from his forehead, with a lock brought forward to form a hook on each temple. Such was his effect on the feminine heart that ladies immediately began sporting what they called "Montague curls." Montague was followed by Charles Coghlan, Miss Coghlan's brother, whom Wallack's great rival, Augustin Daly, brought to the United States. Coghlan was a younger and more modern version of Wallack; an accomplished artist who, specializing in high comedy and romantic roles, also was capable in serious dramatic parts, as Wallack had been in his youth. On the stage, Coghlan was "a miracle of elegance, dress and distinction," and the critic J. Ranken Towse considered him "infinitely superior to any of the leading men of his era." He brought the Wallack company to its highest point of excellence, inciting the other members to equal his own restrained, urbane art. Wallack tried to perpetuate, through his leading men, the school of acting founded by his father and carried forward by himself. To a notable extent he succeeded. Long after his death, the Wallack tradition flourished on the American stage in the persons of Coghlan, Maurice Barrymore (whose children, Ethel, Lionel and John would achieve even greater fame than their father), Osmond Tearle and Kyrle Bellew.

In 1871, Wallack delighted his older patrons by engaging Charles Mathews as a temporary member of his company at a weekly salary of $500. Mathews, nearing seventy, took the role of Dazzle in *London Assurance,* which he had created thirty-one years earlier, and performed other roles equally celebrated. Few playgoers remembered his ill-fated first tour with Mme. Vestris. But many recalled his second tour, and the scandal of his marriage to Mrs. Lizzie Weston Davenport. She had been a dark-haired beauty. She was now a stout, raddled, blonde dowager who fussily tried to curb her husband's ebullient spirits. The following year, Wallack again pleased his older patrons by engaging E. A. Sothern to appear as a star in his famous role of Lord Dundreary. But the outstanding success of the theater was made by Dion Boucicault, who returned to the United States in 1872. Two years later, he put on at Wallack's the best of his Irish pieces, *The Shaugraun.* In this sentimental melodrama, Boucicault at the age of fifty-five took the role of Conn O'Kelly, a roistering scamp of eighteen, with impressive effectiveness. The play had a run of one hundred and forty-three performances, and during its first year in Wallack's repertory brought in receipts of more than $200,000. Often revived there, it was also sent on tour, and produced in Great Britain and the dominions, earning a fortune for Boucicault.

It was his last triumph. His later plays were failures. As a dramatist he was suddenly outmoded. He toured the country at the head of his own company, in his own plays. The results were poor. He felt, but failed to understand, the waning interest of the public. After playing in California, he embarked for Australia with a young leading woman, Miss Louise Thorndyke, to try his fortunes there. The world was incredulous when news came of his marriage to her. For thirty years Boucicault and Miss Agnes Robertson had been known as man and wife, professionally and socially. Three of their children were already on the stage, all of them using their father's name. To establish the legality of her marriage and the legitimacy of her children, Miss Robertson brought suits for divorce in London and New York. The scandal was immense when Boucicault published a letter denying their marriage. However, he did not defend Miss Robertson's suits. It was said that, had he ventured to testify in London, he would have been confronted by documents which he had signed as Miss Robertson's husband—one being a copy of *The Colleen Bawn* which the couple had presented to Queen Victoria, and which the incensed old monarch was willing to have offered as evidence in court. A divorce was eventually granted to Miss Robertson, after which Boucicault, in the United States, went through a second ceremony of marriage to Miss Thorndyke. But the American public did not forgive him.

Even before the production of *The Shaugraun* the supremacy of Wallack's Theater was being challenged. In February, 1869, Edwin Booth opened his ornate theater on the southeast corner of Twenty-third Street and Sixth Avenue. He had taken as his partner in this enterprise a Boston businessman, Richard A. Robertson, without experience in theatrical affairs. Their financial arrangements were notably disadvantageous to Booth. The theater was magnificent, and in its stage equipment far superior to any other, but it had cost one million dollars before its doors were opened, and Booth's career was already mortgaged to a tremendous debt. He had become engaged to Mary McVicker, stepdaughter of the Chicago manager, J. H. McVicker. A short, slender, dark-haired girl of twenty, she was obsessively determined to become a famous actress. At McVicker's Theater in Chicago she had played Ophelia to Booth's Hamlet and then had toured with him as his leading lady. (William Winter, who worshipped Booth, later asserted that "had she chosen to play Irish girls, in farces, she would have succeeded.") To launch Miss McVicker in New York, and to inaugurate his theater, Booth mounted a lavish production of *Romeo and Juliet* which exploited all the new, astonishing effects made possible by its many innovations in stage equipment. His choice of a play, however, was odd. Eleven years earlier he had thrilled Boston audiences when playing Romeo to the Juliet of Mary Devlin, but the effect, like the inspiration, was unique. Romeo had never been one of his best roles. He knew that it was now unsuitable in every way. (A few years later Edward Sothern said to Booth, "The worst performance ever seen was my Armand Duval." To which Booth gravely replied, "The *worst?* Did you ever see my Romeo?") But although some critics wrote

Ada Dyas and Henry J. Montague in "The Shaughraun," 1875

savage reviews of Miss McVicker's Juliet and his Romeo, the play ran for ten weeks and cleared $60,000.

Booth followed it with an elaborate revival of *Othello*. To give this the appeal of novelty, he relinquished his usual role of Iago and played the Moor to Miss McVicker's Desdemona. Booth's poetic, melancholy Othello did not accord with the traditional concept of the role. He was too slight and short to suggest an exceptional physical prowess. He was overintellectual for a character so definitely not a thinker. He was incapable of indicating the sensual element in Othello's love for Desdemona. And he played the murder of Desdemona not as a deed of frenzy, but as a solemn sacrifice, an act of inexorable, abstract justice. Nevertheless, his Othello received high praise. On the night of the forty-second performance the Moor murdered Desdemona for the last time. The deed, on this occasion, was ironically symbolic: Booth was killing Miss McVicker's hope of theatrical fame. They were to be married a week later, and he had insisted that she leave the stage forever. Whether this demand was prompted by his judgment as an artist or his preference as a husband made no difference. Her frustrated ambition was to contribute heavily to his oncoming misfortunes.

His hope of making his theater a national temple of dramatic art was quickly dampened. To meet the debt incurred by its erection, he had to raise money by touring. During his absence, the playhouse was occupied by other stars. Difficulties with his partner accumulated. Booth bought out Robertson, thereby increasing the burden of his debt. At the theater, Hackett played one of his last engagements as Falstaff. (He was sixty-nine. Long a widower, he had lately remarried and become the father of a son who also would take to the stage. An older son was a leading jurist, and a man of wealth.) Jefferson played a five months' engagement in *Rip Van Winkle*. Charlotte Cushman, unseen for ten years and ravaged by illness, played Queen Katharine, Lady Macbeth and Meg Merrilies. The old gods were departing. A few months earlier, in a shabby theater on Fourteenth Street, with a wretched company, Forrest played his last New York engagement to thin houses, appearing as Richelieu and Lear. He wrote to James Oakes that he hoped some member of the audience that had hailed him at the Bowery Theater forty-six years earlier might be present. "If so, how I should like to hear from his own lips if the promises of springtime have been entirely fulfilled by the fruits of the autumn of life!" But no such assurance was forthcoming. To Lawrence Barrett, in the audience, Forrest offered the "strange spectacle of a great light going out in flickers of its old brightness, giving forth only rare intermittent flashes."

Booth returned to his theater in periodic engagements; almost, like the others, a visiting star. He tried to work toward the achievement of his cherished plan. In addition to his usual repertory, he staged unprecedently sumptuous productions of *Hamlet, Richelieu* and *Much Ado About Nothing*, appearing for the first time in New York as Benedick. He offered a splendid restaging of *The Fool's Revenge*. He revived *Othello*, with Laurence Barrett as Iago. He made a spectacularly beautiful production of *Julius Caesar*, in which Barrett won a lasting reputation as Cassius, and in which Booth, during the long run,

Interior of Booth's Theater, showing stage set for *Romeo and Juliet.* From a water color by Charles Witham

appeared at different times as Brutus, Cassius and Mark Antony. He starred Barrett in a costly production of *A Winter's Tale,* and in a modern play. Each season, the receipts at the box office declined. In the spring of 1873, Booth turned over the management of the theater to his brother Junius. The debt on the building stood at $350,000. Booth was convinced that he could soon pay it with profits from tours; then he would make another attempt to carry out his project. That autumn a financial panic brought economic depression to the country. Booth's creditors clamored for their money. His theater passed into other hands, and he was plunged into bankruptcy. The noble dream had ended ignominiously. Booth knew that never again could he hope to create an art theater. Instead, he would have to accept the career of a touring star—which eventually was to bring him a large fortune, but little satisfaction as an artist. He already surmised that his wife was mentally unbalanced. Seven years later, when he was playing in London, she went mad. Three years after that—his wife had died, and he was touring in Germany—Booth learned that his splendid theater was to be demolished to make way for a department store. On the last night, a performance of *Romeo and Juliet* was given, with Mme. Helena Modjeska playing Juliet, Maurice Barrymore playing Romeo, and Mrs. Clara Fisher Maeder (fifty years earlier, the reigning Juliet of the Park Theater) emerging from retirement to play the Nurse.

It was not Booth's grandiose project but another, far more modest, which effectively rivaled Wallack's Theater. In 1869 Augustin Daly leased the pretty little Fifth Avenue Theater on Twenty-fourth Street west of Broadway and began a career that was to make him the leading manager in the United States. At thirty-one he was known as a dramatic critic, a skillful adapter of foreign plays, and the author of several successful melodramas. One of these, *Under the Gaslight,* had a sensational climax which showed an express train rushing toward the hero, bound hand and foot to the tracks. A tall, lean, brown-haired man, Daly was a prodigious worker, high-tempered, absolutely confident of his own judgment, aloof in his manner and arbitrary in his quick decisions. A strict disciplinarian and an unsparing taskmaster—at a dress rehearsal he thought nothing of repeating a long scene as many as seven times—the profession soon took to calling him "the autocrat of the stage." Yet his prestige with the profession was, almost from the outset, so great that only established stars would have declined an invitation to join his company.

Although Daly provided the American stage with a succession of stars whose careers began in his company and were founded on his training, he was inflexibly opposed to the star system and to the practice of featuring actors and actresses. More radically still, he rejected the traditional categories of "lines of business," which confined them to a particular specialty. "There is no line in this theater; you do everything," he informed all applicants, and he frequently required members of his company to take roles for which they thought themselves absolutely unfit. It was his practice, also, whenever a player enjoyed unusual personal success in a leading role, to assign that player a minor role in the next production. "I don't want individual successes in my theater," he explained to a journalist. "I want my company kept at a level. I put them all in a line, and then I watch, and if one head begins to bob up above the others, I give it a crack and send it down again." He wished to make his company a versatile, mobile force, individually adaptable to any roles he chose for them, and invariably performing as a perfect ensemble. To bring this about, he sometimes resorted to ruthless methods and unfair tactics. With the same object, he could bring to bear a prodigal generosity in gifts and attentions while also evading a merited, badly needed increase in salary. He kept himself informed about the doings and sayings of every member of his company, and would have regulated their thoughts if he could. Obsessed by his ambition, his single purpose, his theater took precedence over any person or any relationship. He fascinated the young actresses whose talents he developed. He was thoroughly aware of his ability to enchant them, and used it expertly. Occasionally he was aggrieved when, the enchantment having worn off, they left him. "In love, he was mutability personified," Miss Clara Morris noted; "in friendship, always exigent."

Two members of Daly's original company were to remain permanently associated with him, and both were to rank among the most noted players of their time. Mrs. Anne Hartley Gilbert, who had begun her career in London as a dancer when still a child, closed it seventy years later, in 1904, as "the grand old lady of the American stage." When Daly engaged her she had been in the United States twenty years, and had gained experience as an actress in western stock companies. Mrs. Gilbert had no equal in the roles of elderly women, and she could play the whole range of such parts in classic comedy and modern drama, assuming with equal facility the characters of aristocratic dowagers, domestic martinets, sentimental or pathetic mothers and eccentric, even demented, spinsters. James Lewis played opposite Mrs. Gilbert for nearly thirty years. A short, wiry man with a birdlike face, he was crotchety, sedate, often taciturn. He took a high view of the art of the character actor and would have bitterly reproached himself for revealing his own personality in any of his personations. But in this art he excelled, and all that audiences knew about him was his protean talent. He had the ability to identify himself with any kind of character, and to endow it with convincing individuality; and he used an uncanny skill in make-up to give every character distinctive physical attributes, always unlike his own.

Daly's first season indicated his policies and intentions. He offered revivals of Shakespeare and old comedies; both became permanent features of his repertory. He wanted to produce plays about American life by American writers. Olive Logan provided him with Surf, a light comedy laid at Long Branch, then a fashionable summer resort. Daly had a flair for anticipating changes in the public's tastes and interests. This was reflected in his production of two recent French problem plays—Meilhac and Halévy's Frou Frou and Sardou's Fernande—both daring in their treatment of sexual relations. He had determined to discover and develop American acting talent, and he introduced two young actresses who won immediate favor. Miss Agnes Ethel was a novice who had studied the role of Camille with Miss Heron. Daly gave her the role of Gilberte, the errant wife, in Frou Frou, and the success of the play, which ran for one hundred performances, lifted her to prominence. Miss Fanny Daven-

port, whom he first presented as Lady Gay Spanker in *London Assurance,* quickly became a favorite with the public. A daughter of E. L. Davenport, she had been familiar with the stage from childhood and, although only nineteen, had already acted with her father and had been a member of Mrs. John Drew's stock company in Philadelphia. She was tall, statuesque, auburn-haired; her radiant beauty evoked such widespread admiration that Napoleon Sarony, the leading theatrical photographer, was overwhelmed by the public's demand for his portraits of her. Miss Davenport made her initial reputation as a brilliant, vivacious comedienne, and for several years Daly exploited only this single facet of her talent. Probably neither he nor she divined her gift for the strongly dramatic roles that were to make her a famous star.

For his second season Daly engaged an actress who, in spite of his misjudgment of her, proved to be a spectacular discovery. In order to make her New York debut under his management, Miss Clara Morris accepted a weekly salary of $35, refusing an offer of $100 from Tom Maguire in San Francisco. (Miss Ethel was receiving $100; Miss Davenport, $75.) At their first interview, Miss Morris ruffled Daly's vanity. Her sense of humor was irrepressible. Not aware that he expected reverence from his company, she was guilty of mild levity. He took his revenge when she stated her preference for serious roles. "I never made a mistake in my life," he declared. "You couldn't speak a line of sentiment to save your soul." She tried to argue the point. Daly had never seen her act, but he refused to listen. "Your forte is comedy, pure and simple," he said. He meant the verdict to be final.

Miss Morris was twenty-four, and Daly was probably deceived by her brown-haired, wide-eyed, wistful prettiness. It masked an iron will and a formidable ambition. Her childhood had been spent in poverty with her mother who, deserting a bigamous marriage, had taken employment in the Middle West as a servant. At thirteen, Miss Morris obtained work as an extra in the stock company of John A. Ellsler in Cleveland. She had received no formal education, and she was given no systematic training in acting. She learned what she could from the performances of visiting stars. After some years of playing increasingly important roles, she was engaged as leading woman by Wood's Museum in Cincinnati. Success there determined her to try her fortunes in New York.

She reported to Daly's greenroom under considerable stress. Her money was running low, her clothes were shabby. She would not be paid during rehearsals, and she would have to provide her stage costumes. The ladies of the company— she marveled at their costly attire and jewels—ignored her presence. For his opening bill, Daly had dramatized Wilkie Collins' popular, powerful novel, *Man and Wife*. The heroine of this drama, Anne Sylvester, deserted by her husband, eventually saves another woman from him by proving the legality of her own marriage to the man whom she has come to despise. When Daly's prompter gave out the parts, Miss Ethel received the role of Anne. Miss Morris was assigned the comedy role of Blanche and went home in a state of dejection.

Next morning, Daly abruptly ordered Miss Morris to take the role of Anne. Miss Ethel had capriciously rejected it, on the ground that it was "immoral"— although she had made her success as the adulterous wife of *Frou Frou*. In these circumstances, the part should have gone to Miss Davenport, but Daly did not wish her to play it, and he assigned her the role originally given to Miss Morris. He was extremely dubious about Miss Morris' ability to handle a part that required dramatic intensity and pathos that would move the audience to tears. As the rehearsals progressed, she failed to increase his confidence in her. She could not act to the top of her bent at a rehearsal. Only an outburst of savage temper at the last one—provoked by his many repetitions of a single scene—suggested the possibility of latent power. But on the opening night Miss Morris triumphed and received an ovation. Professionally, she was an

Clara Morris about 1875

anomaly. In private life she gave no indication of temperament. Her colleagues were always impressed by her serenity, her keen sense of fun, her quick laughter. On the stage, she seemed possessed by another personality, wild, passionate, defying all restraints. The sweep and power of her emotional scenes rocked audiences, leaving them shaken and breathless. She could invariably compel them to weep by weeping herself—her voice sounded as if it were flooded with tears, and to shed them she needed only to remember some sad episode of her childhood. For ten weeks, while *Man and Wife* ran to crowded houses, Daly from the prompter's table saw, in the auditorium, a nightly display of damp handkerchiefs that pleasantly turned into more and more dollars.

Miss Morris could tell nothing about her acting except that she "acted from her heart." Some years later, Mme. Modjeska would say that Miss Morris' "art was her own, apart from any rules and routine." This Daly certainly realized, and although he may have abandoned any hope of teaching her technical principles he no longer doubted her talents. (Nor did he doubt her value to him. She needed money desperately. By increasing her pay $5 a week, he persuaded her to sign a contract for the following season at a weekly salary of $55.) He paired her with Miss Davenport in his own play, *Divorce*—the first drama to deal with that subject in an American setting—which ran for two hundred nights. Then he adapted for her Adolphe Belot's melodrama, *Article 47*. This play dealt with a woman shot and disfigured by her jealous lover, who later marries another woman; jealousy and the desire for vengeance drive the discarded mistress mad. Daly told Miss Morris that the success or failure of the play was absolutely in her hands, for its fate would be determined by her mad scene. He advised her to make "a close study of violent madness." She went to the asylum on Blackwell's Island and was permitted to observe the insane inmates. Then it occurred to her that her mad scene could be given a more telling dramatic motive and an added touch of horror. Cora, the disfigured beauty, wore a veil to conceal her hideous scar, and her mind gave way when her former lover, brutally tearing off the veil, stared at the scar. In Paris, the actress who took the role played this scene with her back to the audience, to whom the scar remained invisible. Miss Morris determined that the audience must see the scar. They would then understand that Cora's mind gave way under a shattering blow to her vanity—the instinctive disgust of her former lover. While rehearsals were in progress, experiments were made with make-up; but nobody could produce a scar that satisfied Miss Morris. One day, riding in a Broadway horsecar, she saw a woman whose throat had been gashed; the scar gave her the model she needed, and at home she molded one, of gum and plaster, near her eye. There remained the problem of the crucial mad scene, which she could not act out at rehearsal. At the final rehearsal, Daly insisted that she play it. They quarreled before the company. Her nerves were overwrought, she burst into hysterical tears, the scene was not acted and nobody knew how she intended to play it. On the first night, when her veil was torn away the audience, seeing her dreadful scar, gasped. This was her cue. Staring fixedly at the eyes of the actor who was playing Cora's former lover, she emitted a low, gibbering laugh, swelled it into a long-sustained, blood-curdling shriek, and fell to the floor, raving mad. The effect was overwhelming. When the curtain fell, she surmised that she had reached the goal of her ambition. The critics, next morning, acclaimed her, ranking her as the greatest emotional actress of the time.

The long runs of *Divorce* and *Article 47* enabled Daly to make an experiment. Forming two special companies for Miss Ethel and Miss Davenport, he sent them on long starring tours in *Frou Frou* and *Divorce*. The tours were highly profitable and, two years later, in 1875, he took the entire Fifth Avenue Theater company on a transcontinental tour in a repertory of its most successful plays. The tour began with an engagement in San Francisco, proceeded to Virginia City and Salt Lake City, and continued eastward, during the summer, to New York. Before Daly undertook this pioneering venture, fire destroyed the original Fifth Avenue Theater. He moved his company into temporary quarters while a new Fifth Avenue Theater was built for him on the northwest corner of Broadway and Twenty-eighth Street. This house was opened in December, 1873, by which time Daly had lost the services of Miss Ethel and Miss Morris. These desertions aggrieved him. He blamed both actresses for their disloyalty, their ingratitude; he had discovered them, he alone had "made" them. Yet their departure was almost inevitable. Miss Ethel had seen herself displaced by Miss Morris. Miss Morris, in turn, became jealous of the growing popularity and increasing prestige of Miss Fanny Davenport, whose talents Daly was expertly fostering. When Miss Morris's contract expired, Daly offered her a new one, explaining that he wished to keep her on a low salary but proposed to "make it up to her" by paying for her stage costumes and occasionally presenting her with additional sums of money. She considered this humiliating. "It made me dependent on his whims," she later explained, "and, worst of all, it opened the door to possible scandal." Instead, she offered to sign the contract if Daly would permit her to go on a starring tour in two of her roles. He consented, but later repudiated his verbal agreement with her. After a violent quarrel with him, Miss Morris left the company.

Meanwhile, Daly had discovered a promising young American playwright. Bronson Howard, a native of Detroit who was working as a journalist in New York, submitted to him *Saratoga,* a farce comedy. Daly accepted the play and gave it a careful production, with James Lewis in the role of a likable bachelor pursued by four attractive women. *Saratoga* ran for one hundred nights and was frequently revived by Daly. Charles Wyndham, Howard's brother-in-law, had it adapted for the British stage under the title *Brighton*. It had a long run in London, was also produced in Germany, and was performed in the United States by Wyndham on his first starring tour. Howard subsequently wrote two more plays for Daly. *Diamonds,* a comedy of manners, was laid in New York City and involved a fashionable house party at an estate on Staten Island. *Moorcroft* was a melodrama, the action taking place in Georgia before the Civil War. Neither play was as successful as *Saratoga,* but Howard was sufficiently encouraged to abandon journalism and devote himself to writing plays. In time, he became the outstanding American playwright of his generation and the first to make a fortune from his work. Daly's search for plays dealing with the

CURTAIN TIME

American scene led him to negotiate with such prominent writers as William Dean Howells, Bret Harte and Mark Twain. Harte and Mark Twain collaborated on *Ah Sin,* which Daly produced, anticipating a great success; it failed.

To keep his company supplied with plays, Daly incessantly adapted the works of French and German playwrights, and occasionally wrote plays. Always tailoring his material to the talents of his cast, he wrote his most successful play to advance the career of Miss Fanny Davenport. Under his skillful management, she had become an accomplished and versatile actress. Notably excellent in the old comedies, she was considered a brilliant Lady Teazle. She played Rosaline in the first New York production of *Love's Labor's Lost.* When Edwin Booth came to the Fifth Avenue for a month, as a star, she appeared with him in *The Lady of Lyons, The Stranger,* and Garrick's version of *The Taming of the Shrew.* In modern plays, audiences liked to see her take the role of a fashionable beauty, but Daly gradually released her from this confining pattern. He cast her as Nancy in a revival of *Oliver Twist* and, in W. S. Gilbert's satirical *Charity,* gave her another dramatic opportunity in the part of a ragged outcast. In 1875 he determined to exploit her talent as a dramatic actress by providing her with a strong emotional role. With this object he wrote *Pique,* a melodrama dealing with an unhappy marriage. Because of Miss Davenport's eloquent, powerful acting the play achieved a run of two hundred and thirty-eight performances. This was Daly's last great success in his new theater. Two years later, a series of failures involved him in financial difficulties. He surrendered the theater to its proprietors, disbanded his fine company, and retired from management to make a prolonged visit to Europe.

During the four years that Daly operated his new theater, he met competition from another manager almost as resourceful. At the Union Square Theater on Fourteenth Street west of Broadway, Albert M. Palmer assembled a company which, like Daly's, soon provided the American stage with many stars. Without previous experience in management, Palmer was an able executive and shrewd businessman who believed that he could make a failing playhouse profitable. He engaged, as his dramatic adviser and assistant, A. R. Cazauran, a man long associated with theatrical affairs. Cazauran suggested that the Union Square adopt a policy that would distinguish it from other theaters—make it known to the public as the home of "polite melodrama." The two men quickly built a strong stock company. They lured away from Daly Miss Ethel, Miss Morris and Miss Kate Claxton. They engaged Miss Rose Eytinge, and a talented novice, Miss Maude Granger, who was to remain a popular favorite for fifty years. Their actors included Charles R. Thorne, Jr., as leading man; and McKee Rankin, Stuart Robson and James O'Neill, who became well known as touring stars. From the outset, Palmer's enterprise was exceptionally successful. His first season featured Miss Ethel in Sardou's *Agnes.* It had a run of one hundred performances, at the end of which the star married and retired from the stage. Palmer replaced her, the next year, with Miss Morris, for whom he produced *Camille.* She had never undertaken the role and was daunted by it. Cazauran gave her a detailed account of Miss Heron's performance. "I indignantly declared I would leave a theater before I would do as much," she re-

Richard Mansfield in "A Parisian Romance," 1883

corded. Her Camille was a novelty—a woman of refinement, socially sophisticated—and it brought crowds to the theater. One of Palmer's most spectacular successes was *The Two Orphans,* a pathetic melodrama adapted from the French, in which Miss Kate Claxton, in the role of a blind girl, achieved enduring celebrity. After a run of one hundred and eighty performances in New York, Palmer sent the play on tour with a company headed by Miss Claxton. Later she acquired the rights to it and, as a star, toured the country for twenty years, establishing a record for the performance of a single role. Palmer also produced Bronson Howard's *The Banker's Daughter,* the first serious American "triangle drama," which in 1878 caused an immense sensation, in spite of the fact that its heroine remained throughout, as Howard said, "a pure woman."

As Palmer could not foresee, his most remarkable exploit was to result from a predicament. He planned to produce, in January, 1883, *A Parisian Romance,* which Cazauran had adapted from the drama by Octave Feuillet. In it, James H. Stoddardt, a popular star, was given the role of Baron Chevrial, a decrepit rake. The role was extremely disagreeable and Stoddardt, finding it personally distasteful, asked to be released from playing it. None of the company's leading actors was available for the role, and Palmer had to give it to a young, untried recruit from comic opera, Richard Mansfield. While the play was in rehearsal, Mansfield secretly prepared his characterization. It was painfully realistic in every physical detail and, by bringing it to a hideous climax, he took the first night audience by storm. Largely because of his powerful performance, the play ran for three months. Encouraged by this success, Mansfield proposed to launch himself as a star by taking the play on tour. The venture was disastrous and left him stranded. When he reached New York he returned for a time to comic opera. But he no longer had any doubt about the future, and in this he was correct. The opportunity given him by Palmer had opened the way to a notable career as a dramatic star.

Like Wallack's in New York, the Boston Museum was a civic institution. Situated on Tremont Street, between School and Court Streets, the famous theater was managed by R. M. Field, who believed that it should be a cultural force as well as a place of entertainment. Every season, the repertory featured revivals of standard plays, and Saturday-night performances were devoted to the classics. Many members of the company were associated with it for twenty-five or thirty years, and some for even more. As a result, their ensemble playing attained a degree of excellence seldom equaled on the American stage. Reviewing a performance of *The School for Scandal* in 1874, Henry James pronounced it much superior to a current revival of the play in London. At the Museum, he said, the play was "acted with extreme finish and skill"; the performance "touches the maximum of so-called genteel comedy on the American stage." Bostonians were warmly devoted to the company's principals, whom they affectionately called "the big four." Miss Annie M. Clarke, leading woman; Mrs. J. R. Vincent, player of old women; and Charles Barron, leading man—they were remarkably accomplished, perennially attractive. Yet, as an artist, William Warren, the fourth member of the quartet, towered above them. His prestige in the profession equaled that of the greatest stars.

Warren was the son of the old Philadelphia actor-manager, and was himself an actor of the old school. He had a repertory of six hundred roles that ranged from Shakespeare and classic comedy to farce. His versatility was amazing, but such judges as Booth and Jefferson said that he had no rival in roles which demanded a seemingly natural blending of humor with pathos. Warren was a comedian, but he could draw tears from his audience as easily as laughter. He had the same power over his colleagues, who "often laughed and wept with him almost in the same breath" when performing a familiar play. A tall, portly, dignified gentleman, he was as well known to Bostonians off the stage as on; he shared with Dr. Oliver Wendell Holmes a special veneration. He was a bachelor and lived in the house on Bulfinch Place conducted as a boarding place for touring stars by Miss Amelia Fisher, sister of Mrs. Maeder. Warren's presence made it the preferred Boston residence of Booth, Jefferson, Barrett and McCullough. But only Warren was granted the privilege of a latchkey. Miss Fisher expected her other guests to be in before midnight, when supper was served in the kitchen, and she sat in the hall to admit late comers with a silent reproof. In 1882, matinée and evening performances were given at the Museum to celebrate Warren's fiftieth anniversary on the stage. Elaborate ceremonies were arranged, and thousands of Bostonians turned out to honor him. When he returned to Miss Fisher's, he found a party of eminent colleagues awaiting him. He was presented with a silver loving cup, the gift of Miss Mary Anderson, Booth, Jefferson, Barrett and McCullough. He seemed deeply affected. He looked at the company and, after a long pause, told Miss Fisher, "You better fill this with champagne and pass it round"; he was able to say nothing more. Next day, he went to the Museum for a rehearsal and resumed his work with his usual modesty and simplicity of manner. A year later, when past seventy, Warren retired. He never again entered the theater in which he had passed most of his professional life. To old Bostonians, the Museum no longer seemed the same. But Warren had taught, in their youth, two comedians—Nat C. Goodwin and John B. Mason—who, as stars, carried indications of his acting style into the twentieth century.

The Museum sent its company on annual spring tours through New England, but the Boston Theater maintained, for several years, a special touring company in addition to its resident company. The handsome old theater on Washington Street was controlled by Eugene Tompkins, one of the most progressive managers in the country, who asserted that he never had a season which showed a loss. He booked all the most celebrated stars for annual engagements, and many of them gave their first performances in new roles at the Boston Theater. When stars were not appearing, the stock company played the current successes of New York, London and Paris. Tompkins sometimes commissioned plays for the exclusive use of his company; in this way, he was able to offer his patrons a drama by Sardou before its production in Paris. But in spite of the fact that novelty, rather than the standard repertory, was the feature of his bills, Tompkins presently concluded that the day of the stock company had passed, and in 1885 he made the Boston Theater a "combination house," booking stars with their own companies, and road companies sent out by New York managers. The same conclusion had been reached fourteen years earlier by Mrs. John Drew in Philadelphia, and she disbanded her stock company at the Arch Street Theater, one of the finest in the United States. But as a combination house, she said, the Arch Street "never did so well as before. The public seemed to miss the old favorites and not to care for the new ones."

The first millionaire to enter theatrical affairs made it possible for San Francisco to have an estimable company and a playhouse as magnificent as Booth's Theater in New York. William C. Ralston, a founder of the Bank of California, had a genius for splendor. Belmont, his estate south of the city, was more grandiose than any home in the East. A private telegraph line connected it with his office, enabling him to inform his wife, as he frequently did, that he was bringing fifty guests to dine and spend the night. Ralston decided that San Francisco must have a new playhouse. He had one built immediately, and he appointed Lawrence Barrett and John McCullough to be its managers. The two stars formed a company which included such local favorites as Mrs. Judah and Walter Leman, and opened the California Theater on Bush Street in January, 1869. More than a half-century later a member of the audience remembered that evening as "a grand gala occasion." Bush Street was blocked by clarences and barouches. "The lobby with its mirrors fairly glittered with elated people assembling, long silk skirts sweeping the tesselated marble floor; and the elegant Barrett, in full evening regalia, stood smiling like a host welcoming his guests."

Barrett was not in the cast that evening. He read a dedicatory poem by Bret Harte. Then the curtain rose on a performance of Bulwer's *Money,* with Miss Marie Gordon and McCullough in the leading roles. Miss Gordon's husband, the comedian John T. Raymond, also had a role. Five years later, on the same stage, he was to appear for the first time as Colonel Mulberry Sellers in a dramatization of Mark Twain's *The Gilded Age*—a performance which soon ranked him among the most popular American stars.

The season continued brilliantly with Barrett starring in plays from his repertory. Tall, handsome, vigorous McCullough performed the Forrest roles which were to become his most popular offerings: Damon, Spartacus, Virginius,

Brutus. The partners appeared as co-stars in a series of Shakespearian plays. The engagement of old John Brougham enabled them to produce *The Rivals* with a remarkable cast: Brougham as O'Trigger, Barrett as Absolute, McCullough as Falkland, Mrs. Judah as Mrs. Malaprop and Raymond as Acres. Lotta, returning to San Francisco in triumph, led off a dazzling procession of visiting stars. The first three hundred performances at the California played to receipts of $276,000. It was the most fashionable playhouse in the city, and the two actor-managers were popular socially on Nob Hill. McCullough was convivial, and his high humor ran to pranks. Barrett, always elegant, was sedate and reserved. One night at an after-theater party on the Hill, McCullough was asked to recite. He gave a portion "of the part of one of Shakespeare's women in tones perfectly modulated to its demands." Probably disapproving this genial desecration, Barrett took his host's Bible and chilled the company by reading "that part of Second Corinthians used at funerals." At the end of a year, Barrett withdrew from the partnership and left for the East.

Although he frequently went on long starring tours, McCullough continued as manager of the California. His most notable exploit was to persuade Edwin Booth to return to San Francisco for the first time in twenty years. For Booth's comfort, McCullough provided a private Pullman car from Chicago to San Francisco. Although proud of his own eminence as a star, he took supporting roles during Booth's engagement; "I will always gladly be second to Edwin," he told a friend. The engagement lasted eight weeks and brought in more than $96,000, breaking all records. A Polish actress who had recently arrived in San Francisco went to see Booth play Shylock and Marc Antony. Her English vocabulary was very limited, but she realized that he was the greatest actor she had ever seen. Some of her Polish friends in the city proposed that she play Ophelia, in Polish, to Booth's Hamlet; the role was one of her finest achievements at the Warsaw Theater. An interview was arranged with McCullough, who proposed the scheme to Booth. Booth politely declined it, saying that he was too weary to undertake extra rehearsals; she thought him wise, and was relieved that the performance did not take place. She and her husband went to Southern California where, with a group of their compatriots, they tried to establish an enterprise in communal living patterned on Brook Farm.

A year later, she returned to San Francisco, having learned English and prepared, in her acquired language, two favorite roles: Adrienne Lecouvreur and Juliet. McCullough was persuaded to give her an audition in the last act of *Adrienne*. She was handsome, assured, eloquent. Despite her Polish accent, the beauty of her voice moved McCullough to tears. He engaged her to play the role for one week. She wrote down her professional name: Helena Modrzejewska. It wouldn't do for the United States, he told her, and shortened it to Helena Modjeska. Her debut was sensationally successful. McCullough extended her engagement for an additional week during which she played Juliet and, at McCullough's request, one performance of Ophelia to his Hamlet, playing the mad scene in Polish and the rest of her role in English. On the morning after her debut, Harry Sargent, a theatrical agent, had signed Mme. Modjeska for a starring tour in the East, to open in New York.

McCullough's discovery of Mme. Modjeska was his last important exploit as a manager. Two years earlier Ralston, owner and backer of the California Theater, had attended a directors' meeting at the Bank of California, confessed his insolvency, and later in the day, had gone to North Beach and drowned himself. The financial difficulties which his suicide brought upon the theater increased. McCullough was unable to cope with them. He seemed to be on the verge of a breakdown and when the California finally had to close for a reorganization new managers took it over. McCullough thereafter toured as a star, always successfully. But as the years passed his friends noticed his instability of temper, his dependence on drink, the frequency of his lapses into black depression. In the summer of 1881 he went to London and played at Drury Lane. The venture was not successful. One night, William Winter rode with him in a hansom, and McCullough "suddenly became quite insane, rolling his eyes from side to side and gazing at me, now furtively and now openly, with an indescribable expression of menace—like the look of a tiger." Returning to the United States, he resumed his tours. In New York, one day in 1884, he lunched at Delmonico's with Winter and Steele Mackaye. He talked with them genially and lucidly. But presently his mood changed. He rose and left them, muttering, "Old and wretched; old and wretched; old and wretched." That autumn he played an engagement at McVicker's Theater in Chicago. During a performance of *The Gladiator* he suddenly faltered and was unable to continue. The audience, believing him drunk, broke into laughter and jeers. The curtain was run down. The noise continued. Helped by two members of his company, McCullough came before the curtain. "Ladies and gentlemen," he said, "you are the worst-mannered audience I ever saw. If you had suffered tonight as I have, you would never have done this. Good night." He never acted again. Some months later his condition became hopeless and he was placed in an asylum for the insane. He died soon afterwards.

In 1879, Augustin Daly returned to New York and resumed his career as a manager. He took the former Wood's Museum, on the west side of Broadway below Thirtieth Street, remodeled it, furnished it luxuriously and opened it as Daly's Theater. For the most part, the company he assembled was unfamiliar to New Yorkers. The chief exceptions were old Charles Fisher, veteran of Burton's and of the Fifth Avenue, and young John Drew, who with his sister, Georgianna, and her husband, Maurice Barrymore, had been with Daly during his last seasons. Drew was twenty-six, a man of medium height and athletic figure whose strong features resembled those of his celebrated mother. That formidable lady had taught him acting at her Arch Street Theater. Once when he returned at four in the morning from a disastrous barnstorming tour Mrs. Drew met him at the door with a candle in one hand and a prompt book in the other. Giving him both, she said, "Don't go to bed, John. You play this part tonight." It was a long part, but he played it letter-perfect; his mother would not have forgiven a bungled speech. He was an excellent light comedian whose casual, natural style was the product of technical skill.

To play opposite Drew, Daly engaged Miss Ada Rehan, a girl of nineteen who had been on the stage for six years. She was tall, brown-haired, gray-eyed

John Drew in "The Big Bonanza,"
1875

and not a beauty. But she had "a manner unlike other women, a voice that melted and caressed as it drawled, an awkward grace, an arch expression, a look of mischief." So Otis Skinner thought, when he joined the company a few years later, and Miss Ellen Terry, at about the same time, described her as "the most lovely, humorous darling I have ever seen on the stage." Miss Rehan's rise to fame began during Daly's second season, after Mrs. Gilbert and James Lewis returned to the company. Paired with Drew, and with the older couple as foils, she won praise from the leading critics. Playgoers soon talked of the "big four," and the astute manager felt reasonably certain that any play which presented Miss Rehan and Drew, Mrs. Gilbert and Lewis, in "new and entertaining situations" was likely to be successful. He therefore adopted the policy of tailoring his pieces to this quartet, the elder members usually appearing as a cantankerous, quarrelsome old couple, the younger as lovers who dueled their way to final happiness. In initiating this policy, he abandoned his former position of refusing either to feature individual players or to exploit them in a particular line of business.

This reversal, prompted by his urgent need for immediate financial success, was enforced by a reason even more compelling. Daly detected in Miss Rehan the promise of a great career as he understood one. The fulfillment of that promise became his passion; for the rest of his life it was to be his central purpose. Habitually, he concealed his feelings, and his declaration, many years later, that Miss Rehan "is ever and ever above all others in my thought and hope and pride" was probably only a guarded statement of them. By making her vivacious temperament the basis of an acting style, he enabled Miss Rehan to win fame by means of her personality rather than her personations. She enchanted him just as she was. So he taught her, not how to subordinate herself to a part, but how to express herself in one; not how to identify herself with a character, but how to identify characters with herself. This training had a notable advantage and an unremarked defect. It developed Miss Rehan's technical proficiency, but it failed to enhance her talent. When Daly completed her training, the leading critics, almost without exception, acclaimed her as the foremost comedienne on the American stage. Thereafter, his main problem was to choose vehicles which would brilliantly display her gifts; inevitably, her repertory had little variety. Profoundly loyal, profoundly devoted to him, Miss Rehan never questioned his decisions. Their association was constant and peculiarly intimate. She relied on his direction, and eventually became dependent on it. Apparently, as an actress, she was content to be imprisoned by his image of her as a woman. Her fame was entirely his creation. To the making of it he had devoted all his abilities, his theater, and the resources of the finest acting company in the United States. His gift to her was priceless. It was also fatal. When Daly died, Miss Rehan was not yet forty; his death ended her career. Of Daly, Otis Skinner wrote, long afterwards, that he "carried many secrets to the grave, not the least of which was the story of a broken heart."

Audiences went to Daly's Theater to see sentimental comedies: Daly's adaptations of the works of German playwrights, in which he made the characters and situations credibly American; the early plays of the British dramatist, Arthur Wing Pinero; other similar pieces, British, French or American. That these plays were usually insubstantial and often trivial in theme did not diminish their popularity. They presented four favorite principals and a matchless supporting company. They were invariably performed with great elegance and finesse. Daly's stage settings were always attractive; the clothes worn by his casts were always in the highest fashion; the actresses were celebrated for their

Ada Rehan in "The Country Girl"

beauty. (One of the most beautiful Daly actresses, Miss Edith Kingdon, married George Gould, eldest son of the multimillionaire Jay Gould, and by her tact and charm opened the portals of New York society to a family formerly excluded by it.) As soon as the financial prosperity of his enterprise was assured, and the training of his actors in ensemble playing had been accomplished, Daly began to build a repertory of old comedies, perhaps the more eagerly because these plays furnished excellent opportunities for Miss Rehan—whom he trained, with the rest of the company, to be "natural" in speech, manner and action without sacrificing the "artificial" glitter of wit and rhetoric. Colley Cibber's *She Would and She Would Not,* David Garrick's version of a play by William Wycherly, *The Country Girl,* George Farquhar's *The Recruiting Officer* were successfully revived. (The series culminated in a production of *The School for Scandal* which made Miss Rehan the unchallenged interpreter of Lady Teazle.) Daly also turned to Shakespeare with a magnificent revival of *The Merry Wives of Windsor.* This he followed by the first production of *The Taming of the Shrew* in its original form. With Miss Rehan as Katharina, John Drew as Petruchio, Otis Skinner as Lucentio, Charles Fisher as Baptista, James Lewis as Gremio and Mrs. Gilbert as Curtis, this production was unreservedly praised by the critics and ran for more than one hundred performances. In artistic achievement Daly never excelled it.

Daly's Theater displaced Wallack's as New York's premier playhouse. First nights there brought out the most distinguished audience in the city, drawn from the realms of fashion, literature and the arts. But local supremacy did not satisfy Daly. To make the name of his theater known throughout the country, he sent special companies on tour with his most successful productions, and every spring he took the permanent stock company on a long tour, twice extending it to the Pacific coast. The prestige gained by these tours merely increased his ambition for conquest. In 1884 he took his players to London on the first professional visit ever made by an American company. Two years later he repeated the visit and invaded the Continent, giving performances in Germany and in Paris. In 1888 he made a third European tour, during which he produced *The Taming of the Shrew.* In London, the first performance of a Shakespearian comedy by an American cast was remarkably successful, and led to the first performance of the play ever given at Stratford-on-Avon, where Daly's company produced it at the Shakespeare Memorial Theater.

While Daly's fortunes prospered so spectacularly, Lester Wallack's slowly declined. In 1882, he established his company in a new Wallack's Theater, diagonally across Broadway from Daly's at Thirtieth Street. The playhouse was almost as handsome as Daly's, but apart from its chief players the company was not as brilliant as that of the rival house. Wallack was nearing his seventieth year and his health was failing. He was saddened by the fickleness of the public. He had lost his ability to keep pace with changing popular taste and his revenues diminished. Five years after the inauguration of his new theater, a succession of failures compelled him to relinquish his lease and disband his company. Because of a prior booking at Wallack's, the company's farewell performances were given at Daly's Theater. Wallack went into retirement facing extreme poverty.

Aware of this, Daly and A. M. Palmer proposed to him that they arrange "some public demonstration in your honor." For one year the proud old man declined this proferred benefit. Then he gave in, with a touching effort to save his pride. "If you could point out in the disposing of the pecuniary result," he wrote to his colleagues, "some way by which I could adequately convey my feeling that my chief, and by far my greatest, gratification is the honor conferred upon me, I should take a still greater pride in accepting it." The testimonial performance took place at the new Metropolitan Opera House in May, 1888. *Hamlet* was given, with Edwin Booth in the title role, Mme. Modjeska playing Ophelia, Barrett as the Ghost, John Gilbert as Polonius, Jefferson as the First Grave Digger, Rose Coghlan as the Player Queen. The other roles were filled by eminent actors and actresses, and well-known players came from all over the country to appear as "lords and attendants" at the court of Denmark. Wallack, called before the curtain at the end of the second act, spoke what were to be his last lines on the stage. He received an ovation from the huge audience. And on the following day his pride was spared. A check for the proceeds of the benefit, amounting to $20,000, was given, not to him, but to Mrs. Wallack. Less than four months later, Lester Wallack died.

Meanwhile, theatrical fare of a lighter kind came into vogue throughout the country. In 1866, Henry C. Jarrett and his partner, Harry Palmer, imported a Parisian ballet troupe to perform at the Academy of Music in New York. Before this attraction could open, the Academy was destroyed by fire. The unlucky impresarios then turned to William Wheatley, manager of Niblo's Garden. Wheatley was preparing to produce *The Black Crook,* a melodrama by Charles Barras. He agreed to turn this into an elaborate musical spectacle, using the ballet troupe as its principal feature. Barras, a long-unproduced playwright, objected to this desecration of his work. But a cash payment and a contract providing for royalties secured his consent. (Barras was penniless; his wife, whom he adored, was critically ill. The money came too late to save her life. With the fortune subsequently yielded by his contract he built an imposing country home, went to live there with his mother-in-law and his wife's dog, and soon afterwards in grief committed suicide.) As Wheatley finally produced it, *The Black Crook* was the costliest, most ornate and most daring show that Americans had yet seen. Three lovely young ballerinas—Maria Bonfanti, Rita Sangalli and Betty Rigl—were deservedly acclaimed, though it was not their exquisite art that crowded the theater. One hundred beautiful girls in short diaphanous skirts and flesh-colored tights provided an unprecedented sensation. Here, for the first time, Americans were privileged to see a massive display of feminine charm as nearly as possible unveiled. There were, besides, dazzling and novel scenic effects, culminating in a startling "transformation." In his review, the critic of the *Tribune* reported that, "All that gold and silver and gems and light and woman's beauty can contribute to fascinate the eye and charm the sense is gathered up in this gorgeous spectacle." Attacks by the clergy and the protests of outraged moralists in the press were ignored by an enchanted public, which crowded the huge theater for sixteen months. *The Black Crook* had a run of four hundred and seventy-five performances, breaking all existing records, and its gross receipts exceeded one million dollars. Enterprising managers in other cities soon announced their own productions of the spectacle. In San Francisco, productions were rushed by Tom Maguire at the Opera House, and by the manager of the Metropolitan. Maguire won the race, but his competitor brought a suit against him, charging infringement of copyright. The judge decided that *The Black Crook* did not enjoy copyright protection because it "merely panders to the pernicious curiosity of very questionable exhibitions of the female person."

Visual delights ordinarily obstructed by the fashionable crinoline agitated moralists once again when, in 1868, the Lydia Thompson Burlesque Company of London opened at Wood's Museum in New York. The four radiantly blonde beauties who headed this troupe became, overnight, the sensation of the season. Miss Thompson, blue-eyed and saucy, was an amusing comedienne. Miss Pauline Markham, dark-eyed and statuesque, captivated all sophisticated gentlemen. Miss Ada Harland, a charming dancer, and Miss Lisa Weber, a talented singer, were the other members of the triumphant quartet. These fascinating creatures not only appeared in male attire, but in tights unencumbered by superfluous draperies. In songs, dances and skits they satirized the foibles of the hour, among them, to the delight of male patrons, the "Grecian bend," a new posture

Poster for "The Black Crook"

affected by ladies of fashion. But neither the innocent merriment they afforded nor the widespread admiration they evoked saved them from denunciation by indignant puritans. One critic attacked them so abusively that Richard Grant White, a respected authority on art and music, and editor of Shakespeare's plays, felt obliged to defend their entertainment in *The Galaxy*. "I must confess that I saw no chance of harm in it to myself or to any of my fellow spectators, old or young, male or female," he declared. "Indeed, it seems rather to be desired that the points of a fine woman should be somewhat better known and more thought of than they have been. They seem to me quite as important and I think that they are quite as interesting as those of a fine horse; and I should be sorry to believe that they are more harmful either to taste or to morals."

Miss Thompson and her company played to crowded houses in New York for seven months, then went on tour. In San Francisco, they had a long engagement at the fashionable new California Theater, having presumably won the moral approval of John McCullough and Lawrence Barrett, but they were denounced by Miss Olive Logan, a playwright who was lecturing the city. In Chicago, they played at Crosby's Opera House, and were subjected to incessant attack, on the score of immorality, by the editor of the Chicago *Times*. This proved to be the last straw. Miss Thompson's patience and good humor were exhausted. One afternoon, armed with a horsewhip, she thrashed the offending editor in full view of the crowds on Wabash Avenue, and the same evening lampooned him from the stage in one of her songs. For the pleasure of this double retaliation—and the publicity which it brought her—she willingly paid a fine of $100.

The engagement played by Miss Thompson and her troupe in Boston inspired two young men of that city—Edward E. Rice and J. C. Goodwin—to write *Evangeline,* which Rice, who composed the score, described as a "musical comedy." (It was actually a burlesque-extravaganza.) The collaborators, acting as their own producers, brought it to Niblo's Garden in July, 1874, and its brief engagement there was successful. On the strength of this, Rice obtained sufficient money to mount it more lavishly in Boston, and he embellished it with a female chorus which not only postured and kicked, but performed smart military evolutions—a routine widely imitated and soon considered indispensable. Other elements of the show also indicated Rice's resourcefulness in stagecraft: the playing of the "hero" by a woman; the performance of George K. Fortesque, a fat comedian, in the role of Catherine; the grotesque dance performed by Evangeline's heifer, a beast propelled from within by two men. In its new guise, the piece enjoyed signal success in Boston, had a long run in New York, and Rice soon formed road companies to perform it throughout the country. Touring companies and frequent revivals in New York kept *Evangeline* before the public for more than thirty years. In 1884, Rice scored an even more sensational success with *Adonis,* another piece in the same vein. It played a record-breaking engagement of more than six hundred performances at the Bijou Opera House in New York. In part, this long run was due to the young leading man, Henry E. Dixey, the first matinée idol to appear on the American musical stage. He was handsome, he had a fine figure, and his superb legs were a perennial delight to feminine audiences who obeyed convention by never alluding to them. But propriety did not forbid adulation of Dixey's personality and his "art." Fortunately, this was justified. Equally expert as a singer, dancer and comedian, he remained on the stage well into the twentieth century, and died in 1943 at the age of eighty-four.

With the exception of Rice's pieces, the musical stage was largely monopolized by foreign products. The European invasion began when, at the head of rival companies, Mlles. Lucille Tostée and Irma brought to New York from the boulevards of Paris the delicious operettas of Jacques Offenbach. Although the librettos of these pieces shocked many earnest champions of the proprieties—particularly if they understood French—and there arose a clamor of protest against the defilement of the American stage by "French indecencies," the sparkling music of the composer triumphed over all opposition. The charming rival prima donnas were, as singers, exceptionally talented. They were also skillful actresses, and American audiences were delighted by the novelty of finding dramatic competence and brilliant vocalization united in the persons of two young women who were pretty, piquant, sprightly and irresistibly alluring. Tostée and Irma remained in the United States for several years, touring the eastern states and the Middle West in a repertory that included *La Grande Duchesse, La Belle Hélène, Barbe Bleu, La Périchole, Orphée aux Enfers* and other operettas by Offenbach. When they returned to France, the vogue of opera bouffe, as it was called, had been securely established. An enterprising impresario, Maurice Grau, who later became director of the Metropolitan Opera, formed a French company to present, in addition to the works of Offenbach, those of Edmond Audran, Alexandre-Charles Lecocq, and other currently popular Parisian composers. Headed successively by Mlles. Aimée, Paola Marié and Théo, this company made annual tours that extended from New York to San Francisco. Other companies, performing the same repertory in English, also catered to an increasing demand for light opera.

But the permanent popularity of comic opera in English was chiefly due to William S. Gilbert and Arthur Sullivan. The phenomenal success of their *H.M.S. Pinafore* in London immediately stimulated the imaginations of American managers. Since the work was not protected by international copyright, it could be produced without the consent of the author and composer and, more importantly, without payment of royalties to them. There began a nation-wide race to bring pirated versions of *Pinafore* to the stage. The first American production was made at the Boston Museum on November 25, 1878; the second, at the Bush Street Theater in San Francisco, one month later; and New Yorkers saw it in February, 1879, at the Standard Theater. Before long, *Pinafore* swept over the whole country. Its popularity was such that a "Philadelphia church choir company" was formed to carry it to segments of the public which still refused to patronize the theater, and innumerable juvenile opera companies toured it through small towns. (One of these companies was graced by a future star, Miss Julia Marlowe.) Gilbert and Sullivan themselves brought the London *Pinafore* company to the United States in December, 1879, opening at the Fifth Avenue Theater in New York. On the first night, Sullivan conducted the

Lillian Russell

orchestra and Gilbert, clad as a sailor, figured among the chorus. To prevent American piracy of their new work, *The Pirates of Penzance,* they produced it in New York before it was staged in London. The success of *Pinafore* was duplicated, in 1881, by *Patience,* and it was this comic opera which, indirectly, launched the career of a young woman whose fame was to surpass that of any other American actress.

Miss Lillian Russell (her real name was Helen Louise Leonard) made her debut as a singer of ballads at Tony Pastor's Music Hall in November, 1880. The following autumn she appeared in comic opera for the first time at the Bijou Opera House, winning from the critic of the *Herald* a prophetic notice. "Miss Russell had a beautiful face, a rare figure and a delightful voice that has not been sufficiently trained," he wrote. "If this lady learns to bring her acting up to the level of her other accomplishments, she will be invaluable in comic opera." The success of *Patience* led Tony Pastor to produce a burlesque of it at his establishment, and as the heroine of this piece Miss Russell achieved immediate celebrity; there arose an insistent demand for her photographs that was to continue, unabated, for twenty years. Presently the young prima donna —she was only twenty—was engaged to sing the leading role of *Patience* at the Bijou Opera House. Meanwhile, the Casino Theater, a luxurious playhouse of Moorish architecture, had been erected at the southeast corner of Broadway and Thirty-ninth Street. Its manager, Rudolph Aronson, intended to make it the national temple of comic opera by producing the most notable European successes with the finest casts available. He proposed to gratify the eye as well as the ear; the costumes and scenery of his productions were to be unprecedently sumptuous, and the ladies of his chorus—soon to become nationally known as "the Casino girls"—were to be marvels of beauty.

Aronson's ambitious program inevitably brought Miss Russell to the Casino. She began her long association with this theater in 1883, singing the role of Aline in Gilbert and Sullivan's *The Sorcerer,* and the role of Prince Raphael in Offenbach's *Princess of Trebizonde.* In his old age, one of her youthful admirers, describing her high, silvery soprano voice, declared that "no woman except Lilli Lehman could approach her for loveliness of song." Mme. Lehman was the greatest coloratura soprano of the time, and another, almost equally famous, herself paid an impressive tribute to the excellence of Miss Russell's vocal art. In one of her roles, Miss Russell effortlessly sang eight high C's at each performance, a feat which led the director of the Metropolitan Opera to consider engaging her for his company. Hearing that the engagement was imminent, Mme. Nellie Melba attended one of Miss Russell's performances and afterwards visited her dressing room. She warned Miss Russell not to come to the Metropolitan, for the prima donnas of the opera house had determined to ruin her career if she dared to sing there. Then Mme. Melba expressed her own astonishment at Miss Russell's vocal resources and her reckless use of them. "No prima donna could sing sixty-four high C's every week," she said, "and I would not sing as many in one week as you sing at every performance." Yet it was not primarily with her voice, but with her extraordinary physical beauty, that Miss Russell captivated the nation. Her golden hair and exquisite complexion; her classic features and the opulent curves of her body; her flashing smile and queenly walk—these assured her supremacy in an era of noted professional beauties and made her, for Americans, a symbol of glamour.

In December, 1870, the veteran comedian George Holland died. He had made his American debut at the Bowery Theater in 1827, had been a leading member of Mitchell's Olympic company and, in his eighty-first year, had retired from professional life as a member of Daly's company not long before his death. Holland, in New York, was a public figure and widely beloved. His family wished his funeral to be held at the Church of Atonement, and Joseph Jefferson went there to make arrangements with the Rector. The clergyman refused to conduct services for an actor, but told Jefferson that there was "a little church around the corner where they do that kind of thing." Said Jefferson, "God bless the little church around the corner!" Holland's funeral was held at the Church of the Transfiguration, on Twenty-ninth Street east of Fifth Avenue. Thereafter, the Little Church Around the Corner, as it came to be called, was identified with the theatrical profession. More than eighty years after Holland's death, when his art had long passed from memory, the Little Church, with its beautiful memorials to eminent actors and actresses, and its Guild Hall containing mementos of famous stars, eloquently testified to the honor in which his profession was held.

In the years following Holland's death it became clear that the profession, through the action of its leaders, was adding to its prestige. Harry Montague, the handsome leading man whom Lester Wallack brought from London, suggested the organization of a club like the Garrick Club in London, which had been founded with the object of giving "actors the opportunity of meeting gentlemen and patrons of the drama on equal terms." The Lambs Club, in which this suggestion took concrete form, was organized as a club for actors; but, with Lester Wallack as its "Shepherd," the simple monthly dinners attracted guests of the highest eminence in other fields. Henry Irving, in his Lyceum Theater in London, had a luxurious room where he frequently entertained at supper after performances; his parties were famous, and invitations to them were seldom refused. Augustin Daly installed the "Peg Woffington Room" in Daly's Theater, and the supper parties which he gave there to celebrate his successful productions assembled many of the most distinguished residents of New York.

Edwin Forrest, by provision made in his will, had endowed a home for elderly, indigent actors and actresses where, in the pleasant atmosphere created by his books and pictures and theatrical memorabilia, they could live out their lives in dignity and comfort. But the accommodations of the Edwin Forrest Home were limited, and the need of other forms of relief for distressed members of the profession was urgent. No appeal was made to the public. Instead, the Actors' Fund of America was organized, its founders including Booth, Jefferson, Barrett, Lester Wallack and, as representatives of the managers, Daly and Palmer. At the first meeting, held in 1882, Lester Wallack was elected president. During the following season, a policy of giving benefit performances for the Fund was initiated. Thereafter, for seventy years, the playgoing public contributed to this theatrical philanthropy—always to its own profit—by purchasing tickets.

The moral repute of the theater, and the prestige of the acting profession, were greatly enhanced by two prominent religious leaders. As editors of *The Churchman,* the Reverend George Mallory and his brother, Marshall Mallory, exercised considerable influence on that portion of the public which continued to view the stage and its people with extreme disfavor. When it became known, in 1880, that the Mallorys had embarked on a theatrical enterprise, ancient prejudices were dramatically challenged. The Mallorys not only financed the new Madison Square Theater, on the site of Daly's first Fifth Avenue, but actively participated in its management. The playhouse opened under the direction of Steele Mackaye, who had designed for it novel equipment, including a mechanically operated double stage, which made it the most modern theater in the country. Mackaye was an actor and playwright, and as the Madison Square's opening attraction he mounted his drama, *Hazel Kirke.* Had this play failed, the Mallorys' venture might have had little effect on prejudice against the stage. But, instead, *Hazel Kirke* broke existing records by running for four hundred and eighty-six performances in New York, and was soon carried even to remote communities by more than a dozen touring companies. This made the Madison Square the best-known playhouse in the country. It also reminded Americans everywhere that this theater was not only sponsored, but conducted, by a clergyman.

It was Edwin Booth, however, who furnished the most impressive symbol of the dignity and worth of his profession by founding The Players. His purpose was to organize a club "to represent all that is best in the dramatic profession, to foster the dramatic art, and to exalt the standard of personal worth among the actors of America." He purchased a fine old residence in New York, facing Gramercy Park. After having it embellished by the architect Stanford White, he installed in it his library, paintings and theatrical memorabilia, and in 1888 formally gave it to The Players, reserving for his own use quarters on the third floor. Membership in the club was opened to actors, dramatists and managers; also to authors, artists, journalists and patrons of the arts. Booth realized the need, at that time, of an institution which, bringing together leaders of the nation's intellectual life and its more distinguished artists, might affirm the importance of the arts to the American social order.

CHAPTER 10

The Golden Age of the Road

IN 1875 a stout, vigorous, elderly lady drove into Philadelphia from her suburban home to attend a "morning performance," or matinée, at the Walnut Street Theater. Six years earlier, Mrs. Fanny Kemble had given the last of her Shakespearian readings and had retired, at the age of sixty, to private life. Now she was writing her memoirs—having mastered that new aid to authorship, the typewriter—and this revived her interest in the stage. The matinée promised to be rewarding. The famous Italian tragedienne, Mme. Adelaide Ristori, and her Italian company were giving only one performance. The play was *Elizabeth of England,* which presented Ristori in her most celebrated role.

At the theater, notices had been posted that the performance would be unavoidably delayed. The train on which the star and her company were traveling from Baltimore was late. Bulletins of its progress were several times read from the stage. The large audience endured a prolonged wait, as Mrs. Kemble noted, "with American—unrivalled—patience, good temper and civility." At length Mme. Ristori and her company arrived; they dressed hastily; the performance

Adelaide Ristori in "Elizabeth, Queen of England"

began. Mrs. Kemble had seen Ristori play this role in London and was shocked by the difference in her acting. "Every particle of careful elaboration and fine detail of workmanship was gone," and all that remained was "the broad clap-trap points in the principal situations." Obviously time, not art, was the primary consideration. Mme. Ristori went through an excessively long, demanding part, made several changes of costume, and, as the final curtain fell, "rushed off to catch a train to New York where she was to act next morning, if not, indeed the evening of the same day."

Mrs. Kemble knew that Europeans, when their stars returned from American tours, often complained that they had become "coarse and vulgar in the style of their performances," and attributed this to the deficiencies of the American public. But Europeans were wrong, she reflected indignantly. They ought to blame the financial greed of European stars, who came to the United States only to make money and insisted on giving as many performances as possible to swell their earnings. "Their health is one inevitable sacrifice to this overwork, and their artistic excellence a still more grievous one."

The fact was that a new era had begun for the American stage. In all parts of the country, but particularly west of Chicago, a tremendous expansion of railroads was taking place. New theaters were being built in the metropolitan centers and rapidly growing cities, and along the network of railroads there were few towns of even moderate size which did not have an "opera house." With the disappearance of local stock companies, the whole country was becoming dependent on New York for its theatrical entertainment. In these circumstances managers realized that larger profits could be made from the road than from New York itself. The theater was developing into a large-scale business, national in scope, and audiences throughout the country were to be brought the greatest stars, foreign and American, as well as the most successful plays produced in New York.

Mme. Ristori had made two earlier American tours, performing in the principal cities of the East, Middle West and South. In 1875, embarked on what she announced as a "farewell tour of the world," she was the first great foreign star to play her way across the country from New York to San Francisco. She was fifty-three and entering the twilight of a long, brilliant career. Her company was mediocre, her scenery shabby. Nevertheless, as Henry James reported in the *Nation,* her performances remained "a supreme exhibition of the grand style of acting," and he declared that "no one whom we have seen, or are likely to see in this country, can interpret tragedy in the superbly large way of Mme. Ristori." Her repertory included *Medea, Phaedra, Elizabeth, Mary Stuart, Marie Antoinette,* and in her impersonations of these tragic queens she was able to surmount, by her art alone, the barriers of language, temperament and tradition that rose between herself and her public.

Two years earlier her compatriot, the tragedian Tommaso Salvini, had caused a sensation on his first American tour. He was a handsome physical specimen; tall, imposing in figure, so strong that he boasted of being able to lift with one arm a man seated in a chair and place him on a billiard table. Salvini's face was vividly expressive and his voice powerful and melodious. His most celebrated role was Othello, and his performance of it became a controversial issue. Certain critics denounced his Othello as barbarous, bestial and repulsive. Others praised Salvini's torrential passion and inexhaustible energy. His tigerlike pacing of the stage before the murder of Desdemona; his leap from her body to reach Iago and destroy him; his final despairing agony—in dramatic power, these effects had never been equaled on the American stage. Salvini refused to act more than five times a week, and he said that the actor's life in the United States could be summed up in three words: "theater, railroad, hotel." But he was surprised "that in a land where industry and commerce seem to absorb all of the intelligence of the people, there should be in every city and district, indeed in every village, people who are competent to discuss the arts with such high authority." His tour took him from New York to Philadelphia, Baltimore, Pittsburgh, Washington and Boston. From Boston he went to Albany, Utica, Syracuse, Rochester, Buffalo, Toledo, "that pleasant city, Detroit," and Chicago. From Chicago he toured to New Orleans, taking in the principal cities along the way.

In 1880 John Stetson, proprietor of the Globe Theater in Boston and a manager of touring stars, sent a representative to Italy to engage Salvini for a tour on which he was to play in Italian, but with an American company speaking English. Stetson was convinced that this arrangement would bring greater profits, especially in the road towns. The project astounded Salvini. "But how shall I take my cue, since I do not understand English? And how will your

Tommaso Salvini as Othello,
a caricature of 1875

American actors know when to speak, since they do not know Italian?" The
agent was able to explain. "Our American actors are mathematicians, and can
memorize perfectly the last words of your speeches, and they will work with
the precision of machines." Salvini signed the contract. ("The more difficult a
thing has seemed, the more firmly I have set my mind upon conquering it.")
When announcement of the tour was made, he received many letters of protest
from American admirers. He arrived in New York "nervous and feverish, but
not discouraged or depressed." At the first rehearsal, the American actors were
letter-perfect, but Salvini floundered and retrieved himself only by an effort of
will. Subsequent rehearsals, he claimed, proceeded with an exactitude which
"was due to the memory, the application, and the scrupulous attention to their
work of the American actors, as well as to my own force of will and practical
acquaintance with all the parts of the play, and to the natural intuition which
helped me to know, without understanding, what was addressed to me, divining
it from a motion, a look, or a light inflection of the voice."

In the course of time, Salvini "came to understand perfectly every word of
all the characters; I became so sure of myself that if an actor substituted one
word for another I perceived it; I understood the words of Shakespeare but not
those of the spoken language."

In New York, the bilingual performances failed to attract a large public.
But in other cities, as Stetson had foreseen, the theaters were filled by enthusiastic audiences. For the privilege of seeing the great tragedian they were willing to endure the grotesque mixture of languages, the mediocrity of the
supporting company and the poverty of the stage settings. So gratifying to
Salvini were the financial results of this experiment that he repeated it on his
three subsequent American tours.

Ristori and Salvini came to the United States with the prestige of European
fame, but another star, lacking equivalent repute abroad, achieved it as the
result of American success. In eight years, during which she made four American tours, Miss Adelaide Neilson not only rose to the top rank of her profession
but earned a large fortune which enabled her to retire from the stage. When
she first came to the United States in 1872, she had won favor in the provincial
theaters of Great Britain, and in several roles, notably Juliet, had made an
impression on influential London critics. But on the British stage, although
considered an actress of much promise, her stellar light was somewhat less than
dazzling.

She was twenty-six, a slender, dark-eyed beauty whose chestnut hair had
been dyed golden. A resourceful manager and an inventive press agent aroused
interest in her as a personage. The American public was informed that Miss
Neilson had been born in Spain, the child of a Spanish father and an English
mother. She had been reared in affluence, educated on the Continent; she was
said to speak seven languages; she wrote poetry. Irrepressible genius and her
family's sudden loss of wealth had resolved her to go on the stage. But Miss
Neilson's true story, carefully concealed from the public, was far more impressive than the romantic legend that had been contrived for her. She was the
illegitimate child of a strolling actress who later settled in a Yorkshire town as

Adelaide Neilson in "Romeo and Juliet"

the housemate of a mechanic. Miss Neilson was early put to work in a factory, and subsequently as a nurserymaid. At fifteen, she ran away from home and made her way to London. There she found employment as a barmaid; she gave this up to become a ballet girl. Her beauty drew attention to her and kindly actors gave her some training. She developed a fondness for reading and was advised to study the plays of Shakespeare. From this experience she emerged with a determination to become the leading Shakespearian actress on the British stage. To a friend in New York she confided that she would permit nothing in life to thwart this purpose.

Miss Neilson made her American debut in the role of Juliet and won extravagant acclaim from the critics. She played Rosalind and Pauline in *The Lady of Lyons;* in both roles she was extolled. (On later tours she added Viola, Beatrice and Imogen to her Shakespearian roles.) Critics and audiences alike were captivated by her beauty and her silvery voice. In her impassioned scenes she seemed to be transfigured by the fiery tide of feeling that swept over her. The same extraordinary intensity, in scenes of pathos, made tears well up in her eyes and trickle down her cheeks. She had no gift for writing poetry, but on the stage she could live it, could make it real and vivid for her audiences. This was why, more than fifty years after her retirement and early death, an old playgoer who had seen her in his boyhood wrote: "She was like a dream of love and beauty, the exact repetition of which never came again."

People who met Miss Neilson socially were charmed by her vivacity, modesty and sweetness. But she had a high temper, she was capricious, and in her frequent lapses into sadness and self-pity she was apt to recoil from any show of friendliness. Her British colleagues, knowing her story, made allowances for her vagaries. Just before she left New York for her tour, Edward Sothern called on her at the Fifth Avenue Hotel. During a month's engagement she had triumphed. The news of American acclaim had already reached London, and had swiftly changed her professional status. She had every reason to be happy, but Sothern found her deeply depressed. She asked him for a talisman to bring her luck on her tour; any trifle would do. Sothern may have wished to change her mood by provoking her to a fit of temper; he was, in any case, an inveterate practical joker. He blandly inquired whether she would like to have a grizzly bear as a luck piece. "Yes," she said, "send him up." Sothern went to Wallack's Theater, where a caged young grizzly had arrived that day from California as a gift to the treasurer. He arranged to have it delivered to Miss Neilson "accompanied by four porters with a chain about as big as the cable of a man of war, and a muzzle like a fire-grate." When the beast appeared, Miss Neilson's drawing room was crowded with visitors. Notwithstanding their panic, Sothern later recorded, Miss Neilson kept her temper. She also tried to keep the bear. "But that was an effort beyond her," he acknowledged, "and Bruin was finally presented to the Zoological Gardens in Central Park."

Mme. Modjeska was one of the stars most bewildered by the methods with which tours were conducted. She made a successful New York debut in *Adrienne Lecouvreur,* added to this the balcony scene from *Romeo and Juliet,* and established her drawing power in *Camille*. In this play she refused to present "a common, fallen woman such as one may meet on the streets after dark." It pleased her imagination, she said, to indicate the "delicate style" of Camille's personality; to make her "reserved, gentle, intense in her love and most sensitive—in one word, an exception to her kind." The New York press was unanimous in its praise, crowded houses wept, and Mme. Modjeska's manager promptly put her under contract to tour for thirty weeks during the following season. Before leaving New York, where the tour opened, she asked to see the projected route. The manager had included many one-night stands. Did this mean that she would be required to catch trains very early in the morning? Unhappily it did, and Mme. Modjeska declared that she would do nothing of the sort; she had to have eight hours of uninterrupted sleep or she could not act at all. One-night stands must be excluded from her tour. The manager explained that this was against her interests, since she was receiving a higher percentage of the receipts in those towns than in the larger cities. But, he presently found a way to placate his exigeant star. He rented a private car— "an ordinary Wagner's sleeper, without drawing room"—and Mme. Modjeska and her company were the first actors to tour in relative comfort.

There were, however, other complications. The manager insisted upon providing Mme. Modjeska with a fat pug dog. All prominent stars had pet dogs, he said, and although she disliked small dogs she had to travel with—and constantly parade—this troublesome symbol of her artistic eminence. In Louisville, Kentucky, the manager announced the loss of her stage jewels, allegedly "real diamonds," explaining to her that "every great star always loses hers at least once a year."

Far more distressing to Mme. Modjeska was the requirement that she play

East Lynne—which she despised—every Saturday night, because on that night "a different class of people, fond of popular plays, formed the public." It did not console her that on Saturday nights the theaters were crowded, or that she was repeatedly called before the curtain. And there were occasions when, her scenery failing to arrive at some one-night stand, a performance was ruined by the incongruous sets that were furnished by the theater. "Men and women of culture can be found everywhere, even in the smallest corners of this country," she reflected, and her conscience was troubled whenever she failed to give them her best.

A similar mischance involved Edwin Booth in a notable episode. He and his company were scheduled for a single performance in Waterbury, Connecticut, then a town of some fifteen thousand inhabitants. The theater had been sold out long in advance. The star and his troupe had to make a train directly after the performance. They reached Waterbury before the arrival of their scenery, costumes and other equipment. When it came time to prepare for the performance of *Hamlet,* their equipment had not yet reached the town, and the frightened company manager had to tell this to his star. Instead of raging, Booth took the news calmly. Refusing to cancel the performance, he went before the curtain, explained the situation to the audience, and announced that *Hamlet* would be played on a bare stage, in street dress. The actors were apprehensive. If Booth, in his greatest role, should evoke laughter, the effect on him would be disastrous. "It was one of the greatest triumphs an actor ever had," one of the company wrote amazedly, "for Mr. Booth to compel the vast audience to forget the ludicrous surroundings and think only of the character he was portraying." Their equipment was delivered to the theater in time for the

Helena Modjeska in "As You Like It"

last two acts of *Hamlet* to be performed in costume and with scenery. Yet the enthusiasm was no greater than it had been during the earlier three acts. This was the first known attempt, in the modern American theater, to give a Shakespearian play in street attire on a barren stage. Booth might have been astounded had he foreseen that, nearly fifty years later, productions of *Hamlet* and *Julius Caesar* in modern dress were to be offered to the public, without apology, as examples of the most advanced theory of stagecraft.

Booth's performance in Waterbury demonstrated his ability to rely on a personal art so accomplished and persuasive that it could dispense with all the usual aids to dramatic illusion. The need for this kind of art was diminishing, because of the growing wealth of scenic resource that had become available. Yet many of the greatest actors of the time were capable of exercising a personal art as powerful as Booth's. On one of her tours Mme. Modjeska attended a New Year's Eve supper party that her leading man, Otis Skinner, gave for the company. Each of the guests did a turn for the amusement of the others, but the star's contribution was unique, and Skinner never forgot it. When the festivities were at their height, Mme. Modjeska rose and said that she knew a short recitation in Polish that might please them. "A note of suspense and drama was struck at once," Skinner wrote, many years later. "Her liquid voice became by turns melancholy and gay, impassioned, tragic, light with happiness, and blighting with bitterness. Laughter rang through it, and now sobs and moans. There was not a note in the gamut of emotions she did not touch. She finished with a recurrent rhythm, fateful and portentous. We were clutched by the spell. We didn't know what it was about but we knew it was something tremendous." There was a moment of silence when she sat down. The actors who had been performing with her night after night—technicians who understood the means she used to achieve her effects on the stage—were vanquished by her art. Someone asked her, "What was it, madame? What was it?" She replied, "I merely recited the alphabet in Polish."

But Mme. Modjeska, though able to exercise this purely personal art when speaking her native language, realized that her foreign accent prohibited her from relying on it when using English. Playing in English on the stage, she could illustrate her spoken words by action and facial expression; without these, she could not obtain the same effects. "That was the reason I never liked to give English recitations on a platform," she wrote, "because I had nothing to help out the deficiencies of my pronunciation."

Of the new managers in New York, Henry E. Abbey was the most progressive, and he soon became a dominant figure in show business, as the profession had begun to call it. Actresses were pleased by his dark eyes, black hair and mustache, and charming smile. They approved his air of breeding, his courtly manners—so unusual in a manager—and the impression he gave that, in his dealings, he would always play the *grand seigneur,* never haggling over terms. Abbey was an ingenious, intrepid speculator who knew that operations on a national scale might yield enormous profits. He saw that the methods of big business, particularly its techniques of advertising and publicity, could be used in selling dramatic and musical art to the public. (He was an impresario as well as a manager, and became the first director of the Metropolitan Opera.) Like Stephen Price, Abbey determined to bring the most famous foreign stars of the day to the United States for long tours. A visit to London made by the company of the Comédie Française in 1879 enabled him to embark on this project. During the London engagement one actress in the company, Mlle. Sarah Bernhardt, had made a sensational personal success, a success so extraordinary that it involved her in difficulties with the director of the Comédie and caused her sudden resignation. It was reported that, before deserting the French national theater, she had made arrangements for an American tour, and Henry James, in one of his London letters to the *Nation,* predicted that she would have "a triumphant career" in the United States. She was, he declared, "too American not to succeed in America." She would be recognized as a kindred spirit by "the people who have brought to the highest development the arts and graces of publicity." If the profession of being a celebrity had not already been invented, "it is certain she would have discovered it." Mlle. Bernhardt, James asserted, "has in a supreme degree what the French call the *génie de la réclame*— the advertising genius; she may, indeed, be called the muse of the newspaper."

Abbey had reached the same conclusions even earlier, had made a hasty trip abroad, and had obtained a contract from Mlle. Bernhardt by the simple, though costly, expedient of capitulating to her every demand. Though it pleased Abbey to take a lordly attitude toward money, he was usually astute about his financial arrangements. But he quickly discovered that neither in sagacity nor lordliness could he match the brilliant, temperamental, capricious actress. The new generation of feminine stars were, indeed, perplexing managers by displaying a degree of acumen in matters of business that was both inappropriate to their sex and incompatible with their professed absorption in their art. The terms that Abbey granted Mlle. Bernhardt were unprecedented, and they fixed a goal for every other feminine star of the first magnitude. She was to receive $1,000 for each performance, and in addition half of the receipts in excess of $4,000. Two hundred dollars weekly would be paid to her for hotel expenses. The salaries and other expenses of her company were to be paid by Abbey. And Mlle. Bernhardt was to travel everywhere in a private car containing a drawing room, dining room, kitchen, a commodious bedroom for herself, and quarters for her personal staff.

For months before Mlle. Bernhardt's arrival, Abbey deluged the country with publicity about her. By innumerable articles in the press, by the wide distribution of a lavishly illustrated pamphlet, she was made known as the greatest of tragediennes since Rachel. But, independently of her art, she was in her own right a celebrity, a "personality"—and the rumors about her industriously put in circulation provoked an uproar of moral controversy. Mlle. Bernhardt's eccentricities became notorious. She habitually took her naps in a rosewood coffin lined with quilted white satin. She had domesticated a lion cub (it was, in fact, a leopard) which, with monkeys and other exotic animals, inhabited the garden of her Paris mansion. She practiced sculpture and painting, and had permitted herself to be photographed, in her studio, wearing white velvet trousers and jacket. Perhaps these vagaries were excusable in a genius, but the presumption of genius should not be allowed to cancel out the certainty of sin. Mlle. Bernhardt was the mother of a young son. The story was told that a London dowager to whom she spoke affectionately about the boy asked, in all innocence, whether Mlle. Bernhardt was married. *"Pas si bête,"* the actress replied smilingly. Although this flippant retort had invested her with a legend of flagrant immorality, she was so assiduously courted by London society that her success appeared to stand on "the ruins of a hundred British prejudices and proprieties." Clearly, the precedent established by London must not be followed in the United States. Soon after Mlle. Bernhardt arrived in New York an eminent clergyman denounced her as "the European courtesan who has come to ruin the morals of the American people." Clerical invective pursued her throughout the tour; the violent sermons preached against her by the Bishop of Chicago proved so valuable as advertising that Abbey gratefully sent him "two hundred dollars for your poor."

In New York, where her tour opened, excitement about the tragedienne ran high. On the day when tickets for her four-week engagement were put on sale, a huge crowd besieged Booth's Theater. The high price of $3 was charged for orchestra seats, and increased prices prevailed elsewhere in the house, but within a few hours the advance sale reached $10,000. On November 8, 1880, Mlle. Bernhardt made her debut in *Adrienne Lecouvreur,* and at the end of the performance an ecstatic audience gave her twenty-seven curtain calls. The critics, almost equally enraptured, praised the music of her golden voice, the expressiveness of her face, with its crown of red-gold hair, the eloquence of her gestures, her feline tread. She made her slender, fragile body a dramatic instrument of extraordinary power. (Presently, fashionable ladies, repudiating the current styles, demanded gowns that would give them her "spiral silhouette" —sheathlike robes with high collars, long, tight sleeves and flaring trains.) That she was the supreme representative of "realistic acting" soon became apparent. Her command of pathos, her fiery outbursts of passion, the poignant realism of her scenes of anguish, her death scenes, were unrivaled. She developed her characterizations with a wealth of beautiful detail and a mastery of style previously unknown on the American stage. She appeared in *Frou Frou,* Victor Hugo's *Hernani* and Racine's *Phèdre,* a role in which she had scored her greatest triumph in Paris six years earlier, and which was to remain throughout her long career the finest of her achievements. But her most spectacular success in New York was gained in a role which she had never performed in France. As the heroine of *La Dame aux Camélias* Bernhardt established her American fame. Long afterwards she described it as the role which held "the quintessence of what my personal art can give," and for nearly forty years her *Camille* was one of the classic performances of the American theater. After her last matinée of this play in New York, fifty thousand people waited outside Booth's Theater to see the celebrated actress enter her carriage. In order to spare his star the fatigue of their ovation, Abbey dressed another actress in Bernhardt's clothes, loaded her arms with bouquets, conducted her to Bernhardt's carriage and entered it with her; they arrived at the Albermarle Hotel,

Sarah Bernhardt as Phèdre, 1880

two blocks away, one hour later. Only then was it was possible for Bernhardt to leave the theater and return to her hotel.

The odyssey of her tour was rich in incident. In Boston, two wealthy admirers, collectors of art, decorated her hotel suite with many of their most valuable paintings; she was touched by this instance of American gallantry. She was persuaded to inspect a whale that had been brought in to a Boston wharf, but the consequences of the expedition were exasperating. In each of the major cities where she played engagements the whale also made its appearance as an attraction, advertised with her name. Enterprising manufacturers attached her name, and often her photograph, to a varied assortment of commodities, from cigars to perfume, but this evidence of American popularity failed to please her.

In St. Louis, Abbey insisted that her jewels be exhibited in the store of a leading jeweler. The proprietor added to the display many costly items from his own stock, alleging them to be her property. On the night that she left St. Louis, it was discovered that a gang of outlaws planned to uncouple her car from the train and relieve her of her jewels. The plot was foiled by a band of detectives after a battle with the bandits. As Bernhardt's special train neared New Orleans, Abbey informed her that floods had dangerously weakened a bridge over which it must pass. The engineer offered to attempt the crossing if she would give him $2,500 to be telegraphed to his wife; he doubted that the bridge would hold up. Bernhardt gave the engineer his fee, but only when her train had started across the bridge did she realize that she "was risking without their consent the lives of twenty-seven persons." The bridge trembled and swayed as the train sped over it, and when the last car had cleared, it collapsed. After playing engagements in the principal cities, Bernhardt toured a long series of one-night stands—towns like Leavenworth, Kansas; Quincy, Illinois; Grand Rapids, Michigan; Bradford and Erie in Pennsylvania—"arriving at three, four, and sometimes six o'clock in the evening, and leaving immediately after the play." Her entire tour, which closed with return engagements in Boston and New York, lasted for seven months, and took her to fifty cities in which she gave 156 performances. Her personal profits amounted to $194,-000. Never before had a star made so large a fortune in so short a time.

Soon after "the divine Sarah" returned to France, Abbey arranged an American tour, on terms almost as munificent, for an actress whose dramatic ability was the least noteworthy of her talents. Celebrity had come to Mrs. Langtry as "the Jersey Lily"—the title of her portrait by Sir John Millais—and, with the assistance of an august personage, she had converted it into a more profitable notoriety. She began her spectacular career as the reigning beauty of London society. "Wherever I went—to theaters, picture galleries, shops—I was actually mobbed," she later declared, noting that at social functions "many of the guests stood on chairs to obtain a better view of me, and I could not help but hear their audible comments on my appearance as I passed down the drawing room."

She was a tall, golden-haired young woman whose superb figure, magnificent shoulders and arms, and lovely complexion justified the initial commotion that she caused. The commotion increased when the Prince of Wales showed a marked predilection for her company. Mrs. Langtry had developed an aptitude for leading her private life in view of the public. Her exercise of this unconventional skill brought about the convenient disappearance of her husband and,

Mrs. Langtry, 1882

in due course, the less convenient detachment of her royal admirer. But when financial bankruptcy overtook her, it enabled her to go on the stage "at a very high salary." Money alone reconciled her to the prospect of "a very dull and monotonous existence." Mrs. Langtry's liking for her new profession was somewhat less than tepid: "I had loomed so largely in the public eye that there was no novelty in facing the crowded audience, in which I knew most of the occupants of the stalls and boxes, and all in the cheaper parts knew me." A successful engagement at the Haymarket Theater in London and a provincial tour enlivened by torchlight processions and other displays of public enthusiasm prepared her to come to the United States as a star at the head of her own company.

During her first engagement in New York, Mrs. Langtry was announced to appear in *An Unequal Match,* an old play by Tom Taylor, in *As You Like It* and in *The Honeymoon.* Abbey had so effectively publicized her beauty and her legend that curiosity became irresistible. Americans were eager to pay for the privilege of seeing her, and it made little difference what roles she acted, or whether her performance of them was good or bad. Her Rosalind evoked no enthusiasm from the critics, but it packed Wallack's Theater for two weeks; the public's desire to see her in doublet and hose made adverse criticism irrelevant. Though the aura of illicit romance that surrounded Mrs. Langtry needed no renovation, the newspapers soon reported an event of universal interest. She had acquired an American adorer, Frederick Gebhard, a millionaire and a figure of some social prominence. Her disinclination to privacy proved very helpful to the press, which chronicled in fascinating detail the progress of Gebhard's infatuation.

When Mrs. Langtry took her troupe on tour, Gebhard accompanied her in her private car, and although this caused a tremendous sensation it did not diminish the size of her audiences; in some cities she played to the highest receipts ever taken by the theaters. After a long, profitable tour she returned to New York for a second engagement. An improvement in her art was noted when she performed W. S. Gilbert's *Pygmalion and Galatea,* in which she enacted a marble statue quickened into life by the passion of her lover. She was by now convinced that "purely from the actor's point of view, America is the promised land," though, as she acknowledged, "it was not altogether the idea of continued success that held me." Her determination to remain in the United States may have been strengthened by Gebhard's solicitude. He provided her with a luxurious New York home on West Twenty-third Street, where they entertained lavishly. Few actresses had ever played, off the stage, so melodramatic a role, and Americans, even if scandalized by her conduct, were allured by her personality. Napoleon Sarony, who bought the monopoly of her photographs "for a very large sum," soon found that they were in country-wide demand.

When the Jersey Lily next took to the road she was equipped with a private car built to her order. Except for her acting, which never rose above mediocrity, most expressions of her personality were at least arresting; the car was sensational. Its blue-painted exterior was adorned with wreaths of golden lilies and a large amount of decorative brass wrought into designs of the same flower.

Her bedroom was upholstered in green silk brocade; "the bath and its fittings were of silver, and the curtains of both rooms, of rose-colored silk, were trimmed with a profusion of Brussels lace." A large, ornate drawing room contained a piano. "There were two guest rooms, a maid's room, complete even to a sewing machine, a pantry, a kitchen, and sleeping quarters for the staff." Enormous ice chests under the car made possible the storage of provisions. In this perambulating palace, during the five years of her American residence, the Jersey Lily took her beauty and charm, her fabulous jewels, her extravagant costumes, to every town "sufficiently important to be marked on the map."

However, she failed to visit one town until too late. Langtry, in Texas, was founded and named in her honor, by Sheriff Roy Bean, himself a celebrity by virtue of being "the law west of the Pecos River." Mrs. Langtry offered to present her municipal namesake an ornamental drinking fountain. She was chagrined when Bean informed her that the proposed gift "would be quite useless, as the only thing the citizens of Langtry did *not* drink was water." For one or another reason she kept postponing her visit of ceremony. When finally she was able to spend a half-hour in Langtry, at the Jersey Lily Saloon, "King" Roy Bean had recently died. She was told that it would have been the proudest day in his life had he lived to meet her. This caused Mrs. Langtry professional as well as personal regret. In a career that, surprisingly, had turned out to be neither dull nor monotonous, no audience had ever refused to wait for her. Perhaps she did not recall that, in her previous transactions with royalty, punctuality had been essential.

Americans in the road towns rejoiced in the swift ascent to fame of Miss Mary Anderson, whom they had acclaimed before her first appearance in New York, and to whom, in the days of her greatest glory, they gave the name, "Our Mary." Her beauty exemplified a native ideal, and by the purity of her life and the dignity of her attitude toward her art she increased public respect for the theatrical profession. She was a tall girl, stately and statuesque. Her features were exquisite, and her cloud of brown hair softened their perfect regularity. Her beauty was classic, virginal, passionless; but passion rang out in her rich contralto voice, as if intuitively she understood experiences beyond the compass of her own innocence. At the age of fourteen, in Louisville, Kentucky, she was taken by her parents to see Edwin Booth. "I felt for the first time that acting was not merely a delightful amusement, but a serious art that might be used for high ends," she wrote many years later. Helped only by a few books, she began studying for the stage. She was given an opportunity to read for Miss Cushman. "You have all the attributes that go to make a fine actress," the old tragedienne told her. "My advice to you is not to begin at the bottom of the ladder." Miss Anderson resolved to begin only at the top, and when, not long afterwards, John McCullough heard her read, and offered her a debut as Lady Anne in his performance of *Richard III*, "I answered that I would rather not play second fiddle, even to him."

Her debut was made at Macauley's Theater in Louisville in 1875, when she was sixteen. She played a single performance of Juliet, was praised by the local press, and later obtained a week's engagement during which she appeared in *Fazio, The Hunchback, Evadne, The Lady of Lyons,* all of which, like the role of Juliet, remained in her permanent repertory. A successful engagement in New Orleans followed, and there she was required to undertake Miss Cushman's role of Meg Merrilies—a singular part for a beautiful girl—which became one of her early vehicles as a barnstorming star. For two years, she toured the southern and middle western cities in which stock companies continued to operate. "Though the experience was very hard," she recalled, "I learned little by it, except many of the most irritating of the old-school traditions, and to identify the art with unceasing drudgery." Her most popular role, with the road audiences, was Parthenia in *Ingomar,* and their judgment was later confirmed by New York and London. Miss Anderson appeared in New York for the first time in 1877, with sufficient success to bring her assurance and prestige. A holiday trip to England and France, during which she studied the acting of Bernhardt, Ristori and the leading London stars, increased her store of technical knowledge, and after her return to the United States she always toured at the head of her own company.

She refused to act in plays "that drag one through the mire of immorality, even when they show a good lesson in the end." She declared that anything unfit to be discussed in her parlor had no place in the theater. (W. S. Gilbert once said to her in jest, "I hear that you hate gross things so much that you can hardly be induced to take your share of the gross receipts.") These convictions restricted her repertory: *Fazio, The Lady of Lyons, The Hunchback, Love, Ingomar*—her plays were already old-fashioned, outmoded. Yet the public,

Mary Anderson in "Pygmalion and Galatea"

year after year, came to see her perform them. Her Juliet was a perennial favorite, and when she added *Pygmalion and Galatea* to her list (at the suggestion of General William T. Sherman) the character of the statue-maiden, which initially she disliked, became her most notable role. In 1883, Henry Abbey engaged Miss Anderson to appear for two seasons at the Lyceum Theater in London, during the American tours of Henry Irving and Miss Ellen Terry with the Lyceum company. An excellent company was engaged for her and, for the first time, her plays were mounted lavishly. "How I longed for the simple scenery of the old days," she later recorded, "when the characters were the chief consideration, and the upholsterer and scenic artist very minor adjuncts!" But in London she met with far greater acclaim than she had ever received in the United States. Lord Tennyson and Wilkie Collins proposed to write plays for her. The famous artist, G. F. Watts, painted her portrait; other eminent painters designed her costumes and scenery. She performed Juliet for a run of one hundred nights, and was invited to play Rosalind at the Shakespeare Memorial Theater. Offers for tours in France, Spain, Germany and Australia reached her, and were declined.

It was as a world-famous star that she returned to the United States in 1885, with her magnificent London productions and her Lyceum company, bringing as her leading man Johnston Forbes-Robertson. Her American tour, which carried her to California, was a triumphal progress. Three years later, at the Lyceum in London, she revived *The Winter's Tale,* playing the roles of Hermione and Perdita. It ran for 164 nights, and in the autumn of 1888 she brought the production to the United States. Severely conscientious and a rigorous judge of her own work, she could recall only four performances during her entire career that completely satisfied her aspirations. The practice of her art, though not the study of it, had grown, as time passed, more and more distasteful. "To be conscious that one's person was a target for any who paid to make it one; to live for months at a time in one groove, with uncongenial surroundings, and in an atmosphere seldom penetrated by the sun and air; and to be continually repeating the same passions and thoughts in the same words—that was the most part of my daily life. . . ." She was twenty-eight; she felt that she had reached the peak of her achievement and surmised that she could add nothing to her fame. Without any public farewell, she retired at the close of her tour. One year later, she married Antonio de Navarro, a man of wealth, and settled in England. There, past her eightieth year, she died in 1940.

In bringing Henry Irving, Miss Ellen Terry and the Lyceum Theater company to the United States in 1883, Henry Abbey realized that he was undertaking an exploit of unprecedented difficulty and complexity. But he probably did not foresee its momentous consequences. The visit of these artists was to initiate revolutionary changes in American methods of production, stagecraft, acting style and, eventually, in the taste of the playgoing public. (Their visit antedated by more than two years Augustin Daly's production of *The Merry Wives of Windsor,* the first important illustration of Irving's influence.) All other foreign stars had been satisfied to tour the United States with inferior companies, assembled for a single expedition, and with inadequate scenery.

Irving brought to America a permanent acting company and the productions—eomplete to the most minute accessories—of the plays which they were to perform. American performances were to be precisely like those given at the Lyceum, and this involved a transfer to the United States of nearly one hundred people, for in addition to the acting company, a manager, stage manager and musical director, the necessary staff included lighting experts, stage technicians and even wig makers. No project of comparable magnitude had ever before been attempted.

The fame of Irving and Miss Terry had preceded them. At the age of forty-five, Irving was the acknowledged leader of the British theatrical profession. He had attained this position of eminence during five seasons at the Lyceum where, with Miss Terry as his leading woman, he carried to success the same program that Edwin Booth had conceived for his theater but had been prevented from accomplishing. The careers of Booth and Irving had crossed twice, both times significantly. When Booth made his first professional visit to England, in 1861, he played an engagement at the Theater Royal, Manchester, where Irving, his junior by five years, was a member of the stock company that supported him. Booth's intellectual approach to his art, his poetic imagination, his flexible technique and his extraordinary naturalness deeply impressed Irving. Booth, more than any other actor, influenced him in perfecting his own craftsmanship and in developing a personal style which in no way resembled that of his model. In 1880, when Booth returned to England, Irving was the idol of the London public. Booth's London engagement was played in extremely adverse circumstances. He appeared in a second-class theater and, as he wrote, "with a wretched company, and poorly furnished stage, compared with Irving's superior settings." To make matters worse, his wife's illness reached a crisis and her mind gave way. Though Booth won laudatory notices and found the London public appreciative, he was dissatisfied with the results of his engagement. He told Irving that he would like to give a series of matinées at the Lyceum. Irving proposed, instead, to put on a production of *Othello* in which he and Booth would alternate in the roles of Othello and Iago, and Miss Terry would play Desdemona. Twenty-one of these remarkable performances were given to enthusiastic audiences. The critics, analyzing the differences between Irving's and Booth's concepts and styles, praised both actors for their characteristic merits. But to Miss Terry, Booth seemed, when not acting, "broken and devoid of ambition." She wondered whether his pride had not been more hurt by Irving's "magnificent hospitality than it ever could have been by disaster."

For his part, Booth was struck by Irving's exercise of a talent in which he knew himself to be conspicuously lacking. "At rehearsal his will is absolute law," he wrote, "whether it concern the entry of a messenger with a letter or the reading of a letter by Miss Terry. From first to last he rules the stage with a will of absolute iron, but also with a patience that is marvelous. He sits among his players watching every movement, listening to every word, constantly stopping anyone—Miss Terry as well as the messenger—who does not do exactly right. He rises, explains the fault, and that part of the scene is immediately repeated. His patience holds out against any test. Over and over again the line is recited or a bit of action is done, till all is perfect."

When Booth landed in New York, late in the summer of 1881, reporters questioned him about Irving, whom Americans already believed was his sole rival on the English-speaking stage. "He is a very superior actor," Booth declared, "and is gifted with a remarkable talent for stage management—two qualifications for the stage which are seldom found united in the same person."

Both qualifications contributed to the effect that Irving had in the United States, to which even Booth himself was subject.

Yet Americans knew that, notwithstanding Irving's eminence, he was the subject of heated controversy in England. Few actors had ever aroused comparable dissension—such idolatrous enthusiasm, and such savage detraction. His greatness as a melodramatic actor was acknowledged, but his merits as a tragedian were in constant debate. He was earnest, intelligent, ambitious. ("His work, his work!" Ellen Terry wrote. "He has always held his life, and his death, second to his work.") But some critics pointed out that he was essentially a "picturesque" actor—that he relied for his effects "upon the art with which he presents a certain figure to the eye, rather than upon the manner in which he speaks his part." His roles always bore the peculiar stamp of his personality; his concepts of them were usually "startling, picturesque, irregular, brilliant— sometimes less brilliant than bizarre." Irving's arrogant, hawklike face, and fine, expressive hands were his best physical attributes. He was otherwise unprepossessing; a tall, lean man whose excessively thin legs and extremely long hair were the delight of caricaturists. His strutting stage walk was often derided. His voice was harsh and monotonous. The mannerisms and eccentricities of his delivery became, in the United States as in Great Britain, the butt of ridicule by comedians and mimics. When playing Shakespeare, he habitually interlarded his speeches with what Miss Terry described as "interjections, ejaculations and grunts." His reading of verse was therefore widely attacked, and it was charged that "Shakespeare's finest lines pass from his lips without his paying the scantiest tribute to their quality." Yet in spite of all his failings, Irving was capable of casting a spell on audiences—the spell of a personality which, if not seductive, was incontestably powerful.

About Miss Terry, there was no controversy; she had been recognized as an actress of exquisite genius before associating herself with Irving. She had first triumphed, in 1875, as Portia, with the sense of "being lifted on high by a single stroke of the mighty wing of glory," and remembered, thirty years later, that "everyone seemed to be in love with me." This universal infatuation continued. At thirty-five, when she came to the United States, she was accounted the greatest actress on the British stage. She was tall, very slender, flaxen-haired; though her features were irregular she gave an effect of great beauty. ("Ellen Terry actually invented her own beauty," Bernard Shaw declared.) Her voice, low and husky, was musical and her elocution was superb. Her parents were actors, and at the age of ten she was acting with the Charles Keans. At sixteen, she was married to the painter, George Frederick Watts, who was thirty years her senior; he soon wished to get rid of her and did so. Miserable, and loathing her profession, she went back to the stage, then abruptly retired from it to become the mistress of Edward William Godwin, an architect, to whom she bore two children. After six years she returned to the stage and scored her triumph. Her liaison with Godwin ended; Watts belatedly divorced her; she married an actor, Charles Kelly. His professional jealousy of her, and probably his resentment of her intimate relationship with Irving, brought about their legal separation two years before she came to the United States.

In the United States, as in England, there was much speculation about the relations of Irving and Miss Terry; it would continue long after their deaths. Irving was separated from his wife who refused to divorce him. On the night of his first great success in London, as they drove home from a party, Mrs. Irving asked him bitterly, "Are you going on making a fool of yourself like this all your life?"

He told the coachman to stop, got out of the carriage, never again returned to his home or spoke to his wife. This occurred seven years before the beginning of his partnership with Miss Terry, an artistic union which became one of the classic legends of the stage.

"I think he has always cared for me a little, very little, and has had passing fancies, but he really *cares* for scarcely any one," she once noted, and she surmised that, in spite of his professed admiration, "he has only 'admired' my usefulness to him." There were qualities in his nature, she wrote after his death, "which were unintelligible to me, perhaps because I have always been more woman than artist. He always put the theater first." She acknowledged that, "I, of all people can perhaps appreciate him least justly, although I was his associate on the stage for a quarter of a century, and was on the terms of the closest friendship with him for almost as long a time. He had precisely the qualities that I never find likeable. He was an egotist—an egotist of the great type. . . ."

Yet, as an artist, she admired him unreservedly, obeyed him always, put her own greater genius at his command. To someone who ventured to condemn to her one of Irving's performances, she blazed out, "I am sorry you don't realize that the worst thing Henry Irving could do would be better than the best of anyone else."

If Irving loved her, she soon learned that he loved himself more, and came to resent this. That, in the early years of their association, she loved him deeply seems obvious. "I have the simplest faith that absolute devotion to another human being means the greatest *happiness*," she wrote in her old age. There was no question about her absolute devotion to Irving.

Irving and Miss Terry made their American debuts on successive evenings in October, 1883, at the Star Theater (formerly Wallack's) in New York. Irving chose to present himself in the role of Mathias in *The Bells,* a translation of a melodrama by Erkmann-Chatrian. This was the role which, overnight, had brought him celebrity in London. He played an Alsatian innkeeper who, having murdered a Polish Jew years earlier, is terrified by the powers of mesmerism, which might be used to force a confession from him. Irving's climactic scene was the re-enactment of the murder, by the innkeeper, in a dream, to the insistent jingle of the sleighbells that had originally accompanied it. He acted this to the top of his form, and it evoked tremendous enthusiasm. On the following night, W. G. Wills's *Charles I* served to introduce Miss Terry. It gave her an opportunity for pathos, and Irving a role of quiet dignity in which, as the monarch, he displayed his mastery of make-up. Later, in *The Belle's Stratagem,* Miss Terry revealed her sparkling talents as a comedienne; the role of Letitia Hardy was always accounted one of her finest achievements. In *Louis XI,* adapted from the French by Boucicault for Charles Kean, Irving appeared in one of his most popular and "picturesque" character roles. In *The Lyons Mail,* another piece inherited from Kean, Irving presented a noted melodramatic specialty. He played the dual roles of Joseph Lesurques, a good man falsely accused of murder, and his double, Dubosc, the wicked, degraded murderer. Audiences were astonished by one of Irving's brilliant stage tricks: in one scene, Irving, as Dubosc, unkempt, drunk and raving, made an exit and returned, almost instantly, in the guise of the handsome, slender, saintly Lesurques. The trick was effective; no critic rebuked Irving for its triviality, or for the comparative triviality of his melodramas.

For by this time he had brought forward something of genuine importance. The Lyceum production of *The Merchant of Venice* proved to be the sensation of the engagement. Irving's Shylock, one of the most powerful of all his personations, received high praise in spite of his mannered, eccentric readings. ("My Shylock," he declared to William Winter, "is the best that has ever been given.") His conception of the character broke with established tradition. Unlike Booth, who presented Shylock as a usurer impelled only by personal hatred and greed, Irving made him the representative of a persecuted race, a sympathetic character moved finally to revenge by hereditary wrongs vividly revived in personal injuries. Irving's mastery of theatrical effect in portraying character was illustrated by an innovation in stage business that yielded a moment of intense pathos. He brought the curtain down on the elopement of Jessica in a street ablaze with lights and crowded by maskers. A moment later, the curtain rose on the same street, dark and empty, and Shylock returned from the banquet to knock at the door of his empty home, to realize that he had been robbed and deserted by his daughter, and to stand, mute and hopeless, as the curtain fell.

For Miss Terry, Irving restored the beautiful final scene in the garden of Belmont, always previously deleted from the play. Miss Terry's Portia was acclaimed as a creation of rare sensibility, and her marvelous elocution won lavish praise. (Nobody noticed that she was "self-conscious and uncomfortable" in the casket scene. There, after Bassanio's choice, she gently touched his arm. In London, one critic had rebuked her for this bit of business. "Any suggestion of *indelicacy* in my treatment of a part always blighted me," she confessed. Fortunately she did not know that old Mrs. Fanny Kemble, seeing this at the Lyceum, had been shocked by its vulgarity to the point of exclaiming, in horror, "Good heavens, she's touching him!")

The effect of this production of *The Merchant* was both immediate and enduring. It presented a company trained to individual excellence and ensemble

Henry Irving in "The Merchant of Venice"

brilliance in playing, but for one purpose only: to lift into higher relief the acting of the two stars. Irving did not inaugurate the treatment of Shakespeare's plays as vehicles for stars. But he was the first producer to realize that the performances of great stars could be enhanced by the general excellence of a supporting company whose members were schooled to perfect subordination, even in the most subtle details of acting style. Audiences were impressed by what they took to be a "perfect all-rounded performance," but although this impression was deceptive, it brought discredit on star performances given with inadequate companies whose playing was merely slovenly. Moreover, scenically, Irving's *Merchant* proved to be a revelation. In every detail of pictorial treatment—in magnificence of costumes, in solidity of bridges and buildings, in lighting effects and the dramatic management of crowds—it was a triumph of realistic stagecraft which eclipsed anything previously seen. It heralded an era of strenuous effort to achieve, not illusion, but absolute realism, on the stage—an era of "production" in which plays were treated primarily, not as dramas to be acted, but as opportunities for literal representation. It was the initial impulse to what Otis Skinner later described as "the exaltation of the meticulous."

In the general acclaim that Irving's stagecraft evoked, only one critic pointed to an inherent hazard. "The danger . . . is common," Henry James wrote from London "—the danger of smothering a piece in its accessories . . . The reason is doubtless that the art of putting a piece on the stage, as it is called (as if the only way to put a piece on the stage were not to act it), has lately made an advance . . . which is out of proportion to any improvement that has taken place in the dramatic art proper. Scenery and decorations have been brought to their highest perfection, while elocution and action, the interpretation of meanings, the representation of human feelings, have not been made the objects of serious study."

" *There was a star danced + under that Was I born*": Beatrice :

Ellen Terry :

Ellen Terry in "Much Ado About Nothing"

After a four-week engagement in New York, Irving, Miss Terry and their company went on tour: Philadelphia, Boston, Baltimore, Chicago, St. Louis, Cincinnati, Columbus, Washington, saw them; they returned to Boston, took in the larger cities of New England, played in Canada, and in March, 1884, appeared again in New York. In Philadelphia, Irving put on his *Hamlet,* which he had not given in New York apparently through fear of comparison with Booth. It was well enough received in Philadelphia to enable him to write that "it is a bitter pill to certain Americans that any actor but *one* can be accepted in it." (But when he played *Hamlet* in New York, on his second American tour, he was so severely treated by the critics that he withdrew the play after three performances.) Irving gave Chicago the first showing of the company's elaborate production of *Much Ado About Nothing*. In New York, where Miss Terry's Beatrice was hailed as the finest in the history of the local stage, the play ran for three weeks of the final four-week engagement. During the tour, which had lasted six months, the American public paid more than $400,000 to see the stars and their company, of which Irving's share was one-half. The clear profit to the Lyceum Theater in London was almost $60,000.

The effect of Irving's and Miss Terry's success was most immediately felt by Edwin Booth; but as a theme for reflection rather than as a challenge to contest. Irving in all his roles was always Irving. His personality was his sole medium, and his characterizations were laboriously designed to exploit its resources. He did not attempt to conceive a role independently; he refashioned the character created by the playwright to suit his own peculiar capabilities. The method that Irving applied deliberately, Miss Terry applied spontaneously. As her son, Edward Gordon Craig, was to say, "She played but one part—herself; and when not herself, she couldn't play it." It was this inversion of the actor's traditional craft, this confinement of his medium, which made possible the so-called realism of Irving's and Miss Terry's acting, praised by the critics as an artistic achievement and hailed by the public as an innovation to be emulated. For Booth, this form of acting was not art, and its realism was spurious. He conceived his roles as characters in their own right. It was his obligation to submerge himself in them, not to identify them with himself. His task as an actor was to portray characters convincingly; to endow them with the illusion of reality; this was his doctrine of naturalness in acting. On the stage, he was only the character that he was playing—he was never Booth. He realized that, in Irving, he was confronted by a new theory and a new school. He surmised that their popularity with the public would increase; that literalism and not illusion would come to rule the stage; and that he would be outmoded.

Comparisons were made between Irving's magnificent productions and Booth's shabby staging; between the excellence of the Lyceum company, and the inadequacy of Booth's usual supporting casts. But Booth's tours continued to be profitable, and his personal prestige was undiminished. In 1885, Mme. Ristori, having studied English and played in it in London, came to the United States for a final "farewell" tour, acting in English with an American company. Before returning to Italy, she pleaded for an opportunity to act *Macbeth* "with the Talma of the United States." Two performances were given, at the Academy of Music in New York, and in Philadelphia.

Booth's health was failing, but the following season, when Salvini undertook his fourth American tour, a three-week engagement with Booth was arranged. For one week each in New York, Philadelphia and Boston, the two stars played in *Othello* and *Hamlet;* Salvini taking the roles of Othello and the Ghost, Booth those of Iago and Hamlet, with a superior company. The receipts for their twelve performances were nearly $44,000. But Booth suffered a misfortune. At one of the New York performances, after Salvini, as the enraged Othello, had thrown him to the floor and he had regained his feet, Booth suffered an attack of vertigo. He took several unsteady steps, stumbled, fell down backwards into the footlights. There were some hisses and catcalls. Salvini lifted him to his feet, and the play continued. But in the last act, during Salvini's death scene, the vertigo came on him again. Booth began to mumble, and sank into a chair. Members of the company, gathering around him, screened him from view of the audience. In one of the newspapers, a savage attack was made, charging that Booth had been intoxicated. Lawrence Barrett and other close friends immediately wrote letters to the press refuting the charge. The scandal eventually died down. Salvini wrote: "I cannot find epithets to characterize those twelve performances. The word 'extraordinary' is not enough, nor is 'splendid'; I will call them 'unique'."

Barrett proposed that Booth come under his management; Booth would be relieved of all the responsibilities he disliked; together, as co-stars, they would tour the country. The arrangement delighted Booth. Barrett, to a considerable degree, possessed the two qualifications which Booth thought so remarkable in Irving. He gathered an excellent company and trained it finely, and he provided appropriate scenic equipment for the repertory. The plays were: *Julius Caesar, Othello, Hamlet, Macbeth, King Lear, The Merchant of Venice, Katharine and Petruchio, The Fool's Revenge, Don Caesar de Bazan, The King's Pleasure* and *David Garrick.* The roles of Othello and Iago were alternated. Booth played Brutus, Hamlet, Macbeth, Lear, Shylock, Petruchio and Don Caesar. Barrett acted Cassius, Laertes, Macduff, Edgar, Bassanio, Gringoire in *The King's Pleasure,* and Garrick.

Sharing a private car, the two stars began their first tour in the autumn of 1887. In a period of forty weeks they played sixty-eight cities and towns in all parts of the country; of these, forty-six were one-night stands. Chicago, Philadelphia, Boston, New York and San Francisco each had engagements of approximately two weeks; in a few cities, the stars played for two or three nights. Though prices of tickets were doubled, crowded houses greeted them everywhere. In Kansas City, their single performance opened the new Warder Opera House. The roof of the building had not been completed. They played *Othello* in one set, boxed in to keep out the wind. The audience, shivering with cold, wore hats and overcoats; nevertheless, the stars received an ovation. In places like Oshkosh, Wisconsin; Bay City, Michigan; Macon, Georgia; Waco, Texas; Lincoln, Nebraska, where they played for one night, crowds awaited their arrival at the railroad stations. People who could not afford to attend their performance wanted at least to see the two great tragedians. Two grave, silvery-haired gentlemen wearing astrakhan-collared overcoats and glossy silk hats descended from their private car and walked sedately up and down the platform. This was their exercise, their way of taking the air.

They toured again the following season: longer engagements in the principal cities, and fewer one-night stands. In Rochester, New York, on April 3, 1889, during a performance of *Othello,* Booth, who was playing Iago, suddenly could not utter his lines. He had suffered a light stroke of paralysis. The curtain was rung down. Barrett, overcome by grief, told the audience that America's greatest tragedian would probably never again be seen on the stage. For some days the nation's press carried predictions of Booth's approaching death. Barrett unhappily continued the tour alone, but after a brief rest Booth's physicians permitted him to rejoin the company. His powers were waning fast, and he knew it, yet he could not resign himself to leaving the stage.

Barrett, during the season beginning in the autumn of 1889, wished to tour independently. He arranged a tour for Booth under exceptionally favorable circumstances, with a weekly guarantee of $3,000. A notable company was assembled in which Otis Skinner, leaving Daly's Theater, took the roles formerly assumed by Barrett. Barrett engaged Mme. Helena Modjeska to co-star with Booth, at a weekly salary of $1,500. She had to procure her release from a contract with other managers, and this cost her $400 each week; but, as she noted, "I much preferred to be with Edwin Booth than to play with insufficient support under a commercial management, and I did not think I made a sacrifice in giving up a few dollars for my artistic comfort." (Her artistic comfort had been severely jolted in 1883 when, with high hopes, she added Henrik Ibsen's *A Doll's House* to her repertory, playing it first in Louisville, Kentucky. A very few performances indicated that it "was not relished by American audiences, and we had to take it off.") Booth was fifty-six, Mme. Modjeska was forty-five. Their repertory included *Hamlet, Macbeth, The Merchant of Venice, Much Ado About Nothing* (seldom performed), *Richelieu*. There were also three double bills: Booth in *The Fool's Revenge,* Mme. Modjeska in *Marie Stuart;* Booth in *Don Caesar de Bazan,* Mme. Modjeska in a curtailed *Marie Stuart;* Booth as Petruchio, Mme. Modjeska in *Donna Diana.*

Skinner, who had been in Booth's company ten years earlier, thought him "the shell of the great actor; symmetrical still, but with the echo of youthful inspiration growing fainter." When Skinner went to Booth's dressing room to call him, Booth "rarely laid aside his book or paper without being seized by a vertigo. He would reel like a drunken man, and his first steps would be quite uncertain." Mme. Modjeska, with whom he shared a private car, thought that his health was failing rapidly. "He often seems tired and ill," she noted in her diary. "I heard him saying after some scenes, 'I wish I had all my strength and vigor to play this as I ought to play it.' "

But she recorded her pleasure in his beautiful playing: "He always finds a right measure, even when situations might tempt one to exaggerate, he very seldom oversteps the limit." Often, when they returned to their car after the play, they would ask some of the company to have supper with them, and Booth would talk for hours, causing Mme. Modjeska to marvel at his "narrative gift, his impressionability, brightness and intelligence, of which those who do not know him cannot have any idea." One night at supper, "we spoke of Shakespeare, and then I had an opportunity of learning how deeply and thoroughly Booth studies his parts. He says he has no ear for music, but any mistake in blank verse jars upon him as a false note. Of course he puts a great stress upon pronunciation, emphasis, and inflections of the voice, and he kindly pointed out some of my mistakes in pronunciation, which I gratefully accepted, and tried to correct myself at the next performance."

In the autumn of 1890, Booth and Barrett began another joint starring tour. On March 2, 1891, they opened an engagement at the Broadway Theater in New York. On the night of March 18th, a performance of *Richelieu* was scheduled, with Booth as the Cardinal and Barrett as De Mauprat. Before the performance Booth was informed that Barrett, in his dressing room, seemed to be very ill. He found Barrett in his hat and overcoat, his face hidden; he had been crying. Booth urged Barrett to go to his hotel, but Barrett insisted that he would play. At the end of the third act, when Booth was lying on the Cardinal's bed, Barrett leaned over him and whispered, "I cannot go on."

His understudy took his place and the performance was finished. Booth went to Barrett's rooms next morning. "Do not come near me, Edwin," Barrett said, "for my disease may be infectious, and you must be very careful."

A few hours later, Barrett died. After the funeral, not wishing to throw the company out of work, Booth finished the engagement at the Broadway Theater and played the season's last week at the Academy of Music in Brooklyn. The final performance was a matinée of *Hamlet* on April 4th, and in response to an ovation from the audience, Booth made a brief speech. Outside the theater, a huge crowd had gathered to cheer him. Police made a passage for him to his carriage, and in the tumult he drove away from a stage door for the last time.

He planned to rest for a year, then return to the stage. "I don't know what is to become of me," he told William Winter, one night at The Players. "My strength is going. I grow weaker, all the time; and if I cannot play the parts well, I must quit acting. I don't know what to do."

Winter did not find it easy to suggest that Booth abandon any notion of returning to the stage. Thereafter, Booth's vitality ebbed quickly. In April, 1893, he had another stroke. On June 7th, he sank rapidly. Very late, that night, during a thunderstorm, the electric lights in The Players, and in its neighborhood, dimmed and went out. A few moments after the current was restored, Edwin Booth died.

Audiences in the road cities sometimes declared their independence of the taste of New York. Joseph Jefferson, for example, drew larger houses on tour than in the metropolis. His *Rip Van Winkle* was a perennial attraction, and for a decade his version of *The Rivals* delighted playgoers. (His cousin, William Warren, said that it was "Sheridan twenty miles away," and old John Gilbert, pronouncing it "a sacrilege," hoped that Sheridan's ghost would haunt Jefferson.) In *The Rivals* Jefferson, past his fiftieth year, played Bob Acres. He co-starred with the veteran Mrs. John Drew who, sixty years after her debut as a child prodigy, gave the finest performance of her career in the role of Mrs. Malaprop. It was the road, not New York, that elevated James O'Neill, a handsome, versatile actor, to reluctant one-role stardom. O'Neill triumphed in the role of Edmond Dantes in *Monte Cristo,* and except for occasional appearances in *Virginius,* the public refused to let him perform other plays. Year after year, he toured in *Monte Cristo;* in the end, the play ruthlessly absorbed thirty years of his professional life in more than six thousand performances.

It was the road, defying the dominance of New York, that chose the successor of Miss Mary Anderson. Unheralded, unknown, but offering herself as a star, Miss Julia Marlowe in 1887 gave a matinée of *Ingomar* in New York; shortly afterwards, she appeared at the Star Theater for one week in the roles of Juliet and Viola. She was a girl of twenty-two, tall, slender and very handsome. Dark-haired, dark-eyed, her fine features and deeply dimpled chin gave an effect of beauty to a face that was remarkably expressive. Her low-pitched voice was clear and resonant; she had studied elocution and read verse extremely well. After her engagement at the Star, she went to see Daniel Frohman, manager of the celebrated stock company at the Lyceum Theater on Fourth Avenue and Twenty-fourth Street. Frohman offered her the "juvenile business" in his company for the following season; this she declined.

"Then what do you want?" he inquired, feeling that he had given her a splendid opportunity.

"I want to go out as a star in Shakespeare," she declared.

Frohman was aware that she had caused no sensation in New York, and he did not undertake the management of·her projected starring tour. Miss Marlowe formed her own company and toured for ten years—seldom venturing nearer to Manhattan than Brooklyn—in a repertory that included *Romeo and Juliet, As You Like It, Much Ado About Nothing, Cymbeline, Pygmalion and Galatea, Ingomar* and *The Love Chase.* It was the prestige that she gained outside New York that eventually brought her the accolade of metropolitan stardom. While Miss Marlowe was arduously making her way on the road, her future co-star, Edward H. Sothern, was spending most of each year as a traveling star under the management of Daniel Frohman. He was the son of E. A. Sothern, and a good-looking young man of whimsical nature who had developed a light, engaging style in comedy and in romantic roles. Frohman chose vehicles that were admirably suited to young Sothern's personality, gave him a preliminary season every year at the Lyceum, in the New York, and sent him on tours with the added luster of recent metropolitan success.

Julia Marlowe in "Romeo and Juliet," 1888

It was to the great public of the road that Richard Mansfield carried his campaign for ascendancy. In New York, he believed, a powerful conspiracy against him existed. "I am aware of a cabal," he wrote in 1890, "to keep me from the throne I am striving for—in this cabal are Palmer, Frohman, Daly, Barrett and Booth—the latter maybe innocently." Wild notions of professional hostility often obsessed him. He had a passionate desire to be recognized everywhere as the greatest actor of his time. He wanted wealth because to him it signified power and to the American public, he felt, it signified eminence. "I think *everything* is possible to me if I am helped," he wrote, "and I feel, more and more, that the future—the immediate future—of the American Stage lies very much in my hands. At all events, I intend laying violent hands on *it,* coûte que coûte." As to his artistic aims, he could state them quite simply: "I desire to do great plays and do them greatly, and I desire to do *new* things. The world must move on—on— not back, and I shall move on also; perhaps *up*—perhaps *out.*"

Mansfield was thirty-three, a short, stocky vigorous man who looked like a Prussian officer. He was broad-shouldered, thick-necked, had an aggressive jaw and wore his thinning hair close cropped. Mansfield's mother, Mme. Erminia Rudersdorff, an erratic German singer, settled in Boston during his adolescence. She bitterly resented his wish to go on the stage, and at one of his youthful performances told him that he was "making a fool of himself." The wealthy merchant, Eben D. Jordan, befriended him and later financed many of his costly ventures. In the theatrical profession, and among the critics, Mansfield had acquired a reputation as little enviable as Macready's, not unjustly. His eccentricity and inordinate vanity were notorious. He had an explosive temper and couldn't control it. He was imperious, arrogant, petulant, often morose. He never concealed his contempt for those whom he considered his intellectual inferiors; there were few people whom he didn't include in this category. "Mine was a hard life when I was a child," he once said. "Sometimes I was scolded, sometimes beaten, sometimes starved. God knows it is not strange if I am what they call 'singular.' " These injuries had warped his character, as he realized: "There are times when I feel so barred out by the world, and so hated, that if I could push down the pillars of the universe and smash everything and everybody, I'd gladly do it!" This, he thought, explained his feeling of kinship with characters like Baron Chevrial, and Gloucester in *Richard III.*

If so, it also explained his effectiveness in these roles; a role, to Mansfield, was an opportunity to express some facet of his complex personality. His face was like a mask, and he could make it up to counterfeit any other face. This enabled him, during his career, to play a great variety of character parts, to each of which he gave a distinctive physical individuality; their other attributes were his. Mansfield had a splendid voice—his mother had trained him as a singer— but his inflections and mannerisms of delivery were, like Henry Irving's, unfortunate. He never underplayed, his effects were often bizarre, and to obtain them he sometimes resorted to realistic expedients which fastidious critics thought stagy or merely vulgar.

In *Dr. Jekyll and Mr. Hyde,* Mansfield as Hyde had to leap on Sir Danvers

Carew, hurl him to the floor and strangle him. In early performances, Mansfield lost control of himself, and so maltreated Boyd Putnam, the actor who was playing Carew, that the unfortunate victim of realism repeatedly fainted. In another scene of the same play Hyde had to ask the hag, Rebecca Moore, about the facial appearance of a supposed visitor. Mansfield turned to the actress who played the hag, showing a "distorted, hideous, diabolical countenance," growled the line, "Like *me?*" and drooled. One night the actress was replaced by an understudy who, at the sight of Mansfield's face, began screaming hysterically and almost ruined the scene. When he played Shylock, after his speech to Antonio—"Your worship was the last man in our mouths"—he indicated Shylock's loathing for the Merchant by spitting on the stage, a bit of business for which he was severely censured by the critics.

In 1886, three years after his sensational first performance of Baron Chevrial, Mansfield appeared in a romantic comedy, *Prince Karl,* by Archibald Clavering Gunter. The following year, he commissioned *Dr. Jekyll and Mr. Hyde* from Thomas Russell Sullivan. This dramatization of Robert Louis Stevenson's story was his first decisive hit, and it long remained his most popular piece. Romantic as Jekyll, repulsive as Hyde, Mansfield gave an element of terror to his study of a split personality, and the scene in which—by means of a remarkable stage trick—he transformed himself from one character to the other in full view of the audience, never failed to cause a prodigious effect. In 1888, to gain the prestige of London success, Mansfield appeared in his repertory at Irving's Lyceum Theater and subsequently, at another playhouse, offered an elaborate, costly production of *Richard III.* The London venture was a disastrous failure and left him in debt to the amount of $167,000. For his failure he held Henry Irving responsible and thereafter detested him. On his return to the United States, he appeared in *Richard III,* but his performance of the role was coldly received by most of the New York critics. In 1890, he scored another great success in *Beau Brummell,* a play on which he collaborated with an unknown young playwright, Clyde Fitch.

Soon afterwards, he proposed making an alliance with Augustin Daly. His original project was to co-star with Miss Rehan at Daly's Theater during part of each year; for the balance of the season, they would alternate in remaining at the theater and touring at the head of a Daly company. Daly was eager to make an arrangement that would enable him to present Miss Rehan in a combination as attractive to the public as that of Miss Terry and Henry Irving. But after prolonged negotiations the scheme fell through because neither man was capable of deferring to the other. Mansfield had hoped to inaugurate the project by appearing with Miss Rehan in *The Merchant of Venice,* thus directly challenging Irving. He made his own production of the play. His conception of the character of Shylock—which shifted from that of an abused, sympathetic victim to that of a vengeful demon—failed to please even those critics who, like William Winter, most admired him. At the time, Irving was playing Shylock in the United States, and the memory of Booth's acting in the role was still vivid to playgoers. In New York alone, Mansfield's venture brought him a loss of

$8,000. He usually lost money on his New York engagements. He invariably made money on the road. "I must hammer, hammer, hammer on the hard, hard road," he complained ruefully. The conquest of New York was his goal.

He continued to search for new plays, for new playwrights of genuine importance. In 1889, at the instigation of his leading lady, Miss Beatrice Cameron (soon to become his wife), he had produced for her *A Doll's House,* at special matinées in Boston and New York. But their first contact with the work of Henrik Ibsen caused no commotion in these cities. In 1894, Mansfield wrote dejectedly to William Winter: "I am as far off from the goal of my ambition as ever—and I see no improvement. I open the new Herald Square Theater on September 17, with a satirical comedy, of no particular weight—clever enough; containing no part for me. In fact in the second act (there are three) until the end of it, I do not appear." Notwithstanding these disadvantages, the comedy, by a playwright whose work had not yet been produced in the United States, turned out to be one of Mansfield's major successes. It was *Arms and the Man,* by George Bernard Shaw.

The world, as Mansfield said, was moving on, not back. Conservative critics like William Winter, and all old-fashioned playgoers, felt that it was carrying the drama swiftly in the wrong direction. There was the case of Victorien Sardou, the most successful of French dramatists. In the melodramas that he turned out for Sarah Bernhardt he showed an addiction to heroines chiefly notable for their moral frailty. Could it be denied that these plays were "unpleasant"? Yet, by introducing them to audiences throughout the country, Miss Fanny Davenport established herself as the leading American actress of emotional roles. Her impassioned acting, her spectacular suicide by poison in *Fedora,* crowded theaters from New York to San Francisco. In *La Tosca,* she achieved an even more sensational success. She opened with this play in New York, and the *Herald* devoted two articles to denouncing its immorality. Did it not glorify a Roman actress who, in the first place, had a lover; in the second place, was willing to give herself to another man to save her lover's life; in the third place, committed a murder? In every city where Miss Davenport performed *La Tosca* on tour clergymen preached against it, critics attacked it and moralists condemned it. To their discomfiture, the theaters always sold out.

Worse, far worse, was in store for those conservatives who insisted that "the theater is not the proper place for a clinical disquisition or a detailed, literal portrayal of vicious life." A new realism of subject, character and treatment was insidiously entering the drama; it offered little hope for "the making of good plays out of clean, decent material." Audiences in Boston were subjected to this new tendency in 1891, when the American playwright James A. Herne produced, at Chickering Hall, his drama, *Margaret Fleming,* with the public support of such distinguished writers as William Dean Howells, Mary E. Wilkins and Hamlin Garland. It dealt with the marital relations of a profligate husband and an American gentlewoman who, although adopting his illegitimate child and ultimately taking him back into her home, refuses ever again to live with him as his wife. The climax of the third act, in which Margaret Fleming visits the home of her husband's dead mistress and is disturbed by the crying of their infant, was peculiarly daring. The stage direction read: *Then, scarcely conscious of what she is doing, suddenly with an impatient swift movement she unbuttons her dress to give nourishment to the child, when the picture fades away into darkness.*

New York saw this novelty at a "special matinée" in December, 1891. Three years later, it was again produced there, had a three-week run, and plans were made to send it on a brief tour. But audiences greatly preferred the more "wholesome" realism of Herne's *Shore Acres*. This somber study of Maine villagers was first produced in Chicago, transferred to Boston, and launched on long success in New York. It had a kitchen scene in which a turkey dinner was actually cooked on the stage—the aroma of the roasting bird pervaded the auditorium—and was "eaten for nearly two hundred performances . . . by actors finally too nauseated with turkey to pretend to eat it."

An astonished, profoundly shocked public felt the full impact of the new realistic drama in 1893, when Arthur Wing Pinero's *The Second Mrs. Tanqueray,* after its production in New York, was sent on a transcontinental tour. Pinero had offered the play to Daniel Frohman for production by his Lyceum Theater company. "I wrote him I did not dare present so frank a play in the evening bill," Frohman recalled later, "but that I would like to produce so fine a work at a series of special matinées." However, Frohman dropped the project of matinées, waited until the play had been staged in London, with the beautiful Mrs. Patrick Campbell in the star role, and produced it with other British stars, Mrs. Madge Kendal and her husband, William H. Kendal. They were as well-known for their exemplary respectability as for their talents. Mrs. Kendal was often referred to as "the British matron" of the drama "because of the purity of her domestic life." Frohman recorded that when she undertook the part of Paula Tanqueray "the critics not only deprecated her accepting a part of this kind, but criticized her taste in appearing in a role so at variance with her career as a woman and an actress." Adventuresses, women with a "past," could be excused on the stage only when ultimately defeated by triumphant virtue. The past of Paula Tanqueray was generously populated. Although she had been "kept" by four men, she had an honest desire to live respectably as a married woman, and Pinero invited audiences to feel compassion when her desire was frustrated. Obviously, this was morally intolerable as well as socially dangerous, and the New York *Herald* complained that *The Second Mrs. Tanqueray* "for audacity is nearly without parallel in dramatic literature." The play aroused violent controversy throughout the country except in San Francisco where, according to Frohman, it "fell flat." He was informed that it had no illusion for Golden Gate audiences; "the city was full of Mrs. Tanquerays, and the play seemed to be too much of a moral indictment to find favor as a superb realistic drama."

The production of Pinero's drama created a precedent that was quickly followed. Mme. Modjeska—who was as widely renowned for her virtue as Mrs. Kendal—added Hermann Sudermann's *Magda* to her repertory the following season, another example of the "new drama" which was severely condemned in some cities, but well received in others. "I found in the title-part one of my favorite and most successful personations," she noted. "That which appealed to me was not so much the bohemianism, the plea for woman's rights, as Magda's enthusiasm for art, the consciousness of the high mission of an artist."

And in New York, the most celebrated door in the history of the drama slammed once more, admitting permanently the "unhealthful and injurious" Henrik Ibsen. A single matinée of *A Doll's House*—with certain episodes deleted—was given by an actress who eventually created audiences for his plays in the United States. Four years earlier Miss Minnie Maddern, a popular comedienne, had married Harrison Grey Fiske, editor of the *Dramatic Mirror,* and had left the stage. Now she returned to it, and embarked on a very different kind of career. She had completely changed her style of acting, and some critics who saw her performances at special matinées asserted that her new style resembled that of Mme. Duse. This charge was vigorously denied by the *Dramatic Mirror,* which declared that Mrs. Fiske had adopted the method of "underacting" before the great Italian actress revealed it to the American public.

Mme. Eleonora Duse made her debut early in 1893, in a four-week engagement at the Star Theater in New York. Already famous on the Continent, she was known to relatively few Americans. Those playgoers who followed developments in the European theater were aware that she was an innovator. It was said that she had rejected the entire technical tradition of acting, and had created a wholly new style. For Sarah Bernhardt, with whom Duse was always to be contrasted, acting became an art only when it transcended the natural. It was not an attempt to reproduce the actual, but to transform it, to magnify its significance and intensity. Duse said that she did not "act" her roles; she "lived" them. Her purpose was to create an illusion of absolute naturalness. She repudiated all conventional theatrical effects, considering them "artificial." She refused to use make-up on her face because she was convinced that it detracted from the play of expression. She cultivated a quiet, subdued style which, because of its infrequent resort to overt emphasis and its abstention from any exaggeration, was described as "underacting." She spoke, on the stage, in low, hushed tones, often resorting to an accelerated tempo; her intention was to reproduce the effect of ordinary speech.

Mme. Duse was thirty-four, a slender woman of medium height and not, by the popular standard, a beauty. Her face was magnificently expressive; her great, dark eyes seemed to intimate melancholy and misery; her hands were very beautiful, and she used them, in the marked economy of her gestures, with extraordinary eloquence. Her repertory included only two Italian plays: *Cavalleria Rusticana,* and Carlo Goldoni's classic comedy, *La Locandiera.* (In this, although he did not greatly admire her as a tragedienne, Joseph Jefferson said that "she was perfection itself.") Her other plays included *Camille, Fedora, Fernande, La Femme de Claude, Divorçons* and *Francillon,* all of which she and her company acted in Italian. She was acclaimed by many critics. Among playgoers, she had both enthusiastic partisans and vehement opponents. The controversy over her art was to continue long after her death. "I cared much less for her particular modernistic methods than for her own self and her artistic powers," Mme. Modjeska noted after attending several of Duse's performances. "Whatever school she belongs to, she is a great actress. The intensity with which she abandons herself to the feelings and sufferings of the character she personates makes you forget all surroundings; you do not realize any more that you are at the theater, that there is an actress on the boards; you cease analyzing; you only feel that you are in presence of terrible pain, despair and agony."

Looking backward long afterwards, playgoers realized that 1893 marked a turning point in the history of the American stage. That year brought the death of Edwin Booth, the greatest American tragedian and last significant exponent of the "grand style." It brought to the United States Mme. Duse, whose methods largely inspired the school of acting which dominates the stage today. It introduced the new realistic drama, which was to treat frankly themes previously avoided; and the theory of the "well-made" play, which involved new techniques in writing, and which asserted the supremacy of the play over the actors who appeared in it. At the Columbian Exposition in Chicago, four American actresses were invited to address an international Congress of Women. The appearance before that official congress of Mme. Modjeska, Miss Clara Morris, Miss Julia Marlowe and Miss Georgia Cayvan indicated the honor in which the acting profession was held. In Junius Brutus Booth's youth, reputable folk had classed actors as vagrants. But in 1893, Edwin Booth left a fortune of more than $700,000, and those Americans who identified social eminence with wealth could scarcely deny the reputability of a profession which yielded so impressive an estate. And in 1893, with the opening of a new theater in New York, one of the most powerful forces that the American stage had known began the operations which, within a short time, were to transform it.

Eleonora Duse about 1886

CHAPTER 11

Star-Spangled Stages

ON JANUARY 25, 1893, Charles Frohman inaugurated his Empire Theater on the east side of Broadway below Fortieth Street, in New York. Members of the first-night audience, passing from a spacious lobby through a handsome foyer into the ornate red and gold auditorium, appreciated its elegance. They had no reason to suppose that the Empire would soon rank as the nation's leading playhouse, or that for sixty years it would hold a unique prestige with the public and the profession. Nobody realized that the opening of the Empire marked the beginning of a new theatrical era; yet it ushered in the twentieth century.

First-nighters saw a romantic melodrama by David Belasco and Franklyn Fyles, to which Charles Frohman's older brother, Daniel, had given the title,

James K. Hackett in "Romeo and Juliet," 1899

The Girl I Left Behind Me. The occasion thus united the names of three men, already known to playgoers, who were to become outstanding figures in the American theater. Belasco and the Frohman brothers were first associated a decade earlier at the Madison Square Theater, as employees of the Mallorys. Since then, Daniel Frohman had founded his excellent Lyceum Theater stock company. Belasco had served him as stage manager and house playwright. Charles Frohman had begun the operations that were to make him the world's foremost theatrical magnate. At the height of his career, he controlled six theaters in New York, more than two hundred throughout the United States and five in London. He had twenty-eight stars under his management. He paid thirty-five million dollars annually in salaries; ten thousand people were on his payroll. Yet to the public, Charles Frohman always remained a mysterious figure. He abhorred photographers and avoided reporters; he shunned personal publicity. "I have never known anyone more modest and no one quite so shy," James M. Barrie recorded. "Many actors have played for him for years and never spoken to him, have perhaps seen him dart up a side street because they were approaching. They may not have known that it was sheer shyness, but it was."

So, for the general public, it was not Frohman but Belasco who became the most colorful personality connected with the stage, a living symbol of its glamour. Even his appearance was theatrical. The clerical suit and collar that he affected—some said because as a child he had been educated in a monastery—suggested a costume for a role. It implied an asceticism probably alien to his nature and certainly denied by his legend. He had a fine head, crowned by a shock of black hair in which a single iron gray strand gleamed. His clean-shaven face was pallid; his lips were full and sensual. Under thick black brows, his heavy-lidded dark eyes smoldered. He had been an actor from childhood, but although that phase of his career was now ended he continued to act a role in public until he died. The role was that of David Belasco, a spectacular personality; he acted it so perfectly that it ceased to seem a personation, even to himself. In 1893, at the age of forty, Belasco was launching himself as a producer in New York. His active career in the theater spanned nearly seventy years. He linked the fourth decade of the twentieth century to the epoch of the Charles Keans, with whom he acted in boyhood, and to the period of Tom Maguire's ascendancy in San Francisco.

The public was curious about Charles Frohman and beguiled by Belasco. For Daniel Frohman it had respect and genuine fondness. He was tall, very lean, bald, sparsely bearded, and caricaturists usually made him resemble an amiable crane. He became the accredited spokesman of the theater as an institution, its official representative on ceremonial occasions. Intelligent, genial, deeply devoted to the stage and its people, he served for more than thirty years as President of the Actors' Fund. The entire profession affectionately called him "Uncle Dan." Daniel Frohman dedicated his Lyceum Theater to the production of modern drama. He produced plays by such American dramatists as Belasco and Henry C. De Mille, Paul Potter and Clyde Fitch; by such English playwrights as Oscar Wilde, Arthur Wing Pinero and Henry Arthur Jones. In

1897, he made George Bernard Shaw "an offer to come to America, guarantee-ing him an annual salary, with the proviso that he should write one play a year for my company, and retain for himself the profits of any other work." Shaw refused the offer. In connection with his Lyceum Theater, Frohman established the Lyceum School of Acting, which today flourishes as the American Acad-emy of Dramatic Arts. He was a remarkable discoverer and trainer of native acting talent. His stock company and touring companies furnished a large pro-portion of the new era's most popular stars—including the young woman whom Charles Frohman was to make the most celebrated and beloved actress on the American stage. Albert M. Palmer disbanded his stock company in 1896, and retired as a producer. Augustin Daly, saddened by diminishing audiences and by the failure of his attempt to establish a theater in London, died in 1899, and his stock company was dispersed. Daniel Frohman maintained the Lyceum company until 1902, when "new theatrical conditions began to prevail" and "the era of the regular stock company, the manager's personal family, as it were, seemed to have passed away." The agent who brought about the changes was his brother, Charles.

Charles Froman was thirty-three when he installed his stock company in the Empire Theater. Squat, bald, sallow-faced, his large, melting eyes alone re-deemed him from ugliness. His passion for the theater dated from childhood; at the age of eight, he had sold souvenir books of *The Black Crook*. At thirteen, he sold tickets in a box office. Later, he worked as an advance agent for touring companies, often having to post his own bills and frequently finding himself stranded on the road. He came to know, as Daniel said, "every opera house and lodge hall and hotel and railroad connection" throughout the country; he was "able to book an entire tour without looking at a map"; and, "what was more important, he knew the sort of audience each town could furnish." The knowledge later proved invaluable.

Frohman worked as company manager for Haverly's Minstrels. Then, at the Madison Square Theater, where Daniel was manager and Belasco stage man-ager, Charles booked the tours of fourteen companies that took *Hazel Kirke* to every part of the country. Subsequently, he set up as a booking agent for man-agers of theaters outside New York, arranging for the "attractions" to be toured through their houses. He soon controlled the "open time" of more than three hundred theaters across the continent. These ranged from small-town opera houses chiefly devoted to "10-20-30-cent" melodrama to first-class theaters in the principal cities. Eventually, this business became one of the major sources of Frohman's power, but it did not absorb him. His ambition was to become an independent producer with his own theater in New York. He made tentative experiments. He put on a comedy for Miss Minnie Maddern, a drama featuring Miss Viola Allen, the young leading woman of the Madison Square company. He took William Gillette, the actor-playwright, on a transcontinental tour in Gillette's *Held by the Enemy,* a stirring drama of the Civil War. The success of this play inspired Frohman's first major venture in production. The result was decisive.

In the autumn of 1888, Bronson Howard's drama of the Civil War, *Shenan-*

doah, was produced by R. M. Field at his Boston Museum. Howard was the most distinguished and successful American playwright, but his new work failed in Boston and its withdrawal was announced. At the instigation of Daniel Frohman, who had seen the play, Charles Frohman went to Boston. He was prejudiced in favor of *Shenandoah* by the patriotic theme that had already proved profitable in Gillette's play. Before attending the performance, he negotiated for financial backing to produce it. After seeing the play, he had specific proposals for its improvement; Howard recognized their merit and adopted them in revising his drama. In the autumn of 1889, Frohman produced *Shenandoah* at the Star Theater in New York. The cast which he provided included Miss Viola Allen, Miss Effie Shannon (of the Lyceum company), Henry Miller (formerly of Daly's and the Lyceum), and Wilton Lackaye—all later to become stars. Characteristically, Frohman whipped up excitement about the play with advance publicity. While the company was rehearsing, he put out a rumor that Howard had lost the manuscript of his third act. A city-wide search followed, copiously reported by the press. One week before the opening night, Frohman announced that the missing act had been "found." The play was a sensational success in New York. Frohman quickly organized road companies to take *Shenandoah* on tour. It earned a fortune for Bronson Howard. It made money for Frohman and assured his repute as a producer. More significantly, its success led him to adopt a policy to which, with very few exceptions, he always adhered.

He determined to produce plays only by dramatists of established reputation. (In later years, young American playwrights seldom submitted their scripts to him. One of them, George Middleton, was told by Frohman's play reader that "C. F. had never produced an American play by an unknown dramatist" even when one was highly recommended to him.) Similarly, he decided to employ, as far as possible, actors and actresses who had already won favor. "I have no time to conduct a theatrical kindergarten in developing actors or playwrights, save where the play of the unknown author, or the exceptional talents of the unknown actor or actress appeal to me strongly," he explained much later. "There is an element of safety in considering work by experts, because the theaters I represent need quick results." To Augustin Daly, this contention would have been inconceivable, but Frohman might have pointed out that Daly's theories and methods were obsolete. Frohman had taken to heart Henry Irving's axiom that the theater "must succeed as a business or it will fail as an art." Barrie said of Frohman that, "For money he did not care at all; it was to him but pieces of paper with which he could make practical the enterprises that teemed in his brain." But, convinced that the theater must succeed as a business, he had already charted the course he wished it to take.

In 1890, he leased Proctor's Theater, on Twenty-third Street west of Sixth Avenue, and assembled a stock company. He formed another company to occupy the theater while the resident players made a transcontinental tour. Both groups were composed of well-known actors and actresses; Miss Odette Tyler, Miss Henrietta Crosman, Mrs. Georgie Drew Barrymore, Frederick de Belleville, Emmet Corrigan and Cyril Scott were among them. He recruited from the ranks of "society" amateurs Miss Elsie de Wolfe. He engaged Miss Maude Adams, an eighteen-year-old actress who had been on the stage from childhood. Miss Adams had made her New York debut two years earlier at the Lyceum, in *Lord Chumley,* with E. H. Sothern. With his two companies, Frohman produced plays by William Gillette, Bronson Howard, Belasco and De Mille, and Sardou. Frohman had De Mille adapt *The Lost Paradise,* a play by the German dramatist Ludwig Fulda, transposing its scene to the United States. In De Mille's version, the play dealt with a conflict between capital and labor in a New England manufacturing town, and Miss Adams scored her first notable success in the role of a starved, tubercular factory hand.

Before moving his stock company to the Empire Theater, Frohman formed two projects which produced revolutionary changes in theatrical affairs. Both related, primarily, to the theater as a business; both affected it profoundly as an art. As a producer, he intended to conduct his activities on a national scale. He therefore planned to obtain personal control of a chain of theaters in the country's key cities, where touring companies made relatively long stays. Between these cities, in every direction, were some fifteen hundred one-night stands. Profit or loss on a tour was largely determined by the ability of the company to make consecutive stops on its route between key cities. Frohman's expanding booking business did not cover all the one-night stands. He therefore had no absolute assurance of economical routes for his companies throughout the country. In 1896, he called a conference of the leading booking magnates. They were, in addition to himself, his associate Al Hayman, who controlled a chain of theaters on the Pacific coast; Marc Klaw and Abraham L. Erlanger who, under the firm name of Klaw & Erlanger, dominated booking throughout the South; S. F. Nixon and J. Fred Zimmerman who, as the firm of Nixon & Zimmerman, owned the principal theaters in Pennsylvania. The six magnates organized into a single national chain all the theaters which they controlled or represented, pooling their individual interests. Booking for the entire chain was delegated to Klaw & Erlanger. The Syndicate, as this combine was called, was a theatrical trust. Its monopoly of booking put its members in a position to dominate all phases of theatrical enterprise, from the purchase of foreign and domestic plays to the employment of actors, and the collection of commissions on the receipts of touring companies sent out by other producers.

The operations of the Syndicate precipitated a revolt on the part of insurgent producers, notably David Belasco, and recalcitrant stars. At various times, Jefferson, James O'Neill, Mme. Sarah Bernhardt, Mrs. Fiske, Richard Mansfield and others resisted the Syndicate's demands. Mrs. Fiske, on tour, played in lodge halls and roller-skating rinks. Mme. Bernhardt, always intrepid, played one tour in a circus tent. Four years after the Syndicate was organized, an aggressive opposition, known as "the Independents," appeared. The movement was led by three brothers—Sam, Lee and Jacob J. Shubert—operators of a chain of stock theaters in upstate New York. Acquiring the lease of a single theater in New York City, they soon built others. They gradually acquired a chain of houses from coast to coast. They became producers on a large scale, and financed other independent producers. Bitter warfare developed between the Syndicate and the Independents. It led to overproduction and a surplus of theaters. Towns that could economically support only one first-class house soon had two theaters each controlled by one of the rival groups. In these houses, two similar attractions always competed, thus dividing the local patronage. In 1914, the accumulated losses sustained by both factions convinced them that prolongation of the war would bring them to financial ruin. A working agreement was negotiated and their destructive competition ended. Meanwhile Charles Frohman had built up a personal theatrical empire that not only covered the continent but spanned the Atlantic.

His second project, which he put into execution even earlier, had equally far-reaching effects. He was aware that his public was largely composed of a new generation of playgoers. He surmised that personalities would have greater appeal to their interest than plays. If so, the strongest attraction which he could give any play was the presence in its cast of a magnetic, well-publicized star. "In America we regard the workman first and the work second," he told a British journalist many years later. "Our imaginations are fired not nearly so much by great deeds as by great doers. There are stars in every walk of American life. It has always been so with democracies."

Frohman knew that, with very few exceptions, the great stars of the preceding era had attained their rank only after long and varied experience. For his own purposes, this process was too slow. He could accelerate it by himself "creating" stars. He proposed to become a star-maker. Not many years later the Irish singer Chauncey Olcott, one of the most profitable stars on the American stage, sent a representative to Frohman with an offer to come under his management. Olcott made $100,000 a year; Frohman could name his own percentage. "I greatly appreciate the offer, but I don't care to manage Olcott," Frohman replied. "He is *made*. I like to *make* stars."

As Frohman's producing activities multiplied, star-making became increasingly essential to their success. ("I do believe that throughout the United States a play really requires a star artist, man or woman—woman for choice," he wrote to the British playwright Alfred Sutro.) Although Frohman never forgot that star-making was a business operation, he liked to think of it as an artistic enterprise. It was the activity that best exemplified his personal power, and most enhanced his own sense of it. He seldom referred to his power in theatrical affairs but he did not underestimate it. Once he traveled from Atlantic City to New York with the playwright Paul Potter. "Shall I read you the theatrical news?" Potter inquired, looking up from a newspaper.

"No," said Frohman, "I *make* theatrical news."

Frohman undertook his first venture in star-making in 1892, when he learned that differences had arisen between John Drew and Augustin Daly. Through a mutual friend, Frohman sent Drew an offer to become a star under his management. Drew accepted the offer and signed a three-year contract. (His association with Frohman was to endure until the producer's death, twenty-three years later, but their first contract was the only one they ever signed. This was characteristic of Frohman's dealings with his stars and his playwrights. There were seldom any formal contracts; often, not even a memorandum. Frohman's word was his bond, and the profession knew him as "the man who never broke his word.") As Daly's leading man and a member of his celebrated "Big Four," Drew had won a nation-wide following; he was already a star in all but title. In private life he was a sophisticated man of the world; suave, witty, debonair, a model of sartorial elegance. Drew's off-stage personality was that of a punctilious gentleman, and Frohman shrewdly determined to exploit this professionally.

For Drew's debut as a star, he commissioned from Clyde Fitch an adaptation of a French farce-comedy, *The Masked Ball,* dealing with the effort of a young wife to reform her slightly dissipated husband by pretending tipsiness while at a ball. Drew had been paired with Miss Rehan for fourteen years, and their acting styles fitted so perfectly that it seemed doubtful, whether, deprived of her as a foil, he could be equally effective. As Drew's leading lady Frohman chose Miss Adams, casting her in a sentimental comedy role that contrasted strongly with her previous one of a pathetic factory girl, and in it she again impressed the critics and the public. The play had a run of more than one hundred performances in New York and duplicated its success on a transcontinental tour. Miss Adams continued as Drew's leading lady for five seasons in a series of drawing-room comedies. This was the pattern to which Frohman confined Drew permanently, never permitting him to resume the roles in classic and Shakespearian comedy on which, at Daly's, his repute as an artist had been founded. Drew's earlier admirers declared that Frohman "stereotyped" a versatile, technically accomplished actor to his great detriment. And, as the years passed, the inescapable similarity of Drew's roles gave rise to the charge that he "always acted himself." This charge was hotly denied by some competent technical critics, among them Drew's nephew, John Barrymore. Barrymore asserted that Drew always enacted "the character the dramatist provided," and that his method was to build up a character through subtle gradations of effect.

John Drew

In 1923, when Drew was seventy, he displayed his thorough mastery of the art of acting by returning, briefly, to classic comedy. In an all-star revival of *The School for Scandal* sponsored by The Players for the benefit of the Actors' Fund, Drew played Sir Peter Teazle to the Lady Teazle of his niece, Miss Ethel Barrymore. But during the thirty intervening years Frohman's policy of exploiting Drew's personality had proved to be commercially sound, however misguided artistically. The great public seldom complained about the monotony of Drew's roles. It was Drew that they came to see, and not the play in which he was appearing, and the more he seemed to be acting himself the better they were pleased. Very early in Drew's starring career his supreme elegance furnished American women with a criterion which they applied to American men. As a result, by the turn of the century he had considerable influence on masculine deportment, attire and social attitude. The "Drew reformation" made the male residents of Fifth Avenue and Newport seem almost as distinguished as their butlers, and from these exalted precincts a cult of well-bred worldliness spread over the country.

Playgoers gave Drew the title that an earlier generation had bestowed on James H. Hackett: "the first gentleman of the stage." Frohman's second star, William Gillette, received his title from the profession, which called him "the great aristocrat of the theater." He was nearing forty when Frohman starred him in 1896. Tall, slender, black-haired, blue-eyed, gauntly handsome, he was equally well known as a playwright and an actor. He had toured for five seasons in his farce, *The Private Secretary,* and his drama, *Held by the Enemy,* had brought him national celebrity as well as a considerable fortune. Gillette's father had served as United States Senator from Connecticut, and the future actor's boyhood was passed in circumstances of relative affluence and in an intellectually stimulating environment. Although he left home to go on the stage at the age of twenty, his preparation for a dramatic career differed from that of most of his contemporaries. During his early years as an actor, Gillette found time to take courses at the College of the City of New York, at Harvard and the Massachusetts Institute of Technology, and at Boston University.

This scholarly propensity was reflected in his acting, which he based on a theory of the art that he developed at the beginning of his career and long afterwards set forth in a book. He was one of the first exponents of the modern school of underacting. He realized that "the illusion of the first time in acting," as he described the effect of naturalness and spontaneity, depended on calculated, deliberate artifice. The actor, already knowing all his speeches and "business," must constantly suggest the changing mental and emotional experience of the character he is portraying, who, at any moment, is only becoming aware of what he will next say or do. For Gillette, therefore, acting was always an experiment in psychology. (Referring to the publication of one of his plays, he wrote, "I would much prefer that people read what my characters *do*—how they *behave*—and what is in their minds—than to merely get the words they utter.") He also believed that "actors of recent times who have been universally acknowledged to be great have invariably been so because of their successful use of their own strong and compelling personalities in the roles which they made famous."

This was peculiarly true in his own case, for Gillette's personality was definite and arresting. He took advantage of it, as a playwright, in creating the roles which, as an actor, he intended to perform. Whether in comedy or in melodrama, he usually blended the attributes of urbanity, poise, restraint, and imperturbable self-control—the characters he played were quiet, but gallant and resourceful, men who dominated situations by the power of their intelligence.

Frohman launched Gillette as a star in the actor-playwright's farce, *Too Much Johnson.* The play received poor notices at its tryout performance, but Frohman, who had secretly attended it, surprised Gillette by booking the play for a long run in New York and a long tour. When asked to explain, he said only, "I saw your performance."

His confidence was justified; the play became one of Gillette's most popular vehicles and was frequently revived. Gillette quickly followed it with his two greatest successes, the fine Civil War melodrama, *Secret Service,* and *Sherlock Holmes.* These were hardy perennials which he played in Great Britain and the United States for many years; he made his last American tour in *Sherlock Holmes* in 1931, at the age of seventy-six. He seldom appeared in plays by other playwrights, but one of his best acting achievements was the masterful butler in J. M. Barrie's *The Admirable Crichton.*

Gillette's dislike of society and his fondness for solitude gave the public an impression that he was an eccentric recluse. His intimate friends knew him to be a man of quaint and furtive humor and many hobbies. At his estate at Hadlyme, Connecticut, he maintained a private railroad with three miles of track, and amused himself by driving a miniature train. He spent much of his time cruising on a houseboat, the *Aunt Polly.* He painted, industriously but not too well. He wrote and adapted twenty plays. He retired from the stage four times, making formal farewell tours of the country. Each time, love of his profession brought him back. As an actor, he suffered only one major disappointment. He wanted to play Hamlet, and Charles Frohman made plans for the production. Gillette discusssed his interpretation of the role with Daniel Frohman, who humorously suggested "that the audience would not recognize him in the part unless he smoked a cigar, which he usually did in all his other plays," and flippantly devised a scheme to fit the cigar into Hamlet's principal soliloquy. (He was greatly surprised when, in 1925, Basil Sydney hit upon the same scheme for using a cigarette in his modern-dress production of *Hamlet.*) Gillette's desire to play Hamlet was not gratified. Charles Frohman shelved the projected production, and the public was deprived of an opportunity to see the apostle of "modernism" and realistic method in a poetic role.

Frohman's outstanding achievement as a star-maker was the career of Miss Maude Adams, who for twenty years inspired an idolatry remarkable in the annals of the stage. In 1896, when his novel, *The Little Minister,* was an American best-seller, James M. Barrie made his first visit to the United States. He had earlier written a play, *The Professor's Love Story,* which the British star, E. S. Willard, had successfully presented in New York. On the basis of this prior success American producers, Frohman among them, were urging Barrie to dramatize *The Little Minister,* a venture which he declined to undertake. One

William Gillette in "Sherlock Holmes"

day while in New York, Barrie called at Frohman's office. The producer was out, and his secretary suggested that Barrie go downstairs to the Empire Theater, where John Drew and Miss Adams were appearing in *Rosemary,* a sentimental comedy. Barrie attended the performance, and was sufficiently captivated by Miss Adams's acting to promise Frohman that he would try to dramatize *The Little Minister.* Thereafter, he never wrote another novel. Instead, at Frohman's insistence, he turned out play after play, many of them written expressly for Miss Adams. "He was very dogged," Barrie wrote of Frohman after the producer's death. "I had only one quarrel with him, but it lasted all the sixteen years I knew him. He wanted me to be a playwright and I wanted to be a novelist. All those years I fought him on that. He always won, but not because of his doggedness; only because he was so lovable that one had to do as he wanted. He also threatened, if I stopped, to re-produce the old plays and print my name in large electric letters over the theater."

After meeting a poor reception in Washington during a tryout engagement, Miss Adams brought *The Little Minister* to the Empire on September 30, 1897. This date was, in a sense, historic. It marked the inception of that amazing relationship between the American public and the star which, beginning as a one-sided love affair, developed into a worship without precedent or subsequent parallel. Miss Adams was twenty-five, winsome rather than pretty, slight, frail and girlish. Her lilting speech and muted laughter, the delicacy of her tread, the graceful swiftness of her movement, gave her a quality that soon was described as "otherworldly." Though intensely feminine, she made a curious impression of elusiveness, as if she had an elfin strain. A decade later Barrie was to say of a play that he had written for her, "I could see her dancing through every page of my manuscript." In that play, *What Every Woman Knows,* he gave her lines which defined her appeal for him, and certainly for the public: "Charm is the bloom upon a woman. If you have it, you don't have to have anything else. If you haven't it, all else won't do you any good."

Maude Adams in "The Little Minister"

In *The Little Minister* Miss Adams had a role which blended whimsical humor, sentiment and a veiled implication of pathos. These were the attributes which, in time, came to be asociated with her acting and her personality, so inseparably that critical distinction between them was seldom made. Was it Miss Adams' art which imparted life to Barrie's creations? Or was it Barrie who, through his creations, endowed Miss Adams with her characteristic palette and tonality as an artist? The public never knew and scarcely cared. But the extraordinary, perhaps unique, affinity between actress and playwright was obvious. Frohman once said that, "when one of my stars finishes with a play, that play goes permanently on the shelf, no one ever hoping to muster together an audience for it without the original actor or actress in the star part." Only two of the Barrie plays which Miss Adams acted were ever successfully revived after her retirement.

During its initial showing at the Empire, *The Little Minister* ran for three hundred consecutive performances, to gross receipts of $370,000, a financial record at the time. Before Miss Adams finished with the play, it had three thousand performances throughout the country, earned a half-million dollars for Barrie and more for Frohman. By 1901, when Miss Adams appeared in *Quality Street,* her second Barrie play, she had become the most potent box-office attraction in the American theater. Her name was a magnet that drew crowds, and Frohman, reporting gleefully on her immense success, was able to make such typical observations as, "Miss Adams' receipts last week in Boston were the largest in the history of Boston theaters or anywhere—$23,000."

Yet her most memorable triumph came four years later, on November 6, 1905, when at the Empire she assumed the title role of Barrie's *Peter Pan.* Barrie had offered the play to Sir Herbert Beerbohm Tree for production in London. Tree, after reading it, reported in alarm to Frohman that "our dear friend Barrie has gone mad." The play, he asserted, was a nightmare. There were children who lived in treetops; a character that was only a wandering spot of light; an alligator with an audible clock in its stomach, and a big dog. When Frohman undertook to produce the play in both London and New York, Barrie offered him the script of another, *Alice Sit by the Fire,* to indemnify him for the probable losses to be incurred by *Peter Pan.*

The play was one of the greatest successes in the history of the American theater, and with it Miss Adams completed her conquest of the American heart. She was idolized by children as well as their elders, and in the affection that she inspired there was reverence never before yielded to an actress. "Miss Maude Adams in the only stage personage within my experience," Frohman wrote, "who has a distinct public following, loyal and encouraging to her in whatever she does." This was true, yet it was an understatement of the peculiar fact that, for American playgoers, Miss Adams could do no wrong. Her appearance as Juliet—with the handsome matinée idol William Faversham as Romeo, and the ineffably romantic James K. Hackett as Mercutio—was not acclaimed by the dramatic critics. Nor in Edmond Rostand's *L'Aiglon* did she, in their opinion, rival Mme. Sarah Bernhardt. When, in 1911, Miss Adams assumed the feathers and strut of the barnyard hero of *Chantecler,* a role which Rostand had written for Constant Coquelin, and which Lucien Guitry had created, it seemed probable that her performance would be less than superlative. Yet a line formed at the box office at four o'clock on the day before tickets went on sale; the sum of $200 was offered in vain for a seat on the opening night; and at the end of the play Miss Adams received twenty-two curtain calls. This was not a tribute to her gallantry in assuming a role for which she was obviously unfitted. It expressed an all but universal conviction of her exalted status. Her most fanatical admirers did not claim for Miss Adams, as an actress, equality with Duse or Bernhardt. But the great public claimed for her a distinction far more impressive. They said that she was incomparable.

Millions of Americans saw Miss Adams on the stage, rejoiced in her performances, cherished a sense of genuinely personal relationship to her. Yet, paradoxically, only a handful of people really knew her. Frohman believed that the illusions of the theater would be shattered if the public saw his stars offstage, or knew too much about them. "He spent a fortune sheltering Maude Adams from all kinds of intrusion," his biographer revealed. "With her especially he exhausted every resource to keep her aloof and secluded. He preferred that she be known through her work and not through her personal self." Possibly this was her own preference also, for, as Frohman's biographer noted, "one of his supreme ambitions in life was to gratify her every wish." Miss Adams was not only invisible, but shrouded in mystery.

"C. F. spoke of her as if she were a princess in an ivory tower," Miss Billie Burke, one of his later stars, recalled. "His fine eyes would light up with worship that was almost religious." Like everyone else in the profession, she heard that Frohman was in love with Miss Adams. There was a persistent rumor that they were secretly married, although Frohman lived, as a bachelor, in a hotel. "I think Charles Frohman loved Maude Adams as a hungry spirit loves music and poetry and as a fine boy loves his heroes and their ideals," Miss Burke wrote more than forty years later. "Miss Adams was to Frohman, I imagine, what she was to everyone else: a sprite."

But the rotund little magnate could not help distilling gold from romance. His cherished star and his reluctant playwright were, together, irresistible to audiences, and he made them both millionaires. Miss Burke was by no means the only person who wondered whether any other man "could deal so adroitly with whimsy and so firmly with Mammon."

As Frohman's control of theaters expanded, his annual list of productions increased, mounting from a dozen to eighteen, and after the turn of the century to twenty-five. The output of his "star-factory" at the Empire was not always adequate to his needs. Sometimes, in spite of his preference for making stars, he gathered in stars already established. A few of his best players left him for starring careers under other managements. Some of the stars whom he made also left him. But most of the favorites whose names went up in lights over the marquees of theaters during the first decade of the century were included in his galaxy, however briefly. The rubric, "Charles Frohman presents," was not only a badge of professional distinction but a passport to fortune.

Frohman launched as a star Miss Annie Russell, a petite comedienne who had been leading lady at the Madison Square and at the Lyceum. She delighted audiences in a series of trivial plays, then, under other auspices, surprised the critics by her excellence in the Shakespearian roles of Puck and Viola. Miss Viola Allen, who as a very young girl replaced Miss Russell at the Madison Square, was for five years leading lady at the Empire. She had differences with Frohman and deserted him abruptly to star, under another manager, in a dramatization of Hall Caine's best-selling novel, *The Christian*. It proved to be one of the most profitable plays of the day, and established Miss Allen among the top-ranking stars. A tall, dark, handsome woman, she achieved her most notable successes in romantic roles, chiefly in dramatic versions of such popular novels as *The White Sister* and *The Eternal City*. But she was an ambitious, serious actress and, without hope of large financial profits, she mounted costly productions of *Twelfth Night, A Winter's Tale* and *Cymbeline* which satisfied her aspirations as an artist and enhanced her prestige.

Actors and actresses who felt an obligation to the drama as an art, who wished to appeal to a public presumptively intelligent and cultivated, could not invariably rely on Frohman's encouragement. It was said that "he never read books unless he thought they might become plays." He detested what was coming to be called the "highbrow drama"; the influence of Ibsen, where he was aware of it, repelled him. His personal preference was for melodrama and light comedy. His favorite drama was Sardou's *Diplomacy,* which he often revived with all-star casts. The ideal play, for him, "was always the one he had in mind for a particular star."

In other respects, he was explicit about his demands. "I start out by asking certain requirements of every piece," he said. "If it be a drama, it must have healthfulness and comedy as well as seriousness. We are a young people, but only in the sense of health-mindedness. There is no real taste among us for the erotic or decadent. It is foreign to us because, as a people, we have not felt the corroding touch of decadence. Nor is life here all drab. Hence I expect lights as well as shadows in every play I accept."

He was willing, however, to produce the problem plays of Pinero and Henry Arthur Jones; they were the outstanding British dramatists and Frohman, like Lester Wallack before him, respectfully deferred to British approval. So Americans had the privilege of being mildly shocked by Pinero's *Iris,* in which Frohman starred Miss Virginia Harned, E. H. Sothern's wife and former leading lady, who had risen to celebrity as the heroine of *Trilby,* an actress of great personal dignity and considerable emotional force who long remained a popular favorite. Frohman starred dark, statuesque Miss Margaret Illington, then the wife of his brother Daniel, in *A Wife Without a Smile.* He produced the well-made plays of C. Haddon Chambers, another highly esteemed British dramatist. He brought out Jones's *Michael and His Lost Angel*—an "artistic" success which ran for five performances—and *Mrs. Dane's Defense,* a problem play that stirred up controversy, was often revived and, like *The Second Mrs. Tanqueray,* in little more than a decade became required reading for college students of the drama —many of whom were astonished to learn that these pieces had been held to pose problems in morals.

Miss Margaret Anglin, who created the role of Mrs. Dane, was a talented, intelligent and ambitious artist. Frustrated ambition eventually persuaded her to forsake the security of Frohman's paternalism in order to escape the restrictions which it imposed. Equally proficient in high comedy and in blazing emotional roles that enabled her to dissolve audiences in tears, she had first attained prominence as Richard Mansfield's leading lady in *Cyrano de Bergerac*. When she applied for this engagement Mansfield sarcastically asked her whether she thought she could make up "beautifully enough to play Roxane." She retorted that she could if he could make himself up "ugly enough to play Cyrano." To ntimidate Mansfield required more than ready wit, but Miss Anglin was abundantly equipped with high courage, as her subsequent career proved.

After leaving Frohman, she made arrangements to co-star in the autumn of 1906 with Henry Miller. In the previous spring, while playing an engagement in Chicago, Miss Anglin read the manuscript of a drama, *The Sabine Woman,* by William Vaughan Moody, a poet and teacher at the University of Chicago. The theme of the play was revolt against the crushing authority of conscience and convention. Its treatment of the force of physical passion was daring and poignant. Miss Anglin determined to try it out immediately. She wanted certain changes made to sharpen its dramatic impact, and on the night of the first performance she refused to proceed with the last act until Moody signed the contract she demanded. The following autumn, with Henry Miller, she produced the play as *The Great Divide* in New York. Acclaimed by the critics for its power, beauty and intellectual merit as an interpretation of contemporary American life, the play enjoyed a long, prosperous run in New York and was afterwards toured widely by the two stars. It proved to be a landmark in the history of the American drama, pointing forward to the "renaissance" that was to begin a decade later. Miss Anglin did not always find plays of comparable merit thereafter. But she continued to be an innovator, and among her contributions to the stage were a series of superb productions of classical Greek tragedies: *Antigone, Electra, Medea* and others never before presented to popular audiences.

Frohman starred Miss Julia Marlowe in several "romantic" plays, most notably in Clyde Fitch's *Barbara Frietchie*. An episode in the play required the star to aim and discharge a musket, and during rehearsals in Philadelphia, Byron Ongley, the company's assistant stage manager, was deputed to procure the weapon, take it to Miss Marlowe's hotel, and instruct her in its use. With his characteristic flair for publicity, Frohman notified the hotel management that Miss Marlowe had received a threatening letter from a crank who might possibly appear to make an attempt on her life. When Ongley entered the hotel lobby carrying his musket, four sturdy porters felled him; the police were summoned, and he spent twenty-four hours in jail. The Philadelphia press made a sensation of the attempted crime, and tickets for the engagement were quickly sold out. Although in romantic roles Miss Marlowe became one of the most profitable stars of the time, her large earnings did not console her for the mediocrity of her plays. A similar discontent afflicted E. H. Sothern, who had won his greatest successes in such romantic pieces as *The Prisoner of Zenda* and *If I Were King,* but had also, at the age of forty, undertaken the role of Hamlet with critical approval. In 1904, Frohman brought Miss Marlowe and Sothern together and, guaranteeing each of them $100,000 for a season of forty weeks, the largest fees until then paid to stars, sent them on tour in a repertory of magnificently mounted Shakespearian plays. Thereafter, until Miss Marlowe's retirement from the stage twenty years later, the annual Shakespearian tours of the celebrated co-stars—who were married in 1911, following Sothern's divorce from Miss Harned—were a national institution.

Older playgoers, haunted by memories of Booth and Barrett, Mme. Modjeska, Miss Terry and Miss Rehan, declared that Southern was an able, earnest, scholarly but not inspired interpreter of Shakespeare; that Miss Marlowe, despite the beauty of her voice and person, failed to equal her illustrious predecessors. But for the younger generation, the comprehensiveness of the Sothern-Marlowe repertory, the excellence of their company, the grace and distinction of their playing, established high standards.

For twenty-five years Robert B. Mantell also toured the country in a repertory of Shakespeare's tragedies. He had earlier gained popularity as a romantic actor while performing with Miss Fanny Davenport in *Fedora*. He had a resonant, powerful voice and an impressive physique, and he carried into the twentieth century the acting style of the robustious school of Forrest and McCullough, of which he was the last representative. Beginning in 1910, and for twenty years thereafter, a repertory of Shakespeare's plays, the morality play, *Everyman,* and certain classic comedies were taken to hundreds of communities too small to have a legitimate theater. Under the auspices of the Redpath Lyceum Bureau, a troupe of players directed by the British actor Ben Greet performed Shakespeare in the Elizabethan style on the nation's Lyceum and Chatauqua circuits, providing for millions of Americans their only contact with the professional theater.

The passing of a brief vogue for costume plays created problems for two leading matinée idols, William Faversham and James K. Hackett, who had thrilled feminine audiences in swashbuckling romantic roles. Faversham's flamboyant good looks and athletic figure were not his only assets; he was a talented, adaptable actor; he was also intelligent. He starred with conspicuous success in *The Squaw Man,* a drama of twentieth-century Wyoming, notable chiefly for its acute study of Ute Indian characters and frontier conditions. The play was written by Edwin Milton Royle, an actor who had served a two-year apprenticeship as a member of Edwin Booth's company. Faversham later made a sumptuous production of Stephen Phillips' poetic drama, *Herod,* introduced Bernard Shaw's *Getting Married* to American audiences, put on Shaw's *Misalliance,* undertook the title role of Edward Knoblock's satirical *The Faun,* and emphasized his versatility by giving a meritorious performance of Marc Antony in *Julius Caesar.* The versatility and intelligence which enabled Faversham to keep abreast of changing taste were lacking to Hackett, son of James H. Hackett, who died during the younger Hackett's infancy. Daniel Frohman told a story of rehearsing him to replace E. H. Sothern in *The Prisoner of Zenda,* in which he made his first success. Young Hackett was fond of drink, and whenever the company was ready for one of his scenes he would ask them to wait until he had gone to his dressing room to adjust his collar. This happened repeatedly, delaying the rehearsals, until Frohman finally said, "Jim, bring the entire bottle of collars out here, so we will not waste any time." After that, no further time was wasted.

To act to the top of his form, Hackett needed florid passages; clashing swords and courtly wooing were his forte. In contemporary realistic drama he was insignificant, and his career went into an eclipse when costumed romanticism lost its appeal for audiences. In 1914 he inherited from his niece, the daughter of his deceased half-brother, Recorder John Hackett, a fortune of more than one million dollars. His benefactor was far older than he; she had never approved of him or liked him; but she had died intestate and he was next of kin. Hackett's unexpected inheritance came to him when he was nearing his fiftieth year and made it possible for him to gratify long-cherished professional ambitions. He starred himself, without acclaim, in *Othello* and *Macbeth*. He took his production of *Macbeth* to London, where he engaged Mrs. Patrick Campbell as his leading lady. His success there was sensational; he was praised for restoring to Shakespearian acting the sweep and amplitude of the grand style. Later, Hackett appeared at the Odéon in Paris at the invitation of the French Government, and triumphed there also. The playwright George Middleton, in Paris at the time, read to Hackett a translation of the reviews of his Macbeth, and recalled his comment. " 'Isn't it odd, George!' he said with a twinkle. 'They always called me a ham actor in the States. I seldom got a good notice. And now I come to London and Paris and they call me a great actor. I don't feel I am any different.' "

The actor who most effectively synthesized the resources of the old style and the discoveries of the new was Otis Skinner. He acted with Barrett, Booth, Jefferson, Modjeska; he had been a member of Daly's company for five years. Unlike his contemporary, John Drew, he refused to be stereotyped. Unlike his other contemporary, William Gillette, he would not confine himself to the restricted palette of naturalness. "I had been spending overmuch time with the magnifying glass," he wrote of his decision to leave Daly. "Breadth was what I needed now."

The triumph of a purely realistic drama seemed likely to eliminate breadth from the art of acting. One factor in this triumph was the influence of Ibsen, however indirect or diluted, on a new generation of playwrights. Another was the diminishing size of theaters. In the 1870's new theaters, like the Fifth Avenue in New York or Baldwin's in San Francisco, were built to accommodate twenty-five hundred playgoers. But the Empire, built two decades later, held only eleven hundred, and the trend was toward playhouses of even smaller capacity. This brought the actor into constantly more intimate relation with his audience, and required subtle modifications of acting style. But did it not also reflect a change in the mentality of audiences? "I have often thought," Fanny Kemble wrote seventy years earlier, "that the constant demand for small theaters, which I have heard made by persons of the higher classes of society in England, was a great proof of the decline of the imaginative faculties among them. . . . They have forgotten what human nature really is, and cannot even *imagine* it. They require absolute reality on the stage, because their incapable spirits scoff at poetical truth."

Skinner's most notable contribution to the theater was the insight on which his acting was founded. He saw that the grandeur and amplitude of the old style, stripped of its fustian, could be preserved. Properly applied to the realistic drama, that amplitude and grandeur would, without impairment of naturalness, make factual content yield imaginative and poetic truth. Because of this insight, and his determined cultivation of breadth, Skinner had a range far more extensive than any other actor of the time, and he also had the ability to invest comparatively trivial material with significance. He could turn from a polished performance of Henry Arthur Jones's slender comedy, *The Liars,* to the difficult verse of Robert Browning's intense one-scene tragedy, *In a Balcony,* which he played with Mrs. Sarah Cowell LeMoyne and Miss Eleanor Robson, a gifted and beautiful actress who soon retired from the stage to marry the banker August Belmont. He revived with magnificent effect George Boker's poetic tragedy, *Francesca da Rimini,* in which, twenty years earlier, he had appeared with Barrett. He co-starred with Miss Ada Rehan, who came out of retirement for a melancholy farewell tour, a "sad-faced, white-haired woman . . . taking no interest in anything about her." They played *The Taming of the Shrew, The School for Scandal* and *The Merchant of Venice.* In great plays, Skinner could always render great performances. But a far more impressive demonstration of his art occurred when he appeared in inferior plays and made them seem, as they were not, dramatically, intrinsically, important. Skinner did this again and again: in Clyde Fitch's costume comedy, *His Grace de Grammont;* in Henri Lavedan's *The Duel,* a study of the conflict between religious faith and materialism; in *Your Humble Servant,* by Booth Tarkington and Harry Leon Wilson, which enabled him, as he had long wished, to "portray an actor of the old bad school, one of those simple fellows given overmuch to 'sound and fury'"; and in Tarkington's *Mr. Antonio,* which contrasted the spiritual nobility of an Italian hurdy-gurdy man with the selfishness of a small American town. Skinner's greatest popular success was made in Edward Knoblock's spectacular Oriental fantasy, *Kismet.* This was an implausible piece of theatrical trumpery, but Skinner's performance as Hajj, the beggar, lifted it to the plane of poetic truth. Seldom again was the American public to be furnished so arresting an illustration of the miracle that great acting art can perform with inferior material.

Clyde Fitch, who provided Skinner with two plays, was the most expert purveyor of vehicles to stars. He was also the most prolific, successful and distinguished American playwright of the day. During one season, he had four plays simultaneously running to crowded houses on Broadway. His dramas and social comedies were usually produced in London as well as New York. His best play, *The Truth,* also reached the stages of Italy, Germany, Russia, Hungary and the Scandinavian countries, and he was the first American dramatist to gain prestige in Europe. A small, slender, dark-haired man, Fitch was an esthete who wished to become a millionaire, and had his wish. He also aspired to fulfill the promise of his talent and abundant technical skill, but he could never convince himself that any of his plays possessed genuine, enduring significance. While a demand for historical romances flourished, he wrote the best ones. When taste shifted to realistic drama and high comedy, he excelled in these modes also. "The sensitive predominates in his work," the critic James Huneker wrote, "delicacy, tact and a feminine manner of apprehending the meanings of life." In some ways Fitch understood women almost better than they understood themselves, and as he wrote primarily for a feminine audience this insight accounted for much of his success. His public wanted plays about the fashionable world, and he provided them. The artist in him rendered with marvelous fidelity an opulent background and the glittering surface of life in the realm of the socially elect.

But there was also in Fitch a puritan moralist who was repelled by what he saw beneath the surface. Some of his heroines, for all their elegance and fastidiousness, were deeply tainted. They were possessive, acquisitive and extravagant; climbers ruthlessly intent on social advancement; unscrupulous liars; monsters of jealousy. Miss Maude Adams urged him to "go to some place where the art is dead and life is uppermost—common life," intimating that the characters whom he put on the stage "are real of their kind, but it isn't a red-blood kind." He was aware of this. "I live my life in a mist of shams," he told William Dean Howells. But, as the fashionable painter of a fashionable world, Fitch tried to make the "mist of shams" represent the solid substance of life, and the brilliancy of his craftsmanship often persuaded his audience to accept the substitution.

There was scarcely a woman star of the time whose career Fitch did not advance by writing a play for her. Mrs. Amelia Bingham, a plump actress of

Scene from "The Girl With the Green Eyes," by Clyde Fitch, showing Robert Drouet and Clara Bloodgood (center) 1903

Maxine Elliot in "The Merchant of Venice," 1901

limited talent, rose to popularity with *The Climbers*. Miss Blanche Walsh achieved celebrity in *The Woman in the Case*, a tense and daring melodrama. Fitch wrote *Her Great Match* for Miss Maxine Elliott, and the play induced the public to believe that she was a superior actress as well as a great beauty.

Of Miss Elliott's beauty, there was no doubt. Her stately figure, classic profile, raven hair and luminous dark eyes drew crowds to see her, off the stage as well as on it. An aura of splendor surrounded her, and her caprices were reported by journalists with appropriate solemnity. She was even more imperious than Mrs. Patrick Campbell, the famous English star, who, playing in a theater on Forty-second Street and exasperated by the noise of traffic, demanded that a block of roadway be covered with tanbark. "I wouldn't *dream* of moving from New York to Philadelphia, even, unless it was in my private car," Miss Elliott told Miss Billie Burke. She was, for a time, the wife of the comedian Nat Goodwin, a persistent collector of beautiful spouses who, after their divorce, remarked, "Being married to Maxine is like being married to a Roman senator."

The frigidity implied by this tribute did not accord with Miss Elliott's legend. Gossip asserted that she was the mistress of J. P. Morgan, and when a luxurious theater bearing her name was erected on West Thirty-ninth Street, it was assumed to be his gift. Miss Elliott was also reported to have captivated King Edward VII, and to have received from him a commemorative souvenir in the form of a gold dinner service. These rumors enhanced her glamour, and in London as well as New York she moved in the highest circles. "I may sit below the salt sometimes, dear, but I'm *there*," she said.

Fitch wrote *The Truth* for Mrs. Clara Bloodgood, who had earlier created the title role of his *The Girl with the Green Eyes*. Mrs. Bloodgood came to the stage from the ranks of New York "society," but under Fitch's training she became a skillful and appealing actress. In New York, on its first showing, the merits of *The Truth* were not recognized by the critics, and it was withdrawn after thirty-four performances. A later production in London, with another actress, scored a triumph. Encouraged by this, Mrs. Bloodgood took the play on tour the following season, but the verdict of New York carried authority on the road. Despondent over the failure of Fitch's finest play, and perhaps attributing this to her own performance, though Fitch had praised it, Mrs. Bloodgood caused a sensation by committing suicide at her hotel in Baltimore.

Fitch wrote the play which brought stardom to Miss Ethel Barrymore, who was to have the longest, most illustrious career of any of Charles Frohman's "discoveries." She represented the fourth generation of an American theatrical dynasty. Her great-grandmother, Mrs. Lane, had appeared at the Bowery Theater in 1828, and on the same night her grandmother, Mrs. Drew, had first performed in the United States at the age of seven. Mrs. Drew had acted with "Old Jefferson," with Forrest, Macready and Junius Brutus Booth. She had managed the Arch Street Theater in Philadelphia, and it was in her home there that Miss Barrymore and her brothers, Lionel and John, passed their childhood. Their parents, Maurice Barrymore and Georgie Drew Barrymore, were prominent figures on the stage. So was their uncle, John Drew, who had married the daughter of Alexina Fisher Baker and Lewis Baker, herself an actress. Yet none of the Barrymore children wished to take up the family profession. "We became actors," Miss Barrymore said, "not because we wanted to go on the stage, but because it was the thing we could do best."

In 1896, as a girl of seventeen, Miss Barrymore played a small role in *Rosemary,* with her uncle and Miss Adams. She was sent to London by Frohman, the following year, as a member of the company supporting William Gillette in *Secret Service.* Word reached the United States that her spectacular beauty and charm had taken London by storm. The Duchess of Sutherland, it was said, had sponsored her in society. At different times she was reported to be engaged to several men of title, to the British matinée idol Gerald du Maurier, to Laurence Irving, Sir Henry Irving's son. Old Mrs. Drew had ended her seventieth year on the stage in an all-star revival of *The Rivals* and, shortly before her death, speaking of Miss Barrymore's London success to her grandsons, remarked upon "how far theatrical people had come up in the world during her day"—she could remember a time when they had been excluded from reputable society. Miss Barrymore remained in London to play for one season with Sir Henry Irving at the Lyceum, and it was with the added prestige of this engagement that she returned to the United States.

Frohman engaged Miss Barrymore to play the role of Mme. Trentoni in Fitch's *Captain Jinks of the Horse Marines,* a comedy of New York life in the 1870's dealing with social prejudice against an opera singer because of her profession. The play opened in Philadelphia, home city of the Drews and Barrymores, where it failed. On February 4, 1901, Frohman brought it to the Garrick Theater in New York, believing that it would run no longer than two weeks. Instead, Miss Barrymore captivated the critics and the public. Not only by her radiant beauty and the spell of her low-pitched, husky voice; it was the quiet authority of her

Ethel Barrymore in "Captain Jinks of the Horse Marines," 1901

acting, her unexpected command of her art, that won instant recognition. The play settled into a run that was to last for seven months. Miss Barrymore, who had been living modestly on the top floor of a theatrical boarding house on West Thirty-second Street, celebrated success by moving into a larger room on the second floor. During the third week of the engagement she walked, one night, to the Garrick, on Thirty-fifth Street east of Sixth Avenue. As she approached the theater she chanced to look up and saw her name blazing in electric lights. Without notifying her, Frohman had made her a star. It was, as he told her next day, "the only thing to do."

Subsequent roles emphasized her talent for comedy, although her playing of a one-act piece, *Carrots,* showed that she was also capable of pathos. Comedy was the forte of the Drews. (There was nobody left to remember that old Mrs. Drew, in her youth, had played the entire range of tragic and dramatic roles.) But Maurice Barrymore had made his name in romantic and strongly dramatic parts. Mme. Modjeska said of him that, although extravagantly handsome, he "was too intellectual to be a mere matinée idol," and this was also true of his children. Of Miss Barrymore no less than her brothers. She was not satisfied to play only comedy, and she seemed scarcely aware of a triumph that was reflected by the effort of a generation of American girls to imitate her voice, her stage costumes, the proud carriage of her head which contrasted so piquantly with an invincible shyness of manner, even on the stage. Mme. Modjeska recalled her as "an actress at three. I often saw her eager eyes watching me behind the scenes at a matinée." In 1905, four years after her elevation to stardom, Miss Barrymore persuaded Frohman to let her undertake the role of Nora in Ibsen's *A Doll's House,* and in it first revealed her aptitude as a dramatic actress, her ability to project the unexpressed overtones of a character's feelings, her flair for depth of interpretation. She also possessed a more exceptional gift. She could transform herself inwardly as well as outwardly to meet the requirements of a role.

This she demonstrated when, at the age of twenty-five, she appeared in Barrie's *Alice Sit by the Fire*. There were two important roles in the play; that of a middle-aged mother, performed in England by Miss Ellen Terry, and that of a young girl. Miss Barrymore chose to play the role of the mother who, accepting the verdict of the calendar, turns aside the worship of a diffident young lover—this role being taken by her younger brother, John. She followed this fine performance with a more daring exploit, appearing as the tragic, pitiable charwoman of John Galsworthy's *The Silver Box*. Audiences failed to realize that her performance was not only a display of virtuosity but a proof that Miss Barrymore had the endowment of a great artist. Her public deplored the sacrifice of her youth and beauty, and the play ran for only twenty performances. They were better pleased when she turned to Somerset Maugham's scintillating comedy, *Lady Frederick,* a choice which demonstrated that she was the master of not one, but several acting styles. She proceeded to Pinero's *Mid-channel,* his finest drama, and her performance in this somber study of a marriage meeting with disaster made it obvious that she was the most accomplished dramatic actress on the American stage. Possibly with the intention of defeating any attempt by the critics or public to "type" her, she next appeared in Barrie's *The Twelve-Pound Look*—which so delighted playgoers that she was compelled to revive it frequently for forty years. She first performed it in 1911, and it was already clear that American playwrights had available an actress of the first rank. If, thereafter, Miss Barrymore did not appear in plays that exploited the full range of her art, the fault was not hers.

Meanwhile her brothers, who wished to be painters, not actors, had tried to practice their chosen profession without success, and both reluctantly took to the stage. Lionel established his merits as an actor when playing with John Drew in *The Mummy and the Humming Bird*. In a single short scene in the role of an Italian organ-grinder, he stole the show—an exploit which led his distinguished uncle to reply to an inquiry concerning his health that he was "well enough, considering that every night I have to play second fiddle to that preposterous nephew of mine." But, disenchanted with the theater, Lionel went to work with David Wark Griffith in motion pictures and remained in that field. John Barrymore—erratic, unreliable, intemperate, but indisputably talented—had been placed by Frohman in the company of his star comedian, William Collier, noted for his suave, silky underacting. They had been playing in San Francisco when, in 1906, the disaster of fire and earthquake overtook the city. John Barrymore was reported safe, and working with an army squad in the ruins. This report drew from John Drew the ironical comment that "it took an act of God to get Jack out of bed, and the United States Army to put him to work." But his long apprenticeship to Collier made him an exceptionally proficient light comedian, and in 1909, starring in Winchell Smith's *The Fortune Hunter,* he was already famous, not only as a skillful actor, but as the "handsomest man in America." The full measure of his gifts as a comedian became apparent only three years later, when Winthrop Ames, a cultivated producer, starred him with five leading ladies as the accessible, infatuating, deluded hero of Arthur Schnitzler's mordant *The Affairs of Anatol*. But surprises were in store for Barrymore's adoring feminine public, presently foreshadowed by his powerful characterizations in two unimportant melodramas: *The Yellow Ticket* and *Kick In*.

Frohman had made stars of two actresses who, like Barrymore, were renowned for their beauty; both had served their apprenticeship in musical comedy. Miss Marie Doro was diminutive and ethereal, a wisp of a girl whose great brown eyes, cloud of dark hair and camellialike complexion were disturbing to the masculine heart. Chosen by William Gillette as his leading lady in *Clarice*, she later co-starred with him in *The Morals of Marcus*, founded on a popular novel by W. J. Locke. She gave impressive performances as Dora in an all-star revival of *Diplomacy;* as Oliver in an all-star revival of *Oliver Twist;* and in *The Butterfly on the Wheel*. But the plays in which she appeared made few demands on talent and, perhaps for this reason, she retired from the stage at the height of her popularity, leaving with her judicious admirers a memory of unfulfilled promise. This was also to be the fate of Miss Billie Burke, a young American actress whom Frohman brought from London, where she had risen to playing leading roles with Charles Hawtrey. Miss Burke was twenty-two; petite, red-haired, vivacious and a sprightly comedienne. As leading woman for John Drew in *My Wife*, she scored an outstanding personal success. Frohman promptly starred her in *Love Watches*, adapted from a French comedy by Gaston de Caillavet and Robert de Flers.

There followed a series of roles in which, as she later recorded, "what I had to do was to be as pretty as I could and as gay as I could on the stage, so I did that." She did it to perfection, and to the delight of a tremendous public. She created feminine fashions, evoked masculine adoration, lived in a perpetual barrage of floral tributes. The critics did not encourage her to believe that she might become a great actress; they conceded her charm, but were dubious about her talent. Frohman selected her plays, and she accepted them without question. In most of them she personated "gay girls who moved lightly through society with bright lines to say, expensively gowned and accompanied always by the handsomest and most skillful leading man Charles Frohman could buy." Frohman produced for her Pinero's comedy of backstage life, *The Mind-the-Paint Girl*. It was a play that had substance, and she acted it so well that the critics acknowledged her dramatic talent. For the first time she had an insight into "what the theater could really mean" and felt "an urge to play some of the finer, harder, more glorious parts." How far this aspiration ran counter to the wishes of her public she discovered when she appeared in Somerset Maugham's gloomy drama, *The Land of Promise*. It failed.

She met Florenz Ziegfeld and they fell in love. Frohman, always dictatorial about the private lives of his women stars, detested Ziegfeld and made unpleasant scenes. One evening he came to Miss Burke's dressing room at the theater, hung his hat on a peg, and announced, "I am going to London. I am going to leave my hat. To remind you not to get married. Don't be foolish while I am gone." A few weeks later, between a matinée and evening performance of her play, Miss Burke and Ziegfeld crossed the Hudson River to Hoboken and were married. The news of their wedding made front-page headlines in the press. Miss Burke received a cable from Frohman in London. It read: "Send me my hat." She never saw or heard from him again.

Like Frohman, David Belasco was a star-maker. But whereas Frohman professed to regard his women stars as his children, Belasco acknowledged that he was a tyrant. "I coax and cajole, or bulldoze and torment, according to the temperament with which I have to deal," he asserted. Yet most of his stars gave him unconditional loyalty and absolute obedience. They referred to him affectionately, as "the Governor," or reverently as "the Master." His methods were sometimes painful or humiliating, but they admired the passion for perfection which forced him to be ruthless. The public, however, accepted the legend which, as Belasco said, "made me appear as a ferocious monster who would stop at no limit of physical violence to compel my actresses to do my bidding."

This legend sprang from a widely publicized lawsuit. Belasco had been required to describe, in court, the training he had given Mrs. Leslie Carter, his first star. He told of rehearsing her in the scene of *Oliver Twist* during which Bill Sykes murders Nancy, dragging her about by the hair and beating her head against the wall and furniture. His vivid account of the scene, Belasco asserted, inspired the press to report that he had mauled Mrs. Carter "with fiendishly calculated brutality" in order "to stimulate her emotional fervor."

Emotional fervor was not entirely lacking to Mrs. Carter when she first came to him in a blaze of notoriety. She was twenty-seven, a slender, pale, plain-featured woman who had green eyes and a mass of fiery red hair. The wife of a Chicago millionaire and socially prominent, she had sued her husband for divorce. He brought a counter-suit naming five corespondents, among them the handsome actor, Kyrle Bellew. In 1889, conventional people were shocked by these allegations, which imputed to Mrs. Carter a liberality scarcely to be distinguished from promiscuousness, and a temperament excessively torrid. Her husband was granted his divorce, Mrs. Carter being found guilty of adultery with Bellew. She announced her intention of going on the stage. Carter forbade her to use his name, but she gratified a desire for revenge by adopting his full name for professional purposes. Mrs. Carter went to Belasco and pleaded with him to train her for a stage career. She had to earn a living; she was bent upon becoming an actress; she intended to begin at the top of the profession. "Nothing about her was beautiful or even pretty," he wrote many years later, "but the radiance of her features, the eloquence of her soul, and the magnetism of her highly keyed, temperamental nature convinced me then and there that she would go far, if only her natural abilities could be developed and controlled."

Belasco began a systematic course of training which took five years to complete. At the end of one year, he brought her out in a drama ungallantly titled *The Ugly Duckling,* and a public at first inclined to be hostile applauded her. After another year of study, Belasco adapted for her a French comic opera, *Miss Helyett,* in which she had considerable success. He then withdrew her

Mrs. Leslie Carter in "Zaza," 1899

from the stage for three years in order to give her further tuition. Many of Mrs. Carter's friends in Chicago had deserted her during the scandal of her divorce trial, but her cause had been publicly espoused by N. K. Fairbank, a millionaire, and his wife. Fairbank later backed one of the productions which Belasco made for Mrs. Carter, and it was a lawsuit arising from this financial arrangement which brought to the attention of the public his methods of developing stellar talent.

To launch Mrs. Carter as a star, Belasco wrote *The Heart of Maryland,* a melodrama of the Civil War in which, to save the life of her Northern lover, the heroine swings out from a tower firmly holding the clapper of a bell which was to have sounded the signal for his doom. The play was prodigiously successful. It established Belasco as a producer and Mrs. Carter as an important star. Belasco had decided that violent outbursts of passion were to be her forte, and he had laboriously trained her to the point where she could deliver them at his command, even in an empty theater. He had also drilled her in "sudden transitions of intense emotions." After she had played *The Heart of Maryland* for three years, in New York, on tour, and in London, Belasco provided her with a vehicle designed to display these accomplishments. He made an adaptation of *Zaza,* a drama by the French playwrights Pierre Berton and Charles Simon, in which Mrs. Carter, as a music-hall singer, the mistress of a man already married and the father of a child, had an opportunity to play ardent love scenes, fly into tempestuous rages, and portray a spiritual redemption affectingly brought about by her lover's child. The critics were shocked by the play. So was the public. The theater was crowded for months.

This enabled Belasco and Mrs. Carter to disregard the fact that critical appraisal of her talents had not been entirely flattering; some of the comment was bleakly insulting. Sex, violence and suspense dominated *Du Barry,* the next play which Belasco wrote for his star. He gave her an effective scene in which, as the king's mistress, she hid her lover in her bed while the king and her enemies searched for him; and another in which, dragged through the streets to the guillotine past a jeering mob, she screamed her defiance of them. Mounted in lavish, spectacular style, *Du Barry* ran for many months in New York, and Mrs. Carter afterwards took it on a prolonged tour. For her next vehicle, Belasco collaborated with the novelist John Luther Long. They produced *Adrea,* which purported to be a romantic tragedy. It dealt with a blind princess on an island in the Adriatic after the fall of the Roman Empire, and told a complicated story of love, lust, betrayal and revenge. Though to many playgoers *Adrea* seemed to be composed mainly of bombast and scenery, it had a more than respectable success. This was in 1905, and the alliance between Belasco and his star had lasted for sixteen years. The public believed it to be as durable as that between Charles Frohman and Miss Adams, and assumed that it was based on a romantic attachment. There was a great sensation, one year later, when newspapers revealed that Mrs. Carter, at the age of forty-four, had married W. L. Payne, an actor considerably her junior.

The news took Belasco by surprise, but after he had verified it he refused to forgive her, and they were never reconciled. In training Mrs. Carter, his object had been to develop an actress who would be equal to "Clara Morris at her best." This purpose may have been influenced by nostalgic sentiment about his youthful career in San Francisco. At the time when he was working there as actor, playwright, director and stage manager, Miss Morris had touched the height of her fame as an emotional actress. But Miss Morris' acting style, and the kind of drama to which it was appropriate, were long obsolete. Belasco had given both a temporary plausibility in the plays which he had written for Mrs. Carter. That he could have continued to do this seems improbable, but without his collaboration as playwright and director Mrs. Carter became helpless. Her subsequent ventures as a star met with little success; her meteoric career in effect ended when she broke with Belasco.

During the years of Mrs. Carter's ascendancy, Belasco embarked in a long, costly contest with the Syndicate. This led him, in 1900, to lease the present Republic Theater on West Forty-second Street in New York and, six years later, to build his own theater, the present Belasco, on West Forty-fourth Street, where he installed a remarkable system of stage lighting and also provided himself with an elaborate studio crammed with bibelots, to which visitors were admitted by servitors in livery, their progress toward Belasco being announced by the sound of gongs. But even before this he had won fame as a master of realistic stagecraft. Because of the complete atmospheric illusion he achieved in his productions, the profession took to calling him "the wizard." Actors and actresses considered it an honor to be associated with him. For the privilege of

Frances Starr and Joseph Kilgour in "The Easiest Way," 1909

working under his direction they cheerfully waived the higher salaries offered by other producers. He made Miss Blanche Bates a star, writing for her, with John Luther Long, *Madame Butterfly* and *The Darling of the Gods,* and his melodrama, *The Girl of the Golden West.* He wanted an emotional male star, and he made the improbable choice of a dialect comedian from the company of Weber and Fields, David Warfield, whom he had first met years earlier as an usher in the Bush Street Theater in San Francisco. Warfield had never before played serious drama, but in Charles Klein's *The Auctioneer* and *The Music Master,* and later in Belasco's drama dealing with physical survival after death, *The Return of Peter Grimm,* he became so popular as a specialist in sentiment and pathos that he amassed a fortune and was able to retire from the stage.

Belasco saw Miss Frances Starr play a minor role in a comedy. Impressed by her ability, he sent for her and offered her a contract which she signed immediately. She was a frail-looking girl, brown-haired, blue-eyed, high-strung. He sent her on tour with Warfield in *The Music Master,* then gave her the leading role in his scenically sumptuous production of *The Rose of the Rancho,* a romantic play about the settlement of California which he had written with Richard Walton Tully. Her performance convinced him that she would excel "in roles demanding an intense emotionalism, if only I could contrive somehow to stir her imagination to an even higher pitch." Eugene Walter, a writer of successful melodramas, brought Belasco *The Easiest Way,* a play about a "kept woman." Although Walter had written the role of Laura Murdock for another actress, Belasco decided to give it to Miss Starr as her first stellar part. In the climactic scene of the play Laura Murdock, trapped by her own mendacity and abandoned by the man who sought to redeem her and whom she loves, seizes a pistol with the intention of killing herself but lacks the courage and, with a shriek of terror, throws the weapon down. Belasco felt that this scene had to be worked up to the highest possible pitch of frenzied hysteria. He wanted from Miss Starr "a scream which would denote a soul in torment," but although he rehearsed the scene scores of times she could never satisfy him. To make her respond to his demands he decided to humiliate her before the company, driving her to the point of hysterics. He rehearsed her over and over again, while the company looked on in silent anger and Miss Starr became more and more desperate. Then he recalled that she had often told him of her worship of Sarah Bernhardt. "And you want to be as great as Bernhardt!" he said, sarcastically. "It makes me laugh."

In a flash, Miss Starr screamed hysterically and collapsed on the stage in a faint. When she had been revived, he said, "That's what I want! That's exactly what I've been working for these last three hours."

At the next rehearsal, Miss Starr rose to the climax of the scene with perfect ease.

Belasco's production of *The Easiest Way,* in January, 1909, caused a sensation. Moralists were disturbed by its daring treatment of sex. Impressed by its unhappy ending, but ignoring its inconsistencies and sentimentality, most of the critics and many playgoers praised it as an important American drama. The last line of the play became famous. "Dress up my body and paint my face," Laura Murdock bade her maid. "I'm going to Rector's to make a hit—and to hell with the rest!"

It suggested, at the time, an immense advance toward the social realism of Ibsen and other European dramatists. But the realism of *The Easiest Way* was almost exclusively confined to Belasco's stagecraft. For one scene, he required an exact counterpart of a hall bedroom in a cheap theatrical boarding house in New York. The setting produced by his scene-builders did not satisfy him. "I went to the meanest theatrical boarding house I could find in the Tenderloin district," he wrote later, "and bought the entire interior of one of its most dilapidated rooms—patched furniture, threadbare carpet, tarnished and broken gas fixtures, tumbledown cupboards, dingy doors and window casings, and even the faded paper on the walls." This was the interior which the audience saw on the stage.

Shortly afterwards, in the last act of *The Governor's Lady,* Belasco reproduced on the stage with photographic fidelity a Childs Restaurant, complete even to griddle cakes. He prided himself on "the importance and emphasis I place upon every minute detail which makes for truth in my theater." By truth he meant absolute naturalism in scenic production and, as far as possible, in acting. But the plays he produced were seldom of vital consequence. George Middleton who, as a playwright, knew Belasco well and worked with him on several productions, summed up his limitations: "He had no broad culture and was unaware of social and economic readjustments in the world about him. He produced no important play, I recall, which reflected the new moralities touching on man and society. Preoccupied always with sex, he would dare a bit, as in *The Easiest Way;* but the revolutionary *Doll's House* or any plays which suggested the claims of a mild feminism were beyond him. With few exceptions, the American plays he did were amiably unimportant, though among the best of their kind."

In the years when Belasco's prestige was nearing its height, other prominent people of the stage, rejecting his policies, attempted to develop an audience for plays of intellectual substance. Mrs. Fiske and her husband, who had become her manager, were vigorous opponents of the Syndicate. They leased the Manhattan Theater on Greeley Square in New York and for six years operated it with a splendid company which, at various times, included such eminent players as Miss Emily Stevens, John Mason, George Arliss and Holbrook Blinn. No actress of the day provoked greater critical controversy than slender, carrot-haired Mrs. Fiske, whose brittle, staccato diction, excessively rapid movement and sparing use of gesture were mannerisms that some playgoers found exasperating and others condoned. She was intelligent, idealistic, hard-working and a perfectionist. She was an active propagandist for the prevention of cruelty to animals and for vegetarianism. A young actress whom she took on tour as a pupil vividly recalled that the sum of these attributes, however admirable, was often productive of affliction. The company toured during an excessively cold winter, and principally to one-night stands. Mrs. Fiske called rehearsals almost daily, so that the actors seldom had sufficient sleep. She insisted that her pupil discard her fur coat and restrict herself to a vegetable diet; the young actress was constantly cold and usually hungry. But the magic which Mrs. Fiske exercised on audiences became apparent to her when, delayed by a

George Arliss and Mrs. Fiske in "Hedda Gabler," 1904

blizzard, the company arrived at one town long after midnight to find a crowded house eagerly awaiting a performance that began at two o'clock in the morning.

Some critics asserted that Mrs. Fiske was the most distinguished actress on the American stage. Others declared that she lacked variety and depth, or that she was merely a "personality actress" and monotonously herself in every role. But of her dedication to the cause of a vital and genuinely significant drama there was no doubt. While she maintained her company at the Manhattan Theater she produced Ibsen's *Hedda Gabler* and *Rosmersholm,* and Langdon Mitchell's adroit social comedy, *The New York Idea.* After relinquishing the Manhattan, she produced Ibsen's *Pillars of Society* and *Salvation Nell,* the first play of a young American playwright, Edward Sheldon, who was to become an important influence. Sheldon had been a student in the pioneer course in playwriting established by Professor George Pierce Baker at Harvard University in 1905, an enterprise which would later enroll Eugene O'Neill and Sidney Howard. Sheldon's drama, dealing with life in the New York slums in a spirit of intellectual honesty, was one of the earliest and most successful attempts by an American playwright to make a serious social theme theatrically effective.

It was to Mrs. Fiske's credit that she discovered two native playwrights whose work had a content of ideas, that she took the risk of producing their plays, and that she made these ventures not only artistically, but commercially successful. But Mrs. Fiske, working under conditions imposed by the commercial theater, was skeptical about its cherished orthodoxies. Ibsen was supposed to spell box-office failure. "Our Ibsen seasons have invariably been profitable," she reported, and pointed out that *Rosmersholm,* "the most somber and complex tragedy of its period," ran for one hundred and ninety-nine consecutive performances at a profit of $40,000.

The cause of Ibsen—almost synonymous with that of a "better drama"— was immensely advanced by Mme. Alla Nazimova, a lithe, black-haired, dark-eyed Russian actress. She had come to New York as the leading lady of a Russian company which opened on Broadway, failed, and migrated to a drab theater on the lower East Side. There, Mme. Nazimova's performances of *Ghosts, The Master Builder* and other Ibsen plays attracted the dramatic critics, many Broadway stars, and a large attendance of intellectuals. Her emotional intensity, tragic power and exceptional technical proficiency were obvious even to auditors ignorant of the Russian language. When her troupe sailed for Europe, Mme. Nazimova remained in New York to study English. One year later, in November, 1906, under the auspices of Henry Miller, then playing *The Great Divide,* she made her debut as an English-speaking actress in *Hedda Gabler,* and subsequently appeared in *A Doll's House.* She toured in these plays, and afterward added *Little Eyolf* and *The Wild Duck* to her repertory. Richard Mansfield also contributed to the cause. In 1907, the last year of his life, he introduced *Peer Gynt* to American audiences in an excellent production which met with only moderate success.

While the Ibsen movement was being launched, a parallel effort was being made to create an audience for the plays of George Bernard Shaw. Arnold Daly, who had begun his career as Charles Frohman's office boy, and later had served his apprenticeship in Frohman companies, was fired by an ambition to produce *Candida,* which Richard Mansfield had earlier acquired but had dropped after three disillusioning rehearsals. Daly could obtain no financial backing to put the play on for a run, but managed to secure enough money to give a single performance. In it, Miss Dorothy Donnelly, an actress successful in melo-drama, took the title role; Mrs. Louise Closser Hale played Prossy; Daly played Marchbanks.

(A few years earlier, Mrs. Hale had come to the Frohman office and was told by Daly that the magnate was out.

"May I wait for him?" she asked.

"Yes," said Daly. After three hours had passed she inquired, "Where is Mr. Frohman?"

To which Daly imperturbably replied, "He is in London.")

The trial performance of *Candida* was unexpectedly successful, and with the financial backing of Winchell Smith, a successful playwright, Daly rented the small Berkeley Lyceum, where the play had a run of one hundred and fifty performances. This launched the vogue for Shaw, and Daly subsequently put on *How He Lied to Her Husband,* which Shaw wrote for him, *The Man of Destiny* and *John Bull's Other Island.* In 1905, with Miss Mary Shaw, an ac-complished actress who had been a member of Mme. Modjeska's company, Daly conceived the idea of producing *Mrs. Warren's Profession.* Notice was served on him by Anthony Comstock, head of the Society for the Suppression of Vice, that prosecution would follow if the performance was given. Daly and Miss Shaw decided to disregard the warning. Tickets for the opening night— October 30, 1905—were sold by speculators for $25. Police Commissioner McAdoo was in the audience at the Mayor's request, and next day notified Daly that further performances would be dealt with by the police. None were given. But the critics, with one exception, feverishly denounced the production as an offense to morals, so Miss Shaw and Daly were arrested, brought to trial in the Court of Special Sessions, and acquitted. Two years later, the play was revived without interference. Meanwhile, the British actor Robert Loraine had staged the first American production of *Man and Superman* and, in New York, the play had a run of one hundred and ninety-two performances.

Daly subsequently tried to establish a "theater of ideas" without success. He fell into financial difficulties, had a quarrel with Shaw, and the Shaw plays passed into other hands. Daly's temperamental excesses, his violent outbursts and addiction to drink, his arrogance and impatience, eventually ruined what promised to be one of the most brilliant careers in the history of the American stage. He was a magnificent actor; he was both learned and intelligent; he was uncompromising in his adherence to high ideals. For a time, when the theater stood most in need of such service, Daly took the initiative as its fighting champion of modernism.

A group of millionaires prominent in the affairs of the Metropolitan Opera— they included J. P. Morgan, John Jacob Astor, Harry Payne Whitney, three Vanderbilts and Otto Kahn—decided that the time had come to give the

United States a permanent, national, art theater, conducted on the repertory system, devoted to the production of the finest modern and classic drama. At the cost of many millions, a grandiose and beautiful theater was built in New York, occupying the block on Central Park West between Sixty-second and Sixty-third Streets. Its stage equipment and lighting devices were said to be superior to those of any playhouse in the world, but it was obvious from the outset that the size of the auditorium and that of the stage were excessive for the production of modern plays. As artistic director of the enterprise, the founders chose Winthrop Ames, a Harvard graduate of independent means who had received his initial training with the Castle Square stock company in Boston. Ames assembled a distinguished company of players which included Miss Rose Coghlan, Miss Annie Russell, Miss Beverly Sitgreaves, Miss Jessie Busley, A. E. Anson, Albert Bruning, Louis Calvert, E. M. Holland, Matheson Lang, Guy Bates Post, Oswald Yorke and Ferdinand Gottschalk. The New Theater was opened on November 6, 1909, with a lavish production of *Antony and Cleopatra,* Miss Marlowe and E. H. Sothern appearing as guest stars in the title roles, to which they were unfortunately not adapted. During two seasons, Winthrop Ames was able to find only three dramas by American playwrights that impressed him as being worthy of production. The most important of these, and the only one of permanent significance, was Edward Sheldon's *The Nigger,* a forthright, tragic study of race relations in the South. Of the foreign plays given, John Galsworthy's *Strife,* which dramatized the conflict between capital and labor, and Pinero's *The Thunderbolt* were the most significant. Excellent productions were made of Maurice Maeterlinck's *The Bluebird, Sister Beatrice* and *Mary Magdalene.* There were fine revivals of *Twelfth Night, A Winter's Tale* and *The Merry Wives of Windsor;* and *The School for Scandal* was brilliantly performed with Miss Russell as Lady Teazle and Miss Coghlan, the great Lady Teazle of Lester Wallack's company, as Mrs. Candour. But at the close of its second season the New Theater faced a huge deficit, and its founders determined to abandon the enterprise. The beautiful playhouse (since demolished to make way for an apartment house) was leased to commercial managers and, as the Century Theater, was used principally for spectacles.

The collapse of the New Theater was widely lamented. It indicated that hope for a privately endowed art theater, liberated from the pressure of commercial exactions, was premature. The dispersal of the superlative acting company, the finest that had been assembled since the days of Augustin Daly and Lester Wallack, deprived playgoers of an opportunity to see, year after year, the classic repertory in productions that were handsomely mounted, carefully studied and superbly performed. Had the New Theater succeeded, had it become a national temple of the drama as intended, it might have afforded greater opportunities to the generation of American playwrights who, within a few years, were to bring about a renaissance of the drama. But no important body of native drama existed during the brief life of the New Theater, and its founders, perhaps justifiably, lacked the enthusiasm necessary to profit by their experience and carry on their project in a playhouse better adapted to its purposes.

In the years that followed, significant developments took place within the commercial theater and outside it. The Irish Players of the Abbey Theater, Dublin, a company over which Lady Gregory and William Butler Yeats presided, toured the United States in 1911, presenting the plays of Yeats, John Millington Synge, and other playwrights who had given Ireland a native dramatic literature. Inspired by their example, the "little theater" movement was launched the following year with the opening, by Winthrop Ames, of the Little Theater in New York, the Toy Theater in Boston and the Little Theater in Chicago, directed by the British actor Maurice Browne and his American wife, Ellen Van Volkenburg. Only Ames's playhouse formed part of the professional theater, and as the movement spread over the country (there were nineteen hundred little theaters in 1925) it was nourished, as it had been in Dublin, by amateurs: writers, actors, directors, scene designers.

Of the many little theaters that were founded, two were destined to have a profound effect on the history of the American stage. In 1915 a group of residents of New York's Greenwich Village spent the summer at Provincetown, Massachusetts. Led by George Cram Cook and his wife, Susan Glaspell, they decided to write plays and produce them on a porch for their own amusement; the simple settings were arranged by Robert Edmond Jones. The following summer, they rebuilt an old fishing smack into a theater. Word reached them that a young Villager had arrived in Provincetown "with a trunkful of plays." Eugene O'Neill read them one of his plays, and they produced two that summer. In the autumn of 1916, convinced that they had discovered a genius in O'Neill, Cook and Miss Glaspell determined to found an art theater devoted to the experimental drama. At first in a cellar, and subsequently in a remodeled stable on MacDougal Street, The Playwrights' Theater began operations with a company of actors assembled from the residents of the Village. The works of many young playwrights were produced, but it was chiefly to see the early plays of O'Neill that audiences came to sit on hard benches in a dim, narrow auditorium and watch a company of gifted amateurs perform on a stage little larger than a handkerchief.

Another group of Villagers had formed a producing company in New York during the winter of 1915. Led by Lawrence Langner, Philip Moeller and Edward Goodman, this group, the Washington Square Players, announced that it would confine itself to the production of plays of artistic merit, and that preference would be given to American plays. Two seasons were given at the Bandbox Theater on East Fifty-seventh Street; two more at the Comedy Theater near Broadway on West Thirty-eighth Street, before war conditions forced suspension of the enterprise. During that period the Players performed sixty-two one-act plays, American and foreign, and produced full-length plays by Shaw, Chekhov, Ibsen, Andreyev and Maeterlinck. Among the acting talents which they introduced to the American stage were Miss Katharine Cornell, Roland Young, Glenn Hunter and Rollo Peters. In 1918, the same leaders formed a new group, "to carry out the idea of an expert theater"—a professional, not an amateur institution—and adopted the name Theater Guild.

Meanwhile, in an attempt to improve the working conditions of professional actors, The Actors' Equity Association was organized in 1913. For six years, representatives of Equity vainly tried to come to terms with the producing managers over such issues as minimum wages, a time limit on unpaid rehearsals, payment of transportation, an established maximum of eight weekly performances, and other desired safeguards. When, in 1919, the Producing Managers' Association refused to discuss the issues with Equity's representatives, Equity called a strike of professional actors which closed practically every commercial theater in New York. During the ensuing turbulence, such celebrated stars as John Drew, Ethel and Lionel Barrymore, Lillian Russell and Al Jolson were prominent in working for Equity. George M. Cohan, a beloved figure in the professional theater, was a producer as well as an actor; he sided with the producing managers. At the end of one month, Equity won a complete victory. Thereafter, it was recognized as the official representative of the theatrical profession. Its contract established the conditions under which actors were authorized to work, and exploitation of the profession by its employers ceased. There was one ironical outcome to the actors' strike. George M. Cohan had announced that he would never join Equity. He held to that decision. But Equity, in recognition of his prestige, and perhaps in acknowledgment of his gift of $100,000 to the Actors' Fund during the strike, permitted him, whenever he chose, to appear on the stage as the only professional actor who did not hold its union card.

Within the professional theater, there occurred developments which suggested that the "commercialism" attributed to major producers—most notably, to Charles Frohman and Belasco—was neither as obsessive nor as universal as the public had been led to believe. Frohman, sailing for Europe on the *Lusitania* in May, 1915, met his death when the great liner was torpedoed by a German submarine off the Irish coast. "My own impression about Charles's death," his brother Daniel wrote many years later, "is that it occurred at just about the right time. He had reached the climax of his management career." The fact was that Frohman's policies and Belasco's were already being made obsolescent by a public whose tastes they had largely formed. Other producers had become aware that commercial success and artistic achievement were not necessarily incompatible. No producer of the time was more hard-headed than William A. Brady, for example, who had begun his career as an actor in San Francisco and in his stride toward the New York stage had ventured into such odd byways as the management of pugilists. Brady made no pretense of being an intellectual, but it was he who produced Edward Sheldon's powerful study of political corruption, *The Boss*. It was Brady who backed the attempt of Holbrook Blinn, with his Princess Theater Players, to offer the public "plays of the better type," by American, British and European playwrights. Brady made a signal, even if transient, contribution to the advance of the theater in 1915, when he set up his wife, Miss Grace George, an expert comedienne, as an actress-manager at his Playhouse. Miss George assembled a notable company and offered a season of repertory that included the first American production of Shaw's *Major Barbara,* and revivals of his *Captain Brassbound's Conversion* (first performed eight years earlier by Miss Ellen Terry), Mitchell's *The New York Idea* and Jones's *The Liars.* The season lost money for Brady, but it stimulated later experiments with the repertory principle.

There were also three producers of independent mind and exceptional vision whose activities indicated that incentives to experiment and innovation were not confined to non-professional groups like the Playwrights' Theater and the Theater Guild, but were forcibly present in the professional theater. The plays produced by Winthrop Ames in his Little Theater and other playhouses were radical departures from typical Broadway fare. John D. Williams, like Ames a Harvard man, had been Charles Frohman's business manager before becoming a producer. He resented the charge of commercialism constantly brought against his profession, and he resolved to identify with it, in the public's mind, the element of artistic achievement. Arthur Hopkins had begun his association with the entertainment industry as the operator of a nickelodeon. But his illustrious career as a producer was founded on a principle that contradicted Henry Irving's axiom and Charles Frohman's major policy. Hopkins believed that the theater must succeed as an art or it would fail as a business. It was therefore no accident that Ames, Williams and Hopkins were successively associated with the brief glory of John Barrymore—the greatest American actor of his generation and the theater's most tragic figure.

The demand for musical entertainment constantly expanded and in this branch of the theater foreign products competed with those of a gradually developing American school. In 1895, two years after Frohman opened the Empire Theater, the comedians Joe Weber and Lew Fields established their Music Hall in a little playhouse adjoining Daly's. Neither of them, probably, had heard of the shows produced fifty years earlier by William Mitchell at the Olympic, but the pattern of the shows they staged duplicated Mitchell's, and their Music Hall became as famous over the country as its prototype had been. They assembled a constellation of star comedians, among them David Warfield, De Wolf Hopper, William Collier and Miss Fay Templeton. To these, in 1899, they added blonde, beautiful Miss Lillian Russell, whom they lured from comic opera with a weekly salary of $1,200, and who enchanted audiences by singing such numbers as John "Honey" Stromberg's "When Chloe Sings a Song" and "Come Down, Ma Evenin' Star." Weber and Fields offered a program composed of absurd travesties of Broadway plays, into which they worked their own specialty turn. They also made a feature of the shapeliest, prettiest chorus line to be seen on the American stage. The Music Hall chorus girls were celebrities whose photographs were as widely published and eagerly collected as those of any star. For eight years, the little theater was a temple of drollery which, to the nation at large, expressed the New York that was a city of beautiful nonsense. Then differences arose between Weber and Fields, who had been friends and professional partners from boyhood, and with the dissolution

Scene from "Hokey Pokey," showing Joe Weber, George Beban and Lew Fields, 1912

of their partnership the Music Hall passed out of existence. But during its brief life, it transmitted the tradition founded by Mitchell to Florenz Ziegfeld, the greatest modern master of the revue.

Ziegfeld, a tall, slim, dark young man, was at the time engaged in making his first wife, Anna Held, a reigning queen of musical comedy. She was a petite French girl whose enormous dark eyes, beautiful complexion and arch vivacity were her most noteworthy assets. The stage had many professional beauties and Ziegfeld decided, in order to establish Miss Held securely among them, to equip her with a legend. Presently the nation was startled by the news that, for the sake of her beauty, she took a daily bath in milk. Before this sensation died down there was another. At a party, a gentleman wagered that he could kiss Miss Held two hundred times with undiminished ardor. The scientific experiment ended after one hundred and fifty-two kisses with his defeat. It was delicately implied that no man could sustain longer exposure to such intensity of delight. The furor caused by this story elevated Miss Held to a fame for seductiveness not easily to be equaled by any rival beauty. As Ziegfeld foresaw, her appearance in a musical comedy became a magnet that attracted capacity audiences. And the American public read extremely naughty meanings into her two most popular, and quite innocent, songs: "Won't You Come and Play Wiz Me?" and "I Just Can't Make My Eyes Behave."

Miss Held's greatest rival in musical comedy was Miss Edna May, who, in a single year, rose from a position in the chorus at $15 a week to stardom in Gustav Kerker's *The Belle of New York,* in which she sang the role of a Salvation Army lassie. This was in 1897, and after a long run at the Casino in New York, Miss May took it to London, where it ran for nearly seven hundred performances. This phenomenal success led Charles Frohman to add pretty, ash-blonde Miss May to his list of stars and become a producer of musicals. The pieces in which he displayed Miss May, alternately in London and New York, were manufactured to his order by British composers and librettists. All went well until 1907, when Miss May became engaged to a New York millionaire, Oscar Lewisohn. Frohman, at the time, was negotiating for the English and American rights to *The Merry Widow,* in which he wished to present her, and he asked her to postpone her marriage. This she declined to do, and after a tumultuous farewell performance in London she married. Returning to London after her honeymoon, she began a siege of English society by giving a large reception. She sent Frohman the conventional engraved invitation: "At home Thursday from four to six." He returned it with a laconic, pregnant annotation: "So am I."

But he surmounted the injury of her defection, although he did not produce *The Merry Widow.* He discovered blonde, blue-eyed Miss Julia Sanderson, featured her in a number of musicals and eventually made her a star. She proved to be one of the most durable of his discoveries; after her retirement from the stage, she became a radio star and continued on the air until 1943.

The most successful of all London musicals to reach Broadway was *Florodora,* which owed its run of more than five hundred performances neither to the score of Leslie Stuart, nor to the presence in its cast of charming Miss Edna Wallace Hopper, third of De Wolf Hopper's six wives. The triumph of *Florodora,* produced at the Casino Theater in 1900, was entirely due to its sextette of chorus girls: the Misses Margaret Walker, Vaughn Texsmith, Marie Wilson, Marjorie Relyea, Agnes Wayburn and Daisy Green. Magnificently publicized, they were the lure that brought to the Casino every night the Gay White Way's wealthy beaux and bachelors. Tall, queenly, perfectly matched in height and very pretty, they did one number called "Tell Me Pretty Maiden" which always received at least six encores, in which they wore frilly, pleated pink walking costumes, large black picture hats, long black gloves and carried parasols. It was said that they received, from their admirers, fabulous jewels and other satisfying tributes. Five of them married wealthy men during the engagement, and many of their successive replacements also achieved a financial security which rendered them independent of the arts of the stage. Several companies toured *Florodora* throughout the country, so profitably that it seemed as if the perfect and permanent formula for musical comedy success had been found.

But the next nation-wide hit, *The Wizard of Oz,* was very different. It was an American fantasy, with music supplied by native composers, Paul Tietjens and A. Baldwin Sloane, and its success was made by the remarkable art of two American comedians who had learned their craft in circuses, medicine shows, minstrel companies and music halls. In *The Wizard of Oz* David Montgomery as the Tin Woodman and Fred Stone as the Scarecrow fused the techniques of the clown, the pantomimist, the acrobat and the eccentric dancer into a form of comedy of which they remained the sole masters. Their humor, gaiety and prankishness captivated children, but many adults saw in their performances, as in those of all really great clowns, an element of pathos and a commentary on life. Montgomery and Stone became top-ranking stars on the musical stage, invariably appealing in the successive shows which they played until Montgomery's death in 1917.

A new, assertively native note was brought to the musical stage by George M. Cohan. His parents were barnstorming vaudeville troupers; he and his sister had joined their act at an early age. As an adolescent he wrote sketches and songs, made a specialty of buck-and-wing dancing, and developed the peculiar, nasal style of singing that during his brief career as a star in his own musicals was imitated by every professional mimic. He was twenty-two when he brought his first musical farce, *The Governor's Son,* to New York, in 1901. His friend Ward Morehouse, in one of the best of all theatrical biographies, described Cohan as "fresh, cocky, confident, pugnacious and a hellion." He was a short, blue-eyed, taut-figured man who wore his straw hat or gray derby at a jaunty angle, twirled a bamboo cane, and spoke out of one side of his mouth.

Cohan knew nothing about the conventions of European comic opera, or the stale formulas used by composers of English musical comedy. But the stage had been his life and education, and his flair for the theatrically effective was as remarkable as Belasco's. Having worked only in vaudeville, where the time given to any sketch was brief, he had mastered the technique of a direct attack, a swift pace, a hard punch (this was called "ginger"). Unlike the older vaudeville comedians who still got their laughs by mugging, Cohan was up-to-the-minute in his spirit and methods. He broke all the rules. His delivery was deadpan. He threw lines away. He was brash, breezy, flippant. He used the vernacular of Broadway, and soon made it the vernacular of America. He combined a hard-boiled skepticism about human nature with an unabashed sentimentality about the things in which Americans believed: patriotism, family, love. On the fusty, convention-ridden stage of musical comedy, Cohan's effect was tonic. He was a new, vigorous, independent force working with the materials of American life and giving them an unmistakably native expression.

Like his first show, Cohan's second, *Running for Office,* was only moderately successful in New York, but extremely popular on tour. His third, *Little Johnny Jones,* in 1905, brought him recognition. His fourth, *Forty-Five Minutes from Broadway,* produced the same year, brought him fame. He did not appear in this farce, which took Times Square wiseguys to the sleepy New York suburb, New Rochelle. It featured Miss Fay Templeton and Victor Moore, and it introduced some of Cohan's best songs. Expertly directed and staged by Cohan,

The Florodora Sextette

it became a smash hit. He wrote eight more musicals before 1912, and most of them were outstanding hits. Meanwhile, having formed a producing partnership with Sam H. Harris, he turned to the writing of straight comedy, scored an immense success in that genre also, and created the tightly constructed, fast paced form which was to prevail in popular comedy for many years. But although he had deserted the musical stage, Cohan did not lose his talent for songwriting. In 1917, when the United States went to war, he wrote "Over There," which swept the country—and for which, in 1940, President Franklin D. Roosevelt awarded him a gold medal authorized by Congress.

During the years when Cohan was bringing a new kind of musical comedy to the stage, Victor Herbert skillfully adapted the formulas of European comic opera. Herbert was a native of Ireland; he had received a classical musical education in Germany, and he had been associated with the great conductor Theodore Thomas. Conservative in temperament and cosmopolitan in outlook, he made no attempt to employ characteristically American rhythms. His fluent melodies were always pleasing and always traditional in form and substance.

George M. Cohan in "Hello Broadway"

Herbert's first great success, *Babes in Toyland,* was a fantasy musically superior to *The Wizard of Oz.* He took his place as the leading American composer of operettas in 1905, with *Mlle. Modiste,* in which Miss Fritzi Scheff, a former star of the Metropolitan Opera, enchanted audiences by her singing of "Kiss Me Again" and her vivacious use of a snare drum. Thereafter, until his death in 1924, Herbert usually brought to the stage a new work every year. Among the most notable were *The Red Mill,* written for Montgomery and Stone; *Naughty Marietta,* composed for the opera singers Emma Trentini and Orville Harrold; and *Sweethearts.* The popularity of operetta continued, and two other American composers exploited it with outstanding success. Rudolf Friml made his debut in 1912 with *The Firefly,* and Sigmund Romberg, five years later, scored his first great hit with *Maytime.* Both works were prophetic of the future achievements of the composers. Meanwhile, Franz Lehar's *The Merry Widow* took the nation by storm in 1907. The New York production featured Miss Ethel Jackson and Donald Brian as the amorous waltzers. Chicago, simultaneously, heard the music sung more beautifully by Miss Lina Abarbanell, formerly of the Metropolitan Opera, who was soon to duplicate her success in another operetta, *Madame Sherry.* Touring companies carried *The Merry Widow* to every city in the country, and created a vogue for Viennese operetta which resulted in productions of Oskar Straus's *A Waltz Dream* and *The Chocolate Soldier* (founded on Shaw's *Arms and the Man*); Leo Fall's *The Dollar Princess;* and the *Sari* of Emmerich Kalman, who came to the United States and, as an American composer, joined the school of Herbert, Friml and Romberg.

While European influence dominated the realm of comic opera, Florenz Ziegfeld created, in his *Follies,* the modern and distinctively American form of revue. One of the basic features was suggested by Miss Anna Held, who advised him to "display young and beautiful girls in lavish costumes," but even in his first experimental production, in 1907, Ziegfeld added the elements of comedy, dance and spectacle, if only to a limited extent, and tried to make his show an amusing commentary on the year's events. Over the following years, he constantly increased the elaborateness of his shows, studding them with stars either already established or created by himself. He made Miss Lillian Lorraine a reigning beauty; took Miss Fannie Brice from burlesque and made her a great comedienne; exploited the accomplished Negro comedian Bert Williams. The roster of comedians who figured in successive *Follies* included such remarkably talented but dissimilar performers as Leon Errol, W. C. Fields, Eddie Cantor and Will Rogers, who twirled a lariat while drawling a salty commentary on current affairs. Josef Urban, an Austrian designer familiar with the latest European stagecraft, provided novel, startling backgrounds for the swiftly changing scenes—frequently there were more than twenty—and Ziegfeld achieved spectacular effects with lighting. But the central attraction

Beauties of the Ziegfeld Follies, 1919

of every *Follies* was its parade of feminine beauty. The term "Follies girl" became a national synonym for the ultimate in glamour. Every member of the *Follies* chorus was a featured player, and there was always one supreme paragon: dainty Ann Pennington, or slim, silvery Marilyn Miller, for whom Ziegfeld provided a fresh dancing costume every night at a cost of $175. When Irving Berlin wrote, for one of the *Follies,* a song entitled "A Pretty Girl Is Like a Melody," he stated the theme that was common to all of them.

In the early years of the First World War, two American composers brought out works which launched types of musical comedy that were to be developed after the war. In 1915, Jerome Kern and Guy Bolton collaborated on *Very Good Eddie,* an "intimate," genially satirical, nonspectacular comedy with a plausible story in which the songs were an integral element of the action. One year earlier, Irving Berlin, in *Watch Your Step,* provided the first example of a show conceived entirely in jazz rhythms. Berlin went into the army after the United States entered the war. But in 1918 he brought to the stage one of the finest musicals of the time, with an all-military cast. It was titled *Yip, Yip, Yaphank,* and in it Sergeant Berlin made himself the spokesman of the American armed forces with a song: "Oh, How I Hate to Get Up in the Morning."

CHAPTER 12

The Glorious Years

IN APRIL, 1916, dramatic critics and a first-night audience went to the Candler Theater in New York unprepared for a revelation. John D. Williams was producing *Justice,* a play written by John Galsworthy to bring about reforms in the British penal system. It tells the story of William Falder, an obscure, underpaid bank clerk. For love of a woman unhappily married and abused he steals money. Imprisoned for this crime, he is broken by the cruelty of solitary confinement. After his release, he is driven to suicide by the unremitting, persecutional vigilance of the police. John Barrymore took the role of Falder, and before the final curtain fell an astonished audience knew that, in his debut as a dramatic actor, he had proved that he had no equal on the American stage. Impressive in its restraint, its afflictive passivity, Barrymore's performance constantly suggested an enormous reserve of passion and power. But his playing of the most harrowing scene gave it a meaning that transcended Galsworthy's intention. This was the episode in which Falder, his mind and spirit breaking under the torture of solitary confinement, beats with his fists—helplessly, and with increasing desperation—on the locked door of his cell. As Barrymore played it, nobody could escape a sense that it signified more than the agony of an individ-

George M. Cohan in "Ah, Wilderness"

ual convict. Was it not an enactment of men's discovery that ultimately they are condemned to an isolated existence; that selfhood, in effect, is a prison cell from which there may be no escape? Everyone who saw *Justice* realized that this scene was one of the great experiences afforded by the modern theater. Some surmised that the attribute which made it luminous and never to be forgotten was genius.

Barrymore's previous career offered no reason for supposing that he might be a great artist in serious roles. In 1909 the long run of Winchell Smith's farce-comedy *The Fortune Hunter* had established him as a light—a very light—comedian, and his extraordinary physical beauty had made him a matinée idol. His appearance, three years later, for Winthrop Ames in *The Affairs of Anatol* had given the public an engaging image of his personality. Like Anatol, he was irresistibly attractive to women; an incurable romantic perpetually involved in some new affair. Gossip confirmed this impression. But his personality had darker facets and rumor was busy with these also. There were his prolonged bouts of drinking; his numerous eccentricities; his irresponsibility in the theater; his truculence, explosive rages, and propensity to insult audiences. Only scholars recalled that Edmund Kean and Junius Brutus Booth had also manifested these traits, forgivable in great tragedians long dead but not to be condoned in a young, lightweight farceur. Quite early in his career, Barrymore had unburdened his mind on the subject of audiences to Ashton Stevens, dramatic critic of the *San Francisco Examiner.* "The plural is impossible; whether it be in Butte or Broadway, it's an audience. The same great hulking monster with four thousand eyes and forty thousand teeth. . . .. And that monster unit with one great mind makes or breaks men like me."

Barrymore was thirty-four when his performance in *Justice* brought him fame overnight. Two years earlier his first marriage, to a New York society girl, had foundered. He was playing in a lurid melodrama, *The Yellow Ticket,* starring Miss Florence Reed. One night he made his first entrance on stage dead drunk. Miss Reed, weary of his misbehavior and irresponsibility, ordered the curtain rung down. An announcement was made that Barrymore was ill, an understudy was substituted, and the performance was begun again. Soon after, Barrymore sailed for Europe.

"He was a man who was in flight and in pursuit at the same time," his older brother Lionel wrote, many years later; "no wonder that his path was erratic, like some comet tugged by both earth and sun." In Italy he joined his friend, the playwright Edward Sheldon, whose *Romance,* starring Miss Doris Keane, had rounded out the first year of a success that eventually won for it productions in nine foreign countries. It was Sheldon who dissatisfied Barrymore with his easy success and trivial career, and challenged him to achieve eminence in an art that he disliked. As Lionel Barrymore put it, "Ned Sheldon saw through to something, the real something, whatever that something is when we consider genius, and he set about to develop it in Jack."

The first result was Barrymore's appearance in *Justice,* and when the long tour of that play ended and Barrymore returned to New York, Sheldon had another play ready for him.

He had been writing a play for Barrymore, but abandoned it after reading a script brought to him by the beautiful London actress, Miss Constance Collier. This was a dramatization of George du Maurier's novel, *Peter Ibbetson*, which had been submitted to her in England, which she had entirely rewritten, and had produced with an all-star cast for a single benefit performance at His Majesty's Theater. Sheldon, believing that the play was superior to his own as a vehicle for Barrymore, rewrote *Peter Ibbetson* for his use. He persuaded Lionel Barrymore reluctantly to return to the stage in the ungrateful role of Colonel Ibbetson. Miss Collier was to play the Duchess of Towers, and John Barrymore, Peter. Also in the cast were Miss Laura Hope Crews, a distinguished actress, and Miss Madge Evans, soon to become a film star. Before the play opened at the Republic Theater in New York in April, 1917, innumerable difficulties were surmounted. Money for the production was hard to obtain. John Barrymore objected to playing a romantic role. He was dubious about his lyrical scenes. He declared that in his costume he resembled "a marshmallow in a blond wig." He feared that the public would label him a "pretty boy," and this prospect horrified him. (Long afterwards, Lionel suggested that John, in his scandalous wildness, "was working out some embarrassed defense mechanism in his psyche.") But although Barrymore was skeptical about *Ibbetson,* other noted professionals were not. His prestige and Miss Collier's persuasiveness effected the solution of many problems. Lee Shubert agreed to produce the play. Florenz Ziegfeld furnished equipment which made possible the complicated lighting effects that it required. Miss Maude Adams, who had recently retired from the stage, volunteered to supervise the lighting of the play.

That great art in acting can project an illusion capable of surviving any accident was proved on the first night of *Ibbetson* when, during a lyrical, romantic "transformation" scene, some scenery fell, exposing Miss Collier and Barrymore in a ridiculous situation. There was no laughter from the audience. They sat silently while the curtain was rung down, the scenery was rehung, and the curtain was lifted for the episode to be begun again. In *Ibbetson* the rivalry of the two Barrymores as artists enhanced the splendor of their performances. The leading critics acclaimed John in his first romantic role, and praised Lionel for his superb characterization of the malign, loathsome Colonel. During the long run of the play in New York, John heard that Arthur Hopkins was planning a production of Leo Tolstoy's *The Living Corpse*. Probably incited by Sheldon, he went to see Hopkins and told him that he wished to do the play. Hopkins agreed to produce it if, at the end of Barrymore's tour in *Ibbetson,* the actor had not changed his mind. The tour indicated that addiction to drink was not exclusively responsible for John Barrymore's unpredictable outbreaks. From the opening of the play until the conclusion of the tour he abstained from liquor. Nevertheless, there were frequent recurrences of his violent rages, often provoked by coughing or nervous giggling in the audience, sometimes by mischances backstage, but mainly by one of the fundamental conditions of his profession which to him was so repugnant that he never learned to accept it. When he had fully created a role and had performed it, the necessity for its repetition exasperated him. "Once having accomplished something, from a play to a

woman, he found it tedious and wanted to start a new quest," Lionel Barrymore
stated. And Arthur Hopkins asserted that John "was in no sense what the
theater knows as a trouper, what his forebears had been, what his Uncle John
and sister Ethel were." But, as the tour of *Ibbetson* demonstrated, no matter
what his mood, once on the stage he always dominated it. He invariably possessed his audiences; his power over them seemed hypnotic. Miss Collier
thought him the greatest actor she had ever seen, an authentic genius. During
their Chicago engagement, with a further profitable tour in prospect, he announced to her that he could not continue playing his role. The pattern of
flight from achievement that was to emerge later in his stage career had been
drawn.

After returning to New York, Barrymore conferred with Hopkins. Their
meeting generated a project unique in the annals of the American stage. After
making plans for the Tolstoy play, retitled *Redemption,* Barrymore spoke of
other roles which he wished to perform. Hopkins offered to produce the plays.
He would take the Plymouth Theater for three years, and with Barrymore
would build a great classical repertory. Afterwards Hopkins declared that the
question of profits had not been mentioned or even considered; and their alliance was never cemented by a contract. The project was initiated with *Redemption,* for which Hopkins commissioned Robert Edmond Jones to design the
sets. During the preparations and rehearsals, Barrymore was tireless and
earnest, concentrating his fine intelligence on creating "the picture of a proud
human soul in turmoil and death." Hopkins, who directed the play, described
him as a "director's dream, an actor who asked no special emphasis," and asserted that for Barrymore rehearsals were "a ceaseless quest." His habitual self-
mockery, his sardonic ribaldry—apparently they were hostages to the defeat
which always haunted his imagination—were seldom exercised. The play
opened in October, 1918, and Barrymore's performance was acknowledged to
be more profoundly conceived and more brilliantly executed than any he had
yet given. It was perhaps ironical that his role was that of a man who finds his
soul only after touching the depths of degradation. For thirty weeks *Redemption* played to crowded houses, and the run could have been prolonged in-
definitely. Hopkins closed the play at the height of its success. He and Barrymore were committed to the vision of a great repertory.

Their next play, *The Jest,* was an adaptation by Sheldon and the Barrymore
brothers of a poetic tragicomedy by the contemporary Italian dramatist Sem
Benelli. Laid in the Florence of Lorenzo de' Medici, it concerns the revenge
taken by Gianetto, a young, physically delicate poet, on Neri, a brutal, powerful
bully who has systematically humiliated him. The sets of the four acts were designed by Jones, and the play was directed by Hopkins. Lionel Barrymore took
the role of Neri, John that of Gianetto. "Jack's Gianetto was even more of a
character part than mine, despite the fact that I was full of sweetbreads in the
way of muscle," Lionel wrote in his autobiography. "He was supposed to be an
esthetic, almost effeminate boy who achieved an enormous thrill out of being
in personal danger. Then, as his character develops before your eyes, you see a
person who is not physically supreme triumph over and kick the daylights out of

a brute. This was Jack's personal interpretation of the part and his contribution to the writing of the role. He made his Gianetto bring about the absolute demolition of the great roaring heel Neri—then quailed when he saw how completely he had destroyed him."

The play opened at the Plymouth early in April, 1919, and John Corbin, dramatic critic of the *Times,* spoke for the public in saying that it had "fallen across the sky of a declining season like a burst of sunset color." Benelli, a writer of the school of Gabriele d'Annunzio, had given his drama a decadent cast which Sheldon, in the new scenes that he wove into it, very rightly accented. The beautiful settings provided by Robert Edmond Jones emphasized a contrast between the magnificence of the High Renaissance in its artistic achievement and the cruelty and barbarity of its mores. But it was acting alone that lifted the play above the plane of melodrama, however poetic. Recognizing this, John Corbin praised the "touch of genius" with which Lionel Barrymore made the character of Neri, a monster of malice and ferocity, comprehensibly human. Of John's Gianetto, he wrote, "Except for the white flame of beauty, half spiritual half decadent, with which the actor invests the part, there is no phase which is not inward and subtly complicated. It is only on a second hearing that its involutions become clear." Once again, John's insight had found a philosophical meaning that dictated the acting of his role. His Gianetto was the artist eternally in conflict with his environment; the conflict, in this instance, being the more poignant because it occurred during one of the greatest eras of artistic fertility. "To the future of such actors," John Corbin wrote, "it is impossible to set any limits. Some day we shall see them, perhaps, as Othello and Iago." This hope was not to be fulfilled; *The Jest* was the last play in which the Barrymores acted together.

After a run of nine months, broken only by a summer intermission, Hopkins closed *The Jest* late in February, 1920. By this time the contemplated repertory included future productions of *Hamlet, Richard II, Cyrano, Peer Gynt* and *Faust.* During the long run of *The Jest,* however, Hopkins, Barrymore and Jones had prepared a superb production of *Richard III.* For Barrymore, this required an unusual discipline. His voice, sufficiently effective in romantic and dramatic roles, was not equal to the demands of Shakespearian tragedy. Through John Drew, he was introduced to Mrs. Margaret Carrington, a retired singer, an authority on voice production who had developed novel principles concerning the relation of diction to meaning. "She had come to believe," Barrymore told his friend and future biographer, Gene Fowler, "that it was possible to free the speaking voice to such an extent that one could hear, not the speaker's intention or his personality, but his inner essence, the self, the soul, speaking through him." Barrymore studied intensively with Mrs. Carrington. The defects of his diction were remedied. He gained "the necessary breath control to suspend and sustain the long unbroken phrases of Shakespeare's verse." He acquired a voice of magnificent quality and range, and a command of musical intonation. And, unlike many Shakespearian actors, he learned how to make a distinction, in his reading, between dialogue and soliloquy; between direct speech and the expression of thought supposedly unspoken.

The Hopkins-Barrymore-Jones production of *Richard III* opened at the Plymouth in March, 1920, and was hailed as a masterpiece of stagecraft. In it, scenic investiture and acting achieved an absolute unity of effect, later described by Hopkins as "exaltation, a brief, dazzling sojourn in the high heaven of emotion." Barrymore broke with stage tradition in his interpretation of Richard. He conceived him as a character spiritually warped, finely intelligent and possessed of a sinister, mysterious power. Apparently, he wished to suggest that Richard's deformed body was merely the outward sign of his crippled soul. He did not emphasize the external deformity, but suggested it chiefly by his swift, spidery gait. "I merely turned my right foot inward, pointing it toward the instep of my left foot," he explained to Fowler. "I let it stay in that position and then forgot all about it. I did not try to walk badly. I walked as *well* as I could. . . . A cripple does not try to walk with a worse gait than he has to employ. He endeavors to walk as *well* as he can." He rejected all the declamatory effects traditionally associated with the role, but used a deadly quiet delivery that accorded with his concept of the character's intelligence and iniquity. "It was the first genuine acting I ever managed to achieve and perhaps my own best," he told Fowler long after his desertion of the stage. "It was the first time I ever actually got *inside* the character I was playing. I mean I thought I *was* the character, and in my dreams I *knew* that I was he."

Four weeks after he opened in *Richard III*, Barrymore suffered a physical and nervous breakdown, and the run was abruptly ended. It has been attributed to overwork, to the extreme intensity which he brought to the role, and to his frantic, tumultuous courtship of Mrs. Blanche Oelrichs Thomas, better known by her pseudonym of Michael Strange, who soon became his second wife. When Barrymore was twenty-one, his father's mind had given way; Maurice Barrymore spent the last two years of his life in a private asylum for the insane. Lionel Barrymore believed that his brother "was haunted, in those dark moments which come to all men, by the fear that he too would collapse; and I have been told that it is psychologically sound that the thing you most fear is precisely the thing that is most likely to happen to you." The real collapse did not occur until long afterwards, but Barrymore's sense of identification with Richard, as he had conceived him, may have contributed to his first breakdown.

Barrymore's second marriage was even stormier than his first, and it precipitated him into a singularly ill-advised professional venture. With his sister Ethel, he acted in *Clair de Lune,* a play by Michael Strange which Hopkins refused to produce. The play was justifiably, but savagely, condemned by the critics, whom Barrymore attacked in a letter published by the press. In 1922, two years after his breakdown, he notified Hopkins that he wished to play *Hamlet.* He studied with Mrs. Carrington, who used the method, appropriate for him, of disregarding all stage tradition and forcing him to develop his personal interpretation of the role. Hopkins believed that Barrymore was an actor "who created out of his own texture," always searching within himself for his materials, and never borrowing or copying anything. This devotion to independent creation made him, in Hopkins' opinion, "the only full-grown theater artist of our time." For *Hamlet,* Jones provided one of the finest of all his scenic designs, a single massive set with a great flight of steps, three platforms, and an immense arch at the back framing the sky. Hopkins assembled a cast that included Miss Blanche Yurka as Queen Gertrude; Tyrone Power (grandson of the Irish comedian, and father of the film star) as Claudius; Miss Rosalind Fuller as Ophelia; Whitford Kane as the First Grave Digger.

The play opened at the Sam H. Harris Theater in New York in November, 1922. Barrymore's Hamlet was unanimously acclaimed by the critics, who asserted that it towered above all others in the modern theater. Percy Hammond, in the *Tribune*, remarked that it required no commentary, because "it was so beautiful a picture, so clear an analysis, so untheatrical an impersonation, and so musical a rendering of Shakespearian song."

But Arthur Hopkins long afterwards pointed out that during the run Barrymore "played many different Hamlets." The enormous scope of the role permitted him to indulge his love of creation; "to him, perfection was the aim, and its attainment could not be too much trouble."

Several critics remarked that he played the closet scene between Hamlet and his mother, Gertrude, in the key of romantic love. The theories of Freud were being widely discussed and these critics speculated on the Freudian implications of Barrymore's scene. But, like Marcel Proust in his great novel, Barrymore was probably only transposing into art his most deeply felt personal experience. Between Proust and his mother there had been an excessive attachment; when he wrote his novel, he transformed this into an equivalent attachment between a boy and his grandmother. Barrymore's case was the reverse of Proust's. His grandmother, Mrs. John Drew, had reared him and adored him. He had lived with her and depended upon her until her death, when he was fifteen. She had

John Barrymore as Hamlet, 1922

been his only link with stability and security, and after her death, Lionel Barrymore recorded, "Jack never felt safe anywhere." It seems likely that in his closet scene with Hamlet's mother, Barrymore was acting out the only profound and permanent love in his life.

He played *Hamlet* for 101 performances, then discontinued the run. Much was made of the fact that he carried it to one more performance than Edwin Booth's record; nobody recalled that, ten years earlier, John E. Kellerd had played 102 performances of *Hamlet* in New York. In the autumn of 1923, Barrymore made a brief tour in *Hamlet,* playing to capacity audiences. He gave his final performance in Cleveland, and it was the last time that American playgoers were to see him in a role worthy of his art. During the winter of 1925, he performed *Hamlet* in London, at the Haymarket Theater, for twelve weeks with a British company that included Miss Constance Collier as Queen Gertrude and Miss Fay Compton as Ophelia. The critical reception was excellent. But Bernard Shaw, who attended the opening night with Barrymore's estranged second wife, sent him a letter rebuking him for making cuts in the text and substituting "an interpolated drama of your own dumb show." Shaw wrote: "Instead of giving what is called a reading of *Hamlet,* you say, in effect, 'I am not going to read *Hamlet* at all: I am going to leave it out. But, see what I give you in exchange!' " The rebuke depressed Barrymore, though probably it did not account for his sudden hatred of the role, and his refusal of offers to play it in Germany and France.

When he returned to the United States in the spring of 1925, he had already decided to leave the stage. He was forty-three and at the height of his powers. His career as an artist had been compressed into nine years, and of the six roles which he had performed only two represented his projected classical repertory. Nevertheless, he alone had attained a stature comparable to that of Edwin Booth and a position certainly equal to Booth's. Because there remained the challenge of his unperformed repertory, his retirement amounted to an abdication. Lionel Barrymore surmised that John "was in revolt against the whole insecure pattern of his life"; that "he was at loggerheads with the world and he was at loggerheads with himself and he knew it." Arthur Hopkins put it another way. "He was that rarest of phenomena, the actor who hated to act. He loved to create, but once that had been accomplished, he was like an artist who could not bear to look again upon a finished painting, or a writer who was nauseated by a glimpse of some past creation. This is a feeling that artists will readily understand. That he would have had an unparalleled career there was no doubt, and he knew it. His renunciation was with full knowledge of what he was leaving."

He had failed in painting, the only art in which he wished to succeed; he had triumphed in acting, the only art he despised. So it was perhaps no wonder that his sardonic wit and inveterate self-mockery propelled him to Hollywood with a valet and a small, white-nosed monkey.

The epic of his disintegration had only begun when, late in 1927, George S. Kaufman and Miss Edna Ferber brought to the stage their play, *The Royal Family,* a satirical portrait of the Barrymores. Audiences laughed at the temperamental excesses of the character who represented John, but their laughter, on the whole, was tolerant. Barrymore, however, soon commenced a self-portrait more spectacular and terrifying. He devoted the rest of his years to its composition. His life became the picture in progress; he was not only the artist, but the canvas and the colors. To the great public he became little more than a figure of scandal and an object of derision. The newspapers amply reported on the millions he made in films, and capriciously, ostentatiously, flung away; on his two bankruptcies; on the gigantic scale of his inebriety and eccentricity; on his third and fourth marriages.

Behind the lurid picture continuously presented to the public, there was another, starkly tragic, and not unveiled until after his death in Fowler's moving biography, *Good Night, Sweet Prince*. There were two attempts to play *Hamlet* in films, both defeated by instability of memory. Then came the utter failure of memory, so that in making films he had to read his lines from blackboards. And then his decision to return to the stage, in 1939, at the age of fifty-seven— broken in health, ravaged, weary—in a silly play that made capital of his self-destruction and permitted him to exhibit himself only as a buffoon. He toured in *My Dear Children* for ten months, playing it at the Selwyn Theater in Chicago for thirty-four weeks before, late in January, 1940, bringing it to the Belasco Theater in New York, where it ran for four months. Audiences flocked to the theaters in morbid curiosity. They saw a man who could bring an incisive wit to bear on the ruin he had wrought, and an actor who was still able to dominate the stage; who, when his memory failed to yield the trivial lines he was supposed to speak, improvised lines better and more bitter; who applied to the travesty of his former magnificence the mastery of an art which he had neither ceased to command nor ceased to despise. When the last curtain rang down on the clowning of Hamlet, there was illness, and there were great debts. To pay them, Barrymore offered a caricature of himself on a radio program, inviting the mockery of the public until, one day, he collapsed at a rehearsal. In the coma that preceded death, he often muttered the name by which, in childhood, he had called his grandmother: "Mum Mum."

The presence of John Barrymore haunted the American theater long after he had deserted it. To playgoers who had seen him in his great roles, the vivid memory of his performances furnished a criterion. Like Booth before him, he survived as a standard, a challenge to all aspirants, and more than a decade was to pass before a direct comparison with him was invited. By then, a new generation of playgoers had come to maturity, and to them he was only a name. They ignored his ghostly pre-eminence and chose their own living idols. But the classic and romantic plays which he had never performed were not, meanwhile, neglected. Before Barrymore's retirement Miss Jane Cowl, a dark-haired, dark-eyed, very beautiful star previously associated with popular drama, played Juliet to the Romeo of Rollo Peters in a fine production which he designed, and astonished audiences by the high merit of her performance. She later produced *Antony and Cleopatra*, Maeterlinck's *Pelléas and Mélisande*, and Stephen Phillips' *Paolo and Francesca*. In 1925, Walter Hampden undertook the daring venture of establishing, in New York, a playhouse dedicated mainly to the production of poetic drama. Hampden was Brooklyn-born, Harvard-educated, and British-schooled for the stage. A varied experience had made him exceptionally versatile, and he had a fine voice as well as a commanding presence. For five years, in New York and on frequent tours, he offered a repertory that included *Othello, Macbeth, The Merchant of Venice;* Ibsen's *An Enemy of the People;* Arthur Goodrich's poetic *Caponsacchi,* a dramatization of Browning's *The Ring and the Book;* and, most successfully of all, *Cyrano de Bergerac* in Brian Hooker's felicitous translation.

After Hampden reluctantly abandoned his project, there were no further attempts to maintain an exclusively classic and poetic repertory. But a number of well-known stars made notable excursions into Shakespeare, although none of them ventured to build a repertory of his plays. In 1931 Miss Maude Adams unexpectedly emerged from a thirteen-year retirement to tour the country with Otis Skinner in *The Merchant of Venice.* The two ageing stars—Miss Adams was sixty; Skinner, seventy-three—had become legendary figures to the younger generation, but older playgoers cherished fond memories of both. In many cities they played to capacity audiences, drawing the young as well as their elders, and they received affectionate ovations. They played in Newark, New Jersey, at the end of their tour just before an announced engagement in New York. Several metropolitan dramatic critics attended their performance there and, although disposed to reverence for Miss Adams, were disappointed by her Portia. It was, unfortunately, a role which, had they seen her before her retirement, they might have thought no less unsuited to her. Probably apprehensive about the critical verdict they would receive, Miss Adams and Skinner canceled their plans for a Broadway engagement and abruptly ended their tour.

In 1933, when the nation was afflicted by the Great Depression, and the road was deprived of theatrical fare, Miss Katharine Cornell included *Romeo and Juliet* in the three plays which she performed on a nation-wide tour that took her to seventy-five cities and towns. Notwithstanding the excellence of her cast and production, and the acknowledged beauty of her own performance, it proved to be the least popular of her three plays. Two seasons later, Shakespeare fared better on the road when, under the auspices of the Theater Guild, Miss Lynn Fontanne and Alfred Lunt made a tour on which they alternated a swift, boisterous performance of *The Taming of the Shrew* with a contemporary play. In 1936, thirteen years after John Barrymore's last American performance of *Hamlet,* there occurred the first important revival of the play. It was presented by John Gielgud, a British star, the great-nephew of Miss Ellen Terry. Gielgud's performance of the role was fluent, elegant and eloquent. The dramatic critics acclaimed him and, in New York, his *Hamlet* established a new record of 132 performances.

Another British actor, Maurice Evans, came to the United States to play Romeo in a revival of Miss Cornell's production of *Romeo and Juliet.* He remained, acquired citizenship, and soon took rank as the leading interpreter of Shakespearian roles on the American stage. Evans achieved his first success with a memorable performance in *Richard II,* staged by Miss Margaret Webster. The tragedy had not been produced in New York since Edwin Booth

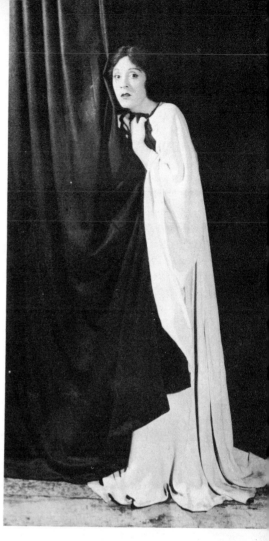

Jane Cowl in "Romeo and Juliet," 1923

performed it, nearly sixty years earlier, and Evans' moving personation of Richard brought the revival to a surprising total of 133 performances. Intrepid as well as ambitious, Evans took advantage of his new prestige to present himself in a series of Shakespearian roles which, in the contemporary theater, were remarkable for their variety. He offered an uncut *Hamlet* which, although the performance required four and one-half hours with a single half-hour recess, met with success. (During the Second World War, Evans played a "streamlined" *Hamlet* for the armed forces, and later produced it in the professional theater.) Evans also appeared as Falstaff in *Henry IV, Part I;* as Malvolio to the Viola of Miss Helen Hayes in a production of *Twelfth Night* made by the Theater Guild; and in *Macbeth* with Miss Judith Anderson. But, although he identified himself with Shakespearian roles more consistently than any other star, Evans did not restrict himself to them, and he was perhaps prevented by financial considerations from offering seasons of repertory at regular intervals. As the years passed Shakespeare, and the classical repertory in general, came to have no more than an intermittent life on the American stage.

The interval between the world wars was made glorious by what has come to be called a renaissance of the drama, though the term is misleading, for the United States had never before produced an extensive dramatic literature either intrinsically important or profoundly related to the national life. But the 1920's, which brought a true renaissance of American fiction and poetry, also launched the creation of a native dramatic literature that soon commanded the respectful attention of the civilized world. Conditions prevailing in the commercial theater, even toward the end of the nineteenth century, had not encouraged playwrights to think of their work as a profession or an art. In 1891, Bronson Howard founded the Society of American Dramatists and Composers with thirty-three members, to promote a sense of solidarity among writers for the stage, and to obtain an amendment of the copyright law, passed by Congress in 1896, which made play piracy a punishable offense. But, during the first decade of the twentieth century, the power of producers over playwrights was extreme, and the position of the dramatist was often little better than that of a hack. So well known a playwright as George Middleton led what he later described as a "double life." As a journeyman, meeting requirements imposed by producers, he wrote plays aimed at Broadway success. The plays which he wrote as a serious dramatist he published in book form, knowing that their production in the commercial theater was improbable.

In 1913, when the Authors' League of America was organized, only a dozen playwrights were included in its membership of three hundred and fifty. The Actors' Equity strike of 1919 encouraged the formation, within the League, of a Dramatists' Guild, whose initial purpose was to draft, and secure acceptance of, a standard contract governing the relations between all dramatists and all producers. Led by Middleton and other prominent playwrights, the Guild unsuccessfully battled for this reform. By 1926, 121 professional dramatists pledged themselves to collective action in withholding their work from any producer who failed to accept, and comply with, the "minimum basic agreement" proposed by the Guild. Faced by the prospect of a drought of plays, the producers capitulated. Eventually Middleton negotiated arrangements between the Guild and foreign organizations of dramatists which effectually nullified the possibility that producers, in the event of conflict with the Guild, could replace the work of its members by foreign imports. Since membership in the Guild was made prerequisite to the production of any playwright's work, and all contracts were required to be approved by the Guild's legal staff, the entire output of American dramatists was controlled by their own collective organization.

Foremost of the new American dramatists was Eugene O'Neill, whose plays, by the mid-1920's, were being produced in Great Britain, the principal countries of Europe, and the Orient. They were not only acceptable to Broadway, but eagerly sought after by commercial producers. For several reasons, this was noteworthy. Although O'Neill most frequently used the medium of prose, he wrote as a poet. His plays often fulfilled the classical requirements of tragedy, and achieved an exaltation and universality long absent from dramatic literature. His attitude to life was that of a mystic. He was acutely conscious of a creative force working upon reality, and he had chosen as his theme "the one eternal tragedy of Man in his glorious, self-destructive struggle to make the Force express him instead of being, as an animal is, an infinitesimal incident in its expression." He felt that the individual's unhappiness in the contemporary world was the result of a spiritual disorientation. In general, the characters in his plays were of two kinds: those who considered themselves identified with something that transcended their personal lives; and those who, having lost the conviction of this relationship, were desperately seeking an equivalent for it. O'Neill was confident that if he could deeply move the emotions of his audiences, he might also persuade them to think. He wished them to become aware of "their ennobling identity with the tragic figures on the stage," even though, in his plays, tragedy often occurred "in seemingly the most ignoble, debased lives."

In their formal elements, as in their theme and subjects, O'Neill's plays were revolutionary. They discarded all established conventions of the "well-made play," defied the accepted rules of dramatic technique, and asserted a new structural freedom. As the years passed, O'Neill also experimented with a series of innovations: expressionism; masks; stylized movement; the soliloquy, used to reveal the flow of a character's consciousness. But his use of these innovations was always functional; they were essential to the expression of what he had to say. And in O'Neill the United States had, for the first time, a dramatist of incontestible genius—a master of his art whose major works, because of their poetic splendor and philosophical significance, became modern classics.

The first of O'Neill's full-length plays, *Beyond the Horizon,* brought him to Broadway. It was produced by John D. Williams, with a professional cast that included Richard Bennett, at a special matinée at the Morosco Theater in New York, on February 2, 1920. The beauty and power of the play were immediately apparent, and in response to public demand it was put on for a run and later sent on tour; it also won for O'Neill his first Pulitzer Prize. Later that year his magnificent *The Emperor Jones,* a haunting, impressionistic drama of fear and terror, was produced at the little Provincetown Theater with the Negro actor Charles Gilpin in the title role. Its success there proved to be so great that the production was transferred to an uptown theater and was afterwards sent on tour. His play *Diff'rent,* a grim, outspoken study of sexual frustration, was produced at the Provincetown and did not reach the commercial theater, but *Gold,* which dealt with a sea captain obsessed by lust for a hoard of gold, received a professional production at the Frazee Theater and failed.

With *Anna Christie,* produced by Arthur Hopkins at the Vanderbilt Theater in New York on November 2, 1921, O'Neill achieved his conquest of the mass audience—a victory that had tremendous significance for the future of the American drama. Hitherto, he had been the idol of the intellectuals. The popular success of *Beyond the Horizon* and *The Emperor Jones* had been initiated by a vigorous campaign that enlisted critics, columnists and other influential leaders of public opinion. Nevertheless, many of his ardent admirers surmised that O'Neill's plays were too "difficult" or "highbrow" or "different" to appeal to the mass audience on whose patronage the commercial theater depends. But the emphatic success of *Anna Christie* on Broadway proved that they—like most commercial producers—had underrated its mental maturity. O'Neill's victory undoubtedly fortified him. Yet it was of even greater consequence to the other playwrights of his generation. It implied that the great public would support plays, seriously conceived and intellectually meaningful, which offered a more invigorating experience than that of transient entertainment. It encouraged playwrights to believe that they would no longer be denied professional production because they had exercised freedom in their choice of subject, theme, or manner of treatment.

Although it was the least revolutionary of his plays, *Anna Christie* exacted, from a popular audience, greater imaginative collaboration than many playwrights would have dared to demand. The stark realism of the first act, in the waterfront saloon; the poetic symbolism of the second, on the barge shrouded in fog; the ironical departure of old Chris and Burke to drink themselves into forgetfulness; the inconclusive ending—these elements, because of their disparity, required an active rather than merely passive response. But only the ending was misunderstood by certain critics who asserted that O'Neill had falsified it by making it a "happy," instead of a "tragic," conclusion. He denied this charge in a letter to the New York *Times,* pointing out that he could have contrived a tragic ending that would have been "superficially right," but untrue to the characters as he had conceived them. "They would act in just the silly, immature, compromising way that I have made them act; and I thought that they would appear to others as they do to me, a bit tragically humorous in their vacillating weakness." He also defined the effect he intended the play to produce: "Three characters have been revealed in all their intrinsic verity, under the acid test of a fateful crisis in their lives. They have solved this crisis for the moment as best they may, in accordance with the will that is in each of them. The curtain falls. Behind it their lives go on." The role of Anna was beautifully performed by Miss Pauline Lord, whose expressive features and hands, hesitant, wistful utterance and indecisive movement made her acting peculiarly evocative. She was elevated to stardom by *Anna Christie,* and the play brought O'Neill his second Pulitzer Prize.

O'Neill presently joined Robert Edmond Jones and Kenneth Macgowan, a dramatic critic, in a producing firm which took over the Provincetown and Greenwich Village Theaters where, for the next few years, all but two of his plays were staged. Three were especially important. In *The Hairy Ape* he treated symbolically, with dramatic force and intensity, the individual's need to believe in the spiritual worth of his existence, to feel a sense of vital attachment to God. In *Desire Under the Elms,* one of his finest plays, he placed what is in effect a Greek tragedy in the New England of the mid-nineteenth century. The story of old Ephraim Cabot, who takes a young third wife only to have her bear a child to his son, then destroy the child to prove to her paramour that she loves him best, closes on Ephraim's surrender to a God that is "hard, not easy . . . hard and lonesome." Walter Huston gave an impressive performance as Ephraim Cabot, but certain segments of the public were shocked by the play, and legal proceedings interrupted its run. Critics, professional colleagues and others appeared in court to champion the artistic merit and moral decency of the play, and the producers were permitted to continue the run. Eventually, *Desire Under the Elms* was transferred to an uptown theater; it was performed in New York for more than ten months.

The success of *The Great God Brown,* which ran for 171 performances to crowded houses, was remarkable. This was the most abstruse of O'Neill's plays, the most mystical in its philosophical implications, and the most symbolical in its treatment. The four characters whom it involves in tragedy are not only individuals. They symbolize attitudes to life which have a long history of conflict. As individuals, each confronts the world with a personality deliberately assumed, and each has a concept of his true personality; the dual aspects of each are symbolized by masks. On its two levels—as human drama, and as a picture of the "conflicting tides in the soul of Man"—the tragedy closes on a note of exaltation; an affirmation of the value of life for its own sake, and an affirmation of the certainty of God's existence. The Greenwich Village Theater, in which *The Great God Brown* was produced, accommodated a moderately large audience, but its location was remote from New York's theatrical district. In these circumstances, the fact that the play ran for more than twenty weeks indicated that the great public was ready and eager to be challenged in the theater; challenged to think as well as to feel. This was demonstrated again by the successful production, at the Pasadena Playhouse, of *Lazarus Laughed,* the fruit of O'Neill's meditation on the meaning of death, which has never been staged in New York.

Meanwhile, the Theater Guild, dedicated to the production of plays "of high artistic merit," had come under reproach for ignoring the work of the most important American dramatist. Justifiably; for five of O'Neill's plays had been submitted to the Guild for production, and all were rejected by a majority vote of its board of managers. This situation exasperated Lawrence Langner, a member of the board and himself a playwright, who was O'Neill's advocate in the Guild. By 1927 the association of O'Neill, Jones and Macgowan as producers had terminated, the playwright was living in Bermuda, and Langner went there to see him. O'Neill had completed *Marco Millions,* and they talked of the possibility of its production by the Guild. O'Neill also discussed the play on which he was then working, *Strange Interlude,* which had been promised to a well-known American actress, but which, in the event of her rejection (which occurred later), he was willing to have produced by the Guild. Langner took to his hotel the first six acts of the play, read them to the accompaniment of a violent tropical storm, and concluded that *Strange Interlude* was "one of the greatest plays of all time."

The Guild's board of managers accepted *Marco Millions* for production, but when the completed script of *Strange Interlude* was submitted to them, they displayed no enthusiasm. With Miss Theresa Helburn and one other member of the board Langner conducted a "frenzied campaign" to secure its production, culminating in a stinging letter to the board. "In *Strange Interlude* we have probably the bravest and most far-reaching dramatic experiment which has been seen in the theater since the days of Ibsen," he declared. And he urged that the Guild's status as the only surviving art theater in the country "places upon us the solemn responsibility of being the first to recognize the work of genius and to dare to experiment, even if it be accompanied by financial loss, if that experiment be in the direction of greatness." Langner's eloquence proved effective; the play was accepted for production. The role of Nina Leeds was offered to Miss Alice Brady, one of the leading emotional actresses of the day. She refused it. The Guild had "great difficulty in securing an actress to play the role," which was generally regarded as unsympathetic. It was finally accepted by Miss Lynn Fontanne, a member of the Guild's acting company and a player of stellar rank.

Early in January, 1928, the Guild produced *Marco Millions* with Alfred Lunt, Miss Fontanne's husband, in the leading role. Like *The Great God Brown,* it expressed O'Neill's disenchantment with modern materialism, and was generally accepted as a satire on contemporary American civilization. Attentive playgoers realized that the dramatist had made it a symbolic statement of the irreconcilable conflict between the philosophies of the Western world and the Orient. Two weeks after launching *Marco Millions* on a successful run, the Guild staged *Strange Interlude.* Its extraordinary length; its device of using the soliloquy to reveal the secret thoughts of the characters, and thereby contrast the reality of their inward life with the unreality of their behavior; its designedly disagreeable tonal coloring—these were features provocative of controversy. O'Neill presented his central character, Nina Leeds, as representative of the contemporary American woman; educated, emancipated, intelligent and eager for personal fulfillment. Tracing her career from girlhood to middle age, he showed her effect on the lives of the five men who stand in closest relation to her—her father, two lovers, husband and son. She is a monster of unconscious selfishness and, except for the son who finally escapes from her possessiveness, she succeeds, unintentionally, in destroying them all. In New York, the play ran for more than four hundred performances. The Guild organized a touring company, in which Miss Pauline Lord and Miss Judith Anderson successively played the role so brilliantly created by Miss Fontanne, and found "that the rest of the United States was just as excited about *Strange Interlude* as was New York."

Nobody was more surprised by the effect of the play than Langner, who had forced its production on the Guild. He "did not dream it would command the popular success it was to achieve." But it earned "nearly $300,000 for O'Neill, and a little more for the Guild," and it brought the dramatist his third Pulitzer Prize.

In October, 1931, the Theater Guild produced O'Neill's masterpiece, *Mourning Becomes Electra.* In it, the dramatist set himself the problem of achieving "a modern psychological approximation of the Greek sense of fate which would seem credible to a present-day audience and at the same time prove emotionally affecting." The story of Electra, "with its complex human interrelationships and its chain of fated crime and retribution, seemed best suited in its scope and in its implications to this purpose." O'Neill adopted "the theme-pattern of Aeschylus and the old legends," and interpreted it "in modern

Glenn Anders, Lynne Fontanne, Tom Powers and Earl Larimore in "Strange Interlude"

psychological terms with Fate and the Furies working from within the individual soul." For the will of the gods, as it functioned in Greek tragedy, he substituted that area of the human mind which lies below the threshold of consciousness. For the Trojan War, he substituted the American Civil War; and for the house of Atreus, the house of Mannon, in New England. O'Neill originally intended his trilogy to be performed on three successive nights. But the decision to perform it on a single night was obviously sound, because it permitted the tremendous cumulative power of the play to become effective.

The Guild commissioned Robert Edmond Jones to design the sets. For the role of Christine Mannon they engaged Mme. Alla Nazimova. Miss Alice Brady, regretting her refusal to play in *Strange Interlude,* was persuaded by her father, William A. Brady, to undertake the role of Lavinia Mannon. Earl Larimore played Orin Mannon. Following the Greek story closely, O'Neill's play presents the murder of General Ezra Mannon, on the night of his return from the Civil War, by his wife, Christine, and her lover, Adam Brant. Thereafter, Mannon's passionately adoring daughter, Lavinia, compels her brother, Orin, to kill Brant; drives her mother and brother to suicide; and, after accomplishing what she conceives to be her duty in enforcing moral justice, immures herself in the Mannon house, condemning herself, by the same moral code which she has applied to the others, to live with the ghosts that will haunt her until she dies. The three principal actors rose to the great opportunities given them by the playwright. Earl Larimore's Orin was a flawless characterization of a man whose values have been confused by war and who, when torn by the contradictory claims of love and duty, is too weak to resist the dominance of a powerful nature. Mme. Nazimova brought to the playing of Christine a masterly resourcefulness in suggesting the character's complexity. Miss Brady's performance of Lavinia achieved magnificence. Her final speech, and her entry into the empty Mannon house to immolate herself on the altar of her conscience, were one of the major triumphs of acting in the modern theater. O'Neill had fulfilled his intention. The action of his play had the magnitude and elevation of classic tragedy, and its characters, by reason of the passion with which he invested them, attained heroic stature.

Two years after producing his great trilogy, the Guild presented O'Neill's *Ah, Wilderness!* Unlike any of his other plays, it is a comedy of family life, nostalgic in tone, probably autobiographical in substance. Laid in a Connecticut town in the year 1906, it tells the story of Nat Miller, father of a family and editor of the local paper, who meets his responsibilities as parent, citizen, and community leader with wisdom and courage. George M. Cohan, appearing for the first time in a play not of his own authorship, undertook the role of Nat Miller. (In San Francisco, it was taken by Will Rogers.) Cohan's performance—gentle, touching and quietly authoritative—won him greater tributes as an actor than he had ever before received. But late in the run, as Langner recalled, "his bad habit of elaborating the comedy made the play seem unnecessarily long."

During a visit to Paris in 1922, Cohan had attended, with George Middleton, a performance by the French star Lucien Guitry, whom he thought "the greatest actor I ever saw." He told Ward Morehouse on his return, "I would strongly advise all American players to study this man and learn how to act without acting." Cohan apparently took his own advice and used his study of Guitry eleven years later, when he played in *Ah, Wilderness!* One of Guitry's technical tricks was to pause before delivering his replies in stage dialogue, to gain the attention of his audience. O'Neill told Middleton that "Cohan had so studied Guitry's 'delay before speaking' that by the end of the run *Ah, Wilderness!* was twenty minutes longer than when we opened." It might have surprised many of Cohan's admirers, as well as the New York dramatic critics, to learn that Cohan, whose whole background, as he said, was "rough and tumble," had tried to model his acting style on that of one of the most subtle and intellectual of French actors.

By 1936, when Eugene O'Neill was awarded the Nobel Prize for literature, a new generation of playwrights had successfully stormed Broadway and, in taking possession of the American theater, had made it the equal of any in the world. They were portraying the national life with courage and insight. The creative vitality of their work was indicated by its extraordinary variety. Realism, social satire, the poetic drama and high comedy flourished simultaneously, and some playwrights cultivated several of these forms. Elmer Rice as a young law student had won celebrity and a fortune, in 1914, with his first play, *On Trial,* a courtroom melodrama in which he made adroit use of motion-picture technique to tell his story. His *The Adding Machine* was an impressive attempt to apply to the American scene the method of "expressionism" with which European dramatists were then experimenting. Turning away from imaginative, stylized drama, he brought vividly to the stage in *Street Scene* the continuous stream of life passing a gaunt tenement in the slums of New York. Many of his subsequent plays were angry sermons on social reform, inspired by sympathy for the urban poor during the Great Depression, but he frequently ventured into the domain of light comedy, and it was in this form that he eventually achieved his greatest artistic success with *Dream Girl,* expertly played by his wife, Miss Betty Field.

In variety of production, Rice was matched by Maxwell Anderson, who began his career by collaborating with Lawrence Stallings in *What Price Glory?,* a melodrama of the First World War which stunned audiences by its hard-boiled cynicism of attitude, feeling and language. The play was an outstanding success, and critics later credited it with having inaugurated the "new" realism which made swift headway on the American stage. This realism was exemplified by Anderson's *Saturday's Children,* a pathetic comedy about the rigors of young married life on a shoestring in a large American city, admirably played by Miss Ruth Gordon. In *Gods of the Lightning,* written with Harold Hickerson, and based on the Sacco-Vanzetti case, he made a grimly powerful plea for social, as well as legal, justice. In *Both Your Houses* his contempt for political corruption was expressed in a savage arraignment of lobbyists and legislators in Washington.

Meanwhile, Anderson had become aware of the limitations of realism. In time, he was to declare his conviction that "the theater is a religious institution devoted entirely to the exaltation of the spirit of man. It is an attempt to justify, not the ways of God to man, but the ways of man to himself. It is an attempt to prove that man has a dignity and a destiny, that his life is worth living, that he is not purely animal and without a purpose." In the light of this ideal, he made a long, valiant and often successful effort to revive the poetic drama. His *Elizabeth the Queen,* composed in a flexible blank verse, dramatized the conflict between Elizabeth's love, as a woman, for the Earl of Essex, and her dire knowledge that, as a queen, she must be "quite friendless, without mercy, without love." Superbly performed by Miss Lynn Fontanne and Alfred Lunt, it achieved great popular success. He met equal success with another tragedy in verse, *Mary of Scotland,* in which Miss Helen Hayes played the ill-fated queen, Miss Helen Menken took the role of the sinister, unscrupulous Elizabeth, and Philip Merivale took the part of Bothwell. Both Miss Menken and Merivale were tall. Miss Hayes's height was a mere five feet, and in order to increase her stature she wore built-up shoes. Even so equipped, she was shorter than Miss Menken, yet in the dramatic scene that brings Mary and Elizabeth face to face, Miss Hayes appeared to tower above her colleague. Asked how she managed to produce this effect, she replied, "I *think* myself tall."

The superior performances of the three actors, the dramatic power of the play and Anderson's ringing verse brought *Mary of Scotland* a run of five months in New York and six months on tour to crowded houses. As if to demonstrate that poetic tragedy need not be confined to historical subjects, Anderson told, in *Winterset,* a contemporary story of a son's effort to clear the name of his father, unjustly executed for murder, and laid its scene in a New York waterside street overhung by a massive bridge. As the young Romagna who offers his life in devotion to his dead father, Burgess Meredith gave a notably sensitive performance. Meredith took the leading role, also, in Anderson's poetic fantasy *High Tor,* which dealt with a young romantic who, hating the modern world and all its works, finds an isolated refuge from it, only to be dispossessed by industrialists who are buying up the region, thereby being condemned to another flight from the encroaching reality that he despises.

The progress from realism to poetry was reversed by Sidney Howard, whose first play, *Swords,* was a poetic tragedy that failed on the stage. He won immediate recognition with his first attempt to portray contemporary American life realistically in *They Knew What They Wanted.* It told the touching story of an elderly Italian wine-grower in California; the gentle, lonely waitress whom he has courted by mail, using the photograph of his handsome young helper; and the consequences of a love affair between the two young people. Beautifully played by Richard Bennett, Miss Pauline Lord and Glenn Anders, the drama ran through an entire season. As his subsequent plays showed, Howard was fascinated by the variety and hazardousness of American life, its perpetual invitation to adventure. In *Ned McCobb's Daughter* he portrayed a courageous, self-reliant New England woman who, faced by the wreck of her marriage, the death of her father, and her helpless involvement in the operations of a gang of bootleggers, manages by virtue of her integrity and intelligence to overcome all obstacles. Howard scored his greatest success with his least characteristic play, *The Silver Cord,* the study of a mother whose perverted, fiercely possessive "love" for her two adult sons promises to wreck their lives unless they escape from her. The fine acting of Miss Laura Hope Crews as the mother, and Miss Clare Eames, Howard's wife, as her daughter-in-law, made the play a duel between two women for men who seemed incapable of self-assertion. In *Alien Corn* he portrayed the life of Elsa Brandt, a pianist who has been trained for a concert career but is bound by circumstance to a dull teaching job in a Middle Western college; who, when defrauded in her love and deprived of her livelihood, goes forth bravely to take up the vocation to which she has been committed since childhood. Miss Katharine Cornell made the character of Elsa appealing, and the play had a gratifying run in New York as well as a successful tour. Howard provided for Walter Huston an effective role in his dramatization of Sinclair Lewis' novel, *Dodsworth.* One of his best plays, *Yellow Jack,* which dramatized the victory of American scientists over yellow fever at the end of the Spanish-American war, failed on its first production but met a more favorable reception when revived, twelve years later.

Unlike Howard, who was seldom concerned with social criticism in his plays, George Kelly soon indicated that he was a powerful and caustic critic of certain aspects of American life. Kelly served an early apprenticeship as an actor in vaudeville, and learned his craft by writing the sketches in which he toured the two-a-day circuits. His first full-length play, *The Torch-Bearers,* satirized the amateur "little theater" movement then sweeping the country. He ridiculed the cultural pretensions and social ambitions of a typical group. He exposed the pompous silliness of a professional lady coach who exploited them; and the intellectual gullibility of the audiences to whom, as missionaries, they were carrying the gospel of "Art." The performance was enlivened by the notable acting of Miss Alison Skipworth as the dramatic coach, and Miss Mary Boland as the ambitious social leader. Kelly dealt, in *The Show-Off,* with a bluffing, boasting, breezy middle-class opportunist bent on acquiring quick and easy wealth in the era of "normalcy." The role was played effectively by Louis John Bartels.

In *Craig's Wife,* he drew a darker picture, a savage portrait of a woman of the upper middle class who marries to achieve security and independence by completely dominating her husband. The intensely disagreeable character of Harriet Craig—Kelly portrayed her with bitter contempt—was revealed with extraordinary subtlety by the performance of Miss Chrystal Herne, daughter of James A. Herne. Thereafter, in his plays, Kelly applied an austere, uncompromising, puritanical moral sense to the criticism of a society which he envisaged as increasingly dominated by women. In *Daisy Mayme,* he showed a prosperous middle-aged bachelor who, in long-standing bondage to his sisters and nieces, meets a shrewd, likable business woman who puts the parasites to rout, and indicates her readiness to substitute her own form of tyranny for theirs. He studied, in *Behold the Bridegroom,* the moral consequences of women's sexual emancipation. In later plays, such as *The Deep Mrs. Sykes,* an amusing portrait of a woman deluded by her intuition, and *The Fatal Weakness,* beautifully performed by Miss Ina Claire, Kelly relinquished the office of a moralist and returned to the vein of satirical comedy that had brought him his early rewards.

Satire, although he professed not to write it, was the medium in which the talent of George S. Kaufman achieved its best expression. In all but one instance, Kaufman's plays were collaborations. (His collaborators included Marc Connelly, Miss Edna Ferber and Moss Hart.) A master of skillful stagecraft, he developed a swift-paced, smoothly finished type of comedy which blended an astringent wit with furtive sentimentality. Like George M. Cohan in an earlier decade, Kaufman interpreted the prevailing mood of his time and, also like Cohan, he became the accredited spokesman of Broadway. He was frequently drafted to rewrite, to "doctor," or direct the plays of less competent craftsmen, and many younger playwrights strove to emulate his work. These facts made him an important influence on the American drama.

In collaboration with Connelly, Kaufman scored an immediate success with *Dulcy,* a pungent comedy about a well-intentioned wife whose abysmal stupidity nearly blights her husband's business prospects. The play elevated Miss Fontanne to stardom in the title role. The collaborators reversed this situation in *To The Ladies,* in which Elsie Beebe saves her husband from the consequences of his conceit, preserves his self-respect, and manages to retain her shaken faith in him. The role of Elsie was given to Miss Helen Hayes after the authors asked her whether she could sing a spiritual and accompany herself at the piano and she assured them that she could. She had never mastered the piano, or sung a spiritual, but with the aid of a music teacher and her Negro cook she acquired the requisite technical competence in six weeks, before rehearsals of the play began. Her touching, reticent performance of the role contributed notably to making the play a success. The collaboration of Kaufman and Connelly reached its highest achievement in *Beggar on Horseback,* an expressionistic dream fantasy which satirized, with an effect of irony, the materialism and oppressive tyranny of efficient big business, voicing the artist's protest against its gospels of standardization and conformity. With Miss Ferber, Kaufman wrote *Dinner at Eight,* a satirical indictment of the moral decadence of so-called good society, the more powerful because it did not pass explicit judgment on the characters whom it portrayed. With Moss Hart, Kaufman collaborated on *The Man Who Came to Dinner,* a savagely cruel portrait of Alexander Woollcott, ebulliently acted by Monty Woolley—but the significance of the play was its implied criticism of a way of thinking, and an attitude to life, exemplified by the character. Also with Hart, Kaufman wrote *Merrily We Roll Along,* his most serious play: a study of the moral disintegration of a dramatist who, by catering to popular taste at the sacrifice of his spiritual and intellectual integrity, gains wealth, celebrity and social prestige and is haunted by the betrayal of his talent.

After terminating his collaboration with Kaufman, Marc Connelly opened a new realm for American dramatists which subsequently yielded a number of notable plays. Fantasy, as a medium for the serious interpretation of life, had not been successfully exploited until Connelly wrote *The Green Pastures.* Initially suggested by Roark Bradford's humorous sketches *Ol' Man Adam an' His Chillun,* Connelly's play was a noble, imaginative treatment of Biblical stories related by a Negro preacher—a study of man's relation to God conceived in the spirit of exalted piety expressed by Negro spirituals. A Negro cast headed by Richard Harrison in the character of "de Lawd" made the play profoundly moving. Paul Osborn's *On Borrowed Time* expressed in terms of fantasy the thesis that unselfish love is a force sufficiently powerful to defeat death. (Osborn's versatility was indicated by his adroit comedy, *The Vinegar Tree,* admirably played by Miss Mary Boland; his idyllic study of American small-town life, *Morning's at Seven;* his realistic dramatization of John Hersey's novel, *A Bell for Adano.*) William Saroyan, in *My Heart's in the Highlands* and *The Time of Your Life,* successfully blended the lyrical, imaginative qualities of fantasy and the ordinary realities of American life, but in later plays his poetic vein ran thin and his propensity to expound trite ideas failed to excite enthusiasm. The most distinguished achievements in the medium of fantasy were effected by Thornton Wilder in two very remarkable, dissimilar plays. His *Our Town*— performed without scenery, on a bare stage—dealt poetically with the cycle of life, from birth to death, in a rural New England community at the beginning of the century, asserting, in the phrase of Maxwell Anderson, that "man has a dignity and a destiny." This was also the theme of *The Skin of Our Teeth* which, symbolically representing the epic of man's mental and social evolution from the dawn of history to the present, showed human life to be continuously threatened by extinction, yet continuously preserved from it by man's blundering efforts.

Three playwrights who began their careers during the Great Depression used the method of traditional realism for purposes of social criticism. Sidney Kingsley's first play, *Men in White,* was an effective melodrama, laid in a hospital, which showed a physician almost instinctively performing his professional duty while under the stress of an emotional conflict. In his second play, *Dead End,* he brought vividly to the stage the social problem crystallized by New York's fashionable East Side, where luxury apartments are adjacent to tenement rookeries, and underprivileged children are early taught the ways of criminality. During the Second World War Kingsley produced *The Patriots,* which dramatized the birth of the nation in the characters of Washington, Jefferson and Hamilton. Later, he returned to more familiar ground in *Detective Story,* laid in a Manhattan police station and, in effect, a powerful indictment of the perversion of justice exemplified by current practices of the police.

Like Kingsley, Miss Lillian Hellman began her career with a melodrama, *The Children's Hour.* It dealt with the havoc wrought on a school and the lives of its two women principals by the slanderous gossip of an evil child. Miss Hellman's expert craftsmanship gave the play an impact which brought it a run of 691 performances. She soon turned to social and political themes. In *The Little Foxes* she etched in acid a family portrait of the rapacious, predatory Hubbards, amassing their wealth in the opening years of the century. (The play offered Miss Tallulah Bankhead the finest role of her career as the implacable Regina Giddens, and Miss Patricia Collinge an equally fine role as Regina's dipsomaniac sister-in-law, Birdie.) Seven years later, Miss Hellman returned to the Hubbard family, in *Another Part of the Forest,* showing them at an earlier stage of their progress. Together, the two plays put into historical perspective a criticism of certain social effects of capitalism. Her *Watch on the Rhine* and *The Searching Wind* brought the terrors and evils of Fascism in Europe directly into the domestic environment of Americans.

Protest, tempered by the vision of a better future, was made explicit in the plays of Clifford Odets, who emerged as a dramatist from the acting company of the Group Theater, which produced his work. His first short play, *Waiting for Lefty,* which showed a labor union meeting in progress, and involved the audience as the supposed membership considering a strike vote, was an immediate sensation. (It was soon being played "in some sixty towns which had never before witnessed a theatrical performance," and with another of Odets' plays was being performed in thirty-two cities.) His first full-length play, *Awake and Sing,* studied with compassion and emotional power the lives of a lower middle-class family in a Bronx tenement, in circumstances of extreme insecurity and poverty, held together by profound loyalty notwithstanding the conflict of their individual ideals and desires. In *Paradise Lost* Odets presented a similar family, confronted by the grim realities of economic disaster but, as he implied, invincible because the persistence of human passion will make them continue living and in the process they may find a new hope and perhaps a new happiness. Odets' later plays—*Golden Boy, Rocket to the Moon, Night Music* and *Clash by Night*—set against the background of the immediate economic situation both the protest of youth at being defrauded of its opportunity and its burning faith in the possibility of a future unlike and better than the past.

The interval between the two World Wars also brought forward a number of playwrights whose work provided the American theater, for the first time, with a literature of high comedy dealing with the native scene. Robert E. Sherwood first experimented with the form in *The Road to Rome,* a pseudo-historical piece possibly suggested by Shaw's *Caesar and Cleopatra,* which gave good acting opportunities to Philip Merivale as Hannibal and to Miss Jane Cowl as a Roman matron who saves her city by the not reluctant sacrifice of her virtue. His *Reunion in Vienna*—strongly influenced by the plays of Ferenc Molnar— was an entertaining bit of frivolity acted to the hilt by Miss Fontanne and Alfred Lunt, for·whom it had been written. In *The Petrified Forest* Sherwood turned to the American scene with a comedy of ideas framed in melodramatic action, played by Leslie Howard and Humphrey Bogart. Although he laid the scene of *Idiot's Delight* in Europe, Sherwood's characters—a vaudeville hoofer and his band of chorus girls, and the beautiful companion of a munitions magnate— were racy of the American soil, and in it he again made comedy serve a serious theme. The delicate balance between comic fable and grave implication was skillfully preserved by Miss Fontanne and Lunt in their performance of the principal roles. Sherwood turned away from comedy in *Abe Lincoln in Illinois,* eloquently acted by Raymond Massey, and *There Shall Be No Night,* a stirring affirmation of democracy and indictment of totalitarianism.

Most of the plays written by Philip Barry were comedies of manners. They dealt with cultivated, sophisticated people, who, enjoying relative freedom from material anxieties, are displayed in situations which compel them to choose between the alternatives proposed by conscience and desire. Barry's light, witty treatment of his stories often disguised the fact that their theme was serious. In *Paris Bound* and *Tomorrow and Tomorrow* he brought into conflict the ethical concept of marriage, founded on a spiritual union, and the current mores which favor individual "liberty," casual love affairs and easy divorce. In *The Animal Kingdom,* his subject was a marriage which does not fulfill its ethical conditions, and in which the integrity of husband and wife requires a dissolution. In *Holiday,* written for Miss Hope Williams, he portrayed a bored, wealthy American girl who finds happiness in escape from her conventional environment. Barry's most popular play, *The Philadelphia Story,* was another treatment of this fable. Written to exploit the talents of Miss Katharine Hepburn, it ran for more than four hundred performances in New York and toured the country for two years. Later he wrote *Without Love* for Miss Hepburn, and it played on tour for a season before being presented in New York. The star's popularity was such that her public bought their tickets far in advance; the theater was sold out long before her arrival in any town; and the company "traveled through the country like a circus, all the comings and goings of Kate being accompanied by the wildest demonstrations on the part of tumultuous admirers." Although the comedy did not receive overwhelmingly favorable reviews in New York, it played to full houses for sixteen weeks, and closed only because Miss Hepburn had to return to Hollywood. That the public preferred the polished surface of Barry's comedies to their content of ideas worked out to the disadvantage of his talent. He wrote three serious plays, all notable, which failed. In *Hotel Universe,* one of the most explicitly philosophical of modern American plays, his theme was the power, for good or evil, of the basic illusions which shape people's lives; in it, Miss Ruth Gordon gave a memorable performance. In *The Joyous Season,* his theme was the effect of religious faith on worldly life, and the difficult role of the Mother Superior of an order of nuns was played with subtle insight by Miss Lillian Gish. In *Here Come the Clowns,* Barry dramatized the contemporary American's search for God, using for his characters the backstage workers in a theater, and making the protagonist, and the prophet of a more spiritual life, a stagehand.

The most accomplished writer of high comedy, S. N. Behrman, produced a body of plays as remarkable for their literary as for their dramatic merits. His characters are too intelligent not to be skeptical. They seldom surrender to prejudices, moral, political, or economic; they distrust all facile formulas. They are enviably free from pressures which warp the judgment of people less fortunate. Their virtue is to see all sides of any complex problem, even if the problem involves their personal fortunes. Because his characters exist in a climate of perpetual debate, Behrman's comedies are primarily intellectual; they express the play of wit and wisdom on social life. His first comedy, *The Second Man,* a study of the dual personality of a writer, was expertly acted by Miss Fontanne, Miss Margalo Gilmore, Alfred Lunt and Earl Larimore, and brought Behrman immediate celebrity. In *Biography,* one of his greatest successes, he presented the case of a woman who, obliged to choose between an opportunist conservative politician and a fanatical radical idealist, refuses both, defending the wisdom of cultivating the greatest possible tolerance for all points of view while committing herself to none. The role of the liberal, or spokesman for tolerance, was brilliantly played by Miss Ina Claire, who also displayed her fine talent as a comedienne in Behrman's *End of Summer,* which analytically studies the relation of wealth to happiness. Because his comedies were not didactic, and because they were deliberately restricted to illuminating discussion, critics sometimes failed to understand that Behrman was dealing with many of the serious issues of the time. In *No Time for Comedy,* written at the outbreak of the Second World War, and acted by Miss Katharine Cornell, he made clear his conviction that the comic spirit and the virtue of discriminating intelligence have their place even in a world where the survival of civilization appeared to be in doubt.

The plays of John van Druten, although conceived in the spirit of high comedy, moved out of the drawing-room world to which high comedy is usually confined. British-born, van Druten came to the United States because his play, *Young Woodley,* having been banned by the Lord Chamberlain, was given an American production. Eventually, he became a permanent resident of the United States and a citizen, but began writing plays about American life only after a long familiarity with it. In *Old Acquaintance,* a study of the professional and personal rivalry of two women authors bound by long friendship, he dealt wittily with literary circles in New York City; the two authors were vivaciously played by Miss Jane Cowl and Miss Peggy Wood. In his most successful comedy, *The Voice of the Turtle,* he balanced the mores of sexual freedom, which permit two young people to drift into what is to be no more than a casual

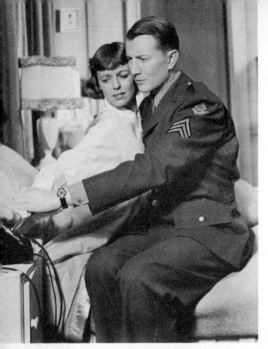

Margaret Sullavan and Elliott Nugent in "The Voice of the Turtle"

love affair, against the eternal human hope for a permanent union founded on love. The young soldier and young actress of van Druten's comedy are prejudiced against love and afraid of being made to suffer by a serious emotion, and the charm of the play is their startled discovery of what their affair means to each of them. The mental maturity of the public was indicated by the fact that the playwright was able, without offending them, to carry the drama of a love affair to a bed, the extinguishing of a light, and a passage of evocative dialogue before ringing down the curtain. Excellently performed by Miss Margaret Sullavan, Miss Audrey Christie and Elliott Nugent, *The Voice of the Turtle* played 1,558 performances in New York and numerous touring companies carried it to audiences throughout the country. In *I Remember Mama*, founded on a sequence of stories by Miss Kathryn Forbes, van Druten brought to the stage the saga of a family of Norwegian immigrants living in San Francisco. Dominated by the character of a wise, gallant mother (played by Miss Mady Christians) the comedy expressed a profound faith in the life of people who meet their problems with high courage, integrity and goodness of heart.

A comedy of manners proved to be the most successful play in the history of the American stage. This was *Life With Father,* adapted by Howard Lindsay and Russel Crouse from the sketches by Clarence Day, with Lindsay in the role of Father, and Miss Dorothy Stickney in that of Vinnie, his troubled, demure and always victorious wife. Although the characters were sharply individualized, the picture of family life achieved by the dramatists was sufficiently universal in its application to bring the play a run of 3,213 consecutive performances at the Empire Theater in New York, and to make it a long-lived road attraction. The talent of the collaborators was later exemplified by an original play, *State of the Union,* the best comedy of American political life to reach the stage in many years.

The effect of the creation, over two decades, of a native dramatic literature was vividly illustrated by the operations of the Theater Guild. This organization was the most powerful single force involved in shaping the character of the contemporary American theater, and it has been in many respects unique. In 1953 it was in its thirty-fourth year of continuous activity as a producer of plays, and except for the successive managements of James W. Wallack and Lester Wallack, had the longest record of service in the history of the American stage. Its present directors, Miss Theresa Helburn and Lawrence Langner, have been

Dorothy Stickney and Howard Lindsay in "Life With Father"

associated with it from its inception, and have been in complete control of its activities for fourteen years. Their associate director, Miss Armina Marshall (Mrs. Langner) has been identified with the Guild since 1922. The Guild was founded in 1919 as an art theater, "to produce plays of artistic merit not ordinarily produced by the commercial managers." Unlike European art theaters, all of which were deliberately cut off from any connection with the commercial stage, the Guild from its beginning has been vitally related to the American commercial theater.

The original object of its founders was to establish "a theater in which plays of artistic merit and adult content could be given to compete with plays which were put on mainly for the amount of profit they could make for their producers." The result was a peculiarly American phenomenon—an art theater animated by the highest ideals, setting new standards of excellence in selection of plays, acting and staging, existing without benefit of subsidy, and carrying on its operations in direct competition with those of commercial producers, in the center of commercial production. It is obvious that the Guild's great influence on the American stage stems from two facts: that it has been from the outset an art theater identified with Broadway; and that, accepting the competitive conditions of commercial enterprise, it has attained, without compromising its standards, a financial prosperity at least equal to that of any other Broadway producer. That the Theater Guild today is infrequently described as an art theater, and is seldom distinguished from other commercial producing organizations, constitutes an index of its remarkable influence on the contemporary American stage. As Lawrence Langner has stated, when the Guild proved its thesis in terms of financial profits, commercial producers began to follow its example, with the result that "what was the artistic theater of those days has since become the most affluent section of the commercial theater of today."

During the first ten years of its activity, the Guild produced sixty-six plays, of which only sixteen were by American playwrights. As Langner recorded, "we were bitterly accused of favoring foreign playwrights, but we stuck to our principle, which was to produce important artistic plays regardless of their national origin." The period from 1919 to 1929 marked the end of a renaissance of the drama in Europe which had begun with the advent of Henrik Ibsen and his contemporaries, and in those years the Guild had "all the literature of the world to choose from," much of it never before produced on the American stage. The Guild brought out twenty plays by British and Irish dramatists, ten of them by George Bernard Shaw, for whom it served as official American producer, and whose *Back to Methuselah* and *Saint Joan* it introduced. It produced eight German plays, including notable examples of the current "expressionistic" drama. It staged plays by the Russians, Tolstoy, Andreyev and Evreinov; the Scandinavians Ibsen and Strindberg; the Hungarians Molnar and Vajda; the Italian Pirandello; the Spaniard Benavente; the Belgian Verhaeren; the Czech Capek; and those of a group of contemporary French dramatists.

In creating a popular audience for so representative a selection of modern European drama, the Guild helped to prepare the way for the new school of American playwrights. Meanwhile, during its first ten years of activity, it did not neglect the work of these new playwrights. The sixteen American plays produced by the Guild included one by Elmer Rice; three by Sidney Howard; three by Eugene O'Neill; and two by S. N. Behrman; and *Porgy,* by Du Bose and Dorothy Heyward, which furnished the libretto for George Gershwin's folk opera, *Porgy and Bess,* produced by the Guild in 1935. The Guild also assembled the finest acting company to play in the United States since the closing of the New Theater in 1911. It included Miss Lynn Fontanne and Miss Helen Westley, Alfred Lunt, Dudley Digges, Ernest Cossart and Henry Travers, and among its later members were Miss Clare Eames, Miss Margalo Gillmore, George Gaul, Glenn Anders, Earle Larimore, Tom Powers, Edward G. Robinson, Claude Rains, Edgar Stehli, Erskine Sanford and Philip Loeb. The nucleus of the Guild's audience was a subscription list which, by the end of its tenth season, had 23,000 members in New York. But the Guild had also begun to take its productions to other cities: Chicago, Baltimore, Boston, Cleveland, Pittsburgh and Philadelphia.

The second ten-year period of the Guild's activity showed a significant change. Fifty-six plays were produced; of these, thirty-six were by American dramatists. In addition to Howard, O'Neill and Behrman, the roster included Philip Barry, Maxwell Anderson, Robert E. Sherwood and William Saroyan. In 1938, Anderson, Howard, Behrman and Sherwood, for whom the Guild had produced sixteen plays, joined Elmer Rice in forming the Playwrights' Company, an independent producing organization to stage the plays written by its members. The dependence of the Guild on these American playwrights is indicated by the fact that Lawrence Langner suggested "somewhat bitterly that they take over the Guild subscription as well, since I saw little prospect of the Guild being able to run the theater"—it was then established in its own playhouse—"without the support of these representative playwrights." Langner's suggestion was not accepted by the Playwrights' Company. The Guild abandoned its costly playhouse, underwent a reorganization which left Miss Helburn and Langner in complete control, and continued its activity. "During our third period of ten years," Langner recorded, "we produced over thirty-five American plays, and only twenty by European writers. Thus, in three decades, we passed from a preponderance of European plays to a preponderance of American plays."

With the onset of the Great Depression and the inability of the Guild to maintain a quasi-repertory system of production with which it had experimented, its splendid acting company disintegrated. It was thus compelled to adopt the policy of commercial producers and engage actors for specific productions. During this period, however, an organization was set up by the Guild and other producers to provide plays for the country at large. This organization, the Theater Guild-American Theater Society, in 1952 had more than 105,000 subscribers in twenty-two cities from coast to coast in which it presented the recent productions of its members. "Many of the cities throughout the country," Langner noted, "would be starved for plays were it not for the fact that the subscription audience underwrites the sending of four or five good plays a year to their towns."

The Civic Repertory Theater founded by Miss Eva Le Gallienne in 1926 was the most ambitious and sustained attempt to revive the repertory system of production. Miss Le Gallienne, daughter of the British poet Richard Le Gallienne and his Danish wife, was educated in France and England, and her ambition to establish a repertory theater may have been stimulated by youthful familiarity with the Comédie Française. She made her stage debut in London, at the age of fifteen, under the sponsorship of Miss Constance Collier, and came to the United States after the outbreak of the First World War. In 1921, she was engaged by the Theater Guild to play the role of Julie in Ferenc Molnar's *Liliom,* which became a colossal popular success and elevated her to stardom. Two years later she starred in Molnar's *The Swan* under the management of Gilbert Miller, son of the actor Henry Miller and grandson of Miss Matilda Heron. Soon afterwards she produced two Ibsen plays in New York, at modest prices of admission, as a preliminary test of the feasibility of her plan to establish "a repertory theater, presenting great plays at popular prices." The results proved to her satisfaction that there existed in New York an audience for such an institution; and that this audience was largely composed of people of modest means —"students, workers, thinking people to whom art and literature in any form were real necessities and not *only* for amusement." As she later recorded: "From the very beginning there was no commercial angle to my plan: the state repertory theaters of Europe are all subsidized; I could not see why America should not have a repertory theater subsidized by private capital in the same way that its opera companies and symphony orchestras are." She secured sufficient capital to engage a company and guarantee its members a first season of twenty weeks. She leased the old Fourteenth Street Theater, west of Sixth Avenue, where, a half-century earlier, Forrest had played his last engagement, and Mme. Ristori had appeared. The house had a seating capacity of about eleven hundred, and Miss Le Gallienne fixed prices of admission from 35 cents to $1.50.

The company assembled by Miss Le Gallienne shared her ideals and her vision, and during the six seasons offered by the Civic Repertory Theater they were joined, for special engagements, by such well-known artists as Mme. Alla Nazimova, Joseph Schildkraut and Jacob Ben-Ami. Thirty-four plays were given a total of 1,581 performances. The repertory included plays by Shakespeare, Moliere, Goldoni, Ibsen, Tolstoy, Chekhov, Schnitzler, Molnar; Barrie's *Peter Pan* and a dramatization of *Alice in Wonderland;* and—the greatest popular success of all—*Camille.* Only one important American play was produced, Miss Susan Glaspell's *Alison's House,* an imaginative dramatic portrait of the poet, Emily Dickinson. Miss Le Gallienne directed nearly all the plays and appeared in most of them. In addition, for three seasons, she conducted a free school for qualified apprentices. But after the first years of the Great Depression, several of the theater's financial guarantors were unable to continue their support of the enterprise. During its sixth season, although box office receipts "had climbed to an amazingly high average," Miss Le Gallienne found that the Civic Repertory Theater required an annual subsidy of at least $75,000 to continue. This sum was not forthcoming, and the idealistic experiment terminated.

Before the Civic Repertory Theater closed, another idealistic enterprise was launched. The Group Theater was projected by Harold Clurman, a young New Yorker who, after studying at the Sorbonne, had worked with the producing organization of O'Neill, Jones and Macgowan, and later was employed as a play reader by the Theater Guild. Clurman's purpose was to form an organization that would "develop actors, playwrights, scene designers, directors" by constituting itself a permanent producing unit maintaining regular seasons in New York. He believed that there existed in New York "a conscious audience to follow the program of a theater that would grow with the years and make a contribution to our social-cultural life in the manner of certain State theaters abroad, or of the Moscow Art Theater . . ."

The company of the Moscow Art Theater, under Constantin Stanislavsky, made a visit to the United States in 1923 and its performances, because of the acting style which Stanislavsky's method of training had produced, made a profound impression on the younger generation of intellectuals. The aim of Stanislavsky's method, or "system," as Clurman defined it, "is to enable the actor to use himself more consciously as an instrument for the attainment of truth on the stage." He determined to employ it, with experienced actors, in all productions of the proposed theater. His ideas fired the enthusiasm of a number of friends in the Guild and in other companies. After preliminary experiments in rehearsing several plays, Clurman formed a group of twenty-eight actors and three directors; Miss Cheryl Crawford, Lee Strasberg, and himself. The initial acting members included Miss Stella Adler, Miss Mary Morris, Franchot Tone, Morris Carnovsky, J. Edward Bromberg and Clifford Odets. (Among later recruits were Elia Kazan and Robert Lewis, both to become well-known directors; Luther Adler, John Garfield, Alan Baxter, Russell Collins and Roman Bohnen.) The Theater Guild assigned to the group its rights in Paul Green's play, *The House of Connelly,* furnished a small working capital to which other benefactors added, and in the summer of 1931 the actors and directors spent three months in Connecticut rehearsing the play.

In September, 1931, under the auspices of the Theater Guild, the Group Theater presented *The House of Connelly* in New York; an inspired ensemble performance took the critics by storm. Notwithstanding the economic stress of the Great Depression, Clurman and his associates hoped to obtain an endowment of $100,000 to finance "a carefully planned program on a long-term or at least a seasonal basis." This hope was never realized. Although, over the years, the Group was able to obtain more than the desired amount, it could only procure money in sums sufficient to finance individual productions. Presently, the affiliation with the Guild ended and the Group was on its own. Several productions were blasted by the critics; Franchot Tone left the group for Hollywood; other leading actors had to take engagements in other companies.

But in the autumn of 1933, with its production of Sidney Kingsley's *Men in White,* the Group achieved a popular and financial success. In 1935, with the production of Odets' *Awake and Sing* and *Waiting for Lefty,* it appeared to be securely established. Although the Group produced the works of many other playwrights, notably William Saroyan's first play, the successive plays written by Odets became its principal resource. Odets was offered highly paid employment in Hollywood and accepted it. Thereafter he divided his time between the financial rewards of the motion-picture studios and the Group, which represented social dissidence and austere artistic ideals. His divided allegiance was symptomatic of the conflicting aims of other members, some of whom attained celebrity and financial prosperity either in Hollywood or the commercial theater. In 1941, after a decade of influential artistic achievement, the Group Theater disbanded. Four years later, writing its history in *The Fervent Years,* Clurman stated: "The basic defect in our activity was that while we tried to maintain a true theater artistically, we proceeded economically on a show-business basis. Our means and our ends were in fundamental contradiction." But the example which the Group Theater gave of a coherent technique of acting and production shared by an entire company was an important contribution to the American stage.

From 1935 to 1939 the United States had, on a nation-wide scale, a theater subsidized and operated by the Federal Government. The Federal Theater Project, established as a division of the Works Progress Administration, was set up for the purpose of taking off the relief rolls employable members of the theatrical profession, and affording them an opportunity to preserve their self-respect by exercising their professional skills as paid workers. Mrs. Hallie Flanagan, director of the Experimental Theater at Vassar College, was chosen to head the project. She held conferences with playwrights, Broadway producers, executives of the various theatrical unions, and representatives of college and community playhouses. The project was then organized on a regional basis to achieve re-employment of professional workers by providing "dramatic entertainment either free or at low cost." Within a year, more than twelve thousand people were employed by Federal Theater units in twenty-nine states and the District of Columbia. During the life of the project some twelve hundred productions of plays were made, ranging over the entire realm of dramatic literature from classical to contemporary. A Negro Theater was established. There were companies presenting plays for children. There were presentations of musicals, dance dramas, puppet shows and revues. The "living newspaper," a dramatization of current events and public issues, was invented and perfected. The most important original play to receive production was Sinclair Lewis' dramatization of his novel, *It Can't Happen Here,* which was made a test of the professional expertness of the project's nation-wide network of playhouses, and was given its first performance simultaneously in twenty-one theaters in seventeen states.

The most significant discovery made by the Federal Theater was "that millions of Americans want to go to the theater if it can be brought geographically and financially within their range." The audiences which it reached were numbered in the millions. Sometimes the results were startling. In Omaha, Nebraska, and its suburbs, the actors learned that 90 per cent of their audience "had never seen a play and could not believe that the actors were not moving pictures," but after every performance "would wait in the doorway to see 'whether the people are real.' " In Valley, Nebraska, a town of one thousand people, eight hundred tried to get into the schoolhouse to see the first play ever given there.

Political opposition to the Federal Theater developed in Congress. When hearings were held by the Senate Committee on Appropriations with a view to its discontinuance, support for the Theater came from the New York dramatic critics, Actors' Equity, commercial producers and prominent stars. Miss Tallulah Bankhead, appearing before the committee as a witness, cried out, "But actors are people, aren't they? They're people!" Congress terminated the Federal Theater on June 30, 1939, by specifically prohibiting its continuance under a new appropriation voted for the Works Progress Administration. "This singles out a special group of professional people for a denial of work in their profession," President Roosevelt told the press. "It is discrimination of the worst type."

Yet in the Second World War, as earlier in the first, the Federal Government gratefully accepted from the theatrical profession the unique services which it alone could furnish and promptly, voluntarily, offered. At New York's celebrated Stage Door Canteen, every well-known player of stage and screen appeared; famous stars and minor performers alike waited on the men in uniform who thronged there. Broadway productions were sent out for Sunday performances at camps within traveling range of New York, the casts giving up their day of rest and performing without pay. And, under the auspices of USO, great stars as well as the rank and file of the profession went out to entertain the armed forces in Africa and Europe, the Middle East, the remote islands of the Pacific, the Aleutians, Alaska and Iceland.

The period between the two wars brought about a decline, not in the star system, but in the efficacy of its appeal to the public. During the era of Frohman and Belasco there were many stars who, by virtue of their personal prestige, were able to fill theaters on the road, even if their plays were poor and their supporting companies inferior. A number of factors radically changed this situation. The competition of feature motion pictures in luxurious playhouses was an ominous threat to the touring company. The invention of the talking picture, and the almost simultaneous incidence of the Great Depression, sharply reduced the number of "legitimate" playhouses throughout the country as well as in New York. Meanwhile, the rise of a native school of dramatists had the effect of making plays, rather than stars, the primary interest of audiences. As Miss Katharine Cornell put it: "First and foremost, always, is the play. And the play can only be served by having each part cast as well and played as carefully as the leading roles." Good plays with fine ensemble acting would lure a wary public to the theater. The day of the third-rate touring company, even in a recent Broadway success, and of stars who were personages rather than performers, came to an end.

The stars who achieved nation-wide prestige were therefore fewer in number, and most of them were women. Among the first to emerge was Miss Helen Hayes, who began her professional career at the age of five in a Washington stock company; made her Broadway debut in a musical comedy with Lew Fields four years later; and at fourteen played a young girl's role with John Drew in *The Prodigal Husband.* After touring the South and West at the head of a company playing *Pollyanna,* she was given her first dramatic role in 1918, when she played Margaret, the "dream daughter," in Barrie's fantasy, *Dear Brutus,* with William Gillette. Three critics described her performance as "exquisite"; it was, in effect, so poignant that her role displaced Gillette's as the central element of the play. Heywood Broun, in his review for the *Tribune,* mentioned Miss Hayes's "amazing equipment of natural charm and technical skill," and in doing so·pointed to the attributes which served as a foundation for her distinguished career. She took "flapper" roles in Booth Tarkington's *Clarence,* which made Alfred Lunt a star, and Edward Childs Carpenter's *Babs,* which elevated her to stardom at the age of twenty. During the Boston engagement of *Babs,* Miss Hayes was visited in her dressing room by Lotta Crabtree, long retired and past her seventieth year. The famous soubrette of former days told the young star that she was "a born comedienne," and that she possessed "three great qualities": she spoke so distinctly that every word could be heard in the gallery; she had a beautiful natural speaking voice; and, most important of all, on the stage she was "a good listener." Her manager, the veteran George Tyler, told Miss Hayes's mother that Miss Hayes "never makes a mistake in her reaction to a line or thought, but she doesn't know why she doesn't. It is an unerring instinct."

But Miss Hayes realized that, to become an artist, she would have to supplement instinctive technical skill with conscious technical resource and, although an established star, began intensive study with Miss Frances Robinson-Duff, a dramatic teacher. Thereafter, she resolutely enlarged her acting range by undertaking a series of roles remarkable for their variety. She played Elsie Beebe in *To the Ladies;* Cleopatra in a revival of Shaw's *Caesar and Cleopatra;* Maggie Wylie in a revival of Barrie's *What Every Woman Knows,* which had not been performed since Miss Maude Adams first appeared in it eighteen years earlier. Miss Hayes played the role for sixty-two weeks in New York and on tour. In *Coquette,* a melodrama by Miss Ann Bridges and George Abbott, she undertook her first strongly emotional role, with sensational success. The play ran for twenty months in New York, and Miss Hayes toured in it across the country for another year. Later she turned to poetic tragedy in Anderson's *Mary of Scotland,* and immediately afterward to her greatest triumph of virtuosity, Laurence Housman's *Victoria Regina.* In this she personated Queen Victoria in a series of episodes that carried the character from girlhood to her eightieth year. Housman's piece was literature, not drama. Its powerful impact when transferred to the stage was not intrinsic but contributed by Miss Hayes's acting. Her achievement was therefore exceptional: through the exercise of her art, she created a play. Her performance of *Victoria Regina* was a display of bravura seldom equaled on the modern stage. In it she made no use of her "amazing equipment of natural charm"—which often caused her to be compared with Miss Maude Adams, and sometimes resulted in the underrating of her craftsmanship. Entirely dissociated from Miss Hayes's personality, it established her as one of the most remarkable technicians in the American theater.

Miss Katharine Cornell, who made an inconspicuous debut with the Washington Square Players, acquired the fundamentals of her craft by playing, for three summers, with the stock companies conducted in Buffalo and Detroit by Miss Jessie Bonstelle. The discipline was severe: "ten performances a week

Katharine Cornell in "The Barretts of Wimpole Street"

and a new play every Monday night." But long afterwards Miss Cornell asserted its value as training, and also specified its peculiar hazard. "You learn all the tricks—to do them quickly. Of course, it can be dangerous. You can't go on getting your effects with counterfeits, using obvious devices. As you mature, and have time to develop a part, you've got to discriminate—decide what methods to use and what to discard. If you don't go on to learn to act creatively, you are bound to become permanently stocky—a ham."

That she had overcome the danger of superficial technical fluency was obvious when, in 1921, she played her first significant role on Broadway in *A Bill of Divorcement,* a study of hereditary insanity by the British novelist-playwright Miss Clemence Dane. Miss Cornell, playing the adoring daughter of a supposedly shell-shocked British veteran, had the problem of indicating to the audience that the girl was a victim of the family inheritance, yet doing this so subtly that the audience "would only realize subconsciously that there was something different about her until that stark moment when they, too, discovered the truth." She was convinced that the effect could be made only through a slight overemphasis of all the character's emotional reactions. "As I tried to work out a technique for projecting such an esoteric and elusive pathology," she recorded later, "I suddenly found my hands doing a great deal of my acting." In the climactic scene during which the girl learns the truth, "my hands again became for me the living symbols of that terrible doom and that despair." Her performance, hailed by Alexander Woollcott as one "of memorable understanding and beauty," was largely responsible for making the play a hit on Broadway.

Her personal success in *A Bill of Divorcement* brought Miss Cornell an offer of immediate stardom from the producer Al H. Woods. She was already skeptical about the star system. "Authentic stardom means a good deal more than having one's name in lights or being billed above the play. It is something which rarely happens overnight, something for which one needs maturity and long stage experience. Also, it is a gift which, if it is to have any permanent significance, must be bestowed by a public rather than a manager." She declined to become a star, and there followed, within two years, "the inestimable benefit of playing seven parts—all very different." In reviewing her performance of one of them, the critic Burns Mantle declared that Miss Cornell "has more of the Duse quality than any of the other younger women of the stage." This suggestion was amplified by H. T. Parker, the erudite critic of the Boston *Transcript,* when Miss Cornell played Shaw's *Candida,* in 1924. He asserted that she "achieved the part by mental and spiritual sensibility." Mantle and Parker thus detected, early in Miss Cornell's career, the two most distinctive attributes of her art: her ability to reveal the complex inward life of a character; and her ability to endow a character with greater meaning than the text or indicated action make explicit.

It was the latter of these attributes that lifted her performance of the role of Iris March, in Michael Arlen's *The Green Hat,* to the plane of artistic achievement. The play was a dramatization by Arlen of his best-selling novel about a glamorous, neurotic, female libertine. The novel expressed, vulgarly, a post-war mood of desperation. The play was sheer trumpery, but Miss Cornell wanted to undertake the role, and her performance brought her stardom. She determined "to make Iris unobvious," and by rejecting all easy methods of portraying the character as seductive, she gave it a measure of tragic significance. In New York, and on the road, *The Green Hat* absorbed two years of Miss Cornell's time. Remarkably, she did not become tired of the preposterous role; she remembered it gratefully because it "gave me a public." Subsequently, she played Somerset Maugham's melodrama, *The Letter;* a dramatization of Edith Wharton's novel, *The Age of Innocence,* by Mrs. Margaret Ayer Barnes and Edward Sheldon; *Dishonored Lady,* a melodrama by the same collaborators. None was a drama of outstanding merit, yet Miss Cornell's performances led Richard Watts, critic for the *Tribune,* to assert that she possessed "a dramatic power, a keen sensitivity, a sharp intelligence and an emotional vigor that are not terribly far from overwhelming," and to declare that she was "our First Actress."

In 1931, with her husband, Guthrie McClintic, Miss Cornell formed a producing company which, in effect, became "a foundation for producing plays which seem worth doing and in the way we think it worth-while to do them," rather than "a business venture for personal gain." Their first production was Rudolf Besier's *The Barretts of Wimpole Street,* with Miss Cornell in the role of Elizabeth Barrett and Brian Aherne in that of Robert Browning. Her magnificent performance in an exceptionally difficult role brought Miss Cornell critical acclaim, establishing her as "an actress of the first order." The play ran for a full year in New York, and Miss Cornell toured it across the continent.

Two years later, with a notable company, she played *The Barretts, Candida* and *Romeo and Juliet* on a nation-wide tour of thirty-one states, performing in cities and one-night stands, in some towns using theaters which had been closed for twenty years, in others resorting to motion-picture houses. Due in Seattle, Washington, for a performance on Christmas night, Miss Cornell and her company were prevented from reaching the city until nearly midnight by a washout on the railroad. They were met by the manager of the theater, who told them that the audience was still waiting. They rushed to the theater, and Miss Cornell gave instructions to have the curtain rung up so that the audience might see the setting and lighting of the stage while she and the company dressed. At one o'clock in the morning their performance of *The Barretts* began, and the final curtain fell at four. "I don't think we ever gave a better performance or played to a more divine audience," Miss Cornell recorded. "They cheered and cheered; gave us curtain call after curtain call. It was all so remarkable—we couldn't believe it—I've never heard of anything like it."

New York saw Miss Cornell's Juliet one year after the rest of the country. It was her first attempt to meet the challenge of a great classic role and her performance, extolled by all the critics, proved that her art was equal to this ultimate test. One of the most significant features of Miss Cornell's activity as an actress-manager was the variety of her productions. Over the years she offered plays by the American dramatists Howard, van Druten, Anderson and Behrman; Shaw's *St. Joan* and *The Doctor's Dilemma* as well as frequent revivals of *Candida;* a translation of Friedrich Hebbel's *Herod and Mariamne,* Chekhov's *The Three Sisters,* in which she appeared with Miss Judith Anderson and Miss Ruth Gordon.

The joint starring careers of Miss Lynne Fontanne and Alfred Lunt, who were married in 1922, extended over a longer period than those of such celebrated stage partners as Miss Terry and Henry Irving and Miss Marlowe and E. H. Sothern. From 1924, when they first co-starred in Molnar's *The Guardsman,* they appeared together in more than twenty plays, of which the great majority were light comedies. This tended to obscure their equally notable talents for other forms of drama, displayed only infrequently, as in their performances of *The Brothers Karamazov, Elizabeth the Queen,* and Chekhov's *The Seagull* or, in the case of Miss Fontanne, by her creation of the role of Nina Leeds in *Strange Interlude.* They brought to the contemporary theater the remarkable interplay of acting and unity of style which earlier had been exemplified by Miss Ada Rehan and John Drew. Like their distinguished precursors, they usually appeared in plays which, founded on an affectionate duel, enabled them to exhibit a unique aptitude for verbal fireworks. In comedy, the Lunts could range from the delicately sentimental to the brilliantly cruel, "from moods of gaiety and light laughter to the savage laughter of satire or irony."

Recognizing their virtuosity—a diminishing element in the modern theater— the public responded by attending their performances in any play, demanding of a Lunt-Fontanne comedy only that it provide an opportunity for the two stars to exercise, as brilliantly as possible, their technical mastery. This mastery, as their professional colleagues were aware, was nourished by their conviction that every performance is of equal importance, and their ceaseless efforts during the run of a play "to deepen their parts and to find better ways of playing them." Lawrence Langner recorded an example of this extreme conscientiousness which, when it is cultivated by actors, is seldom known by the public. "After playing *O Mistress Mine* for three years, during the last Saturday matinée Alfred said to young Dick Van Patten, playing the juvenile, 'I have a new idea for this scene. I think it will improve it. We have one more chance to try it before we close the play!'"

An equally talented and proficient comedienne, Miss Ina Claire, achieved celebrity for her vivacious, sparkling performances of high-comedy roles, carrying on a tradition represented by the French actress, Mme. Gabrielle Réjane, and Mrs. Fiske. David Belasco saw Miss Claire give, in the Ziegfeld *Follies of 1916,* an astonishing impersonation of Miss Frances Starr, and at

Lynne Fontanne and Alfred Lunt in "Amphytrion"

Tallulah Bankhead in "The Little Foxes"

once engaged her to play the title role of *Polly With a Past,* a comedy by George Middleton and Guy Bolton. The play was a great success and launched Miss Claire's career as a star. Her performances in Frederick Lonsdale's *The Last of Mrs. Cheyney,* and in a revival of Maugham's *Our Betters* with Miss Constance Collier, established her as the pre-eminent actress of her generation in roles that required a continuous play of wit to be carried with an effect of naturalness and spontaneity.

Of the outstanding stars of the period, Miss Tallulah Bankhead alone exemplified, for a fascinated public, the old tradition of the actress as a coruscating personality. The extraordinary legend that attached to her, although perennially exciting to playgoers, often made them singularly heedless of her great talent. Probably no star commanded an equally enthusiastic personal following. Like Miss Maude Adams, she was accounted superior to criticism by her adorers. Yet their devotion worked out to the disadvantage of her art because, on the stage, they wished her to "be herself" rather than play her role, and although she never gratified this demand, its insistence offered little encouragement to her creative ability. After unhappy early ventures on the New York stage, she became a star and a popular favorite in London; eleven years passed before she again faced a New York audience, in 1933. Unlucky in her choice of plays, she nevertheless revealed brilliant gifts as a comedienne, and her performance in a revival of *Rain* suggested the power which, as an emotional actress, she had displayed when acting *Camille* in London. Her performances in *The Little Foxes* and *The Skin of Our Teeth* established her as a dramatic artist of the first rank, with a talent of exceptional range, a remarkable physical and vocal eloquence, an impressive reserve of power and passion, and great technical resources. That Miss Bankhead could dominate an audience by her art rather than her personality was obvious, and to judicious playgoers her decision to retire from the stage in 1950 represented an abdication almost as lamentable as John Barrymore's twenty-five years earlier. Two years later, Miss Bankhead published her autobiography, a document which candidly exposed her frustration as an artist and which, as a commentary on the theater of her time, expressed an embittered sense of its deficiencies. "In the thirty-three years that I've been on the stage," Miss Bankhead wrote, "I have appeared in thirty-five plays—only three of which had any merit." On the basis of this appraisal, only one conclusion was possible. One of the finest dramatic talents in the American theater had been denied its potential achievement, and to lovers of the stage this represented a deplorable loss as well as a scandalous waste.

Musical comedy and the revue continued to flourish, introducing some new and spectacular talents. Beautiful, magnetic Miss Marilyn Miller was elevated to stardom by Florenz Ziegfeld in *Sally,* in 1920, scored a sensational success with Jerome Kern's song, "Look for the Silver Lining," and thereafter, until her last appearance more than a decade later in *As Thousands Cheer,* remained a reigning favorite. In 1924, the importation from London of *André Charlot's Revue*—the sketches, lyrics and music provided mainly by Noel Coward—brought to the United States for the first time Miss Beatrice Lillie and Miss Gertrude Lawrence, who were to have long and distinguished careers on the American stage. Miss Lillie was an inspired comedienne with a style peculiarly her own, in which parody, pantomime and clowning were fused so expertly as to conceal the fine technical skill of her performances. Her sketches usually expressed a coolly satirical attitude to human nature; she made its follies amusing and absurd without evoking contempt for them; and she persuaded her audience, while laughing at her subjects, to realize that they were also laughing at themselves.

Miss Lawrence won immediate acclaim for her singing of "The Limehouse Blues," a characteristic example of her ability to express the subtle overtones that accompany a dominant emotion. With a limited vocal equipment, she gave the illusion of being a great singer, and with probably slender technical resources as a dancer, she created the effect of beauty when she danced. Her talent was fundamentally dramatic and interpretive; she was a comedienne whose gaiety and vivaciousness had an undercurrent of pathos, as if the darker aspects of experience were always present to her imagination. As the years passed, she often turned from musical comedy to the legitimate stage, giving brilliant performances of light comedy in Noel Coward's *Private Lives* and *Tonight at 8:30,* and showing that she was equal to the more exacting requirements of Shaw's *Pygmalion*. One of her most impressive achievements was her creation of the role of Liza Elliott in *Lady in the Dark,* in 1941. Though presented as a musical comedy, with a libretto by Moss Hart, music by Kurt Weill and lyrics by Ira Gershwin, *Lady in the Dark* was a play containing interludes of song and dance that illustrated the fantasies of its heroine, confronted with them during the progress of psychoanalysis. Miss Lawrence's role required her to move, continuously and almost uninterruptedly, from the world of actuality to the world of fantasy and back again. The role was not only protean, but every dissimilar incarnation of fantasy had to be vividly related to Liza Elliott's character in the dramatic episodes that took place in her environment of daily life. Miss Lawrence gave a performance as amazing in its dramatic versatility as in its artistic virtuosity.

Two other musical-comedy stars attained outstanding prominence. Miss Ethel Merman first claimed public attention in 1930. Appearing in *Girl Crazy,* for which George Gershwin provided the music, she electrified audiences by her singing of Gershwin's "I Got Rhythm." She had received no training as a vocalist. The power of her voice was more remarkable than its beauty, but her use of it achieved dynamic, exciting effects which no other singer of her type was able to match. Her diction was perfect and, given a slightly ribald, humorous lyric, she made every word contribute its precise value. Better than any other singer of the time, she knew how to "put over" a song. She appeared, with increasing success, in a series of musicals by Cole Porter: *Anything Goes, Red Hot and Blue, Du Barry Was a Lady, Panama Hattie* and *Something for the*

Jimmy Durante, Ethel Merman and Bob Hope in "Red, Hot and Blue"

Boys. In *Du Barry,* she attempted for the first time to characterize and act her role as well as sing her songs. Thereafter, improving her personations, she developed gifts as a comedienne. These gifts were as largely responsible as her singing for a triumph, in 1946, as Annie Oakley, the famous sharpshooter, in Irving Berlin's rousing *Annie Get Your Gun,* for which a coherent libretto was supplied by Herbert and Dorothy Fields, son and daughter of Lew Fields. Berlin's *Call Me Madam,* with a book by Howard Lindsay and Russel Crouse, gave Miss Merman an even more varied role, and in it she displayed her talents in full maturity.

In 1938, Miss Mary Martin made her New York debut in Cole Porter's *Leave It to Me.* She achieved celebrity overnight with a single song, "My Heart Belongs to Daddy." Critics noted that she delivered a witty, suggestive lyric with an air of demure archness that indicated unusual artistic tact, but did not specially remark her attempt to dramatize a role which afforded little opportunity for acting. Miss Martin was soon starred in *One Touch of Venus,* for which Kurt Weill provided the score. The story dealt with the coming to life of a statue of Venus, and in the role of the ancient goddess reborn in modern New York Miss Martin displayed impressive dramatic talent, proving her ability to dominate an audience by her acting alone, as well as by her singing. Her gifts, which resembled those of Miss Lawrence, made it clear that she would have a notable career.

The traditional form of comic opera, with few deviations from the standard formulas of the European product, was successfully cultivated, in the postwar decade, by Rudolph Friml and Sigmund Romberg. Friml composed *Rose Marie* and *The Vagabond King;* Romberg, *Blossom Time* and *The Student Prince.* But the form had little attraction for the major composers of outstanding talent. Jerome Kern reached the height of his career in a series of collaborations with Oscar Hammerstein 2d, a librettist and writer of lyrics who possessed remarkable gifts and created a new kind of musical. The new form was first revealed in *Show Boat,* a dramatization of Miss Edna Ferber's romantic novel, produced in 1927. In it, Hammerstein provided a genuinely dramatic libretto, with characters plausibly real, and so carefully integrated the songs in the action of the play that they became components of its drama. This inspired Kern to compose his finest score; one of his songs, "Old Man River," was a permanent addition to American music, and others were only slightly less notable. The collaborators continued developing their concept in *Sweet Adeline, Music in the Air* and *Very Warm for May.*

George Gershwin, with his brother Ira as writer of lyrics, began his most characteristic work with *Lady, Be Good* in 1924, and continued to treat the contemporary American scene in *Oh, Kay*—which starred Miss Gertrude Lawrence—and *Funny Face.* In 1930, he reached a new peak of development with *Strike Up the Band,* for which Morrie Ryskind provided a libretto satirizing current economic and political conditions, and prophetically showing the nation involved in war. Gershwin's finest musical comedy—*Of Thee I Sing*—was written in collaboration with George S. Kaufman and Morrie Ryskind, who furnished a superbly satirical libretto dealing with American politics. Produced in 1931 with Victor Moore in the role of a melancholy Vice President who could find no duties to perform, *Of Thee I Sing* was not only a tremendous popular success, but the first musical play to win a Pulitzer Prize for drama. Thereafter, Gershwin determined to write an opera. The result of this ambition was *Porgy and Bess,* his last work, produced by the Theater Guild in 1935, and frequently revived. Described as an "American folk opera," it was not a composition in the traditional form of grand opera, but a landmark in the development of a native form of musical comedy, an advance on the road first opened by *Show Boat.*

The highly individual talent of Irving Berlin, which during the post-war decade was employed on a series of *Music Box Revues,* was applied, in 1932, to *Face the Music,* for which Moss Hart wrote a libretto which dealt bitterly with the Great Depression, and savagely indicted the corruption of the police in New York City, recently exposed in an official investigation. The collaborators next produced *As Thousands Cheer,* a revue which satirized with ebullient hilarity many conspicuous features of the American scene at the time.

Meanwhile, another team of collaborators—Richard Rodgers, composer, and Lorenz Hart, writer of lyrics—were also concentrating on American subjects. Their first important work, *A Connecticut Yankee,* with a libretto founded on Mark Twain's novel and written by Herbert Fields, was produced in 1927. They wrote other delightful musicals—*On Your Toes, Babes in Arms, The Boys From Syracuse*—but their talents took a new turn, in 1937, in *I'd Rather Be Right.* For this musical, George S. Kaufman and Moss Hart col-

Illustration by Marcus from the Program of "Showboat," 1927

laborated on a book that dealt humorously with the politics of the New Deal, and brought President Franklin D. Roosevelt to the stage in an impersonation by George M. Cohan.

At sixty, Cohan was disgruntled by the failure of his recent plays; his kind of comedy had been outmoded. He realized that his career as an active force in the theater had ended. He was embittered by the conviction that the recognition he deserved had been denied him. (Three years earlier he wrote to George Middleton: "I've been fortunate, however, in having a full life—Plenty of money—Plenty of fun—Plenty of Everything except a certain classification I never achieved.") He disliked appearing, for the first time, in a musical of which he was not the author and composer; the new school of musical comedy was, in fact, repugnant to him. He resented the tremendous popular success of the show, which was the greatest musical hit since *Show Boat,* a decade earlier. In these circumstances, it was ironical that, as an actor, Cohan attained a new and widespread fame in *I'd Rather Be Right,* evoking enthusiasm throughout the country from a generation not yet born in the days of his early celebrity.

In 1940, collaborating with the novelist John O'Hara, Rodgers and Hart brought to the stage *Pal Joey,* in which the new school of musical comedy entered its maturity. A witty, sophisticated and realistic treatment of one segment of the American scene, it proved that there was no phase of contemporary life which was not susceptible to the musical stage. It was clear by then that the United States was producing, in this department of the theater, works of an importance comparable with its drama.

Toward Tomorrow

A SECOND world war ended; the fifth decade of the century was passing, and the sixth approached. The great flowering of creative vitality in the drama had not yet run its course. Its continuity was signalized by the return to the theater of Eugene O'Neill, and the almost simultaneous emergence of a young generation of playwrights whose work promised to carry forward the revolution which he had inaugurated.

O'Neill returned to the theater in 1946, thirty years after the production of his earliest one-act plays in Provincetown, thirteen years after the production of his last full-length play on Broadway. Once again, in *The Iceman Cometh,* he invited compassion for "all man's blundering unhappiness." But this long tragedy expressed no affirmation of life, no exaltation of the spirit; it was the most pessimistic and despairing of his plays. In a waterfront lodging house and bar on Manhattan's lower West Side are assembled a group of derelicts, to whom drunkenness and their few pathetic illusions offer the only refuge from the abject misery of their existence. There arrives their occasional patron and boon companion, Hickey, who astounds them by preaching a gospel of regeneration. He undermines the illusions of one after another, sending them out to

Vivienne Segal and Gene Kelly in "Pal Joey"

face the world that has defeated them. One after another they return, defeated
again. Hickey also returns, having murdered his wife and summoned the police.
They will come to take him to his death—to free him forever from his last
illusion and his last futile hope—and the others will find relief, as before,
through escape into drunkenness and their tattered, baseless dreams. That man,
as O'Neill put it, is "a victim of life's ironies and of himself"; that his existence
is a desolation, and his death a release—this was the apparent import of the
play. It was admirably produced by the Theater Guild, with James Barton in
the role of Hickey, and Dudley Digges in that of Harry Hope, the bemused,
fear-ridden proprietor of the lodging house and bar. Another play by O'Neill, *A
Moon for the Misbegotten*, was performéd on the road in 1947 but soon withdrawn. Later, word reached the public that although he had completed other
plays, none would be produced during his lifetime. In effect, *The Iceman
Cometh* was his valedictory to the theater.

O'Neill's greatest influence was exercised belatedly, not through his theory of
tragedy, but through his repudiation of the dramatic conventions established by
Ibsen. The "well-made play," the modern realistic drama, assumed the stage
to be a room from which the fourth wall had been removed, and the aim of the
playwright was to reproduce in that room the effect of actual life. O'Neill was
the first American dramatist to profit by the psychology of Freud and Jung,
which indicated that the sources of human action—the compelling motives that
determine it—are to be found in the unconscious, rather than the conscious,
mind. O'Neill felt that this not only added a new dimension to the drama, but
made necessary an entirely new technique. It showed the realism of Ibsen and
his followers to be merely superficial, for what they translated to the stage was
no more than the external appearance of reality. If reality is subjective, internal
rather than external, literal reproduction of appearances on the stage is irrelevant. So O'Neill believed, and in many of his plays he tried to discard the
methods of pseudo-realistic or representational treatment, and transfer the
locale of the drama from a room to a mind. Few playwrights of O'Neill's generation made any consistent attempt to find a new form for the drama, especially
one adaptable to the new dimension that had been opened to it. But O'Neill's experiments provided a tradition, and even a foundation, for the work of a number
of playwrights who entered the theater after the Second World War. Meanwhile,
experiments like his had been conducted in the dance-drama, notably by Miss
Martha Graham, and in the more purely dramatic form of the mime, or acted,
wordless play. The art of the mime, highly developed in both Europe and the
Orient, had only one exponent in the United States, Miss Angna Enters. A
writer and painter as well as an actress, Miss Enters herself composed the large
repertory of monodramas in which she appeared. In subject they ranged from
the medieval to the contemporary; in substance, from comedy to tragedy; but
they had in common a single fundamental concept. Each presented a character
at a moment of crisis in subjective experience, or inward life—sometimes when
the character's behavior was deliberately intended to conceal the interior conflict. Using only costume and a few simple properties, Miss Enters was able, by
means of her powers of expression and her command of physical eloquence, to

Shirley Booth and Sydney Blackmer in "Come Back, Little Sheba"

make psychological drama vivid and explicit in pantomime. She was a precursor of the new school of dramatists.

The most remarkable feature of the work of the younger playwrights was their use of the stage in a new way to dramatize the subjective experience of their characters. This effort to bring to light the hidden worlds in which individuals live—often sharply unlike the supposedly "real" world which they inhabit—was first exemplified in 1945 by Tennessee Williams' *The Glass Menagerie*. The play deals with three characters: a mother who retreats from the drabness of her existence into fantasies of her girlhood as a Southern belle; a crippled daughter who diverts to a collection of glass animals the passion which she knows that no man will ever reciprocate; a son who provides their livelihood by working in a warehouse. He is a would-be poet who hates his job, his environment and his burdensome family, and is determined to contrive his escape from them. Williams used the device of making the son, long after his escape, a narrator who addresses the audience; the play takes place in his memory. This enabled Williams to ignore the conventions of realistic drama and thereby concentrate and sharpen his tragedy of frustration on the planes of inward and outward life. In the production, Eddie Dowling took the role of the son, Miss Julie Hayden that of the daughter. The mother was superbly played by Miss

Laurette Taylor, who had enjoyed her most conspicuous success more than thirty years earlier in *Peg o' My Heart,* a sentimental comedy by her husband, J. Hartley Manners. After his death, she had done little to advance her career. The role of Amanda in *The Glass Menagerie* was her last one, and the splendor of her performance indicated that a very great talent had been deplorably wasted. Williams' next play, *A Streetcar Named Desire,* was another study of frustration, even darker because of its relentless picture of loneliness driving a woman ever deeper into a world of personal fantasy until her mind gives way. His later plays were *Summer and Smoke, The Rose Tattoo* and *Camino Real*— the last, an apocalyptic picture of the contemporary world as he conceives it to be.

In *All My Sons,* Arthur Miller proved his ability to write a powerful play within the conventions of realism, but his far more significant *Death of a Salesman* demonstrated that he was capable of inventing a dramatic form for the expression of a tragedy wholly subjective. Miller's pathetic drummer represents, in his modest ambitions, the middle classes of the nation. His personal tragedy is brought about by his unquestioning faith in that "success" which is the national dream, myth and ethos. His frustration results from the intensity of his faith, which compels him to translate into subjective reality the public creed in which people profess to believe but, if wise, do not attempt to live by. With an oblique reference to contemporary conditions, Miller in *The Crucible,* dealt with the consequences of mass hysteria and mass delusion, using as his subject the tragic story of witchcraft in colonial Salem. Arthur Laurents vividly dramatized the interior life of a character in *Home of the Brave,* a psychiatric study of a soldier, and drew a touching portrait of a spinster's frustration in *The Time of the Cuckoo.* Like Laurents, William Inge used the traditional form of a realistic drama for two eloquent, moving plays—*Come Back, Little Sheba* and *Picnic*—based upon conflict between the inner and outer lives of characters. The glowing performance given by Miss Shirley Booth as a disillusioned, slattern wife in *Come Back, Little Sheba* brought her to stardom after a stage career of more than twenty years during which she had shown exceptional versatility in a wide range of roles.

Two novelists, Miss Carson McCullers and Truman Capote, joined the younger group of playwrights with dramatizations of novels. Both rejected the formulas of realism and used experimental forms dictated by their material. Miss McCullers' *The Member of the Wedding,* memorably acted by Miss Ethel Waters, Miss Julie Harris and Brandon de Wilde, was a haunting study of adolescent loneliness which met with great popular success. Truman Capote's *The Grass Harp* translated to the stage an adolescent's conception of the adult world and a fable of certain characters who, because they are pure in heart, revolt from it. The play failed on Broadway, but was successfully revived in an "arena theater" in Greenwich Village. The work of all these younger playwrights indicated that the revolution initiated by O'Neill was still going forward, and that it might result in an entirely new kind of drama. The belief that the drama, in order to achieve serious relevance, must escape from the limitations of realism was apparently shared by two playwrights of the older generation. Moss

Hart testified to this conviction in *The Climate of Eden*. John van Druten, after two notable successes in *Bell, Book and Candle* and *I Am a Camera*, wrote a moving, mystical celebration of faith in life, *I've Got Sixpence*. Although both these plays failed on Broadway, they made positive contributions to the advancing art of the drama.

The art of the musical stage advanced to new heights with the production, by the Theater Guild, in 1943, of *Oklahoma!*, the first of a series of collaborations by Oscar Hammerstein 2d, and Richard Rodgers. This idyll of rural America, which involved such novelties as a murder and a dream ballet which enacts a conflict taking place in the mind of its heroine, went begging for backers when the Guild's depleted treasury could not alone finance its production. Money was eventually raised in small amounts and with great difficulty; when the piece was tried out on the road, many Broadway sages predicted its failure in New York. But *Oklahoma!*—actually a popular opera in which, for the first time, dramatic action, song and dance were absolutely welded—became a classic of the American theater, running uninterruptedly for five years on Broadway and for ten on the road. The collaborators adapted Molnar's *Liliom* to the locale of New England in *Carousel,* used an original story for their *Allegro,* and achieved another triumphant success in *South Pacific* (founded on James Michener's *Tales of the South Pacific*) in which Miss Mary Martin and Ezio Pinza, a former star of the Metropolitan Opera, gave distinguished performances. In *The King and I* they brought to the popular musical stage for the first time a drama with tragic overtones and a dominant mood of pathos. Artistically, it was the finest

Scene from "Oklahoma!" showing the original company

example of the new form of music-drama which they had invented, and it gained added luster from the superb performances of Miss Gertrude Lawrence and Yul Brynner. In *Me and Juliet,* produced in 1953, they dealt with backstage life in the theater; the action of Hammerstein's play occurred during the production of a musical show.

The popular musical stage had an important accession in Leonard Bernstein, composer and conductor of concert music, who provided notable scores for *On the Town* and *Wonderful Town,* two exhilarating panoramas of New York. Meanwhile, Irving Berlin and Cole Porter continued to be productive. Berlin's *Call Me Madam,* Porter's *Kiss Me Kate* (for which Bella and Sam Spewack provided an exceptionally fine libretto) and *Can-Can* represented these composers at their best. The creative vitality of the musical stage was no less remarkable than that of the drama.

Though Americans were seldom sentimental about the destruction of old buildings rich in historical associations or reminiscent of departed glories, the passing of an old and famous New York theater brought nation-wide expression of regret. In 1953, after sixty years of illustrious service, the Empire Theater closed its doors, to be demolished and replaced by an office building. When it was opened, Broadway was known as "the Great White Way," the nation's theater street, and the name of the thoroughfare became a synonym for show business. With the disappearance of the Empire, there remained on Broadway not one playhouse devoted to the drama. For the public as well as the theatrical profession, noble traditions clustered about the handsome old Empire. Mme. Bernhardt and Miss Ellen Terry had played there; so had Mme. Modjeska, John Drew and William Gillette. It was the theater in which Miss Maude Adams, Miss Ethel Barrymore and other reigning stars of their generation had enchanted audiences. It was associated with the careers of Miss Helen Hayes, Miss Cornell and the Lunts. Before the theater closed its doors, a festival evening of "farewell to the Empire" was organized under the auspices of the American National Theater and Academy. The program was made up of scenes from plays which had been produced in the theater during its long history. One scene from the opening attraction, *The Girl I Left Behind Me,* was performed and for this, touchingly, Miss Edna Wallace Hopper returned to the stage to play the role in which she had appeared on the Empire's first night, in 1893. The razing of the Empire left the beautiful old Walnut Street Theater in Philadelphia as the nation's principal shrine of stage tradition. Opened in 1809 for the use of a circus, and rebuilt in 1820 as a playhouse, it had provided a stage for "Old Jefferson" and his colleagues; for the debut of Edwin Forrest; for the performances of Miss Cushman and Rachel, and for nearly every distinguished actress and actor since their time.

In 1953, the American theater appeared to be in the full noon of a golden day. Yet, as always before in its history, there was no lack of gloomy predictions about its future, and some of them came from professional authorities whose devotion to the stage could not be questioned. The great drain of Hollywood on the living theater, which first became a serious threat when John Barrymore deserted the stage for motion pictures, increased year by year. One after another, the most promising acting talents of the younger generation succumbed to its lure. The grave danger that resulted was described by Harold Clurman. "The older generation were people trained in the theater—who remained there. The younger generation is composed of people who begin in the theater and usually leave it shortly after their first 'triumph'—or five years after their debut. Having acquired an industrial psychology, and being therefore more money and publicity conscious than is good for an artist, they hope to reach the top of the heap in Hollywood or in another of the mass production media. If they succeed in this, their return to the theater is a kind of courtesy call. . . . Ten successful years in pictures may make an actor ten times as popular as when he left the stage; it will not necessarily make him even twice as good. Actors grow only through practice—persistent, varied, constant." Clurman also drew attention to

Gertrude Lawrence and Yul Brynner in "The King and I"

the restrictive effect on the actor's art of the prevalent system of "type casting," and to the failure of our theater to provide a repertory sufficiently comprehensive for the training of young actors in versatility—the command of a range of acting styles. Acting, he asserted, had become "limited, almost uniform, producing a new kind of pathetic naturalism or theatrical journalism for which the highest encomium seemed to be conveyed in such terms as 'lifelike,' 'natural,' 'real,' 'touching.' " Because actors were being trained only for the current style, many of the great plays of the past, and especially the classics, could no longer be adequately produced. If our theater is not to be diminished, Clurman declared, there must be restored to American acting "originality and depth of interpretation, grandeur, passion, daring, sweep, color, brilliance, grace, above all, the magic gift for inner and outer transformation."

Another indication of attrition, and its dark import, were pointed out by Brooks Atkinson, dramatic critic of the New York *Times*. During the season 1952–1953, only twenty-nine new plays were produced on Broadway. (The peak of production occurred during the season 1928–1929, which brought two hundred new plays to the stage.) "No lover of the theater can read the annual statistics without a feeling of awful apprehension," Atkinson remarked. "Fewer productions every year, frightening costs of production and operation—these are the facts that consistently eat a little further into the vitality of the theater." In the light of the record, Atkinson surmised that "It is quite possible that the serious play of artistic independence may die, at least on Broadway, and bequeath the commercial theater to popular comedies . . . popular melodramas . . . and the big musical dramas." He asserted: "There is no place in our commercial theater for interesting plays that do not arouse many thousands of people to immediate action." The shrinking activities of Broadway in production—Walter Kerr, dramatic critic of the New York *Tribune,* characterized the 1950's as an "age of gingerly sporadic and painfully nursed production"— found a dolorous echo in the annual statistics of employment published by Actors' Equity. During the calendar year 1952, the union had a membership of slightly less than seven thousand, the largest in its history. Yet only one out of every six of its members had been professionally employed for as long as six months. The "average stage actor"—according to the statistics—had worked ten weeks during the year, and had earned $825.

But the outlook was not altogether dark. The theatrical profession had been stirred to action in a campaign undertaken by the American National Theater and Academy, known as ANTA. This organization, chartered by Congress in 1935, was working for a decentralization of the professional theater by means of the establishment of regional playhouses with resident companies throughout the country. Evidence was rapidly accumulating that such playhouses could prosper. The successful operation of "arena theaters" in a number of cities, including New York, suggested that the professional stage could flourish independently of Broadway. The first arena theater was opened on the campus of the University of Washington, in Seattle, in 1940. The best-known professional playhouse of this type was conducted by Miss Margo Jones in Dallas, Texas. In arena theaters the audience was seated on four sides of an acting area, and simplified methods of production imposed by this structural feature enabled the managements to operate them far more economically than a conventional playhouse.

Although the road still suffered from a dearth of attractions, whenever the original company of a recent Broadway success went on tour, it was likely to play to capacity houses, not only in the larger cities but in the one-night stands. The fact was that throughout the country there existed an immense and expanding audience for the living theater. This audience had been created, principally, by the community, university and college playhouses, which were functioning in all parts of the land. Some of these playhouses, in addition to carrying out impressive production schedules, also maintained touring companies which carried their plays to the smaller towns of their regions. The example of the University of Washington was both remarkable and suggestive. It operated two theaters on its campus, both offering public performances on six nights every week throughout the year, thus furnishing the city of Seattle continuous dramatic fare and, in a measure, making it independent of Broadway. Nothing more clearly indicated the genuine interest of the nation in the living theater than the fact that nearly three hundred colleges and universities were offering professional courses in the arts of the stage—drama, acting, scene-designing; and the techniques of production also—and, in connection with these courses, were carrying out programs of production and performance for receptive audiences. In 1953, an intention to train for a career in the theater seemed no more unusual than a similar intention with respect to the practice of law, medicine, or engineering. This in itself implied that, as always before, the American theater would survive all predictions of its approaching demise.

The long-waged, cruel, often disheartening battle of the theatrical profession to attain prestige had been won many years earlier. Their belief in the dignity and social value of their art was corroborated by the attitude of the American public. It was not without significance that when Miss Gertrude Lawrence died, in the autumn of 1952, a sense of grief was felt across the country, or that in New York, on the day of her funeral, five thousand people crowded into the streets near the church in which services were held to pay silent homage to her. "She cheerfully dedicated her own life," Oscar Hammerstein 2d said in his eulogy, "to a series of elaborate and glorious imitations of life—imitations that were just a little better, a little brighter, than life itself. . . . This was her mission." He might have been describing the dedication of all those innumerable actresses and actors who, since the time of George Frederick Cooke, had carried the mission of their art to the American people—to the little settlements of the frontier, to San Francisco and the mountain mining camps of California, and to the road. To provide imitations of life which have a grandeur greater than that of life itself—this was the function of the theater, and lacking its unique service and continued vitality the nation would suffer a spiritual loss. Because, year by year, more Americans were coming to realize it, the glories of the theater in the future might well excel those of its illustrious past.

About the Author

BORN and raised in New York City, Lloyd Morris received his education at the Ethical Culture School and Columbia University. A man of letters in the best sense of the phrase, he has written biography, fiction, criticism, history and drama. Among his works are *The Celtic Dawn,* a study of the Irish renaissance; *The Rebellious Puritan,* a biography of Nathaniel Hawthorne; *The Damask Cheek,* a comedy written in collaboration with John van Druten; an autobiography, *A Threshold in the Sun; Postscript to Yesterday* and *Not So Long Ago,* social histories of America; *Ceiling Unlimited,* a history of American aviation written in collaboration with Kendall Smith; *Incredible New York: High Life and Low Life of the Last Hundred Years;* and *Curtain Time: The Story of the American Theater.* He has also written extensively for the magazines, has served as drama critic, taught at Columbia and lectured throughout the country.

In his spare time, of which he has very little, Mr. Morris collects records and contemporary prints and takes pleasure in the theater, good food, good wine and good conversation.